MARKETING ON THE INTERNET

Fourth Edition

Other titles of interest from Maximum Press

101 Ways to Promote Your Website: Sweeney,
   1-885068-37-9

Business-to-Business Internet Marketing: Silverstein,
   1-885068-35-2

E-mail Marketing: Kinnard, 1-885068-40-9

Exploring IBM's Bold Internet Strategy: Hoskins, Lupiano,
   1-885068-16-6

Exploring IBM Technology, Products & Services, Second Edition:
   edited by Hoskins, 1-885068-31-X

*Building Intranets With Lotus Notes & Domino 5.0, Second
   Edition*: Krantz, 1-885068-24-7

Exploring IBM Personal Computers, 10th Edition: Hoskins,
   Wilson, 1-885068-25-5

Exploring IBM AS/400 Computers, Ninth Edition: Hoskins,
   Dimmick, 1-885068-34-4

Exploring IBM S/390, Sixth Edition: Hoskins, Coleman,
   1-885068-30-1

Exploring IBM Client/Server Computing: Bolthouse,
   1-885068-04-2

Exploring IBM RS/6000 Computers, Ninth Edition: Hoskins,
Davies, 1-885068-27-1

Exploring IBM Network Stations: Ho, Lloyd, and Heracleous,
   1-885068-32-8

For more information, visit our World Wide Web site at:
www.maxpress.com
or e-mail us at *moreinfo@maxpress.com*

MARKETING ON THE INTERNET

Fourth Edition

Jan Zimmerman

MAXIMUM PRESS
605 Silverthorn Road
Gulf Breeze, FL 32561
(850) 934-0819
www.maxpress.com

Publisher: Jim Hoskins

Manager of Finance/Administration: Donna Tryon

Production Manager: ReNae Grant

Cover Design: Lauren Smith Designs

Compositor: PageCrafters Inc.

Copyeditor: Andrew Potter

Proofreader: Julie Cameron

Indexer: Susan Olason

Printer: P.A. Hutchison

This publication is designed to provide accurate and authoritative information in regard to the subject matter covered. It is sold with the understanding that the publisher is not engaged in rendering professional services. If legal, accounting, medical, psychological, or any other expert assistance is required, the services of a competent professional person should be sought. ADAPTED FROM A DECLARATION OF PRINCIPLES OF A JOINT COMMITTEE OF THE AMERICAN BAR ASSOCIATION AND PUBLISHERS.

Recognizing the importance of preserving what has been written, it is a policy of Maximum Press to have books of enduring value published in the United States printed on acid-free paper, and we exert our best efforts to that end.

Library of Congress Cataloging-in-Publication Data

Zimmerman, Jan.
   Marketing on the Internet / Jan Zimmerman. -- 4th ed.
   p. cm.
   Includes index.
   1. Internet advertising. 2. Internet marketing. 3. Internet
(Computer network) I. Title.
   HF6146.I58 M38 1999
   658.8'4--dc21
                        99-6691
                         CIP

*For my Uncle Ben, who has
encouraged me more than he knows*

Acknowledgments

This book would not have happened without months of assistance from Alex Knox, who provided extraordinary research and Web skills, searched for art, obtained copyrights, and assembled the Resource Appendix. I again enjoyed the additional research support, copyright clearance talent, and business acumen of Margaret Keller. I am enormously grateful for their skills, their commitment, and their patience. My appreciation also to Lawrence Feinberg for CompuServe research. There is no thank you big enough.

As always, my critique group—Phil Jackson, Cliett Kight, Joe Quattro, and Linda Salomone—provided invaluable input, editorial vision, and support. And I want to thank my clients, from whom I learn every day about innovative ways to market on the Internet. They provide me with a reason to perpetually search the Web for new discoveries.

My thanks also to all the vendors and organizations that answered endless questions and gave copyright permission. The companies discussed in Chapter 9 were generous with their time and information, and Barb Tomlin of Westward Connections (*http://www.westward.com*) graciously provided some valuable information.

With the Internet changing so rapidly, I can only hope that all my errors and omissions will be overtaken by a new reality before they are noticed.

Disclaimer

bilities of the products mentioned in this book. The manufacturer's product documentation should always be consulted, because the specifications and capabilities of computer hardware and software products are subject to frequent modification. The reader is solely responsible for the choice of computer hardware and software. All configurations and applications of computer hardware and software should be reviewed with manufacturer's representatives prior to choosing or using any computer hardware and software.

Trademarks

The words contained in this text that are believed to be trademarked, service marked, or otherwise to hold proprietary rights have been designated as such by use of initial capitalization. No attempt has been made to designate as trademarked or service marked any personal computer words or terms in which proprietary rights might exist. Inclusion, exclusion, or definition of a word or term is not intended to affect, or to express judgment upon, the validity of legal status of any proprietary right that may be claimed for a specific word or term.

Foreword

The World Wide Web has emerged in the 1990s as the preferred mass medium, one that uniquely combines interactivity, content, and commerce. The Internet is unique in that it is an information network that is ubiquitous, global, and decentralized. It is quickly becoming not only a "commercial" medium, but also a mass medium that rivals TV, radio, and other vehicles for information dissemination and exchange. The Net is the only medium in which users can both receive information as they can in the broadcast medium (by going to Web sites like Yahoo!) and communicate with others individually through e-mail.

Several trends are pushing the Internet toward a bigger and brighter future. The first trend is that there is a very healthy and competitive Internet access provider market. With the telecommunications market in the United States being deregulated, it is expected that the access-providing business will be even more competitive, as local and long distance phone companies, as well as cable providers, are expected to jump into the game. The net result will be a faster, cheaper, and more user-friendly service for the average consumer.

The second trend is that the transmission speeds available to businesses and homes will rapidly be increasing. This means that delivery of more demanding content such as full-motion video and other forms of multimedia content will be a better experience for users. Another trend is the development of more sophisticated software and technology, such as future generations of browser software (Java, VRML, etc.).

Last, because of the development of inexpensive standardized tools for publishing on the Web, more and more people will be putting content on the Web. Content will be increasingly more compelling and of higher quality, as models for content being funded get established.

The big promise is for the Internet to become the premier medium for information, entertainment, and business transactions. The intranet is the current rush, as businesses are quickly adopting the Internet as the platform for conducting communication and document management. This, combined with the mass media aspect, makes the Internet a truly ubiquitous and standard information medium. Given these factors, the future of the Net is indeed bright. However, this is still a rapidly developing medium. Pricing models for supporting quality content development are still lacking, although some form of advertising, transactions, or subscription is developing. Furthermore, regulations imposed on the still nascent industry could seriously affect the potential growth of this medium.

The Net will continue to draw millions of new users every year. The powerful thing about the Net is that it is a very organic, user-driven medium. The users can shape what the Net looks like through their interaction and feedback. What will sustain the Net and its businesses will be the creativity and participation of its users. The users and businesses of this new-found medium and community must not take the growth and freedom for granted. Without responsible actions, this medium can go away as quickly as it came. The future of the Net depends on the people as much as it depends on technology.

Jerry Yang
Yahoo! Cofounder

Contents

Chapter 2:
The ABCs of Internet Marketing   36

Chapter 3:
Creating and Distributing Info-Tools   74

Chapter 5:
Maintenance and Monitoring Results   177

Chapter 7:
Multimedia on Your Web Site   276

Chapter 8:
Dollars and Legal Sense   308

Chapter 9:
Model Web Sites for Internet Marketing   348

Chapter 10:
Conclusion 381

About This Book

Whether your business is already on the Web or you're trying to make the online decision, the fourth edition of *Marketing on the Internet* will provide you with invaluable advice, worksheets, and hot tips to ensure success. This edition has been updated to keep owners, CEOs, and marketing managers current on the status of online sales and marketing. Use this book as a one-stop information source on all aspects of Internet marketing, from how to select vendors to how to assess the effectiveness of a Web site. It is organized to work equally well whether read straight-through, or consulted as a reference on specific points of research.

The popular first edition, published in 1995, sold over 10,000 copies in the first two months and went on to become the publisher's bestselling title. The third edition, with its expanded focus on the Web and emphasis on business-based decision making, sold out its printing in one year. This fourth edition will help you make the best possible choices for your online marketing. It contains

- The latest statistics to give you a solid base of information on Internet demographics, user buying habits, and business transactions

- Many new Web sites to stimulate your imagination and serve as models for Web development

- Lessons in looking at sites, to understand their effectiveness from design, navigational, marketing, and promotional points of view

- In response to popular demand, a comprehensive selection of free features you can add to your Web site to improve performance and draw repeat visitors

- A brand-new section about improving ranking on search engines

- More information about online advertising, bought and sold

- A complete section on creating a transaction site, from shopping cart and checkstand software to auctions and catalogs

- Increased emphasis on international marketing and spotting trends to prepare you for the fast-changing world of electronic commerce

- A complete index of all URLs in the book

Here is what's inside:

- Chapter 1 reviews the growth of commercial activity on the Internet and the World Wide Web, with emphasis on its potential value for sales and marketing.

- Chapter 2 outlines seven basic steps for online marketing success, starting with a business plan, knowledge of direct marketing principles, and online research.

- Chapter 3 describes low-cost, non-Web electronic tools to initiate Internet marketing efforts and complement your Web presence.

- Chapter 4 details the process of creating a Web site, from selecting a Web designer and/or Web hosting service to estimating costs and analyzing site effectiveness.

- Chapter 5 explains the importance of maintaining and updating a Web site, and monitoring the traffic it receives.

- Chapter 6 tells how to promote a Web site using the site itself, other Web resources, non-Web Internet tools, advertising, and off-line publicity.

- Chapter 7 shows how to add sizzle to a Web site with the latest multimedia technology.

- Chapter 8 discusses the security, transaction, payment, and legal considerations of marketing online, from credit cards to copyrights.

- Chapter 9 looks at model Web sites that successfully apply specific online marketing techniques.

- Chapter 10 looks at long-range trends that may affect electronic commerce, the growth in international online marketing, and the importance of integrating online marketing with other business operations.

- Appendix A is a list of helpful Internet resources organized by topic.

- Appendix B provides a glossary of acronyms and technical terms boldfaced on first use in this book.

- Appendix C provides a page index for all the URLs that appear.

Your "Members Only" Web Site

The online business world changes almost every day. That's why a companion Web site is associated with this book. On this site you will find the latest Internet commerce news, book updates, expanded information, and other Internet marketing–related resources. However, you have to be a member of the Marketing on the Internet Club to gain access to this site.

When you purchased this book, you automatically became a member (in fact, that's the only way to join). To access the companion Web site, go to the Maximum Press Web site located at *http://www. maxpress.com* and follow the links to the Marketing on the Internet companion Web site area. When you try to enter the companion web site, you will be prompted for a user ID and a password. Type in the following:

- For User ID enter: *mktint4e*

- For Password enter: *handlebar*

You will then be granted full access to the "Members Only" area. Once you arrive, bookmark the page in your browser and you will never have

to enter the user ID and password again. Visit the site often and enjoy
the Internet marketing news and information with our compliments—
and thanks for buying the book. We ask that you not share the user ID
and password for this site with anyone else.

Introduction

Outer space may be "the final frontier" for Star Trek, but cyberspace is the new frontier for marketing. Since 1993 a whole new way of doing business has unfolded on the Internet, a crazy-quilt connection of computers worldwide. That's when Hypertext, a graphical programming language, and Mosaic, the first software for viewing graphics online, enabled the creation of the World Wide Web portion of the Internet. The Web has expanded economic activity of all types from physical space into cyberspace.

By March 1999 the Internet reached over 240 countries and territories, and more than 159 million people. With commercial companies now operating over 85% of all Web sites, the Internet has opened a whole new dimension for promoting, selling, shopping, browsing, and buying products and services.

More than $300 billion changed hands on the Web through infrastructure development, direct marketing and media sales in 1998. Internet commerce exceeded expectations by topping $100 billion last year. It is expected to account for 6% of the global economy by 2003.

Those statistics explain why the Baby Bells, AT&T, MCI, and Sprint have joined Intel, Microsoft, Compaq, and others to push new telephone-based, high-speed interconnections via digital subscriber lines. They explain the furious merger activity among telephone, cable and Internet companies seeking to control broadband Internet access, not to mention the acquisition of all but one of the top 15 Internet companies by large corporate interests.

Multinational companies such as Ford, J.P. Morgan, Dun & Bradstreet, J.C. Penney, Mitsubishi, General Motors, Sony, and Philips have expanded onto the Web, along with Prince Andrew, the rock star Prince, travel agencies, breweries, movie studios, Girl Scout Cookies, and pizzerias. There are nearly 1,000,000 active commercial Web sites on the Internet today, up from only 50,000 in 1995.

Not only can you make money using Internet technologies, you can save it. Companies such as Federal Express have found that enabling customers to track packages online not only meets their needs, it is cost-effective. Internet technology can be used on an intranet, a closed network limited to the employees of any given company, to produce information for internal use, such as inventory records, price lists, and benefit packages. Instead of spending millions on corporate training materials, for example, companies can make programs available online at a much-reduced cost. Cost savings from reduced expenditures for communications, smaller inventories, customer support, and reduction in the number of middlemen is expected to save companies billions of dollars.

The first organizations to exploit this technological frontier were high-tech companies, but now businesses selling everything from socks to socket wrenches see the information superhighway as a route to profits. The best kinds of businesses for selling online tend to be those that offer

- Hard-to-find specialty products, one-of-a kind products, or regional items

- Computer-related and high-tech products, from software to mouse pads to CD players

- Information products, such as reports, news, or data

- Products with broad geographic, especially international, appeal

- Items that can be sold less expensively over the Internet than elsewhere

- Products with a high enough price tag to cover the cost of Internet selling in time, infrastructure, and shipping.

You needn't be limited by the notion of selling directly to customers. Although some find the Web a great way to generate revenue, many more use it to

- Increase brand or product awareness

- Enhance corporate image

- Provide information or display samples of goods or services

- Generate lists of prospects

- Build relationships with customers and prospects

- Improve customer service

- Gather information about customer needs and preferences for future product development

- Better understand customer demographics

- Test consumer response to discounts or special offers

- Find business partners, dealers, franchisees, or suppliers

- Recruit talent, members, employees, or subscribers

- Save money by lowering the cost of customer communication and support, reducing the cost of order fulfillment, shortening the time frame for acquiring inventory, reducing stock on hand, and simplifying distribution channels

Several themes echo throughout this book. First, you need a good business plan before investing marketing dollars online. There is no point in establishing an e-commerce Web site if you don't have a reliable supplier, the infrastructure to handle orders, and the financial resources to keep updating your site. A good business plan confirms that you've covered all these bases.

Second, you must commit to constant online research and continual site updates. Cyberspace changes so quickly that a decision that's right today may be wrong tomorrow. Monitoring technology and the online activities of your competitors, suppliers, and customers is essential to successful online marketing.

Third, Internet marketing is just another part of your overall marketing effort. Staying customer focused is just as important online as it is off-line.

This book will help you decide whether the Internet and the Web can make your business more successful and more profitable. If the answer is yes, it will help you implement your electronic vision. Use this book as a reference. Read it with your own marketing plan in mind, and your own marketing staff involved.

By all means read this book with one eye on the screen and the other on your business, one hand on a mouse and the other on your financial statement. Seriously, read and surf simultaneously, checking out the many Web sites illustrated or called out in the text to obtain an overall picture of what's happening in cyberspace.

The Web is a great place to have fun—but it's more fun when it grows your bottom line.

1

The Internet: A Technology Means to a Marketing End

The lifetime of the Internet is a brief 30 years, yet it has profoundly changed how we search for knowledge in an age when knowledge is power. The **World Wide Web** (also known as **W3, WWW,** or the **Web**)—that graphical, easily accessible portion of the Internet—has energized its growth over the past six years.

In this chapter we'll look at how the Internet, especially the Web, is redefining business communications, modifying consumer behavior, and mediating the relationship between a business and its customers.

Overwhelming all expectations, Internet revenues of all types topped $300 billion in 1998. Retail sales alone could reach $108 billion by 2003, with business-to-business electronic commerce at least triple that amount. Combined, these numbers would represent about 6% of global commerce.

Should part of these revenues be yours? Should you invest your time, energy, money, and other resources to market and/or sell over the Internet? Or should you expend those scarce resources on off-line marketing techniques that you know will work?

To help you make a good decision, this chapter provides basic background information about the Internet. We'll cover a little history, a few statistics, and some technology. Armed with this information and the review of your business and customers in Chapter 2, you can determine whether the Internet is a place for you. Specifically, we'll discuss

- The technology and history of the Internet and World Wide Web

- The range of activities available online

- Business opportunities online, including market research, advertising, and sales

- How new technologies may affect Internet use in the future

- Efforts to measure the Internet audience and the effectiveness of advertising to it

What Is the Internet?

Computer networks link two or more computers to allow their users to share information, programs, and equipment, and to communicate with one another. Networks come in two flavors: **LANs** (**Local Area Networks**) link computers in the same building or area, and **WANs** (**Wide Area Networks**) tie together distant computer systems.

The Internet is simply the worldwide interconnection of many different networks. By hooking together **servers**, the large computers that manage individual networks, the infrastructure of the Internet allows millions of people to access information stored on tens of thousands of computers around the world. The Internet transmits messages between servers much the way the telephone system does, using satellites, microwaves, and dedicated cables such as Ethernet lines, fiber optic cables, cable television lines, or even the simple phone lines in your home.

There is one absolutely critical difference. Unlike the telephone system, the Internet lets you send messages not to just one person, but to everyone on the Internet or to a specified group of people. The Internet turns every individual or business into a broadcaster, able to communicate from one to many, a privilege previously reserved for television, radio, and publishing companies.

Originally, computers on the Internet could exchange only text messages. Now the Web portion of the Internet allows users to exchange graphics, still photos, animation, voice, and even full-motion video. Think of the Web as a virtual publishing company through which anyone can distribute the electronic equivalent of glossy magazines or short films.

The Web is the fastest-growing, most user friendly, and most commercially popular segment of the Internet. Any computer on the Internet equipped with a **browser** (software designed to look at Internet resources) and small pieces of specialized software called **plug-ins** can access different kinds of text, images, and sound. A **page** (part of a site) on the Web can be connected to another page with related information using a **link,** even if the computer hosting the other page is halfway around the earth, orbiting in the space shuttle, or sitting on Mars. How did all this come to be?

History of the Internet

The Internet owes its existence to the Pentagon and the Cold War. To solve the problem of a centralized computer system vulnerable to a single well-placed bomb, scientists at the Rand Corporation developed the concept of a **centerless network** in 1964. They envisioned thousands of computers connected with communication redundancy, much the way the human brain is wired, so that the loss of a few "neurons" or connecting cables would not result in a total loss of function.

In 1969, two **nodes** (computers connected to a network) were linked for the first time on the ARPAnet, the precursor to today's Internet. (ARPAnet was named after the Defense Department's Advanced Research Projects Agency, which sponsored its development.) Researchers at UCLA, MIT, Stanford Research International, Bolt Baranek & Newman, and the British National Physical Laboratory defined a way to bundle information into structures called **packets,** which were labeled with the **network address** of the recipient's electronic mailbox. Like a message in a bottle, a packet of information is cast adrift in the sea of computers on the network. Each computer forwards the packet closer to the address on the bottle. Once the packet reaches its destination, the packet structure (i.e., the bottle) dissolves, leaving the message intact. All computer networks now use this packet scheme to package and deliver messages reliably. The **protocol** that moves these packets of information along Internet pathways is called **TCP/IP** or **Transmission Control Protocol/Internet Protocol.**

When the ARPAnet was decommissioned in 1989, NSFnet supplanted it as the main high-speed transmission line, or **backbone,** with support from the National Science Foundation. The Internet is now self-sustained by a network of interested parties, both public and private. Perhaps because its original government funding mandated public ownership of the enabling technology, or perhaps because of an open development process through public Requests for Comments (**RFCs**), the Internet grew of its own accord to meet the needs of its users.

Without a doubt, the rapid spread of sophisticated desktop computers in the 1980s and 1990s enabled the Internet to take off. ARPAnet was founded in the days of large mainframes located at universities and major corporations; NSFnet was originally funded to connect five supercomputer centers. Without PCs there never would have been so many computers to connect!

The 1993 release of Mosaic, the first browser capable of reading graphical information, provided the mechanism for user-friendly access and gave birth to the Web. Suddenly, Internet usage parameters that had been doubling each year began doubling in three months. Even with the enormous base now in place, the rate of doubling has not yet begun to slow. It will have to ebb eventually—at this rate, facetious forecasts predict that everyone in the world would be connected by July 31, 2003!

Curious? For more information on the history of the Internet, try

http://info.isoc.org/internet/history

http://www.pbs.org/insidepbs/pbsol.html#timeline

Spectacular Growth

In its first 15 years, the Internet barely topped 1,000 **hosts** (computer systems connected to the Internet, whether full-time or part-time, by direct or dialup connection). In its second 15 years, it exploded like a supernova. As seen in Figure 1.1, by January 1999, the Internet comprised nearly 45 million hosts. These hosts represent over 100,000 interconnected networks and over 159 million users in 240 countries and territories around the world.

If the average annual growth rate of 40 to 50% over the past three years continues, the number of hosts on the Internet is projected to reach 90 million by the year 2000. The Internet, which has grown faster than any other communications technology in history, is one of the truly remarkable stories of the 20th century.

The rate of growth of the Web exceeds that of the Internet as a whole. The total number of **domain names** (registered Web site names) now tops 5 million globally and 4 million in the United States, though nearly half of those are registrations without an active site, as seen in Figure 1.2. Over 60,000 new names are registered every week; that

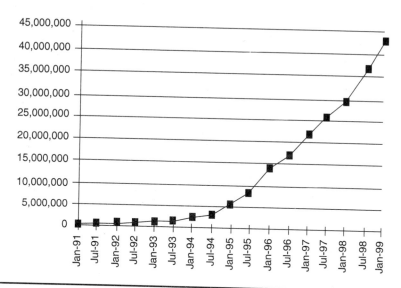

Figure 1.1.   Internet domain survey host count, *http://www.nw.com/zone/ host.gif*. Produced by Network Wizards.

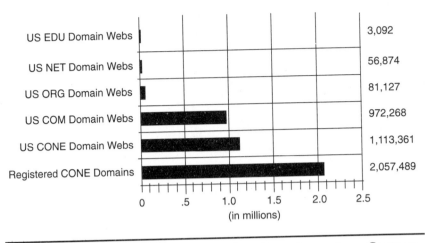

US EDU Domain Webs	3,092
US NET Domain Webs	56,874
US ORG Domain Webs	81,127
US COM Domain Webs	972,268
US CONE Domain Webs	1,113,361
Registered CONE Domains	2,057,489

0 .5 1.0 1.5 2.0 2.5
(in millions)

Figure 1.2. Live domains distribution, *http://www.internet.org*. Courtesy Michael Bauer, Internet.org.

means over one million names were registered in the first four months of 1999 alone. (We'll discuss registration in Chapter 4.) The expansion of Web sites in the commercial (*.com*) domain has far outpaced that of not-for-profit organizations (*.org*), network servers (*.net*), and educational institutions (*.edu*).

Figure 1.3 shows the growth of domain types by host count, recognizing that hosts may now represent multiple domain names, and a domain name may use more than one host. (In other words, Internet statistics are inherently imprecise.) Commercial domains represented about 87% of all active domains in December 1998, up from about 65% in 1996 and only 5% in 1994.

As of 1998, about 50% of all U.S. businesses and 34% of small ones had Web sites. Altogether, there are an estimated 320 million pages on the Web, with 1.5 million new pages going up daily worldwide. For marketing purposes, the implications are staggering.

For current statistical information, check out

http://www.nw.com/

http://www.ngi.org/trends.htm

http://www.mids.org

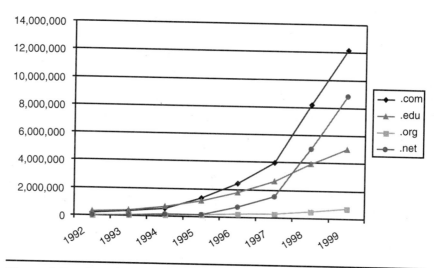

Figure 1.3. Distribution of top level domain names by host count, *http://www.nw.com/zone/WWW/top.html*. Produced by Network Wizards.

Before Going Further: Get Access

Whether it's the past, present, or future of the Internet and the World Wide Web, the best way to learn is to get online. If you already have access, great. If not, here's what you'll need:

- A *computer:* the faster the machine and the larger its hard drive, the better it can handle graphics, sound, and video.

- A *modem:* hardware that enables computers to communicate with each other over telephone lines. The faster the speed, the more rapidly information can be downloaded from the Web. Modem speed is measured in thousands (kilo or K) of **bits per second (bps)**. Sometimes bps is called the **Baud** rate. A 28.8 Kbps modem is considered minimal for receiving graphics from the Web in a reasonable amount of time. Modems usually come packaged with communications software.

- *Browser* software, such as Netscape Navigator or Internet Explorer.

- An *Internet connection,* either directly through one of more than 5,000 **Internet Service Providers** (**ISPs**) or through a commercial online service, such as Prodigy, CompuServe, or America Online (AOL). In addition to acting as ISPs with full Web access, these services offer a private network of information services, shopping malls, advertising channels, and entertainment.

If you're uncomfortable selecting an ISP, you can easily start with one of the major online services summarized in Figure 1.4, all of which also offer access to the Web. Almost always, you can obtain 50 to 100 hours of free use for exploration. Or check a site like *http://www.cnet.com/Reports/Special/ISP/index.html* to obtain rankings of ISPs in your service area. (If you need Internet access for this type of research, try your local public library; most now offer free Internet time.)

Getting an account with an ISP or online service is very simple: Sign up online or call and ask for one. You will receive communication and browser software, along with an account number, and will be asked to supply a password to get online. Although most services offer lower monthly rates for limited time online, there is no point for most businesses to sign up for anything but unlimited use. For the purposes of this book, you'll be an electronic looky-loo. Once you're set up, read this book with your browser on and mark favorite sites for future use.

How Do People Travel to Cyberspace?

Access to cyberspace matters to you as a marketing person. How your customers obtain Internet access and the kinds of information

Service	# Subscribers	Contact	Monthly Fees	Extras
America Online	17 million	(800) 827-6364	$21.95	100 hours free
CompuServe	2 million	(800) 848-8900	$19.95	100 hours free
Prodigy	505,000	(800) 213-0992	$15.95	50% off 3 months

Figure 1.4. Subscription rates for online services.

they are able to receive affects your ability to reach your desired audience. It matters that by the year 2000 the installed base of computers will be over 164 million in the United States and 579 million worldwide. It matters that more than 50 million new machines, many of them replacing outdated equipment, are now sold each year in the United States.

Of course it matters that new technologies, such as personal digital assistants, "screen" phones with built-in browsers, and intelligent cell phones will become alternative forms of Web access in the future. Even Yahoo is planning to build hand-held devices and Internet appliances!

It matters that more than 45% of U.S. homes (45 million) have a PC. Prices have fallen so low that an estimated 17% of homes will have more than one computer by the year 2000, sometimes connected to each other with a phone-based, mini-networking card or by Intel's newly introduced AnyPoint Home Network, which plugs into the outside of the computer.

Almost half these homes have a modem. The number of households using the Internet is projected to increase from 23% in 1997 to over 36% (36.5 million homes) by the year 2000. It matters to you as a marketing person that every day more than 52,000 Americans log on to the Internet for the first time, with Internet traffic doubling every 100 days.

Figure 1.5 shows that users are connecting to the Internet at faster and faster rates. Nearly two-thirds use 33.6 or 56 Kbps modems, and only 12.2% of modem users try to access the Web with a modem that is 28.8 Kbps or slower. Since faster modems mean users can receive graphics and multimedia from the Web more quickly, this information influences Web design.

Since customers' connection options may affect your online marketing methods, it matters that for the first time in 1997, more Americans (17.6 million) sought Internet connections from an ISP rather than from a major online service like America Online.

An estimated 52% of small businesses are online, with 25% of them using a commercial service provider exclusively. Projections show that over 71% of small businesses will be online by the year 2000.

It even matters to you which hardware platforms and browsers people use, since many Web sites don't look equally good in all environments. Typical platform and browser distributions are shown in Figures 1.6 and 1.7.

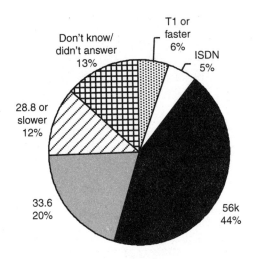

Figure 1.5. Internet connection speeds, *http://www.compare.net*. Screen shot reprinted by permission from Microsoft Corporation.

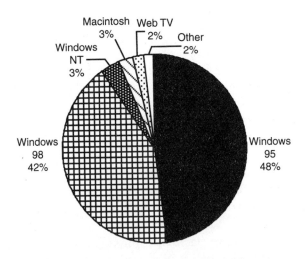

Figure 1.6. Platform distribution, *http://www.statmarket.com/page .cgi?computers*. Courtesy Statmarket.com, a WebSideStory Production.

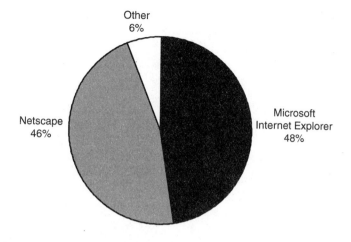

Figure 1.7. Browser distribution, *http://www.statmarket.com/page.cgi? computers.* Courtesy Statmarket, a WebSideStory Production.

The most popular browsers, Netscape's Navigator and Microsoft's Internet Explorer, have long since supplanted Mosaic. These browsers (but not all the older ones) allow access to other Internet functions such as e-mail, news groups, and mailing lists, as long as an ISP handles these functions.

What Happens in Cyberspace?

What's going on that has more than 10 million Americans logging on every day, many of them multiply times? (See Figure 1.8) A survey by Forrester Research Inc. of 100,000 North American households that had been online at least three times in the previous three months concluded that e-mail, going to the Web, and researching product purchases were the most popular reasons for being online. But time spent doesn't correlate directly with reasons, as seen in Figure 1.9. While 26% of Internet-using households give shopping as one reason for being online, individuals spend only 1% of their online time buying.

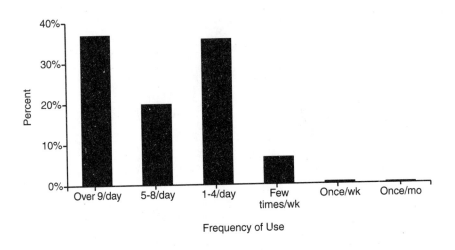

Figure 1.8. How often browser is used for discreet set of tasks, *http://www.gvu.gatech.edu/user_surveys/survey-1998-10/graphs/use/q01.htm.*
© 1994-1998, Georgia Tech Research Corporation. All rights reserved.
Source: GVU's WWW User Surveys at *http://www.gatech.edu/user_surveys.*

The Forrester survey also looked at the distribution of sites visited, as seen in Figure 1.10.

Electronic Mail

Electronic mail, or **e-mail,** is one of the original and still essential uses of the Internet and online services. With e-mail, one person sends a message to the computer mailbox of another. E-mail also allows someone to broadcast a message to many people simultaneously. Most e-mail programs permit users to attach a computer file containing any type of information, from spreadsheets to software programs. Over 100 million people now use e-mail, sending or receiving an average of 26 personal messages per day. This does not count over 7 billion commercial messages per day, a large percentage of which are unwanted. Worldwide e-mail traffic in 1998 was estimated to total between 2.7 and 3.4 trillion messages.

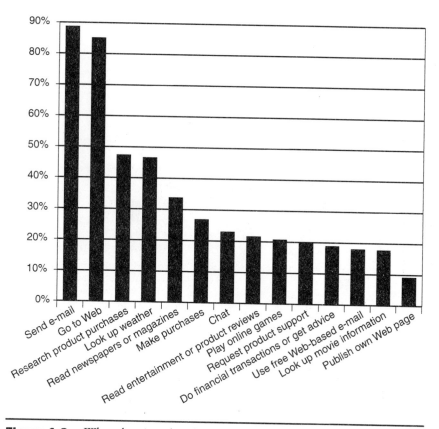

Figure 1.9. What the virtual audience does online. Source: 1999 Technographics ®, Forrester Research, Inc.

Mailing Lists

An Internet **mailing list** stores the names and associated e-mail addresses of users with a common interest in a particular topic. Once a mailing list is started, Internet users can add their names and e-mail addresses to the list (called **subscribing**). They can exchange e-mail messages simultaneously with everyone else on the list, regardless of the e-mail program being used. About 21% of e-mail users are on mailing lists, which can range from a few hundred to tens of thousands of subscribers.

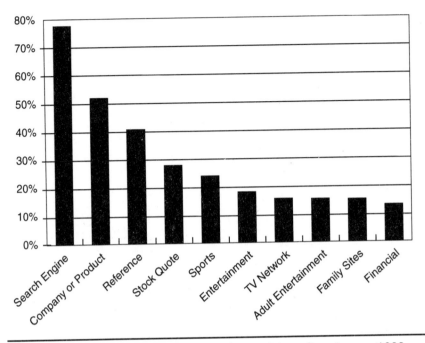

Figure 1.10. What sites the virtual audience visits online. Source: 1999 Technographics ®, Forrester Research, Inc.

Over 90,000 mailing lists cover every subject imaginable. Scientists use mailing lists for peer discussion of theories and experiments. Philosophers use them. Priests use them. Techies and Dead Heads use them. Even marketers use them. On the Internet all kinds of people use mailing lists to stay informed of important events, exchanging data on everything from the flight path of killer bees to changes in concert schedules.

News Groups

Mailing lists are accessed via e-mail, but **news groups,** a worldwide system of about 35,000 discussion groups on a portion of the Internet called USEnet, require full Internet accounts and news group reader software provided by an ISP. News groups function like mailing lists in some ways, but they offer several different methods of sending messages. A user can **post** a message for everyone in the group or respond to someone else's comments. In the latter case, only those who read the original comments see the response.

A few of the more popular news groups have as many as 300,000 at a particular time. More commonly, subscribers range from 200 to 10,000. A recent survey by the Graphics, Visualization and Usability (GVU) Center at Georgia Institute of Technology showed decreasing use of news groups, with 20.8% of all Internet users accessing at least one per week. However, 21% of Internet users seldom access them. Women and 19- to 25-year-old users are the least likely to access a news group. Whether a news group will be a valuable marketing tool for you depends on your business and your target market.

The World Wide Web

The World Wide Web consists of those servers on the Internet programmed to handle specific information requests from browser software. To locate any resource on the Internet that is part of the Web, you enter an address into your browser in a standard format called a **URL** (Uniform Resource Locator). Typical Web addresses look like this: *http://www.maxpress.com*. The **http** (**HyperText Transport Protocol**) indicates a special method of moving **hypertext** files, which contain links to other Web pages, across the Internet. It is one of the most important methods used on the Web. The **www** after the double slash (*//*) means that the information is located on a dedicated Web server. Most browsers allow users to **bookmark** (save the URL address) any sites they want to recall in the future.

By the Numbers: Business on the Internet

About 26% of Web households report purchasing something online in 1998, up from 19% in 1997 and 15% in 1996, according to GVU survey results (shown in Figure 1.11). This steady increase is encouraging more businesses to sell online. Even if they don't actually buy on the Web, about half of online consumers obtain product information or research future purchases, especially for computers, travel, and cars. Some 12% do so daily. These numbers are a persuasive argument for going online even if you choose not to sell there.

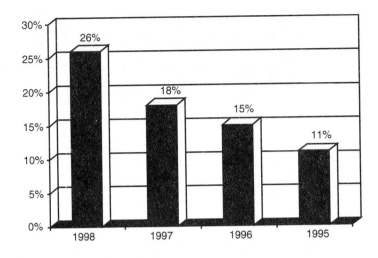

Figure 1.11. Percent of Web households purchasing online, *http:www. gvu.gatech.edu/user_surveys/*. © 1994-1998 Georgia Tech Research Corporation. All rights reserved. Source: GVU's WWW User Survey at *http://www. gvu.gatech.edu/user_surveys/*.

Perhaps the most interesting statistic about commerce on the Web, however, is that most of it is not retail, but business-to-business. More than 435,000 businesses are expected to engage in some form of interbusiness electronic commerce by the year 2000, more than triple the number in 1997. The volume is astonishing: The Department of Commerce forecasts business-to-business online purchases at $336 billion by 2002, or about 9% of total business commerce, up from only $7.8 billion in 1997. To stay abreast of Internet statistics, watch sites such as the Internet Index at *http://www.openmarket.com/intind ex.cfm*, *http://www.internet.com*, or GVU at *http://www.gvu. gatech.edu* (shown in Figure 1.12).

Who's Selling What?

Some products sell better on the Web than others. Hardware, software, books, CDs, travel, and toys are among the most popular items, as seen in Figure 1.13. Auction sites with a range of products are attracting large numbers of shoppers. Flowers do well on the Web.

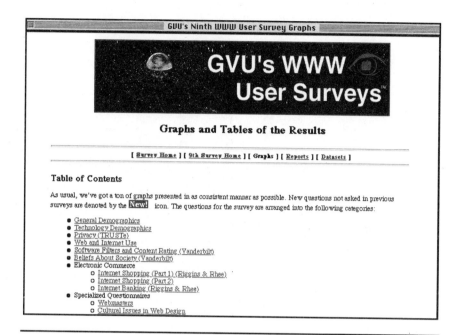

Figure 1.12. GVU user survey home page, *http://www.gvu.gatech.edu/ user_surveys/.* © 1994-1998 Georgia Tech Research Corporation. All rights reserved. Source: GVU's WWW User Survey at *www.gvu.gatech.edu/ user_surveys.*

For instance, *PC Flowers & Gifts* at *http://www.pcflowers.com/pcf/ default.asp* pioneered with Prodigy and other online services, and then added the Web. Over 40% of its annual revenues now come from online sales.

Travel is another growth story. By the year 2000, online commerce related to travel is estimated to reach 41% of Internet sales, with visitors attracted by such sites as *centralamerica.com* (see Figure 1.14) at *http://www.centralamerica.com/cr/parks/index.htm.* Close to 90% of online consumers use the Web to find out about their travel destinations, over 80% have visited travel Web sites, and tens of thousands of plane tickets are now purchased online.

The number of real estate sites has also grown, from huge sites like *http://www.realtor.com* to individual agents' sites. It is difficult to quantify the dollar value of real estate sold because sales are initiated online but closed off-line. However, with real estate sites attracting more than 6 million visitors per month, getting a property featured

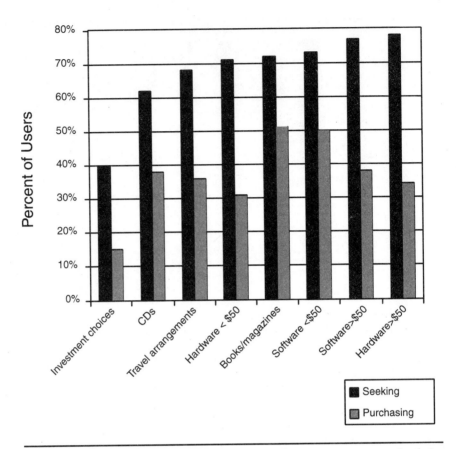

Figure 1.13. Online seeking and purchasing, *http://www.gvu.gatech.edu/ user_surveys/survey-1998-04/graphs/shopping/q3.htm.* © 1994-1998 Georgia Tech Research Corporation. All rights reserved. Source: GVU's WWW User Survey at *www.gvu.gatech.edu/user_surveys.*

online has become the fourth most effective residential selling technique, after signage, multiple listing services, and referrals.

How People Find Sites

It's important to understand how people find the Web sites they visit, because this will affect your Web promotion strategy. Already newspapers and TV shows review Web sites and announce Web happenings, from scheduled chats with stars, athletes, and political

Figure 1.14. Travel site, *http://www.centralamerica.com/parks/index.htm*. Courtesy centeramerica.com.

personalities to live Webcasts of entertainment events. News programs, movies, and all forms of advertising now include URLs in their promotional matter—just watch an evening of television or tabulate the print ads with URLs in your favorite magazine.

A GVU survey in October 1998 ranked users' common strategies for locating a Web site in the following order, from highest to lowest:

- Links, 88.3%

- Search engines, 84.8%

- Friends, 64.7%

- Printed media, 62.6%

These numbers remain fairly consistent from prior surveys, with the exception that the number of viewers who use links increased by over one-third.

If you sell online, you may also find that potential customers locate you through price-and-feature comparison sites like *http://www. compare.net* or price-based sites like *http://www.priceline.com* to find the best bargain on their desired products. Others offer shopping-specific search engines, like *http://shopping.yahoo.com* or Jango (*http://www.jango.com*), an Excite!-owned site devoted solely to retail sales. After the user enters a desired product, the engine returns information about locations and prices. Shown in Figure 1.15, Jango adds source sites when site owners click on "Add URL" at the bottom of the page.

Advertising on the Web

Viewers are often enticed to sites by Web advertisements, which 42% of online businesses use to promote their URLs. The total spent on such advertising in 1996 was a significant, but not astounding, $267

Figure 1.15. Shopping search engine, *http://www.jango.com/xsh/index. dcg?* Jango is a trademark of Excite, Inc. and may be registered in various jurisdictions. Excite screen display © 1995-1999 Excite, Inc.

million. Another $40 million was spent to advertise on non-Web services such as AOL.

Internet ad revenue exceeded $1.3 billion in 1998 and is forecast at $3 billion annually by the year 2000. For comparison, look at the distribution of $40 billion in total annual advertising expenditures shown in Figure 1.16. In spite of the increase from $400 million in 1997, the Internet still accounts for only a small percentage of advertising dollars.

Although more and more sites are seeking advertising, only about 20% attract ad revenue, with most of the money going for standardized **banner ads** (short, wide display ads). These are particularly popu-

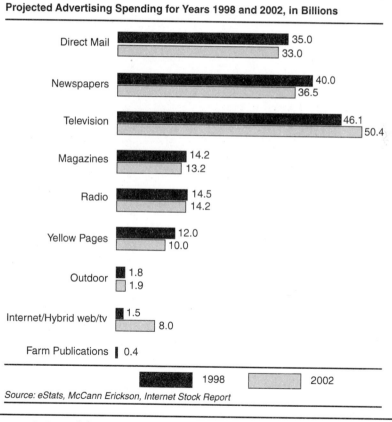

Projected Advertising Spending for Years 1998 and 2002, in Billions

Media	1998	2002
Direct Mail	35.0	33.0
Newspapers	40.0	36.5
Television	46.1	50.4
Magazines	14.2	13.2
Radio	14.5	14.2
Yellow Pages	12.0	10.0
Outdoor	1.8	1.9
Internet/Hybrid web/tv	1.5	8.0
Farm Publications	0.4	

Source: eStats, McCann Erickson, Internet Stock Report

Figure 1.16. Advertising spending by media, *http://www.estats.com/estats/ad_rev_persp_2.html*. Source: eMarketer at *http://www.emarketer.com*.

lar on large gateway sites like Netscape's NetCenter or Time Warner's Pathfinder at *http://pathfinder.com/time/digital,* as seen in Figure 1.17), since recent research shows them to be as effective as television in building brand awareness.

Banner ads are now responsible for only 53% of Web ad revenue, down from 80% in 1997. Sponsorships at 30% and **interstitials** (larger display ads between Web pages) at 6% are responsible for most of the remaining ad dollars. As their novelty wears off, banner ads are losing their appeal, with click-through rates now below 1% for static ads.

Even so, the cost of banner advertising may be out of the ballpark for small- to medium-size businesses except on small sites. Banner ads have become part of the imaging game for large companies, who

Figure 1.17. Banner ad on a major site, *http://www.pathfinder.com.*

rely less on actual click-throughs to their site and more on the subconscious recognition of brand names. As an alternative, we'll discuss how to exchange free links and banner ads with complementary businesses in Chapter 6. Sites like *http://www.emarketer.com* shown in Figure 1.18 or *http://www.adresource.com* or *http://cyberatlas. internet.com/segments/advertising/ad_index.html* are good sources for up-to-date information about online advertising.

Mass vs. Target Marketing

A perennial advertising debate rages over Web promotion: is the Web 90% brand imaging? Or is it 90% niche marketing? Should you aim for mass markets, maximizing your total exposure and the total number of viewers who see your name? Or should you aim at narrow demographic prospects who are more likely to turn into customers?

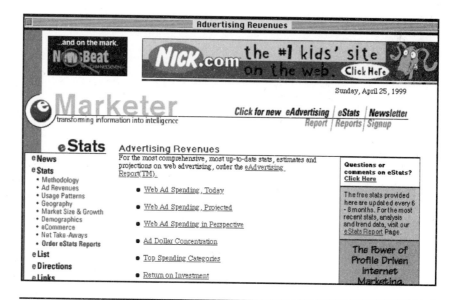

Figure 1.18.   Source for Internet advertising statistics, *http://www.estats. com/stats/net_ad_rev_exp.html*. Source: eMarketer at *http://www. emarketer.com*.

As a rule of thumb, unless you are a major corporation already managing brand imaging in national newspapers, network TV, radio, and glossy magazines, you will be better off with a target marketing approach. Spend your precious dollars where they will reach the most likely buyers. The cost of exposure-driven marketing is likely to empty all but the deepest pockets.

Advertisers use the term **CPM** to represent the cost per thousand possible viewers or listeners (M is the Roman numeral for 1,000). Generally, the higher the CPM, the smaller, but more targeted, the audience is in terms of geography or demographics. The table in Figure 1.19 compares typical CPMs for various media. The key, as always, is whether the viewers you reach are the right targets for the product or service you sell.

Even though its CPM may be low, the actual costs or minimum rates for an ad may not be. A 30-second Super Bowl ad, with a CPM of $12.30, sold for $1.6 million in 1999 to reach 130 million viewers. Over 30 different companies thought it was worth this price to include their URLs in the 1999 Super Bowl broadcast; 5 of these companies exist only online.

By comparison, the average CPM for a Web banner ad is $35, down for the second year in a row, partly due to the rapid growth in the supply of online advertising space. Actual costs range from a few hundred dollars per year to a few thousand dollars per week. You'll need to balance your budget against your desired audience size and demographics.

Advertisers apportioning their budgets must think hard about a 1997 Price Waterhouse Consumer Technology survey that showed

Form of Media	CPM Range
Web site (depends on number of impressions, demographic selection)	$18-$70
National Newspaper/Magazine	$30
Primetime Network TV, e.g. The Oscars	$27
Super Bowl	$12-$14
Typical Network TV Show	$7

Figure 1.19. CPMs by media.

that over one third of respondents used the Internet instead of watching TV and nearly one third used it instead of reading a book, newspaper, or magazine.

A similar survey by GVU indicated that 55.4% replace TV viewing time daily with the Internet; another 24.8% do so at least weekly. This statistic, combined with the fact that e-mail is now used as often as the phone, makes it clear that many people have already integrated the Internet thoroughly into their lives.

Push vs. Pull Technologies

Most Web marketing is based on **pull.** Your Web site or banner ad waits for users to link to your site, download your information, subscribe to your mailing list, or otherwise pull the information to themselves. One way to increase the value of your advertising dollar is to look at **push** technologies, which may help you reach your desired demographic profile. Push technologies on the Web are more like broadcast ads. People have to watch or listen to them whether or not they want to.

Recently developed push technologies, such as Marimba's *CastaNet,* incorporate advertisements with automatic downloads of information that a user has requested. An ad for golf clubs, for instance, might reach only those who requested sports news about golf. Such narrowcasting technology allows you to send ads to the specific demographic groups—segregated by categories, such as interest, income, age, and gender—that best fit your target market. This turns Web advertising into very familiar territory. You can implement this technology on your own Web site, allowing those who register to decide what kind of products interest them. You can then send them information on a regular basis, without waiting for a specific inquiry.

The best-known commercial user of CastaNet is PointCast (*http://www.pointcast.com*), a news service free to users. PointCast automatically downloads news to appear as a screen saver as often as the user requests. The stories are accompanied by animated ads. Figure 1.20 is typical of what a PointCast user sees, and Figure 1.21 shows frames from a typical animated ad. To use this particular service, an Internet aficionado must have fairly sophisticated equipment with lots of storage space and fast communication access that is al-

Figure 1.20. What PointCast users see, *http://www.pointcast.com*. PointCast is a registered trademark of PointCast, Incorporated.

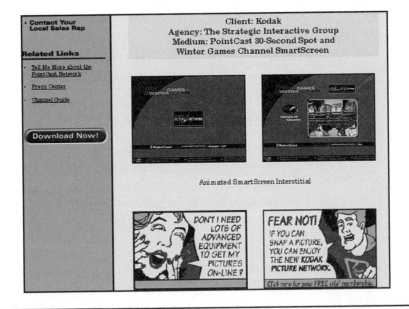

Figure 1.21. Animated ad at PointCast, *http://www.pointcast.com*. PointCast is a registered trademark of PointCast, Incorporated.

ways turned on. Lanacom, which was recently acquired by BackWeb Technologies, Inc., also offers software for delivering information to the desktop. (*http://headliner.com/index.html*). Push techniques are just one of many new technologies that will affect how you design and implement your Internet marketing strategy.

A Glimpse of the Future

The Internet couples a new broadcast medium with the allure of interactivity. The Internet demands that viewers constantly make choices, whether jumping to a new page or selecting something from the page they are on. From a marketing perspective, there is nothing like the opportunity to communicate with potential customers at the very moment when they are looking for information or making a purchasing decision.

In the near term, high-end computing capabilities combined with high-speed Web access will remain for most viewers a tantalizing feast they are unable to consume. A certain fraction of potential customers will get so annoyed waiting for an image to download that they will click away from a site or log off the Internet. You've probably done it yourself. Sites may lose customers who do not have adequate equipment to view a video-laden Web site or anger those who lack the know-how to install a plug-in needed to enjoy an expensive, animated Web site.

Let's look at some near-term technologies that may make the Web feast a little more affordable, a little more accessible, and a little more enjoyable for users. We'll discuss the technologies involved and what they imply for your company. Improvements are coming in two main areas:

1. Faster access to information from the Internet

2. Ease of use

First, you can assume that the enabling technologies of faster microprocessors, larger memory, and fast-access, economical storage will continue to offer better computer performance at the same or lower cost—multimedia PCs are already sold on specials for as little as $600.

Remember that the overall system can run only as fast as the slowest piece in it. Think of a stream of digital data as if it were a stream of water. The only way more water can flow through a pipe in a fixed length of time is to make the pipe bigger or the water smaller. Making water smaller is not an option in the physical world, but in the digital world, both options are available. You can make the pipe—bandwidth—bigger, or you can make information smaller through **data compression** technologies. Whichever way it is accomplished, running more information through a "pipe" translates to more connections, overcoming the well-known sluggishness of the Internet at busy times of the day. It also means that more information can be delivered to the same number of connections. For instance, graphics or sound can be transmitted in the same time it used to take to send only text. Let's look at some ways of obtaining bigger data "pipes."

Pipe Dreams

You may have heard in the press about four technologies for improving Internet access. The first three come from the telephone world; the fourth option derives from the perennial battle between phone companies and cable TV. All increase the size of the "pipe," allowing more data to flow more quickly between individual computers and the Internet. Collectively, these **broadband** technologies were used by only 310,000 U.S. households in 1998 (1.3% of online households). This is forecast, perhaps optimistically, to grow to 15.6 million households (30% of online households) by the year 2002.

ISDN

ISDN (Integrated Services Digital Network) is available now as a dial-up service in metropolitan areas for a base rate of about $30 a month plus installation. There is usually a per minute charge after a certain number of hours. Practically speaking, ISDN guarantees users an access rate of 56 to 64 Kbps. While current phone modems over **POTS** (Plain Old Telephone Service) offer up to 56 Kbps connections, there is no guarantee that rate will be obtained at busy times of day.

ISDN also works fine for several users at a time, though it is not fast enough to run a server. ISDN, which requires a separate line and an ISDN modem (I-modem) costing several hundred dollars, remains primarily a business option. Expect to spend about $200 for one-time setup and at least $30/month for ISDN service.

Leased Lines

Another business option, a **leased line,** requires rewiring an office building, which can be logistically and financially difficult. Leased lines come in assorted sizes: 56K lines, equivalent to one 128K connection; T1 lines, roughly equivalent to 6 ISDN lines or 1.5 M (million) bps; and T3 lines carrying 44.7 Mbps. T1 connections are often used to connect networks to the Internet, but it takes a T3 line to carry full-motion, full-screen video. T1 service is expensive: $500 to $1500 a month. Additional equipment is needed to divide the resources among different servers.

ADSL

ADSL or **DSL (Asymmetric/Digital Subscriber Line)** is poised for the big time, though there were only 100,000 users in 1998. An updated residential version of ISDN, ADSL takes advantage of advances in compression and other technologies to cram even more information into a standard telephone line. It promises faster, cheaper Internet service, with performance up to 6–8 Mbps. Unfortunately, ADSL speed is mainly for downloading information; sending back a request for information is much slower. Now available in some major metropolitan areas, monthly ADSL costs start at about $40 for 256 Kbps, $65 for 512 Kbps, and $125 for 1 Mbps.

One word of caution: These high-speed access lines, and sometimes even adequate copper phone lines, often are not available in thinly populated rural areas. For more information on ISDN, T1, and ADSL telephony, check out these Web sites:

- *http://www.PacBell.com/Products/business/fastrak/net working/ISDN/*

- *http://www.specialty.com/hiband*

- *http://cyberatlas.internet.com/big_picture/hardware/broad band.html/*

Cable Modems

Cable television lines are obviously capable of handling full-screen, full-motion video in real time; that's exactly what they deliver now as an analog signal to a television set. Cable companies joust with phone companies over who will provide broadband connections into the home. As a result, the corporate structure of the digital communication industry is in constant flux. AT&T has added cable operators Media One and TeleCommunications, Inc. (TCI) to its holdings, thus becoming the largest cable company in the United States with the potential to reach 60% of U.S. households. TCI, in turn, has an alliance with the independent cable-based ISP access service Cox@Home, which has 210,000 subscribers.

Some cable operators plan to integrate Internet services through investment, such as Time Warner, which has invested in a cable modem service called RoadRunner. Investments run the other way as well. Microsoft, for instance, has invested in cable operator Comcast Corp. and AOL is talking to Time Warner Cable. Cable companies and ISPs are battling over whether cable companies can require consumers to use their own bundled Internet service, or whether they should be required to allow multiple ISPs access to their lines.

Of course, it doesn't help to have faster transmission over an existing cable connection to your house if you don't have a way to connect to the computer. Cable modems with speeds of 128 to 256 Kbps cost $75–$200 for the hardware and/or installation, plus monthly charges of $30–$50, about the same as an ISDN line. When connected through a digital fiber optic network, such as Cox@Home (*http://www.cox.com/CoxatHome*), cable modems can download from 1.5 to 3 Mbps, bringing up sites instantaneously and downloading 10 MB files in well under a minute. (Uploading speeds are slower, ranging from 33.6 Kbps to 1 Mbps.)

Like ADSL, receiving information via standard cable modem is much faster than requesting it. Unlike a private ADSL line or other telephone service, a cable line is shared with other subscribers, slowing transmission as the number of users increases. On the other hand, a cable connection is always on. Cable modems claimed an installed base of 500,000 units in 1998, though they are predicted to surpass 2.4 million units by 2002.

In any case, it will be several years before this broadband Internet access becomes commonly available: Broadband access of some type will be rolled out to only 60% of the country by 2004. For more information on cable modems and other options, try the following Web sites:

http://www.multichannel.com/bband.shtml

http://www.iconocast.com/whatis/whatis.html

http://cyberatlas.internet.com/big_picture/hardware/hardware_index.html

Faster regular modems, which use ordinary copper telephone wires, are already on the market, with speeds of 56 Kbps most common. Like cable modems, uploading and requesting information is often slower than downloading. A 56 Kbps modem can be purchased for under $100.

Users of such ordinary modems outnumbered users of more advanced devices by a ratio of almost 20 to 1 in 1998. By 2003, some studies predict this ratio will decrease, with ordinary telephone modems projected to account for only 63% of those connecting to the Internet, cable modems 14%, DSL 12%, ISDN 8% (mainly at companies or institutions), and hybrid satellite 3%. Cabled sections of rural areas may find cable modems and/or Internet TV their best option in the near term. Satellite connections are becoming more affordable, but remain only one-way.

Telephones, Teleconferencing, and Multimedia, Oh My!

High-speed, broadband connections increase expectations. Improved capacity allows more complex messages to be sent more quickly. Today's graphics-based marketing message will become a multimedia message replete with video, animation, and high-quality sound. The nature of computing could change, with users accessing software on the Web instead of installing applications on their hard drives.

Internet teleconferencing may someday dramatically reduce the need for business travel. Large companies such as Microsoft are already experimenting with such extended teleconferences, offering **sitecasts** that include real-time video, prerecorded graphics and slides, and real-time text chat lines. From a marketing perspective, the changes in technology translate into:

- The potential to attract new customers with sophisticated, value-added sites

- New forms of product and service delivery with value-added features like voice and video teleconferencing and live performances

- New products and markets in the form of pay-per-use software applications, like word processing and spreadsheets

- More satisfied online customers, which implies more online sales

Alternate High-Speed Networks

One innovation may reduce the number of Web surfers, though not by much. Frustrated by the increasing commercialization of the Web, the explosion of sites and users, and subsequent slow transmission speeds, the military long ago created MILNET, a network independent of the Internet. In addition, some 60 corporations and academic institutions turned on an alternative Internet called the Abilene Project in February 1999.

The Abilene Project will run at 2.4 gigabits (billion bits) per second—43,000 times faster than a 56K modem—making high-speed video and audio a reality. The prototype for the Internet of the future, this 10,000-mile fiber optic network is part of a larger research effort known as the Internet2 Initiative. Internet2, founded in 1996, is a public/private sector consortium, funded partially with federal dollars under the Next Generation Internet Initiative and partially with investment and equipment from high-tech companies.

Just in case you're thinking of joining this exclusive club, plan to prove that your company is a viable research entity and expect to pony up a $100,000 membership fee and $25,000 annually for maintenance and overhead. For more information, check out

- The Abilene Project at *http://cgi.pathfinder. com/time/digital/daily/0,2822,20462,00.html)*

- Internet2 Initiative at *http://www.internet2.edu*

- Next Generation Internet Initiative (NGI) at *http://smithsonian.yahoo.com/nextgeneration.html*

If academics, high-tech corporations, and the military are part of your target market, you need to consider whether you will lose exposure from MILNET and the Abilene Project, or whether those populations will simply use two networks for different purposes.

Ease of Use: The "Internet Appliance"

At the low end of the market, companies are competing to test whether a marriage of the Web and the tube can be made in cyberheaven. If the fusion advocates have their way, using the Internet will be as easy as sitting on your sofa, clicking your remote control to channel surf for a classic flick.

Internet TV products use a regular television set, a special Web terminal that sits on top of the TV, a standard phone jack, a remote control unit with a "Web" button, a subscription to an Internet TV service, and an optional wireless keyboard and/or printer adapter. Forecasts for the year 2000 indicate that about 12 million households are expected to use Internet TV to reach the Web, although that number may be unrealistic.

Some see Internet TV as an opportunity to create a new form of interactive entertainment; others see an endless version of the Home Shopping Show. But almost all Internet TV advocates envision direct tie-ins between television shows, their sponsors, and related Web sites, such as clicking on a TV guidebook, reading reviews, or checking out the Web site of a hit show. Internet TV users can surf the Web like a pro, join entertainment chat groups, read fan mags online, send e-mail to their favorite star, and order any product advertised on TV that's available on the Web.

Made by Sony, Philips, Curtis-Mathes, and Mitsubishi, set-top terminals for Web browsing run $300–$400, with up to $100 additional for the keyboard. The units contain a 1.1 GB (gigabyte) hard drive and modems to download special Web content during available intervals in television transmission. Subscriptions to one of the Internet TV services run about $20 a month, which is competitive with standard rates for an ISP.

Large companies are trying to cover all bases. In 1998 Microsoft bought WebTV, a service that has garnered 150,000 subscribers since its launch in 1996. About the same time, Internet rival America Online bought NetChannel, a competing Internet TV service.

An alternative approach, Worldgate, blends the Internet and television by offering Internet service through a standard cable converter box and television remote. Faster to set up and less complicated than the options just discussed, Worldgate also expects to be cheaper—$12 a month—without any additional equipment required. Of course, unless there are significant improvements in psychic technology, you'll still have to type your e-mail with a keyboard. Trials are scheduled for 1998. Stay tuned.

For the Internet marketer, these Internet TV alternatives, which counted perhaps 600,000 combined users in 1998, open the possibility of reaching a group of users somewhat different from those currently on the Web. When the price drops from a $600 computer to a $300 box, when the computer is as familiar as the TV, when the interface is simplified—advertisers take note.

First, these viewers will have absolutely no problem receiving multimedia content. In fact, they will expect it, once again ratcheting up the cost of Web presence and promotion. Second, the demographics of Internet users will change, bringing an audience to the Internet that is more diverse in income, age, education, and employment, an audience more reflective of the overall population. For up-to-date news about what's happening with Internet TV, see such Internet information sites as *http://www.ruel.net/settop_news.html*, shown in Figure 1.22.

One of your tasks in the next chapter will be to profile your target customers. Among the questions you'll need to answer is whether they are on the Internet now, whether they are likely to become participants if Internet TV catches on, or whether they are likely to drop off if they become users of private, high-speed networks.

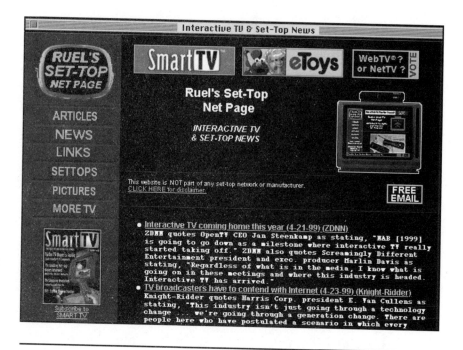

Figure 1.22. Internet TV information site, *http://www.ruel.net/settop_ news.htm.* © 1999 Ruel T Hernandez, *http://ruel.net* or *http://ruel.com.*

The Bottom Line

Using an array of online data to enhance your marketing efforts may seem a daunting challenge, but it is just another method for achieving your business goals. As always, the most complex problems will not be technology based, but business based: finding your target market, turning prospects into customers, and keeping those customers as repeat buyers of your product or service.

In the following chapters, you'll find more detail about how to evaluate and implement your Internet marketing options, from developing an Internet marketing plan (Chapter 2) to non-Web electronic marketing (Chapter 3) and the implementation of a Web site (Chapter 4).

2

The ABCs of Internet Marketing

To demystify the Internet, you should evaluate it as you would any other marketing or sales opportunity, such as an advertisement in a trade journal, a new product brochure, or a booth at a street fair. The Internet offers all those options to a creative businessperson: It is at once an advertising medium, a form of sales literature, and a distribution channel.

One thing is certain: Don't use the Internet unless it makes sense for your business. As a form of communication, the Internet is a means, not an end. Avoid the temptation to go online simply because everyone else is doing so. A manicurist whose clientele all work in one high-rise office building might not get much business from the Internet, but someone who sells glue-on nails with rhinestone studs or painted desert scenes might do very well indeed!

By the end of this chapter you will understand

- The importance of good business practices to online success

- The elements of an Internet marketing and/or sales plan

- The parallels between online and direct marketing

- The seven steps to Internet success

Your Business Plan: Internet and Otherwise

You do have a plan, don't you? A **business plan** is a written description of your business goals and how you will achieve them. If you don't have one, write at least a short draft before you go online. If your plan is sitting on a shelf, dust it off and update it. If you plan to start a new enterprise that exists only on the Internet, having a business plan is absolutely critical.

For help with business plans, check out your local Small Business Development Center. These centers are often located at community colleges. For the one nearest you, call the Small Business Administration Answer Desk at 1-800-827-5722 or check out the SBA Web site at *http://www.sbaonline.sba.gov.*

Obviously, the business plan for a Web-based purveyor of cookie "bouquets" will differ from the plan for a minority executive search firm. A distributor of natural health products needs to resolve different business issues than a factory-direct seller of hot tub covers, but all these businesses can use the Internet to enhance their marketing. Look at their Web sites in Figures 2.1 through 2.4 to see how these businesses have taken advantage of the Internet's potential.

Many businesses write a plan only when they go to a bank to borrow money, but wise business owners write one annually as an internal gyroscope. They use the plan to set milestones for the coming year, to introduce a new product, or before entering another geographic territory. In many ways, going online is like adding another business location, albeit an electronic one.

If you are in business, you can use the plan to evaluate critically what is currently working and what is not. Be honest about business problems when you write or revise your plan. For instance, if you've been getting complaints about the slow shipment of products, you need to find out whether the problem is order processing, the lack of goods in stock, a poor supplier, or a backlog in the shipping department. Taking orders electronically might only compound these problems.

Question all the elements of your business. Is your current advertising successful? Do you need to move to a different manufacturing facility or add another storefront? Are you being pressed by a competitor with deep pockets who can afford to undersell you? Understanding the problems you already face is essential before deciding whether the Internet would help overcome them or would merely

Figure 2.1. Sample business Web site, *http://www.cookiebouquets.com.*
Courtesy Cookie Bouquets.

Figure 2.2. Sample business Web site, *http://www.minorityexecsearch
coml.* Courtesy Minority Executive Search, Inc.

Figure 2.3. Sample business Web site, *http://www.mytwohomes.com.* Courtesy LadyBug Press.

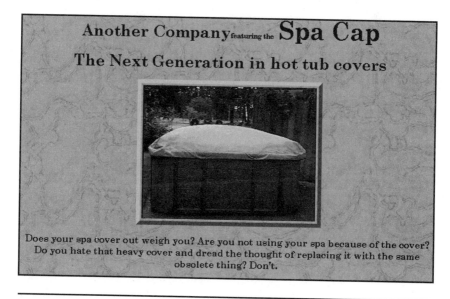

Figure 2.4. Sample business Web site, *http://www.spacap.com.* Courtesy Another Company.

magnify them. The Internet is not a panacea for other business difficulties, nor is it a get-rich-quick scheme. For that, stick to late-night infomercials.

Elements of a Business Plan

The content of a business plan may vary with the type of business, but it generally includes the following sections:

1. Mission/type of business (e.g., manufacturing, wholesale, retail, catalog, service)

2. Description of product or service

3. Competition

4. Marketing

    a. Target market (customer description)

    b. Objectives

    c. Methods

    d. Advertising detail

5. Sales plan

    a. Objectives and methods

    b. Distribution channels

    c. Sales methods (e.g., sales force, agents, reps, telemarketing)

    d. Pricing

    e. Fulfillment process

6. Operations

    a. Facilities (e.g., location, size, equipment)

    b. Manufacturing methods (if applicable)

    c. Suppliers

    d. Customer service and support

    e. Staff

7. Projected revenues and expenses (one to five years)

The Internet itself can help you write your business plan. For instance, through online research you might find new suppliers who could give you a better price, faster delivery, or higher-quality goods. You could check whether the Internet has created new competition. With manufacturers, wholesalers, and retailers all selling on the Web, distribution channels—and price points—are shifting rapidly. You may need to adjust sales projections accordingly.

Stories of easy dollars flowing in Internet commerce may leave you fantasizing about the cyberwealth of Bill Gates, or at least of Midas. However, if you can't fulfill customer orders quickly with good products, you may easily go through cyberbusiness failure. A well-thought-out business plan is the best way to increase your likelihood of success.

The Importance of Good Business Practices

The media tend to write about Web winners. But it is not all a bed of cyber-roses. The $3 billion crush of online orders in Christmas 1998 caught even the big "e-tailers" off-guard. Booksellers Amazon.com and Barnes and Noble, auction house eBay, and Toys 'R' Us all had problems processing orders online and making timely delivery.

By early 1999 surveys showed that the season had taken a toll. Customer satisfaction, though still high, slipped among Web walkers, according to Jupiter Communications, a media research firm in Greenwich, Connecticut. It found that satisfaction with online shopping ranked at 74%, a downslide of 14% between July and the end of December 1998. Only 37% of the households in their survey said they would spend more money online the following Christmas.

It's worth noting that customers most appreciate shopping online for its convenience, as you can see in Figure 2.5 from a Department of Commerce survey conducted in 1998 (*http://www.ecommerce.gov/ emerging.htm*). Consequently, poor performance that interferes with convenience is a sure way to lose a customer. Sites that make their products hard to find, forcing people to go through page after page on the Web, are just as discouraging as stores with similar products scattered all across several departments on different floors.

A company that doesn't fulfill promises of next-day delivery or falsely says a product is in stock can't expect satisfied buyers. Jupiter Communications also found that 42% of sites they surveyed didn't provide adequate customer response to e-mail, taking five days or more answer or blowing off e-mail inquiries altogether.

If purchasing data and credit card information gathered online is not kept private and secure, customers will lose confidence about shop-

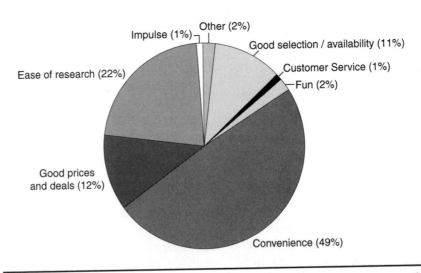

Figure 2.5.   Best thing about online shopping, *http://www.ecommerce.gov/ danc5.htm.*

ping in cyberspace, just as they would if their credit card numbers were stolen after charging dinner at a local restaurant. The implications are clear: If you plan to sell online, you need to focus on service and attracting repeat customers. There's nothing new about that.

You Can Do Much More Than Sell Online

Selling electronically instead of through a print catalog is usually the first thought that comes to mind with the Internet, but you can do much more. The marketing section of your Internet business plan may reflect many other goals:

- Increasing brand or product awareness

- Enhancing corporate image

- Providing information and/or displaying samples of goods or services

- Generating a list of prospective customers

- Building relationships with customers and prospects

- Improving customer service

- Gathering information about customer needs and preferences to guide future product development

- Better understanding customer demographics

- Testing consumer response to discounts or other special offers

- Finding business partners, dealers, franchisees, or suppliers

- Recruiting talent, members, employees, or subscribers

- Saving money by lowering the cost of customer communication and support through automation, simplifying distribution channels, lowering the cost of order fulfillment, or reducing inventories.

Keep such goals in mind as you write the marketing section of your business plan. They determine which methods you will use, Internet or otherwise. Even if you are a truly virtual company, one that exists only in cyberspace, the Internet will be only one of many methods needed to achieve your targeted goals. The fastest-growing companies already understand this. As seen in the 1998 survey in Figure 2.6, almost all companies view their sites as multipurpose in nature. Only 32% reported selling products or services directly as one of the functions of their Web site.

You must also determine what constitutes successful completion of your goals, at least in broad terms. Whenever possible, quantify those successes. For example, $25,000 in sales over the first year, 600 people a day learning about your business, speeding order fulfillment by two days, obtaining six new bookings as a wedding photographer, hiring three new employees.

Is the Internet Right for Your Business?

What kinds of businesses work on the Web? All kinds: genealogy search services (*http://www.itw.ie/roots*), career and outplacement (*http://careerlab.com/letters/default.htm*), private investigators (*http://www.fraudfinders.com*), reference support (*http://www.surfchina.com*), coupon services (*http://www.ecentives.com*), crafts (*http://www.origamido.com*), gifts (*http://www.candlelightgifts.com*).

If you're thinking of starting a computer-based, virtual company but not sure what you want to do, try browsing through such lists as Work-at-Home Ideas on the news group *biz.general*. (See Chapter 3 for more information on news groups.) Be creative as you think about what an audience looks for online. Remember Marshall McLuhan's dictum, "the medium is the message." As users become more sophisticated, they search out applications that make the best use of the Web for itself, not as a way to repackage content appropriate to another medium. In other words, people crave interactivity online,

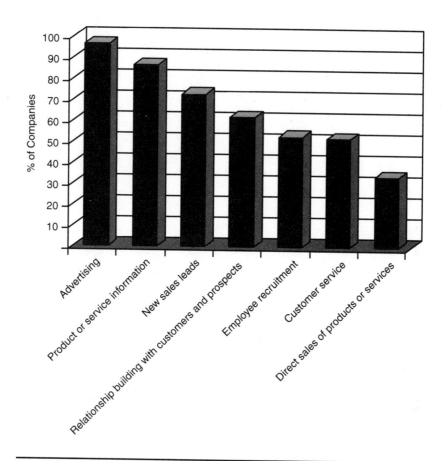

Figure 2.6. Purposes of corporate Web sites, *http://www.barometer surveys.com*. Courtesy Pricewaterhouse Coopers' "Trendsetter Barometer."

whether through an auction, a chat room, buying, online planning, or creating their own home pages.

Can you marry a business concept to entertainment, creating not the info-tainment of television news or the edu-tainment of educational software, but the busin-tainment of interactive marketing? Can you figure out a way to create an online community that will flock to your bazaar? Search the Web to see what businesses similar to yours are doing online. Then write your business plan, adding your creative vision to the pot.

Essential questions

With a clear picture of your business goals and an understanding of the operations of the Internet and the Web, you can decide whether to add those capabilities to your sales and marketing tool kit. To start with, the American Institute of Certified Public Accountants suggests you ask yourself the following questions, particularly if your intent is to sell, as well as to market, online:

1. Is your business local in nature?

2. Does your business depend on face-to-face contact with customers?

3. Could you benefit from a national or global reach?

4. Do you have an unusual product that's difficult for customers to find?

5. Can your product ship by mail or courier service?

6. Are your customers able and willing to use the Internet to get obtain service?

A "yes" answer to the first two questions indicates that the Internet may not be for you, unless you are planning to expand your business or use your site for purposes other than sales. A yes answer to the last four questions is a positive indicator for Internet marketing.

Take time to think through your answers. Whether your product is appropriate for the Web is more than just a matter of shipment. Does it need extensive setup or installation time? If so, can you coordinate a service call with an online order? Is it a made-to-order or customizable product? Made-to-order is possible online: Levi-Strauss sells custom-fit jeans on its Web site (*http://store.us.levi.com: 80/store/home.asp*). Just make sure that you can handle such orders, perhaps by an immediate callback from a sales rep.

Above all, review your business plan. Is growth the right move for your company? Are you capable of handling expansion that might ensue from Internet-based marketing? Do you have excess capacity now? Would you need space? personnel? equipment? inventory? financing?

Here's the ultimate question: Will an investment in Internet marketing pay off by increasing the value of your company? If the answer to that question is "no," then satisfy your Web cravings as a buyer, not a seller.

Know Thy Business Universe

You need to gauge the electronic savvy of your business universe in every direction. First, analyze your competitors' Web sites and the methods they use to communicate with customers. Just because they are online, doesn't mean they are turning a profit! One of the most famous business stories on the Web, Amazon.com (*http://www.amazon.com*) projects 1999 revenues of $1 billion, but it has yet to break even.

Second, research your suppliers to see how many of them are on the Internet. You may find a potential for comarketing or other business opportunities. You might find potential links to and from your site, or identify other Web sites that would refer potential customers to you in exchange for a small commission.

Finally, compare the target audience described in your business plan to the profile of online users described later. If you sell to other businesses, see if those customers have an electronic presence. Remember, the really big story in Internet commerce is business-to-business selling, which accounts for triple the revenue of retail sales.

If your customers aren't using the Internet, should you be there? This isn't an automatic no, but it should make you pause. Consider whether online marketing is important to other target audiences, such as suppliers, potential employees, or possible business partners.

Is your target audience more likely to use the Internet at work or at home? Currently, about 70% of American users access the Internet from home and 43% access it from work, at least part of the time. If you don't know whether your audience meets this profile, ask them! A little market research, even randomly calling some existing customers, will give you critical information. See what Internet services besides the Web your customers use. e-mail? News groups? Do they subscribe to mailing lists? Use AOL or CompuServe? If you don't have customers yet, you can still conduct simple research calls to define your target audience.

Know Thy Target Audience

Internet users over the age of 16 in the United States and Canada now number more than 92 million, representing 37% of all adults. Worldwide, there are 159 million users, with growth forecast to reach 320 million by the year 2002—almost 5% of this planet's inhabitants. The amount of time spent online is shown in Figure 2.7, with about 60% of users spending more than 10 hours per week. One fifth to one quarter of users go online daily.

No Internet demographic study is 100% reliable because everything changes so rapidly. With that caveat, consider the statistics from a January 1999 survey by the Pew Research Center seen in the table in Figure 2.8. It compares the newest Internet users with those who

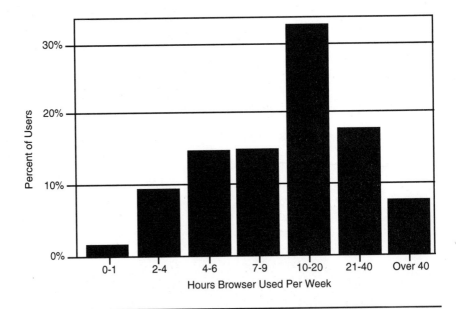

Figure 2.7. Time spent online, *http://www.gvu.gatech.edu/user_surveys/survey-1998-04/graphs/use/q20.jpg.* © 1994-1998 Georgia Tech Research Corporation. All rights reserved. Source: GVU's WWW User Survey at *www.gvu.gatech.edu/user_surveys.*

were online before. The results, with the significant exceptions of race and income, bear out a comment made by the author of a similar *Business Week* study in April 1997, "As more people get online, cyberspace begins to look more like Earth."

The data show that over half the Americans surfing the Web today are between 30 and 49 years old. Don't discount seniors over 50 though: The fastest growing group on the Internet, they comprise about 20% of Web users.

Educational and income statistics for Internet/Web users have declined to more closely mirror those of the population as a whole. Thirty-three percent of the overall population has a household in-

	Went Online in the Past Year	Online More Than a Year	In U.S. Population as of (7/98)
Percent of Adult Internet Users	46	53	
Percent of Users Who Are Age			
18-29	25	30	16.2
30-49	52	50	30.9
50-64	16	15	14.2
65+	4	4	12.7
Percent of Users by Gender			
Male	48	55	49
Female	52	45	51
Percent of Users With Income			
$50,000+	35	45	14.7
$30,000-49,000	23	22	16.5
Under $30,000	23	16	68.8
Percent of Users With Education			
College Graduate	29	46	26.1
Some College	32	30	29.1
High School Grad	33	19	32.7
Less than high school	6	3	12.1
Percent of Users Who Use Internet for			
Work	24	30	
Pleasure	52	39	
Mix	22	31	

Figure 2.8. Demographics of Internet users, *http://cyberatlas.internet.com/ big_picture/demographics/mainstream.html.* Reprinted with permission © 1999 Internet.com, LLC. All rights reserved.

come over $50,000; 35% of Internet users do. Internet users still outdistance the percent of the population with some college attendance by 61 to 46%, but of those planning to go online in the future, 49% have a high school education or less.

Most significantly, the gender gap has closed: Slightly over half of Internet users are female, up from 39% in 1997 and from 5% only six years ago. Furthermore, they've become the driving force in Internet buying. The increasing number of women signifies one of the most important trends for Internet marketers, since women traditionally control household budgets and are responsible for 70% of retail sales. Undoubtedly, these statistics account for the increasing number of major Web sites aimed at women:

http://www.oxygen.com/ (as seen in Figure 2.9.)

http://www.ivillage.com

http://www.women.com

http://www.womenswire.com

http://www.chickclick.com (a Web ring that includes the "grrls" sites that follow)

http://www.webgrrls.com

http://www.cybergrrl.com

http://www.femina.cybergrrl.com (a search engine for women)

These sites are not slouches. iVillage, which went public in March 1999, counts NBC among its investors and claims 73 million page views per month. Oxygen Media has funding from AOL, ABC TV, and Oprah Winfrey's media company. Women.com has Hearst Corporation (*Redbook* and *Cosmopolitan* magazines) backing. Like their male-counterpart sites, these Web darlings have yet to turn a profit. A number of sites also aim at the increasing online presence of preteen and teenage females:

http://www.smartgirl.com

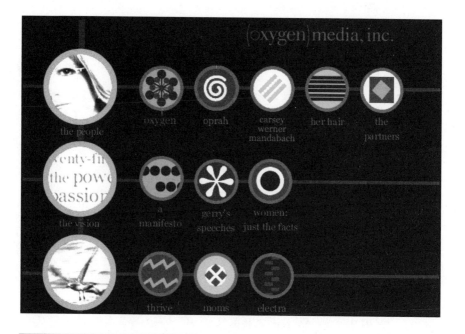

Figure 2.9. Web site aimed at women, *http://www.oxygen.com*. Courtesy Oxygen Media, Inc.

http://www.teengrrl.com

http://www.gurl.com

http://www.dELiAs.com

One word of dismay: The Internet does not look like the world when it comes to race. Internet and Web users are overwhelmingly white compared to the demographics of the U.S. population, as seen in the table from GVU in Figure 2.10. It's not just a matter of usage. Computer ownership and Internet access are not equally distributed across racial lines either. Whites in America are twice as likely to own a computer and more than three times as likely to have Internet access as African Americans. According to a Commerce Department survey "Falling Through the Net," racial disparity in use is not accounted for just by income. To reach an African-American audience, you might

Background	% U.S. Users	% U.S. Population	% European Users	% Other World Users
African-American	1.9	12.1	—	0.3
Indigenous	0.3	0.7	—	0.8
Asian	2.9	3.7	0.8	13.5
Hispanic/Latino	1.9	10.4	1.4	3.3
Multiracial	1.6	1.0	0.8	3.0
Other Minority	1.6	—	1.6	4.3
Caucasian	89.8	72.1	93.2	72.2
Not Identified	—	—	2.2	2.6

Figure 2.10. Percent of Internet users who are minorities, *http://www. gvu.gatech.edu/user_surveys/survey-1998-10/graphs/general/q48.htm.* © 1994-1998 Georgia Tech Research Corporation. All rights reserved. Source: GVU's WWW User Survey at *www.gvu.gatech.edu/user_surveys.*

want to search out such sites as AfroNet and African American Internetwork.

If your audience is Hispanic, you might want to focus your efforts on Prodigy, which offers a Spanish-language Internet access service ($19.95 per month), hoping to bridge the language barriers that have the kept the number of Hispanics online so low (see Figure 2.10 again). In addition to customer service and technical support in Spanish, Prodigy incorporates Spanish-language advertising, news, and links to Hispanic Web sites and Spanish-language search engines. Promoted initially in Chicago and Miami, the service eventually will be promoted nationwide.

New Hispanic-oriented portals, like *http://www.quepasa.com* have started to spring up. Other companies with Spanish services generally focus on Latin America, although the content, being virtual, is available in the United States. Star Media, out of New York, and AOL's joint venture with a Venezuelan company both serve that market.

Finally, users overwhelmingly have white-collar occupations, with only 15% in the "Other" category (except for seniors) as shown in Figure 2.11. Now that the Internet has spread from academia to the business world, students have become a smaller percentage of users overall, but they remain nearly half the audience ages 19 to 25.

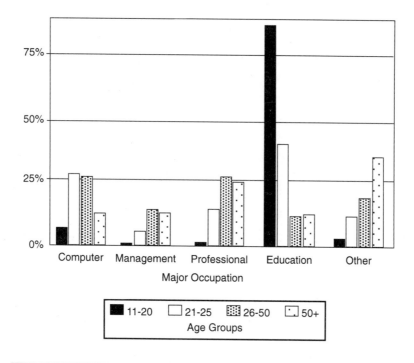

Figure 2.11. Occupations of Web users by age, *http://www.gvu.gatech.edu/ user_surveys/survey-1998-04/graphs/general/q27.htm.* © 1994-1998 Georgia Tech Research Corporation. All rights reserved. Source: GVU's WWW User Survey at *www.gvu.gatech.edu/user_surveys.*

Matching Methods to Research

If your research shows that it makes sense to start marketing online, look closely at the various methods available to you for achieving the marketing goals and objectives in your business plan. Which methods will work best for each goal? Make a list of both electronic and non-electronic means. If you want, organize this material in a chart, with your goals along the side. Check off the appropriate methods for achieving each one, as seen in Figure 2.12.

For instance, news groups are not a good choice for retail sales. If you are trying to build brand name recognition, where the number of impressions counts more than making a sale, then adding online ad-

Possible Marketing Goal	Online Mailing Lists	News Groups	Direct E-mail	Online Services	Web
Build Customer List					
Display Sample of Goods or Services					
Enhance Corporate Image					
Find Business Partners, Dealers, or Franchisees					
Gather Customer Preferences					
Improve Customer Service					
Improve Supplier Relations/Performance					
Increase Brand/Name Awareness					
Obtain Better Demographic Information					
Product Development and Testing					
Recruit Employees, Members, or Subscribers					
Research Competitors, Marketplace, Suppliers					
Sell Goods or Services					
Test Consumer Responses to Marketing Offers					
Understand Customer Needs					

Figure 2.12. Online marketing worksheet.

vertising in addition to a Web site makes sense. However, you'll still need a regular advertising budget for print, radio, or television. On the other hand, if you want to display a sample of your wares, then a Web site is the best electronic way to go. If you want to test market a special promotion, try targeting e-mail to people who have registered at your site. Only you can decide which methods will fit your objectives.

Marketing on the Internet is a business decision. Is it cost-effective for *you*? Can you find *your* audience? Are there losses if you *don't* do it? The answers to these questions need to be considered as part of your online marketing plan.

Online Marketing Is Direct Marketing

While selling on the Internet is similar to catalog sales, marketing online is similar to direct mail. Consider the Internet as direct media.

- Direct mail sells by sending people information. The Internet provides an expanding universe of information delivery possibilities.

- In direct mail marketing, you attempt to identify people who are most likely to want your product or service. You need to locate prospects and turn them into customers. You must do the same when marketing over the Internet.

- With direct mail marketing, you might mail brochures or sales letters to 100,000 people all over the country. When marketing over the Internet, you deal in the same kinds of numbers, but the Internet is global, not local.

You may already be familiar with the acronym AIDA to remember the key points of direct mail marketing. It stands for

- Attention

- Interest

- Desire

- Action

In any marketing approach, first you have to get the attention of prospective customers. Then, you must create interest in your product. Third, you build desire for your product. Finally, you ask the prospect to take action. He or she must fill out a form, call an 800 number, or send in a coupon—any action will do as long as it demonstrates intent.

The same techniques apply online. Gaining attention, creating interest, and building desire actually may be easier on the Internet than in other media because your prospective customer has already gone to the Web to find something or is browsing through cyberspace like a window shopper strolling through a mall.

Attention

On the Internet, you use hypertext, video, sound, graphics, and animation to make your point. Good graphics, attention-grabbing headlines, and a good lead draw people to your page.

Information Creates Interest

Internet viewers have a remote control device in front of them all the time—their mouse or trackball. The instant they determine there is nothing in your site for them, they will use this device to dismiss your contribution and move to other sites. Whenever you are tempted to become overly enthralled with your Web offerings, remember those "couch potatoes." They change channels at every chance if they are not entertained or informed. It's the same on the Internet. Web pages have to be constantly updated, and kept exciting and different, to ensure that viewers linger on your site and that they return to visit often. The Internet is called the Information Superhighway, not the Advertising Superhighway. Keep your customers interested, your pitch soft. As long as you provide the information or entertainment people want, they will return to your site.

Interactivity Builds Desire

The combination of the Internet and the personal computer is a very interactive experience, so you can build into your display all manner of techniques that allow a prospect to uncover and discover even the subtlest feature of your product.

Interactivity is the most intriguing part of this new marketing medium. The viewer actually builds desire by moving through your site to locate the answers that are needed to make a buying decision. For example, look at the interactive materials calculator at *http://www.todayshomeowner.com/calculators/index.html* or the room planner at the Herman Miller office furniture site seen in Figure 2.13 (*http://www.hmstore.com/planner/index.html*). Be a little patient. Most product purchases, in any medium, take place after seeing a product several times. It's the same with the Internet.

Action

Having a prospect take action is sometimes easier to do on the Internet than in other media. When you advertise on the radio, you have a real problem getting listeners to take immediate action because they are often driving. When you advertise on TV, your prospects are generally relaxing on a sofa; they are not likely to make a phone call just for you.

On the Internet, though, you are reaching prospects already sitting up and paying attention. Whether they are using their computer at home or at the office, your prospects are in the right frame of mind

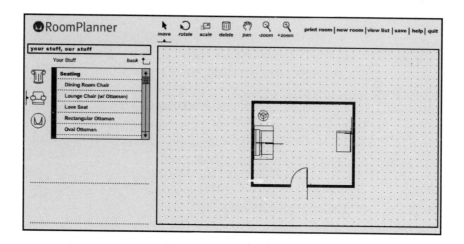

Figure 2.13. Interactive online tool (room planner) *http://www.hmstore. com/planner/index.html*. Courtesy Herman Miller, Inc. Herman Miller for the Home.

to take action, so ask them to do something like registering on your site. After completing a short form, the customer merely clicks on a button to e-mail it back. There is no postal middleman here. You don't have to wait two or three days for notification of the prospect's interest in your product or service.

The Seven Steps to Internet Success

With your business plan, knowledge of direct marketing, and Internet research in hand, you can start building a detailed marketing plan that will increase your chances for online success. As with any other form of marketing, the old maxim holds: Plan your work, work your plan.

There are seven important steps to success:

1. Get online and observe.

2. Evaluate your current situation.

3. Define online objectives, products, and markets.

4. Create and distribute info-tools.

5. Create or upgrade your Web site.

6. Measure your results.

7. Market your Internet presence.

We'll discuss the first three steps in this chapter, with a brief overview of the remaining four.

Step 1.   Get Online and Observe

It's time for research. You've looked at the online presence of your customers, competitors, and suppliers, and made a first estimate of which methods might make sense. If you need more information, try to include some enticement for customer response and/or completion of a short survey. Consider a giveaway or a discount coupon that can be used online or off.

Your research won't be wasted. Once you have customer information, including e-mail addresses, you can develop extremely personalized, targeted marketing campaigns to inform potential customers of products they might find appealing or of discounts available. You can solicit customers' input on future product design or enlist them in test marketing special promotions.

By obtaining feedback from your electronic marketing experiments, you'll learn for yourself the best way to reach your target audience. Now it's time to get a feel for the way information, advertising, and sales move across the Internet. This may confirm your instincts, or it may lead you to change your plans.

First check out the online services, such as AOL or CompuServe. Evaluate how companies advertise and how they place their ads. Are they catching users when they first sign on with a special offer? Does a display ad interrupt a quarter of the viewing screen as you click on a new page? What types of ads appear on a news page? On a search page? Can you figure out whom these advertisers are trying to reach?

See how companies provide customer support through online services. What would you need to do to provide support this way? Look at the electronic shopping malls, too. What would you have to do to showcase your product? Figure 2.14 is an example of an AOL shopping site; Figure 2.15 shows a technical support page.

Now go to a forum in your area of interest, whether it is computer hardware or travel. Observe the chat groups. Sign up with several mailing lists and see what kind of mail you receive.

Finally, go to the Web to review good sites. Analyze sites that appear on the Cool Links or HotSite lists at such locations as *http://www.coolcentral.com*. Your goal is to educate yourself about the variety of Web sites, to develop an eye for the designs you find appealing.

Step 2. Evaluate Your Current Situation

With online research animating your brain, evaluate your current situation. Do you fully understand where your customers congregate on the Internet, the best way to reach them, the best way to deliver to them, and how to support the sale?

Figure 2.14. AOL shopping mall. "America Online," "AOL" and the Logo design are all registered trademarks of America Online, Inc. © 1997-1999 America Online, Inc. All rights reserved.

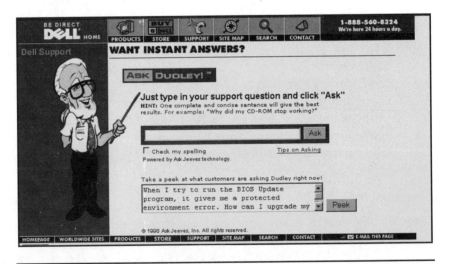

Figure 2.15. Tech support site, *http://support.dell.com/askdudley.* © 1999 Dell Computer Corporation. All rights reserved.

You might use this initial effort to survey customers about what they would most like to buy, or you may decide that your current product or service won't sell well over the Web. Be prepared for surprises. At first, used cars seem an unlikely item to sell online. Could there be a place for a used car dealer on the Web? You bet!—if the purpose is to trade classic cars, locate parts, or buy and sell vehicles with a high market value, such as an old Studebaker. It works for the folks at *http://www.oldcars.com,* whose site is shown in Figure 2.16. New cars are a hot item for online purchase, too. Look at *http://www.autobytel.com* or *http://www.autoweb.com.* After processing customer information and arranging financing online, the new car sites direct people to a local outlet or auto buying service for actual delivery.

Figure 2.16. Unlikely business to find on the Web, *http://www.oldcars.com.* Courtesy *www.inetcity.net.*

Decide whether this type of niche marketing fits into your business plan. Use good old-fashioned market research to determine whether buyers would be willing to pay your costs as a broker for such goods and when they want to manage such trades themselves. How many such buyers might you reach online compared to advertising in a specialty car magazine such as *Hemmings,* which has a monthly circulation of 260,000?

Remember that marketing on the Internet may be faster and cheaper in absolute dollars than traditional bulk mail, but it is not always as cost-effective. Test the results carefully: Try a similar promotion using both methods. You may find that not enough of your customers use the Internet or that your true clientele is local, not international. You must look at the cost of sales in both methods. It is tempting to avoid dealing with printers, mailing houses, bulk mail regulations, and the post office, but coping with a poor ISP, bugs in Web page programming, and slow Internet access can be just as aggravating.

You may find from your research that you also need to rethink your concept of the competition. With the Web, it's easy to sell directly to the final consumer. If competition from manufacturers and wholesalers has surfaced, will you be able to match the prices they offer? If not, you have several choices. First, grow your business another way. Second, link up with some of your competitors, acting as a megaphone and a funnel, broadcasting and expanding their message while directing customers to their site—for a fee, of course!

A third option has popped up within the past 18 months: online auctions. You can work either side of the auction equation, either creating a site that supports auctions or selling your products through an existing retail auction site. For the former, take a look at specialty retail auction sites like G.B. Tate & Sons at *http://www.gbtate.com,* which offers fine antiques, or Sporting Auction at *http://www.sportingauction.com,* which focuses on sporting apparel, equipment, and memorabilia. Even traditional sites are opening an auction alternative: Budget Rent-a-Car Corporation has created an auction site (*http://www.drivebudget.com*) to let customers bid for a specific car, city and date.

To become one of many "auction-preneurs," head for the big sites, such as *http://auctions.yahoo.com,* its recently launched competition on Amazon.com, or the pioneering auction site, eBay Inc., at *http://www.ebay.com.* eBay is now worth more than $7 billion, and has sold over 39 million items since its founding in 1995. The site, shown in Figure 2.17, logs 600 million hits per month from 2 million auction addicts (that's an average of 10 hits a day per person). Typically, auction sites collect a token listing fee and a commission of 1.25% to 5% on every completed transaction. It remains to be seen whether major distributors and manufacturers, who provide most of the low-cost merchandise sold on these sites, will decide to sell to the public themselves, cutting out the auction middleman.

A parallel auction market has flourished in the business-to-business arena. Sites like Egghead at *http://www.surplusdirect.com,* BidCom at *http://www.bid.com,* and OnSale at *http://www.onsale.com,* shown in Figure 2.18, offer discounted or surplus computer and office equipment. Industry-specific auction sites now abound, such as *http://www.metalsite.net* for the metal industry. Traditional surplus auctioneers, such as Norman Levy and Associates (*http://www.nlainc.com*) or the Defense Department's surplus disposal

Figure 2.17. eBay™ auction site, *http://www.ebay.com* is a trademark of eBay Inc.

Figure 2.18. Business-to-business discounted equipment, *http://www. onsale.com/atcost/atcost.htm.* Courtesy Onsale Inc.

site at *http://www.drms.dla.mil,* also post notice of auction opportunities online. In Chapter 8, we'll discuss software that allows you to set up your own Web site to handle auction transactions, as well as some of the problems that arise from unscreened matches between buyers and sellers.

Some predictions for auction dollar volume go as high as $129 billion in 2002, about one third of all Internet commerce, with 70% of that in the business-to-business auction markets. These optimistic estimates are based on the Web's unique ability to link a critical mass of buyers and sellers in real time to establish market-driven prices on a dynamic basis.

You must be willing to say *no* if the Internet does not make good business sense, but there are many online avenues worth exploring before you reach that point. Be flexible in learning about other ways that the Internet can help you grow your business. Whatever you decide about your online approach, review and revise your entire business plan, not just the marketing section, to ensure that you have a cohesive and comprehensive program for online success.

Step 3. Define Online Objectives, Products, and Markets

Conservatively assess what objectives you want to achieve and in what order, given what you have learned. Let's assume you've decided that online marketing should be part of your future. Now what? As with almost any new project, it makes sense to start in a small way and then expand your efforts as you learn what works. For instance, you may decide to establish an online presence for six months before selling your product.

If you are going to sell, select one or two items from your product line to start. If possible, pick a product with a successful and reliable sales history through direct response marketing, thus removing one of the variables in your online marketing experiment. Later, you can expand to hundreds of products or put your entire catalog on line.

By the same token, if you want to expand your corporate presence, think what aspect of your company is best portrayed through the Web. With multimedia capabilities, it's possible to showcase everything from musical talent to video histories. Consider the geographic area in which you want to provide your service. Decide whether you can or should create an auxiliary product, such as an audio CD for customers located too far away to hire your jazz trio to play at their next Christmas party.

If you don't receive at least minimal interest after three months, whether measured in terms of hits or sales, you may need to rethink your project. Perhaps your Web design isn't drawing the audience you expect. Perhaps people have not found your site and you need to expand your online and off-line promotion efforts. If you're getting hits but not making sales online, perhaps your retail prices are too high for this electronic location. Alternately, perhaps others too easily match your product or you haven't asked for the sale effectively.

Step 4. Create and Distribute Info-Tools

The Internet's historical and still most popular function is research in the broadest sense: searching for information, whether it is academic, personal, or business. To succeed online, you need to restructure existing promotional material or create new materials to meet the Internet's insatiable demand for information. In many cases, the marketing value of a site comes from perceiving your company as a source of useful information, completely independent of point-of-sale activity. As you well know, nothing happens for free: You will need to budget both dollars and time for preparing collateral information.

Plan to create auxiliary online info-tools and an electronic publicity campaign. You will need to publicize your site to ensure that large numbers of Web surfers continually learn about you, whether through search engines, hotlists, news groups, mailing lists, or direct e-mail. As you'll see in Chapter 3, info-tools in these non-Web settings can be short messages, reports, books, newsletters, or excerpts from longer works.

Whether you have a new way of making peanut butter or you sell an old-fashioned item like paper clips, tell people about your product with an interesting, informative angle. Describe how to make the world's longest paper clip chain, or list 1001 things that can be made from recycled peanut shells. Find a way to make your business sound fresh to the world, or at least new to the Internet universe.

Graphic versions of these info-tools can later be placed on your Web site. One site that successfully uses such tools is Virtual Vineyards (*http://www.virtualvin.com,* shown in Figure 2.19), which provides ever-changing information from trivia to serious discussions of oenology. The folks at Virtual Vineyards educate their customers with info-tools. They plan soon to track customers' purchases, following up with e-mail suggestions of special bargains, related gourmet foods, or fine wines.

Step 5.   Create or Upgrade Your Web Site

Some sites get great exposure; others provide great service to their customers. A few make sales, a few make money, and many save money through more efficient business operations. How do you develop a site that will work well for you? Do you do it yourself or get help?

In most cases, unless you have pre-existing technical sophistication or can utilize a prepackaged template, you're better off contracting with a Web designer to create your site and a Web hosting service

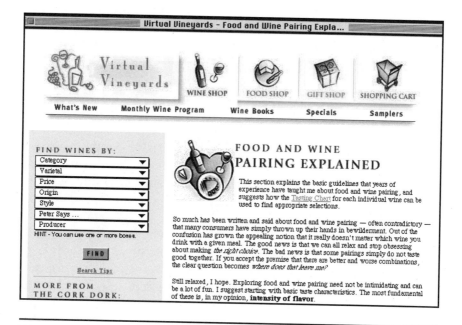

Figure 2.19. Info tools, *http://www.virtualvin.com.* ©1994-1999 Virtual Vineyards, Inc.

to maintain it. To manage more than a simple home page in-house, you may need a local area network, server hardware and software, a high-speed connection to the Internet, and access to technical support, including a Web programmer, a graphic artist, and an MIS (management information system) specialist to oversee the project.

As you'll see, there is plenty for you to do on the business side, even when you hire an outside Web designer and Web Hosting Service Provider (WHISP). Often, one facility will provide both: More than 85% of WHISPs currently provide some type of Web site design as a value-added service.

Anything truly valuable takes time or money to develop—often both. As a guideline, 1998 estimates of the national median cost for building a straightforward e-commerce Web site were $25,000 for a small site, $33,000 for a medium one, and $78,000 for a larger one. These numbers are exclusive of ongoing costs, such as Web hosting, which begins at around $25 a month, or the costs of maintaining, monitoring, and promoting a site, and handling additional customer demands. There are low-cost alternatives. Many WHISPs offer free, template-based Web site development when you sign up to use them as your Web host. We'll talk about these and other procedures for developing a Web site in Chapter 4.

Step 6.   Measure Your Results

There is no way to discover whether you have met the goals of your plan unless you build in measurement methods. In Chapter 5 you'll learn about specific services that are available through your WHISP or other companies to measure precisely how well your Web site is working.

Everyone thinks about counting simple **hits** (total number of times any file on a site is accessed), but it may be more valuable to know how many unique visitors reached your site. You might also want to track how long people stay on your site, the path they follow through it, and whether they return. You will certainly want to know how they reach you (referral links) and which specific pages interest them.

Sites that accept advertising should be able to track both the number of visitors who see each ad and those who actually link to your site from the ad. All major services and **portals** (large Web sites used as a launching pad for other sites) offer sophisticated demographic analysis of their users. (A list of portals is found in Figure 2.20.)

http://www.yahoo.com	http://www.infoseek.com
http://www.AOL.com	http://www.lycos.com
http://www.hotbot.com	http://www.northernlight.com
http://www.galaxy.com	http://magellan.excite.com
http://www.excite.com	http://www.altavista.com
http://www.snap.com	http://www.webcrawler.com
http://www.go.com	http://www.net-find.com
http://www.netcenter.com	

Figure 2.20.   Major portals on the Internet.

PointCast's screensaver audience, for instance, is more male, better educated, and more affluent than Internet users as a whole. Because PointCast's users request specific news topics, advertisers start with a well-targeted list of viewers.

Automated statistical tools are available only for the Web. For e-mail and mailing lists, you have to maintain your own records of responses to posted or e-mailed information.

If you are selling online, be sure to track the source, amount, and item number(s) of each sale. This enables you to compute your cost of sales more accurately and to compare the value of selling online with the value of selling through other methods, such as traditional mail catalogs.

Step 7. Market Your Internet Presence

No matter how successful a Web site you create, you must attract people to it. It does you no good to have the best site on the Web if no one knows how or why to find you. One of the most important parts of successful marketing on the Internet is achieving exposure amid overwhelming amounts of information. The Web is such a busy intersection on the Information Superhighway that you have to tell potential visitors which way to turn.

To get the maximum effect from your online marketing, all other advertising in print media, TV, or radio should mention your Web address. This off-line supplement to your Web presence lets the world know you are an electronic player, thus making a statement about your company's involvement in contemporary technology.

Web addresses now appear everywhere in all kinds of advertising. You might expect Mitsubishi to advertise its URL in *Newsweek*, but did you realize that over two thirds of the ads in the first 20 pages of a typical issue of *Good Housekeeping* or *Sunset* also carry Web addresses? Be sure to place your Internet address on your letterhead, mailers, flyers, business cards, and promotional items as well.

As you get more sophisticated, you can coordinate Web site activities with traditional advertising and promotional activities, such as an event, special sale, contest, customer feedback line, or PR campaign. Using standard target-marketing techniques, you could write a press release about the unique contents of your Web site to drive additional visibility in print. Chapter 6 is devoted to techniques for marketing your Internet presence.

A More Level Marketing Field?

Any business can appear significant and powerful online. By following the design concepts discussed later in the book, you can have a Web site as effective as Ragu's at *http://www.eat.com*, shown in Figure 2.21. The look and feel of your site can have all the flash of the big guys—for a price.

You can market online at all levels: very cheap, the equivalent of a photocopied handbill (black ink on colored stock); moderately inexpensive, like a used car commercial on cable TV; moderately ex-

Figure 2.21. Sample large site, *http://www.eat.com/dining.html.* Courtesy Lipton Investments, Inc. and Unilever USA, Inc.

pensive, the Web equivalent of a four-color, glossy brochure with lots of photos; and the all-out extravaganza, the electronic equivalent of a one-minute spot broadcast in prime time on the three major networks. The amount you spend will depend on your available budget, the nature of your company and its products or services, the kind of audience you are trying to reach, and the extent to which you need to use interactive multimedia on your site.

How many people will use your site? One of the most popular sites in Internet history, NASA's Pathfinder photographs from the 1997 mission to Mars (*http://mpfwww.jpl.nasa/gov*), received more than 100 million hits from all its mirror sites combined in just one day, and 500 million during the month of July.

Dell Computer (*http://www.dell.com*), which sells $14 million a day in equipment, receives some 25 million site visits per quarter. Even a moderate-size site like Global Change at *http://www.globalchange.com/futurenorthernl.htm* claims 550,000 hits in 8 weeks.

However, few sites attract these numbers. The Internet viewing population for most businesses is closer to the number of viewers that an infomercial receives on late-night television. Even if your Internet marketing is solely designed to provide corporate presence, set a goal for the number of viewers you want to attract.

The bottom line is that the Internet and the World Wide Web are wonderful tools when used in conjunction with traditional marketing methods. The keys to success in Internet marketing are simple:

- Plan carefully.

- Pay attention to how this new medium can help you meet your business goals.

- Understand how an online presence will affect your overall business operations.

Internet Marketing Affects All Business Operations

Think about the impact of hundreds of thousands more prospects cruising the Internet. Do you have the staff to respond to a large volume of requests for information? Will you need to hire telecommuting subcontractors? Bring on more employees? Expand space? Do you have the infrastructure in your office, in terms of computers and modems, or maybe even a LAN? How will this affect your cost of sales?

If you are selling, consider in advance how you will fulfill increased orders promptly. In addition to the personnel issues just mentioned, do you have access to the needed inventory or the space to store it? Can you arrange just-in-time contracts or drop shipping with your suppliers? Can you process orders efficiently? Because of the increased competition on the Web, you can expect significant price pressure. Can you meet it? Will you be able to renegotiate pricing with your suppliers? Cut costs elsewhere? Do your forecasts show that you can increase volume to counteract a smaller profit margin?

There is no point in selling more goods if it means losing money. These are old-fashioned marketing questions, but they don't go away just because you are using new-fangled technology.

As you experiment online, *don't* stop marketing your products and services in ways that currently gain sales. If you succeed online, you may decide to shift your marketing mix or to open an all-online division, but wait for proof. In the meantime, keep doing what works. As you'll see throughout this book, a well-conceived Internet marketing strategy will complement your traditional marketing efforts and vice versa.

Keep Your Promises

Whatever you promise—quick shipment, high quality, cheap price, individual attention—do it. Promises can be explicit (free monogramming) or implicit (write us). Don't risk customer goodwill by falling down on the job.

Customer Service Is the Name of the Game

The Internet doesn't free you from doing what every business must do to get and keep customers: provide good service. Think not about how Internet marketing differs from what you are already doing, but about how your successful business practices can be incorporated online. You know the basic rules quite well. Certainly you know that it is easier to make a repeat customer from a satisfied current customer than to attract a new one.

Now it's time to turn your plan into reality. We'll look at the four remaining steps to Internet marketing success one by one in the following chapters: non-Web marketing tools; creating an effective Web site; monitoring performance and promoting a Web site successfully. This is a good time to create folders on your hard drive to bookmark sites for various service providers, model sites, and potential advertising or link sites. You might also want to start a large three-ring binder to track your Internet marketing efforts. Make 10 dividers for

1. ISP and Web Hosting Service Providers

2. Web Designer/Subcontractor Selection

3. Site Development

4. Site Statistics and Maintenance

5. Site Feedback and Bug Reports

6. Info-Tools

7. Web Site Promotion

8. Web Site Advertising

9. Schedules

10. Budget

3

Creating and Distributing Info-Tools

In this chapter we'll discuss the next step to Internet success: creating and distributing info-tools. These are specific messages that provide an ever-changing stream of information to generate interest and attention. You give something away to get noticed while you tie in products related to the information you give away. Handled properly, the information you cast upon the waters will come back as customers.

Although establishing a Web site gets the most commercial attention, there are many other ways to take advantage of the Internet for marketing purposes: e-mail, news groups, listservers, classified ads, and display ads on commercial online services. A good Internet marketing plan selects from all these possibilities to enhance online presence. Some companies test these less-risky, less-expensive alternatives before launching a full-scale marketing effort on the Web. The largest companies continue to integrate them into a spectrum of online activities.

To provide concrete examples, you'll look over the shoulder of the fictional Gadsby's Popcorn Company. Gadsby's, a maker of organically grown gourmet popcorn, has annual sales of $2.5 million and employs 25 people. Marketing Manager Jane Ogilvie has been assigned the task of developing and executing an online marketing plan for Gadsby's new line of flavored popcorn. By the end of this chapter, you'll know how to

- Create info-tools, from signature files to FAQs

- Distribute these tools via e-mail, mailing lists, listservers, and news groups

- Use online, off-the-Web marketing, such as classifieds

- Take advantage of opportunities available on major online services.

Creating Info-Tools

Before you wade into the whitecapped marketing waters of cyberspace, you should create six electronic info-tools related to your product or service:

1. Signature files

2. Blurbs

3. Reports

4. Newsletters

5. Press releases

6. Lists of frequently asked questions (FAQs)

These simple tools, which can be kept in the Info-tools section of your notebook, will be valuable regardless of the marketing methods you select. You can create them with your word processor as simple text files, without any special formatting. If you later establish a Web site, you can add graphics and other features.

Signature Files

The electronic equivalent of your business card, a three- to six-line, text-only, **signature file** can be appended to the end of every e-mail message, blurb, report, or other posting. Not only does it include all critical information about how to reach you, it also incorporates a brief marketing phrase that positions your business. Like your business card, your signature file is left as often as possible. This little self-promotional file is not considered advertising, so you can use it everywhere you go on the Internet.

Be sure to include all feasible ways to contact you. If you have a toll-free number, show it. If you want users to visit your Web site, provide the URL. If you can be reached by carrier pigeon, give directions a bird can follow. The make-believe signature file that Jane Ogilvie creates for Gadsby's is shown in Figure 3.1. She may change the addressee line to direct responses to appropriate individuals or to track the source of the inquiry.

Most e-mail programs have their own simple procedure for creating a signature file. Look up *signature* in the documentation, member services, or Help facility to find instructions. Once you have created a signature file, it can be attached to every message you send. On some online services, such as AOL, you can append a signature file automatically to a news group posting, but for e-mail, you must create a text file and paste it in manually.

```
Jane Ogilvie
Gadsby's Gourmet Popcorn
Specializing in Naturally Grown popcorn
1234 Main Street, Waterloo, Iowa 50701
T: 800-555-POPS        F: 319-555-6666        E: Ogilvie@pop-popcorn.com

After Gadsby's has a Web site, she'll add:
Discover our latest flavors at http://www.pop-popcorn.com

(If Gadsby's has a separate listserver address, she'll show that too.)
```

Figure 3.1. Signature file for Gadsby's.

Blurbs

Blurbs are short electronic messages about your business, products, services, or a related topic. The text can be lifted from an existing news release, newsletter, or brochure, or created from scratch. Be sure to tell readers how to contact you to place orders or get more information.

Your blurb will eventually enjoy wide distribution online—a kind of electronic word-of-mouth—so check it for spelling and typographical errors, and edit it for readability. Follow basic principles for "revving" your copy with energy:

- Use the first person (I, we) or second (you), not the third.

- Use positive phrasing, such as "buy now" instead of "don't hesitate to buy."

- Use short, commonly used words.

- Use active verbs; try to avoid forms of the verb *to be*.

- Use numbers and details, such as "ultramarine, mint green, and mango," instead of "many colors."

- Spark your text with vivid words (e.g., munchies, sun-dried, guilt).

- View your blurb both on screen and in print to ensure there are no problems.

Jane at Gadsby's Popcorn created the blurb in Figure 3.2 for use in electronic marketing. She will append her signature file, coding the addressee line to track the source of resulting inquiries.

Reports

Longer than blurbs, reports are information-intensive files for the interested reader. However, they don't contain much more marketing content than a signature file. You will upload these report files to

Gourmet popcorn, a low-fat alternative to other munchies, is great for your entire family. With only 5% of calories from fat and almost no cholesterol, popcorn is a healthy way to snack without guilt. Our new flavors, like cheddar, sun-dried tomato or green chili, tease the taste buds with grown-up flavor. Gadsby's Gourmet Popcorn places good health and good taste at the top of our priorities.

For a free sample of Gadsby's organically-grown flavored popcorn, just hit REPLY. Type ONLY your name and address in the message filed.

Figure 3.2. Sample blurb for Gadsby's.

strategically placed areas on the Internet that attract your target audience.

These reports should not be particularly time critical, or you will have to update them continually. They might be short feature stories that could appear in a trade journal or product fact sheets that are appropriate in a few news groups. Or you could create such items as a trivia question game about your industry, questionnaires with a free gift for completion, or industry-related crossword puzzles. Be creative, but soft-pedal marketing appeals in these reports. Since they may appear in places that restrict advertising, keep the content factor high. People can always go to your Web site or contact you by phone or e-mail for more information.

For example, if you manufacture any kind of product, write a report about the process. Chronicle the history of your industry. How about a report on the inventor of the product? If you sell cars, create reports about Teflon coatings or racing or tune-ups. If you sell houseboats, create reports about hull design, outboard engines, or how to go through locks on the St. Lawrence Seaway.

For Gadsby's, Jane creates several reports from her own knowledge or with input from others in the company. One deals with cultivation of corn by Native Americans; another describes different corn species used for popcorn, animal feed, and corn on the cob eaten on the Fourth of July. A third covers how popcorn is made, and yet another talks about the wide variety of flavored popcorns now available. As always, Jane appends her signature file.

Newsletters

Like their print counterparts, electronic newsletters may appear either regularly or irregularly, but change their content. Soft marketing also applies to newsletters. Don't oversell your product or service in a newsletter, but let readers know subtly what you have available. As before, include your signature file.

If you are an electronic publisher, a newsletter might be your end product. You could send sample newsletters over the Internet to get people interested and ask for a subscription to future issues, whether free or paid. If reports and newsletters are unique, add a copyright notice at the bottom, indicating whether others need permission to redistribute the newsletter or can do so as long as you are credited. (For more information about copyright, see Chapter 8.) Figure 3.3 shows excerpts of an online newsletter distributed via e-mail by Bidcast (*http://www.bidcast.com*), a company that notifies small businesses and contractors of Federal government procurement opportunities.

Press Releases

One of the most-used forms of self-promotion, the press release is as effective online as off. Update old press releases for electronic placement. Create new ones as you go along, covering everything from product announcements to news about changes in your Web site, to notices of promotions or awards. You'll post these releases, along with reports, in appropriate areas of the Internet. Be sure to include your signature file, designating a different contact person if appropriate for your organization. (Figure 3.4 displays one of Jane Ogilvie's fictional press releases.) If you have the budget, check out services that will distribute your press releases to multiple online and offline media outlets:

- Business Wire (*http://www.businesswire.com*)

- PR NewsWire (*http://www.prnewsire.com*)

- Digital Work (*http://www.digitalwork.com/index.asp*)

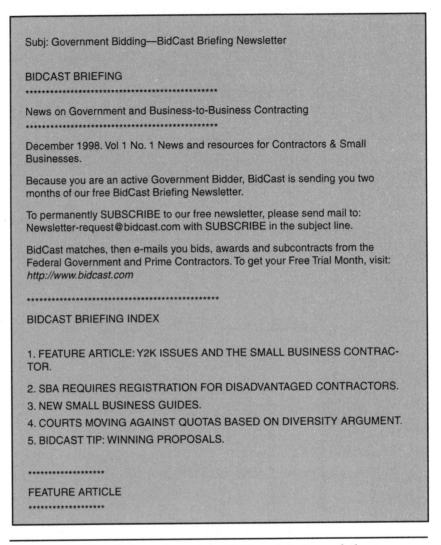

Subj: Government Bidding—BidCast Briefing Newsletter

BIDCAST BRIEFING
****

News on Government and Business-to-Business Contracting
****

December 1998. Vol 1 No. 1 News and resources for Contractors & Small Businesses.

Because you are an active Government Bidder, BidCast is sending you two months of our free BidCast Briefing Newsletter.

To permanently SUBSCRIBE to our free newsletter, please send mail to: Newsletter-request@bidcast.com with SUBSCRIBE in the subject line.

BidCast matches, then e-mails you bids, awards and subcontracts from the Federal Government and Prime Contractors. To get your Free Trial Month, visit: *http://www.bidcast.com*

****

BIDCAST BRIEFING INDEX

1. FEATURE ARTICLE: Y2K ISSUES AND THE SMALL BUSINESS CONTRACTOR.

2. SBA REQUIRES REGISTRATION FOR DISADVANTAGED CONTRACTORS.

3. NEW SMALL BUSINESS GUIDES.

4. COURTS MOVING AGAINST QUOTAS BASED ON DIVERSITY ARGUMENT.

5. BIDCAST TIP: WINNING PROPOSALS.

****

FEATURE ARTICLE
****

Figure 3.3. E-mailed newsletter from BidCast, *http://www.bidcast.com.* © 1999 Bidcast, the powerful Internet bid service.

FAQs

Files of answers to **frequently asked questions (FAQs)** can be extremely useful with Internet news groups and some mailing lists. Create several of these files in question-and-answer format. FAQs usually con-

---

FOR IMMEDIATE RELEASE   CONTACT: JANE OGILVIE
DATE: MARCH 23, 1999   **ogilvie@pop-popcorn.com**

Lip-smacking, finger licking, apple-cinnamon-caramel popcorn. Fragrant memo-
ries of amusement parks, dunking for apples, and Thanksgiving pies burst from
freshly-popped kernels of Gadsby's latest popcorn flavor.

Caramel Crunch joins the Gadsby's product line-up on Monday, March 29, 1999. It
initiates a "Sweet String" of flavors to come. Gadsby's current "Savories" line
includes white cheddar, sun-dried tomato, and green chili.

President Katherine Gadsby says, "This new line will satisfy the sweet tooth of
baby boomers, without adding fat, cholesterol, or high calorie count. Our studies
show this population worries more about salt than sugar."

Gadsby's Popcorn (Pop-Popcorn) is the premier supplier of gourmet popcorn to
upscale movie theaters, restaurants, gift shops, and specialty food distributors.

For more information, call Marketing Manager Jane Ogilvie at 800-555-POPS, or
go to our Web site at *http://www.pop-popcorn.com.*

Figure 3.4. Sample press release for Gadsby's.

---

tain little about your company except "Provided by" and your signature file. Users often read FAQ files to become familiar with a news
group, so create FAQs that provide valuable information about your
industry or innovative ways to use your product. Also create several
product-specific FAQs to be used in locations other than news groups
or to respond to e-mail.

FAQ files for news groups must conform to a specific format. To
obtain this information, read the FAQs for the news group you want
to join. Like all postings to moderated news groups, your FAQ will
be reviewed and either approved or disapproved. Files that smack of
blatant advertising or promotion generally are not acceptable. Once
FAQ files are posted, you can update them whenever you want. (Later
in this chapter, you'll learn more about news groups.)

For instance, point your browser to a listing of news groups and
browse for likely ones, such as *biz.general*. Select the desired group(s)
and read their FAQs. With most systems, you just click an icon to

post your message. If it's useful and interesting, your own FAQ or report might be copied to thousands of Internet sites. That could generate many new customers indeed!

E-mail Marketing

E-mail is a good way to start exploiting the Internet. If you haven't already, you need to join the estimated 100 million people who exchanged some 2 billion messages a day in 1998! E-mail reaches everyone on the Internet, even the several million customers with free e-mail-only accounts from Juno, Hotmail, or any one of many Web sites. (To subscribe to one of the first two, write *webmaster@juno.com,* go to *http://www.juno.com,* or call 1-800-654-JUNO. For Hotmail, go to *http://www.hotmail.com,* or call 1-408-222-7000.)

Using your online service, your browser, or a freestanding e-mail program, practice sending messages to others following the directions given. Be sure you know how to attach your signature file, either automatically or manually. In preparation, set up an organized method of folders and files on your hard drive to categorize your saved e-mail correspondence.

To simplify your e-mail tasks and reduce the time it takes you to respond to inquiries about your product or service, create a standard greeting that you can personalize quickly as a preface. This can be as simple as

Dear____,

Thank you for your interest in _____. You will find the answer to your question in the report that follows. Let me know if I can be of further assistance.

Then create a series of text files for the most common replies or use any of your FAQs, reports, or blurbs to speed up response time. Without such tools you could easily spend hours, rather than minutes, responding to e-mail each day. Try to include a **call to action,** such as inviting individuals who send an inquiry to join your mailing list or asking viewers to visit your Web site (include your URL with a hypertext link, if at all possible). As always, end with your signature file.

Figure 3.5 provides excerpts from a marketing e-mail sent by AOL in response to a request for information. Large companies especially take advantage of this low-cost method of communicating with their customers. As noted in the last chapter, your company could be perceived as nonresponsive if you don't handle e-mail response well. You could easily start to lose customers.

Managing e-mail can become a daunting task when the number of messages reaches 45,000 a month, as it does for Dell Computers. The task has become so complex that firms like MessageMedia (*http://www.messagemedia.com*), seen in Figure 3.6, have grabbed

---

Subj: AOL Advertising

Thank you for your interest in America Online (AOL). I have outlined some of AOL's advertising opportunities below. You have several options, however I recommend you look at the "search term" area of NetFind as one of the most cost effective forms of advertising on AOL. Please review the information and feel free to call or e-mail me with any questions.

You can find more advertising information online at AOL keyword MediaSpace , or on the web at *http://media.aol.com* (also fax on demand 800-832-8220). AOL offers special packages for any investment to help you harness the power of this medium. AOL can either drive traffic to your existing web site with banners located in highly targeted content areas or give you opportunities for content sponsorship.

Please feel free to contact me soon, if possible, as our most popular Search Terms are selling out rapidly. I have a number of success stories about businesses like yours who have used AOL very profitably. Please call me and tell me about your business so that I can help craft an online strategy with you. Thank you for your interest in advertising with AOL.

Best Regards,

Exxxx Tyyyyyyyy

AOL Interactive Marketing

415-XXX-XXXX, ETyyyyyyyy@aol.com

Figure 3.5. Responsive e-mailed blurb from AOL. "America Online," "AOL" and the Logo design are registered trademarks of America Online, Inc. © 1997-1999 America Online, Inc. All rights reserved.

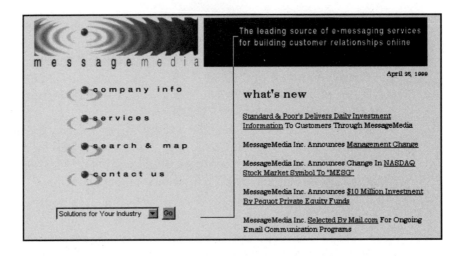

Figure 3.6. E-mail management program, *http://www.messagemedia.com.* Courtesy Message Media.

this opportunity to manage e-mail for large companies. Products like Dr. Bean (*http://www.db2nt.sideware.com*), LiveContact (*http:// www.balisoft.com*), and Right Now Web 2.0 (*http://www. rightnowtech.com*) offer expensive software ($6,000–$15,000) to track inquiries and generate automated responses in-house. The latter two also offer hosting options with a fee based on monthly volume or per customer service agent.

Mailbots

There is another option for responding to a high volume of e-mail. Some ISPs can help you respond automatically to routine messages by using a program called a **mailbot** (a cross between *mail* and *robot*) or **auto-responder.** As seen in Figure 3.7, a mailbot automatically sends an appropriate message to anyone who sends an e-mail. Mailbots are often used to confirm receipt of an order placed at a Web site or to acknowledge a support inquiry.

The easiest way to set up a mailbot is to designate a separate e-mail address under your master account or create an alternate one.

Hello. (This is an automated response. There is no need to reply.)

Your message regarding:

[NMT Web Help #514] /TBD/stats

has been received and assigned a request number of 514.

We will respond to this problem as quickly as possible.

In order help us track the progress of this request, we ask that you include the string [NMT Web Help #514] in the subject line of any further mail about this particular request.

For example:

Subject: [NMT Web Help #514] /TBD/stats

You may do this simply by replying to this email.

Figure 3.7. Service mailbot (New Mexico TechNet), *http://www.technet. nm.org.* Courtesy New Mexico Technet.

When a mailbot is active, you can't receive regular e-mail messages, so put only the alternate address into **vacation mode.** (Vacation mode is usually used to respond tell senders you are away and direct them elsewhere for immediate assistance.)

However, you can change a vacation message to information about a product or service. You could put your blurb into a "vacation" mailbot, along with a list of other info-tools and instructions on how to get them. If you want to get more specific, you can create different mailbots at different addresses, each used for a particular purpose. Jane Ogilvie's fictional mailbot is shown in Figure 3.8. You can see why this powerful and inexpensive Internet tool may be worth your time.

To set up your mailbot, coordinate with your ISP. (Not all have this service.) Many offer users about 5 MB of free space on their computer system to store a predefined mailbots. Others charge a setup and/or a monthly fee. You can usually find information about vacation mode in your ISP's own FAQ file.

Your free sample of Gadsby's Flavored Popcorn is on the way! For a full list of products, check out our Web site, Pop-Popcorn (*http://www.pop-popcorn.com*). You may place your order online or by fax. In a hurry? Call 800-555-POPS. Thank you for your interest in Gadsby's Popcorn. (Follow with signature file).

Figure 3.8. Sample mailbot for Gadsby's.

Listservers

A sophisticated mailbot called a **listbot** or **listserver,** a program that automatically processes requests, is even more useful. The advantage of a listserver over a regular mailbot is that a listserver can be **concatenated.** That is, prospects and customers who mail to it are asked to do something that will result in another document being mailed to them without further intervention. A listserver acts as an automated sales clerk or fax-back service, responding to requests for more information by sending the appropriate document. You can have hundreds of different files sent to different classes of customers, all automatically.

A newsletter is a perfect way to utilize a listserver. Place announcements around the Internet giving the listserver address, which will be something like *info-newsletter@pop-popcorn.com*. When a person requests something from this address, the listbot will send out a sample newsletter. At the bottom of the newsletter, you tell people how to subscribe for a year. When customers have confirmed (and paid, if required), their e-mail addresses will be added to another mailing list that automatically sends out monthly issues of the newsletter.

Price sheets, catalogs, and current inventory records are also excellent uses for listservers. You can change listserver files daily, weekly, or whatever it takes to keep users up-to-date. Because people have specifically found your address and are requesting information, you can provide all the marketing materials you want with as hard or soft a sell as you find appropriate. Be sure to include your signature file and your URL, if you have one.

Subscribing to Mailing Lists

On the Internet, a mailing list consists of people who have subscribed by sending their e-mail addresses to a listserver. There are over 90,000 mailing lists on the Internet packed with prequalified prospects whose enrollment establishes an interest in a subject area related to your business. As such, mailing lists can be an effective channel for promoting your company.

To see some of these lists, go to your browser and type one of these addresses:

http://www.liszt.com (seen in Figure 3.9)

http://www.yahoo.com/business_and_economy/companies/marketing/direct_marketing/direct_mail/mailing_list

http://nsns.com/MouseTracks/tloml.html

As seen in Figure 3.9, these sites have facilities for searching lists in various ways.

You can either subscribe to a list from one of these sites or e-mail the listserver with the prescribed text. Once you have subscribed, you will receive an updated list of the most recent messages. From then on, you will get a copy via e-mail of anything posted by any other subscriber and you can send a single e-mail message that will be distributed to everyone else.

As an exercise, subscribe to the RITIM-L list, which deals with telecommunications and information marketing. Send an e-mail to

listserv@uriacc.uri.edu

In the body of the message, type

subscribe RITIM-L

That's it!

Before you start posting e-mail to a list, always study incoming messages to understand the nature of the list and acceptable commu-

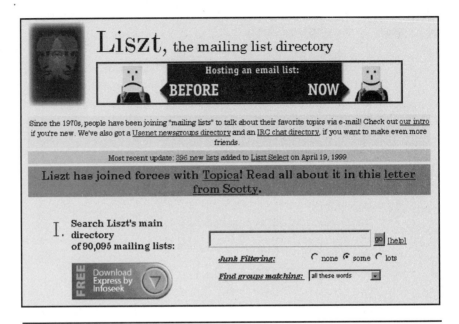

Figure 3.9. Mailing list source site, *http://www.liszt.com.* Courtesy Scott Southwick.

nications. A few (very few) of these lists allow specific advertising or promotional materials, such as a discount for members who purchase from your Web site. Others strongly resist such messages. Be sure to observe the protocol for the list!

Although you can usually find the e-mail addresses of others who are on the list, *never, never,* send them unsolicited, private e-mail (**spam**). However, you can scan that information to confirm that you are participating in a list with appropriate potential customers for your company.

Back at Gadsby's, Jane Ogilvie decides that a mailing list should be the next step in her strategy. After subscribing to her own list, Jane sends her first message to list members.

Creating Your Own Mailing Lists

To build a "snail mail" list, you purchase multiple direct mailing lists, mail a flyer, and get a response from one or two percent of the recipients. You may buy many mailing lists to have a significant number of "real" prospects for your products and services. Considering the expense of designing, printing, and mailing your literature, old-fashioned direct mail can cost anywhere from several dollars to several hundred dollars per lead. For much less money, you can create a mailing list on the Internet. When properly used, you'll find that electronic mailing lists can be a very effective marketing tool.

First tell your ISP that you want to establish a mailing list regarding swimwear, space aliens, wok cooking, Elvis Presley—whatever is related to your product or service. Each ISP has different rates for setting up a mailing list or listserver. Typical prices range from $25 to $50 for setup and $1 per transmission, up to several hundred dollars for setup but no transmission or monthly fee. Some ISPs offer a modest monthly or annual rate. LinkExchange, seen in Figure 3.10, offers a free listbot at *http://www.listbot.com/p_notsure.shtml,* complete with signup direct from your Web site, as long as you're willing to let people see ads. For $99 per year, you can sign up for ListBot Gold.

You'll be asked to choose among options like those that follow so that the ISP can put together the appropriate listserver for you. It may take an administrator several days to set up your mailing list.

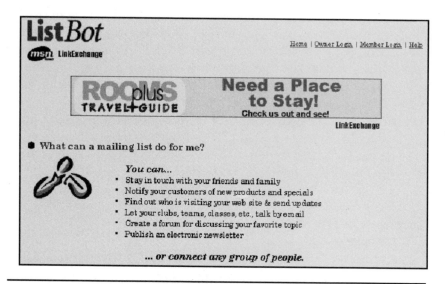

Figure 3.10. Listbot service, *http://www.listbot.com/p_notsure.shtml.* Screenshot reprinted by permission from Microsoft Corporation.

- **Auto:** The listserver performs all subscription requests without your prior approval.

- **Open:** Users can add or drop themselves, but not someone else, without prior approval.

- **Closed:** You, as owner, approve all subscriptions. This is often used for a paid subscription list.

- **Private:** Only people who are on the list can see who else is on the list.

- **Fully moderated:** You approve any incoming message before it can be mailed to the list.

- **Externally moderated:** You approve only messages from outside the mailing list.

- **Maximum message length:** You must approve any e-mail larger than the preset length you've established.

As the list owner, you receive e-mail notification of all "subscribe" and "unsubscribe" requests. Like bulk mail at the post office, mail sent out to lists is usually given a lower priority than regular e-mail and will take longer to be sent from a server. Most list software allows you to send an automatic "probe" message to confirm the e-mail addresses of subscribers and remove any faulty addresses.

You can use your own mailing list to advertise your product or services as aggressively as you want, whereas you can't advertise on somebody else's mailing list unless they specifically allow it. Be sure that recipients understand they can elect not to receive your e-mail. *Above all, remember to subscribe to your own list!*

Posting to a List of Lists

Once your mailing list is running, add it to a List of Mailing Lists. Your mailing list address will be copied to hundreds of thousands of nodes where major network users reside. This distribution enables you to build a large list. Some services ask you to send an e-mail message with your announcement to the mail master. Others have you fill out the questionnaire, such as at *http://www.liszt.com,* where you add your list by selecting *Liszt Link* or *Web Link,* and filling in the blanks. Another way to announce your list is by filling out a form at *http://www.mail-list.com.* A similar method is used to announce your mailing list on the online services.

You should soon receive dozens of messages telling you that someone has joined or dropped off your list. Neither requires any more attention on your part. To find out how your list is doing at any given time, simply send the message *Who* to your own list. The e-mail addresses of all subscribers should bounce back to you. Unless you have restricted access, any subscriber on your list can do the same thing.

You will need to nurture your list. Set up a regular schedule to monitor the traffic. This is a good time to create a chronological **infolog,** like the one in Figure 3.11, to include under the Info-Tools heading in the binder you created in Chapter 2. Note each scheduled task, compile copies of each tool, and log when tools are created, posted, and the volume of response each one generates.

If responses to your list start to flag, it's up to you to keep the postings hot and encourage others to do the same. If the messages get boring, your subscription list might start to shrink. Invite important and interesting people to subscribe, or take several aliases and stir up discussion yourself.

This is your list, so you can end each of your messages with a call to action. Invite recipients to ask for your sales literature through private e-mail, to visit your Web site, or to request ordering information. Of course, include your signature file.

Reaping What You've Sown

You can use the power of e-mail to follow up on hundreds of leads by posting the appropriate, already-created info-tool to your own mailing list. When you see from a message that someone is ready to become a customer, you may want to individualize the response or close the sale off-line. You have everyone's e-mail address on your own mailing list, so you can easily send an individual message.

At this point, basic business practices come into play. Use your sales force to "farm and feed" the list. Leads are precious, so don't waste them. They won't turn into sales unless someone telephones

Scheduled Task	Description	By	Date Created	Date Posted	Location & Notes (e.g. # responses)
Signature File	J. Ogilvie; master	jo	11/14/98		
Signature File	P. Piper for CompuServe	jo	11/17/98		
Signature File	E. Taylor for Web	jo	11/17/98		
Blurb #1	healthy value	jo	12/1/98		
Blurb #2	short #1 for news groups	jo	12/3/98		
Report #1	Native American cultivation	jo	12/5/98		
Report #2	Corn species	jo	12/5/98		
CompuServe	Subscribe ($21.95/month)	jo	12/6/98		
Report #3	Popcorn manufacture	jo	12/8/98		
Blurb #3	New flavor announcement	jo	1/6/99		
Signature File	Modify Ogilvie, Dept QA, for news groups	jo	1/6/99		
Press Release	Corporate backgrounder	jo	1/12/99		
Press Release	New flavor announcement	jo	1/14/99		
Report #4	Flavored popcorns	jo	1/14/99		
FAQ	Where to find Gadsby's products	jo	1/15/99		
FAQ	Making good popcorn	jo	1/15/99		
E-mail	cover response	jo	1/16/99		

Figure 3.11.   Chronological Infolog (continued on next page).

Scheduled Task	Description	By	Date Created	Date Posted	Location & Notes (e.g. # responses)
Upload reports	Gourmet Food Forum, CompuServe	jo	1/20/99		
Newsletter	January issue	jo	1/23/99	1/23/99	
Subscribe RITIM-L	mailing list on information marketing	jo	1/26/99		
Check news group	alternate college food	jo	1/27/99	1/27/99	
Answer e-mail		jo	2/2/99		
e-mail response	franchisee response	jo	2/9/99		
Answer e-mail		jo	2/9/99		
FAQ	franchising	jo	2/13/99		
Answer e-mail		jo	2/16/99		
Check news group	rec.food.recipe	jo	2/18/99		
Answer e-mail		jo	2/23/99		
New mailing list	healthy snack food eaters	jo	2/26/99		
Announce list	at mail-list.com	jo	2/26/99		
Post Report #1	to mailing list	jo	2/27/99		
Answer e-mail		jo	3/2/99		
Create mailbot	for auto-response to list	jo	3/4/99	3/4/99	

Figure 3.11. Chronological Infolog (continued from previous page).

when a call is requested, sends out literature or samples, and makes sure that customers' needs are met.

This process works for Gadsby's. A few days after announcing her own list, Jane watches it begin to grow. When she reaches 100 members, she posts some of her previously created info-tools and starts to participate actively. Over time, her list increases to more than 3,000 people and the volume of retail sales goes up by 10 percent due to electronic orders.

You now have several distribution channels for your info-tools: standard e-mail for manual responses, mailbots for automated responses, other mailing lists, and your own list on an automated listserver. Whenever you change or add to your info-tools, be sure to post them to all the various lists and news groups you've joined. Record these postings in your activity log. If you have a listserver address, don't forget to show it in your signature file, all info-tools, traditional promotions, business cards, and letterhead. Now let's turn to another inexpensive way to establish an electronic presence on the Internet.

News Groups

News groups are virtual communities of people who choose to discuss a shared interest on the Internet. Called USEnet, this portion of the Internet hosts discussions on over 35,000 topics, with millions of people participating worldwide. A given news group that reaches even 1 percent of the Internet population is extraordinary—that's over a million prequalified prospects interested in something related to your business. About 1 **gigabyte** (**billion** bytes) of new information is circulated every day through this Internet function.

To find a list of news groups, point your browser to one of the following sites:

http://www.liszt.com/news

http://tile.net/news/viewlist.html (seen in Figure 3.12)

At these sites you can search for news groups by keyword. In most cases, you don't even need to subscribe; just click to read the mes-

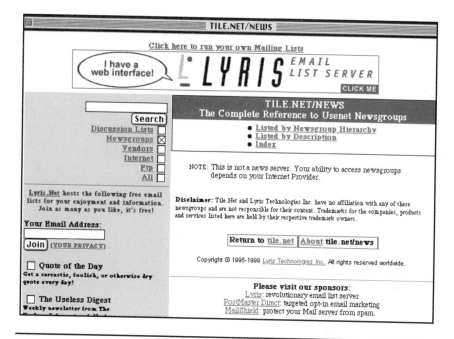

Figure 3.12. News group source site, *http://tile.net/news/*. Courtesy Lyris Technologies, Inc.

sages that interest you. Try one or two that appeal. As an exercise, try out the *biz.general* news group shown in Figure 3.13. You can find out which of the *biz* newsgroups allow advertising by looking at their FAQs at *http://www.bizynet.com/faq-news.htm*. The Internet changes so rapidly that you should search for relevant news groups at least every six months. Put that task in your info-log! You can even buy special software, such as News Rover (*http://www. newsrover.com*), to search news groups for you.

In a news group you can post a message of your own or respond to a message someone else has submitted. The former is better because everyone in the group will receive your response. An answer to a message on a prior topic, called a **thread,** is sent to those who have read the prior message.

The information you distribute online, called a **posting,** can be as short as one or two sentences or as long as a multimedia presentation. If you post a message that is nothing more than an ad, you will be considered a **spammer**—someone who abuses the Internet by post-

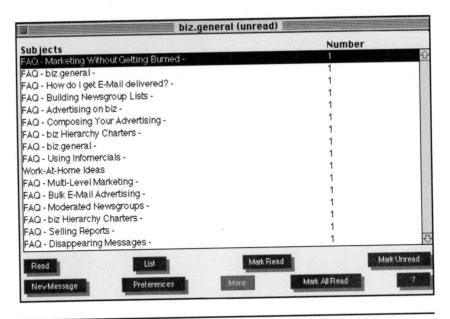

Figure 3.13.   Biz.General FAQs, *http://www.bizynet.com.* Courtesy Chris Gunn, Bizynet Coordinator.

ing unsolicited advertising in inappropriate news groups. Generally, you will be effective as long as your postings contain real information of value to news group readers, not just promotional material. Posting plain ads without monitoring the group for answers will probably not yield good results anyway. Press releases and product announcements are acceptable in some news groups.

Major news group categories are shown in the table in Figure 3.14. Each of these categories is divided hierarchically into minor groups and then into more detailed subgroups, like an outline. Groups are named by continually appending other words to the right of the prior word, separated by a period. The longer the name, the more focused the group. You can often check all the FAQs in a news group category at once. Jane Ogilvie might find news groups related to Gadsby's Popcorn at *rec.food.recipes* or *alt.college.food,* for example.

Some news groups are moderated by people or groups of people who review messages for relevance before posting. Many people prefer moderated groups because they tend to have higher-quality, less-

BIZ	Business	SCI	Science topics
COMP	Computer-related topics	SOC	Social issues
MISC	Miscellaneous topics	TALK	Like Talk Radio—anything goes
NEWS	Current events	ALT	Other topics not covered above
REC	Recreation-related topics		

Figure 3.14. Major news group categories.

repetitious content. Although most news groups are not moderated, they may still have rules about what you can and cannot post; be sure to check their FAQs. In general, the best way to gain attention in this environment is to participate actively in a good discussion thread. As always, play observer initially. Stay in the background for several weeks, reading messages without sending any of your own.

Once you find a few appropriate news groups, post messages asking for names of related groups. The members themselves will lead you to more and more focused news groups. Take their leads until you think you have located the majority of news groups appropriate to your business. Don't forget that asking questions enables you to leave your signature file, which builds recognition for your business.

Some people advocate using fake names in signature files and "From" lines of newsgroups to avoid receiving junk mail, but you may regret it from a business perspective. As Chris Gunn of Bizynet puts it, "that's like trying to do business with an unlisted phone number." For more general information on news groups and mailing lists, go to the Internet FAQ section at *http://www.bbn.com/support/resources/internetfaq.htm.*

Netiquette

When you participate in the news group part of the Internet, you're invading an area of cyberspace that people guard avidly against commercialization. If you don't honor the rules, you will get **flamed** (sent derogatory messages). Hundreds of people in the news group who have been told about your infraction may send you **mail bombs,** useless mail that clogs your mailbox. You can be dropped from a moderated news group for violating its rules. If someone in a news group replies angrily to one of your postings, telling you to cease and desist, try to re-establish harmony with the group (or drop out). Here are a few basic rules to follow:

- If you decide to use news groups (or other people's mailing lists or listservers) as part of your marketing strategy, you must be subtle.

- Never post any blatant advertising in news groups. Use the third-party technique of a satisfied customer talking about your products or services in a positive way. If you have a satisfied customer, ask for a testimonial in the appropriate news group. You can also answer a question asked by someone else in the group.

- Keep your contributions full of real information.

- Never use CAPITAL LETTERS; they are considered rude in the news group community.

- Distribute information through news groups and listservers only to those who have expressed an interest in receiving it. For direct e-mail, use only names received through registration or by request. Always let customers remove their names from your e-mail address book.

Other Non-Web Marketing

Over 17 million people currently subscribe to one of the "Big Three" online services: America Online (AOL), 17 million; CompuServe, 2 million; or Prodigy. Although the online services also act as ISPs, offering access to the Internet, online subscribers who are timid or have slow modems may use only the service itself. Since the majority of subscribers to these services are families, the online services may represent a significant market for you.

Broadly speaking, CompuServe, which was acquired by AOL in 1998, has a reputation for having more business customers, whereas Prodigy aims exclusively at the home market. AOL has the largest customer base, easiest user interface, and best graphics, but has problems with busy signals to local servers due to rapid growth. If you choose to market directly to online service customers, be aware that membership changes rapidly and that demographics can be difficult to nail down. Web portals have to some extent replaced these services as destination points and gateways. Online services are fairly competitive with ISPs, averaging $20–$22 per month for unlimited user access.

Depending on your business, you may want to subscribe to all or none of these services. Of course, you will drop any online service whose marketing results after several months do not cover at least the monthly expense of that service. As with everything else on the Internet, the best way to learn about online service customers and culture is to observe quietly in the background.

Forums

Browse forums and message boards, which operate like news groups for the online services, to read the info-tools of others. There are forums on everything from aquariums to zoology, from politics to pop stars. Major computer companies, such as IBM and Microsoft, also maintain forums on the online services. And, of course, Web-related forums are very popular. You will need to search the available forums to select the ones most likely to attract users who fit your profile of a good prospect. Each forum has a system operator, or **Sysop,** who is responsible for managing forum activities. Each time you move to a new forum, study it until you understand its style and the quirks of its Sysop.

To see a list of useful forums on AOL, type in the keyword BUSINESS KNOW-HOW, choose Message Boards or Forums, and select a relevant topic from the list, as seen in Figure 3.15. You might also want to check out the keywords SOHO (small office/home office) or ONLINE BUSINESS. On CompuServe, select GO FORUMS from the Main Menu. The Public Relations and Marketing Forum on

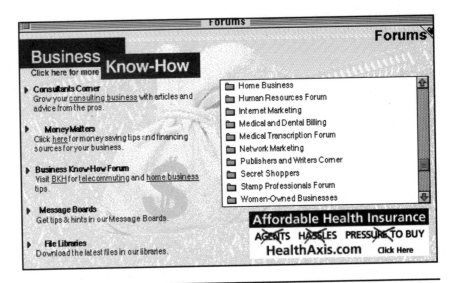

Figure 3.15. Business forums on AOL. "America Online," "AOL" and the Logo design are registered trademarks of America Online, Inc. © 1997-1999 America Online, Inc. All rights reserved.

CompuServe is particularly valuable because you can upload a press release. A good release may be picked up and reprinted by the country's top magazines and newspapers.

Remember, the purpose of all this is to create easy pathways to the largest possible number of potential customers. Jane at Gadsby's Popcorn decides to start with CompuServe, then add the other online services, and finally build a Web site. She finds that CompuServe forums contain three areas:

1. *Libraries* packed with files uploaded by individuals, marketers, and experts on any given subject. Some files are highly useful shareware programs; others are informative text.

2. *Messages* is a section for posting messages and reading messages posted by others. The message section can be thought of as a no-host radio call-in program, limited only by the topic.

3. *Conference rooms* where people gather simultaneously to hold moderated, scheduled chats. Set up with the support of the

Sysop, who publicizes conferences over the online service, these can be very useful to a creative marketer. If you are an expert on any given subject, you can use these to become better known, to establish credibility, and by extension to promote your company.

Posting to Forum Libraries

With the online services, the main strategy is to upload info-tools, such as reports, newsletters, and press releases, to the library section of each useful forum.

On CompuServe, choose the option LIBRARIES or FILES from the main Forum menu. Select the library you want and choose the Upload or Contribute Files option, following the directions onscreen. Select keywords carefully to make it easy for others to find your file. Back at Gadsby's, Jane uploads her previously created reports to the library section of the COOKS ONLINE forum on CompuServe.

On AOL you upload a file by going to the keyword Upload, which takes you to the Uploading Center with multiple libraries. Follow directions for the library you select.

Prodigy, which has no ability to store info-tools, strongly discourages advertising and promotion. You might try the Small Business/Home Office board, as long as you are subtle. Otherwise, your Prodigy marketing will be restricted to purchased advertising.

You can obtain a count at any time of how many people have downloaded your report from the library. If your report is interesting, expect hundreds of downloads per month. If you see only a few, go back to the drawing board. Don't give up, just learn from the experience and try again.

Forum Messages

Once you contribute a report or any other info-tools to an appropriate forum library, announce where your report is and how to get it. Start by making a short announcement inside the message section of the forum. You can also place your message in any other appropriate (meaning on-topic) forums, whether or not you uploaded your info-tool to those forum libraries.

Now is also the time to become an active member of the appropriate forums. Read their postings regularly, respond to questions if you know the answer, and comment on the messages posted by others. Always include your signature file so that forum members will be exposed to your company name and know how to reach you.

If people ask for information about your products, forward a blurb and tell them where to find other info-tools you have uploaded. If their request appears in the forum message section, post your blurb there. If the request comes from private e-mail, send your blurb to the individual's e-mail address only. This combination of posting files and sending e-mail messages can be an effective and inexpensive method of marketing. Be sure to track all these actions, as well as the number of responses from each source, in your info-log.

At Gadsby's, Jane sends a notice about her report to participants in the Cooks Online Forum and begins to respond to queries raised online. As her e-mail box fills with requests from CompuServe subscribers for more information, Jane responds to each message and sends out her blurb. All this interaction gives Jane more ideas for info-tools, blurbs, and reports, which she adds to her online marketing arsenal.

Although Jane's search for more forums related to popcorn turns up empty, she finds several CompuServe forums that are indirectly related. The forum Building Your Business catches her attention when she realizes that many of its participants are looking for business opportunities. As it happens, Gadsby's offers franchises to qualified people who want to distribute its popcorn or open a storefront of their own. Jane creates a report and blurb related to franchising, and she uses similar methods to spread the word online. As a result of her Building Your Business forum activity, Jane sells six franchises around the country over the next few months—excellent results from these early online marketing steps.

Conferences

Conferences on either AOL or CompuServe allow you to showcase your own and your company's experience. (Prodigy has no facility for conferences, although you can become an Information Associate.) Conferences are like chat rooms, but they have a focal point—you.

You can always participate in conferences arranged by others, which at least permits you to leave your signature file. It's better, however, to host a conference in your area of expertise. The Sysop of the particular forum or board arranges conferences. Sysops may be hard to reach, and it can be difficult to schedule a conference on a particularly busy forum.

As the moderator, you will make a presentation, with files delivered beforehand to conference attendees. Participants could number from several dozen to several thousand. During the conference, any attendee can type in a comment, which is then commented on by the rest of the group.

Make sure all attendees know how to reach you afterward, since you can't market your services directly during the conference. Conference participants are a self-selected list of likely prospects. You're on your own, though, to follow up on leads from people who contact you later.

Classifieds

Classified ads, ads that appear in a section organized by subject, are available on all the online services as well as on USEnet. Classified ads, like the one in Figure 3.16, can be one of the best advertising buys in the world. They are relatively inexpensive—often free or just a few dollars per week—and can reach a potential audience of millions. Most of all, people who read classifieds are often ready to buy: they are the ultimate in prequalified customers.

AOL's classified charges, which are category based, range from $7 to $13 for two weeks for a multiline ad that fits in the box shown in Figure 3.16. Monthly and annual rates are also available, as are free "message board" classifieds for items under $100.

By comparison, print classifieds may run anywhere from $12 per day for a paper with a circulation of 200,000 to $53 for one with 500,000 readers, up to $240 for a paper with a circulation of several million. (Most print advertisers now include an online ad for free or for a small additional charge.) Depending on your target audience, classifieds may be a better buy than display ads; viewers of classifieds preselect themselves by searching specifically for the category that interests them.

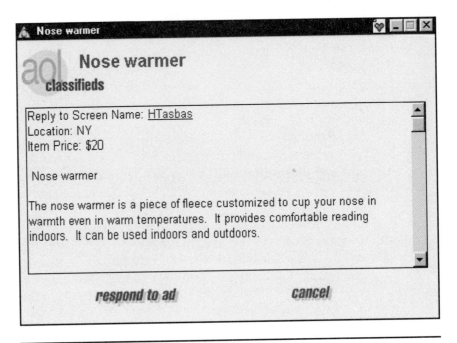

Figure 3.16. AOL classified ad. "America Online," "AOL" and the Logo design are registered trademarks of America Online, Inc. © 1997-1999 America Online, Inc. All rights reserved.

If you have a larger budget, you can opt for a display ad (discussed later) on most online services' classified pages. Figure 3.17 shows display ads from a classified sub-index on AOL.

Writing a good classified ad is an art. You'll need a good headline as well as concise body copy. Study the ads that appear online, check out the tips for writing an ad at AOL Classifieds, get a book from the library, or run a comparison ad in a newspaper. Remember to track your ads so you know which ones work best. You can do this by coding e-mail response addresses, or even by creating a separate Web entry page for each ad. You'll know within several days if your classified ad is successful. Change the language if it doesn't draw.

Most people get an excellent response if they offer anything worthwhile. If you sell only several items, you may break even; a few more and you've made money.

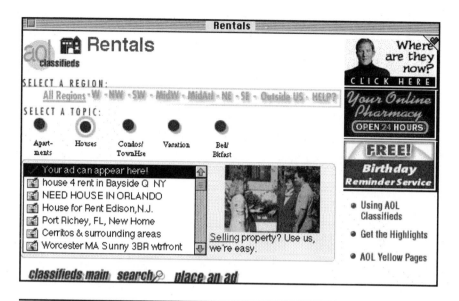

Figure 3.17. Display ads in AOL classified section. "America Online," "AOL" and the Logo design are registered trademarks of America Online, Inc. © 1999 America Online, Inc. All rights reserved.

USEnet and Web Classifieds

If your budget is really tight, consider USEnet classifieds, which are free to both buyer and seller. USEnet classifieds are found mainly in the *.forsale* news group, but some other news groups accept them (check, for example, *.wanted, .jobs,* or *.marketplace*). Starting with the *.forsale* news groups, ask members for their help in locating others that accept classifieds.

You can regionalize your ads by going to regional news groups. For example, if you want to sell your old family car in Chicago, the *chi.forsale* news group would be the best place for you. All you do is join the group and type an article that becomes your ad. As always, post only items for sale that are relevant to the subject of a news group. Use a news group search program like the one at *http:// www.liszt.com/news* or *http://tile.net/news/viewlist.html* to locate good "for sale" sites.

Web-based classifieds, such as Classifieds 2000: The Internet Classifieds (see Figure 3.18) have more features than those on USEnet. Most, for instance, have the capacity for photos and parameter searches. Classifieds 2000 is free. The Online Classifieds (*http://www. srv.net/toc/*), charges $25 for a six-month ad, with an additional $2.50 charge to appear in multiple categories. Rates for a year are only $40, with $5 for each additional category.

Display Advertising on Online Services

You can always purchase advertising contracts with the online and free e-mail services, which rely on ads to pay their costs. The options range from display ads on shopping related pages, to banner ads con-

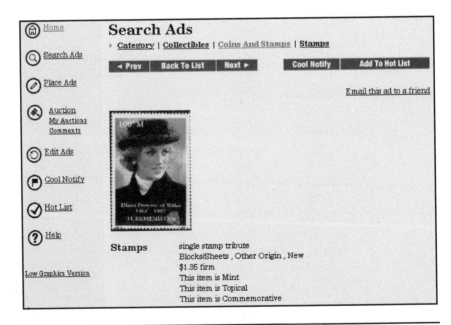

Figure 3.18. Internet classified ad from Classifieds 2000, *http://www. classifieds2000.com*. Excite, Jango, and Classifieds 2000 are trademarks of Excite, Inc. and may be registered in various jurisdictions. Excite screen display © 1995-1999 Excite, Inc.

nected to specific search words, or placement tied to focused services, such as Chat Rooms or Check Mail pages.

Costs run anywhere from $2 to more than $60 per thousand impressions—but minimum payment might be $10,000 per month or more! (For a description of AOL's advertising alternatives, go to keyword MEDIASPACE or see *http://media.aol.com*.) With minimums like these, display rates on the homepages or other primary screens of online services may easily exceed the reach of a small business. You'll learn in Chapter 6 that advertising rates increase for more selectively targeted audiences, though the total number of viewers may be smaller. (Figure 3.19 is an example of a full-page display ad on AOL.)

By comparison, a Monday-through-Thursday, black-and-white, 1/16-page print ad in *USA Today* now runs $19,000 per week.

As you review your marketing plan in light of all this information, you may decide that these off-the-Web methods alone will consume your time and financial resources. If they produce sales, that's

Figure 3.19. Full page display ad on AOL. "America Online," "AOL" and the Logo design are registered trademarks of America Online, Inc. © 1997-1999 America Online, Inc. All rights reserved.

terrific. Even if you later decide to go on the Web, these tools—e-mail, listservers, news groups, forums, and classifieds—will extend your marketing reach.

Choose the online method and info-tools that work best for your business and your budget, regardless of what anyone else does. In the following chapters we'll look in detail at the remaining three steps to Internet success: creating a Web site, monitoring results, and promoting your Internet presence.

4

Creating Your Web Site

As you've realized by now, the World Wide Web is a decadently rich marketing tool, particularly when served with the non-Web online marketing methods described in the previous chapter. Now it's time to detail the fifth step for Internet success: creating or upgrading a Web site. We'll analyze what makes a good site, evaluate Web Host Service Providers (WHISPs), and explore all aspects of development, from registering a domain name to estimating costs.

Although this discussion assumes that you will contract with other companies for Web design and hosting, we'll consider whether it's reasonable and cost-effective for your company to execute these responsibilities instead. Should you decide to undertake some or all of the Web creation and hosting tasks in-house, you can adapt the following guidelines. Once again, we will focus on the importance of planning and research before you start spending money. In this chapter you'll learn about

- Analyzing Web site design and navigation

- Planning your site, including budget, timeline, staff, and infrastructure

- Hiring service providers: ISP, Web host, and designer

- The steps of the design process

- Suggestions for a successful site

- Free features and resources

There's More to a Site Than Meets the Eye

Before you can create or upgrade your Web site, it will be helpful to learn how to evaluate the design of other sites. As with art, you can move beyond the perspective of "I don't know anything about it, but I know what I like." The better you can articulate what makes a particular Web site effective, the better you can communicate with your Web designer, colleagues, customers, and even your boss.

Start a collection now of sites that you like or dislike. Print out pages whenever you're surfing the Web and save them in your Web notebook for the initial design conference described in "Initial Design Conference and Review Schedule." By the end of this section, you should be able to analyze the four elements of a site, identifying what features of each are worthy of praise or need improvement:

- Concept

- Content

- Navigation

- Decoration

Concept

Concept is the beginning, but not the end of a Web site. Keep in mind the dictum, "form follows function." In Chapter 2, you learned the importance of defining the purpose(s) your Web site will serve (function) and what audience(s) you want to reach. When you look at any Web site, you should be able to decode the audiences and purposes the site is intended to serve. Who is expected to look at the site? What message are they expected to take away? Only in the context of its goals and audience can you evaluate how effective a site is and whether the most appropriate means of communication have been used.

Behind every great Web site is a unifying theme or concept. Here's where the creative folks play an essential role, transforming their understanding of your business into a visual metaphor that will carry through all the pages of your site. As you surf sites on the Web, you quickly realize that the good ones maintain the same look and feel throughout. This consistency not only makes it easier for the viewer to navigate the site, it also reinforces the chosen image of the company.

The concept may be a concrete metaphor, like that of Grant's Ale *(http://www.grants.com,* shown in Figure 4.1), or a matter of style, as with New York Cabbie *(http://www.nycabbie.com,* shown in Figure 4.2). It can be friendly or formal, avant garde or retro, academic or playful, sophisticated or slapstick, droll or determined. Most important, the concept should be consistent and accurately reflect the company and purpose of the site.

Figure 4.1. Concrete metaphor, *http://www.grants.com.* © 1999 Yakima Brewing and Malting Co.

Figure 4.2. Style metaphor, *http://www.nycabbie.com/.* © MLK (TPS), Paul Wallace, Webmaster; Frank Palmenat, Digital Artist.

Content

A site unfolds for a viewer not just on the screen, but in time. Like a story, a site should have a beginning, a middle, and an end. This may seem counterintuitive given all the links and random navigation on the Web, but if you think about time, instead of space, it makes sense. The beginning grabs viewers' attention, the middle is the value-added, content portion of the site, and the end is the payoff (when viewers' needs are satisfied, e.g., by downloading a file) or the **call to action** (a specific suggestion of what step to take next, e.g., register now.)

To fulfill the purpose of a site, content—the words, pictures, and multimedia on the screen—must be relevant, stated clearly, and communicated quickly. What the creator intends should be what the viewer perceives, even subconsciously. For instance, what data does your target audience need to decide to buy your product? To differentiate you from competitors? To be satisfied with customer support?

Consider *http://www.supplierlink.com* in Figure 4.3. You know the purpose of the site immediately from the opening graphic. The

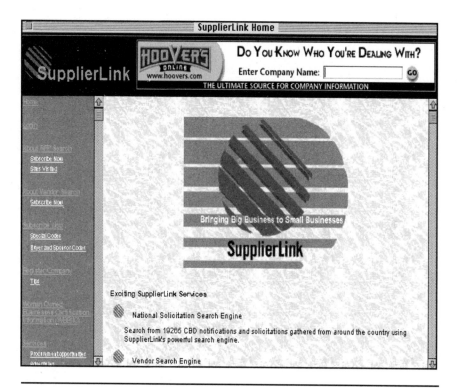

Figure 4.3. Sample site, *http://www.supplierlink.com.* Courtesy POD
Associates, Inc.

homepage also instantly defines the target audiences and functions
available on the site.

Whatever the Web site, someone must conceive the initial content; almost always that someone will be within the business, not a
contractor. An outside designer rarely knows a company's products
or services well enough to start designing from scratch. The inside
person will probably also suggest external links and provide an initial hierarchy of information, structuring what should be on the sur-
face, and what belongs several clicks down.

Sometimes you can tell that the content of a site consists of a pre-
existing ad or brochure copied without change. Often, this doesn't
work. The copy may be too wordy, too long, or too passive for the
inherently interactive Web. As Marshall McLuhan noted long ago in
his analysis of media, the initial tendency is to make previous media

the content of the newest one. (For example, people tried to put theater-style stage productions onto television or read print ads on radio.)

While you can sometimes adapt older content to save time and money, almost always you will need to tweak or "repurpose" it for the Web. Graphics may not transfer well to a lower-resolution screen; photos may take too long to download. You'll want to reorganize content, creating links or putting some information farther down in the site.

Don't feel that you have to overwhelm visitors with every single bit of information ever created about your company. In fact, a site that stays tightly focused on your marketing mission will be more satisfactory to both the viewer and your bottom line.

Navigation

How well can the viewer get around a site? Is it obvious? Intuitive? Does it leave a trail of "bread crumbs" so viewers know where they've been in case they want to go back? Does the site provide clues to what users will find at future destinations? Are they led gently along a garden path to the next panorama or left to wander through a maze?

Site designers can facilitate navigation in many ways:

- Structure the site consistently, with similar elements always appearing in the same place on different pages.

- Organize content logically and directly through topics and subtopics, like the table of contents in a book or the outline of an essay.

- Guide a typical user with such cues as buttons, layout, and prompts.

- Develop an identifiable menu structure, such as Envirolink's icons (shown in Figure 4.4 at *http://wwww.envirolink.org)*.

- Always provide a site index (sometimes called a map or directory) that affords an overview of the entire site in terms of both structure and content.

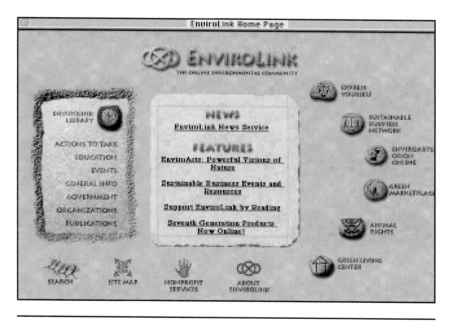

Figure 4.4. Clear menu and structure, *http://www.envirolink.org.* Courtesy of The Envirolink Network.

- Make the site index available from every page.

- Ensure that the site index contains active internal links to the desired page(s).

- Restrain the number of main on-screen options to no more than 6 to 10.

- Use pop-up or pull-down menus to provide additional detail.

- Keep any point on the site reachable within two or three clicks.

- Maintain an intuitive structure, like hub and spokes or tree branching.

- Offer a clear, complete home page that is always accessible.

- Assist users with on-screen help, especially for complex, information-dense sites.

- Consider an on-screen search engine so users can enter keywords they are seeking (see *http://www.teefinder.com*, shown in Figure 4.5).

- Change the color, shape, orientation, or type style of links on the menu and index so users can always tell where they have been and where they currently are.

- Take advantage of click actions to reinforce messages (i.e., ask viewers to request something specifically by clicking).

Figure 4.5. On-site search engine, *http://www.teefinder.com*. © 1998 Teefinder; Web design and development by Circle-R Designs at *http://www. circle-r.com/webdesign*.

Of course, like anything else creative, there are reasons to break all the rules. If the purpose is to entertain users and create an on-the-Web experience, a designer may choose to amuse, confuse, confound, and mystify the viewer, as underwear manufacturer Joe Boxer does in its site map at *http://www.joeboxer.com/Joeboxer2/map/map freak.html*, shown in Figure 4.6.

Decoration: Backgrounds, Buttons, and Bars

The unique style of a site—what most people think of as Web design—is actually the servant of concept, content, and navigation. Decoration refers to the graphic and multimedia elements that are as unique to your site as your logo is to your name.

A designer has almost infinite options for color, buttons, backgrounds, textures, rules, typefaces, illustrations, photos, and multimedia. Should the buttons be three-dimensional, flat, or beveled?

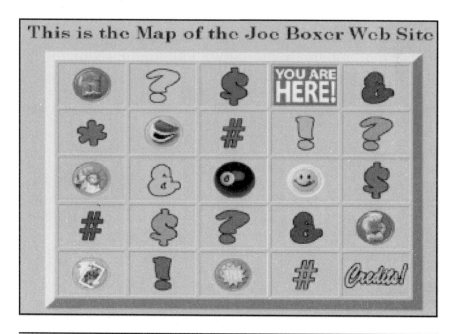

Figure 4.6. Site map, *http://www.joeboxer.com/Joeboxer2/map/map freak.html*. Courtesy Joe Boxer Corporation.

Should the imagery be realistic, abstract, or a combination of the two, like the surreal paintings of Magritte? Are cartoons or logotypes appropriate? Imagination is the only limit. Corporate colors, logo, and/or standard typefaces should probably be repeated on a site. Designers are fond of a saying by the architect Mies van der Rohe, "God is in the details." Make your corporate image sparkle through the decorative details on your site.

Take a look at the four screenshots in Figures 4.7 to 4.10 *(http://www.bohos.flypaperpress.com, http://www.flaxart.com/, http://food.epicurious.com, http://www.finecoffee.com)*. Would you be likely to confuse the corporate identity of any of these sites, each of which has its own unique Web style? Figure 4.11 is a rating sheet that you can adapt to evaluate your own or others' sites.

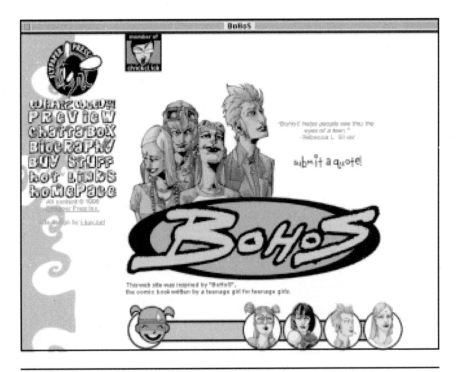

Figure 4.7.   Unique style, *http://www.bohos.flypaperpress.com*. Trademark & © 1999 FlyPaper Press at *http://www.temp24-7.com*.

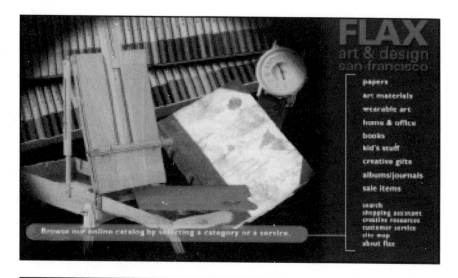

Figure 4.8. Unique style, *http://www.flaxart.com.* Courtesy Flax Art & Design.

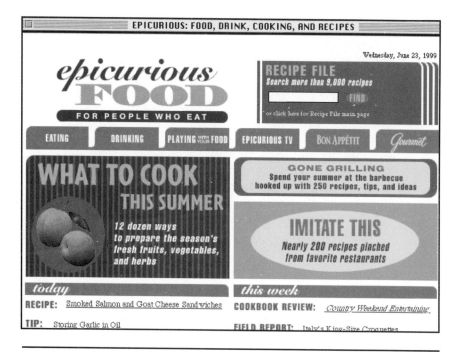

Figure 4.9. Unique style, *http://food.epicurious.com.* Courtesy Epicurious Food © 1999 Conde Nast, Inc. All rights reserved.

Figure 4.10. Unique style, *http://www.finecoffee.com* or http://*www.alvan houtteusa.com.* Courtesy Fruba, Inc. dba College Hill Coffee Shop.

Preplanning Pays Off

A strategic Web plan includes the standard elements of any project management task:

- Budget.

- Timeline for development.

- Identification of key personnel and task estimates for site development and upkeep.

- Analysis of internal resources and needs, in this case for hardware, software, and telecommunications infrastructure.

Based on the imagery and the content, who is the audience for this site and what purposes does the site serve?

Rank each item below from 1-5 with 5 being best. Subtotal each category, then total the site overall.

CONCEPT

How well is a coherent visual metaphor carried through the site?	1	2	3	4	5
How well is that metaphor carried through on each screen?		1	2	3	4	5
How well does the metaphor fit the company image?		1	2	3	4	5
How well does the metaphor suit the purpose of the site?		1	2	3	4	5
How well does the metaphor suit the target audience?		1	2	3	4	5

Concept Subtotal_____

CONTENT

How appropriate is the text-intensiveness of the site?   1 2 3 4 5
How well does the site answer any questions you may have?   1 2 3 4 5
If you have unanswered questions, how easy is it to ask questions
via e-mail and/or phone? How prompt is the response?   1 2 3 4 5
How well does the content suit the purpose of the site?   1 2 3 4 5
How well does the content suit the target audience?   1 2 3 4 5

Content Subtotal_____

NAVIGATION

How consistent is the navigation?   1 2 3 4 5
How obvious, simple, or intuitive is the navigation?   1 2 3 4 5
How easy is the access to the menu, site index, and home
   on each screen?   1 2 3 4 5
How accessible are navigation tools (screen visibility/position)? 1 2 3 4 5
How effectively are internal links used to move through site?   1 2 3 4 5
How well arranged is the content (e.g. number of clicks needed)? 1 2 3 4 5

Navigation Subtotal_____

DECORATION

How attractive is the decoration?   1 2 3 4 5
How well does the decoration support the concept?   1 2 3 4 5
How well does the decoration support the content?   1 2 3 4 5
How well does the decoration support the navigation?   1 2 3 4 5
How well does the decoration suit the purpose of the site?   1 2 3 4 5
How well does the decoration suit the target audience?   1 2 3 4 5

Decoration Subtotal_____

Figure 4.11. Web site evaluation form.   Site Total_____

Before handling these elements, return to the initial plans for your Web site in Chapter 2. Transfer your goals and objectives onto a concise Web worksheet, like the sample in Figure 4.12. You will need this worksheet for internal planning and as the basis for a **Request for Quote (RFQ)** from various designers and Web service providers. The worksheet helps to encourage team buy-in, forge consensus, or justify the project to higher-ups. When you look for people to assist with the project, either inside or outside the company, the Web worksheet provides a succinct recruitment message. And whenever you come to the inevitable decision forks in design, the worksheet will help you maintain focus.

Do you remember cereal box contests? The ones where you had to complete the phrase "I like fruity SugarOhs because..." in 25 words or less? Writing the summary for the worksheet is much like that. If you can't say what you want your site to accomplish and how you will do it in less than one page, you haven't fully thought it through.

A Web worksheet starts with the site's goal and objectives, and includes a description of the audience and the methods to be used. Specify the payoff and/or calls to action. As you go through various planning steps, complete the sections about resources, revenue, staffing, and budget. The worksheet and all the cost estimates belong in your Web notebook.

Preliminary Budget

Prices for Web development vary by size and complexity of the site, geographic region (vendors on the coasts are more expensive), and the size and reputation of the design house you select. Given that prices for developing and maintaining the same Web site may be separated by an order of magnitude or more, one approach is to start with an internal estimate of how much you are willing to spend. After your first round of bids, finalize a budget—and stick to it. Try not to pay for what you don't need.

If you don't establish a limit, Web costs can quickly balloon out of control. A budget not only allows you to manage expenses for the Web site, it allows you to compare estimated costs for this form of advertising, sales, and/or customer support against off-line forms. It ensures that you have thought through potentially hidden expenses and forces you to set priorities in terms of features and time. Think-

WEB SITE PLANNING WORKSHEET

Web Site URL: _____

Page Name: _____ Date: _____

Goals: _____

Objectives (quantifiable) in the form of:

1. _____ (units) within _____ (time frame)
2. _____ (units) within _____ (time frame)
3. _____ (units) within _____ (time frame)

Target Audience:

Call(s) to Action:

Site/Page Description (Include estimated number of pages, number of multimedia elements, i.e. animations, audio, video. Specify whether live, downloadable or streaming technologies will be used. Indicate frequency of live events.)

Resources

	Needed for Development	Avail? Y/N	Needed for Operation	Avail? Y/N
Hardware				
Software				
Server				
Communication				
Client	Not Applicable	N/A		

Content Sources:

Development Staffing:

Maintenance Staffing/Frequency:

Estimated Costs:

$ _____ Start-up $ _____ /mo. Maintenance

Figure 4.12.   Web site planning worksheet.

ing about money makes you ask whether the investment of time and dollars for a Web site will produce the desired results, or whether there are better ways to expend resources.

NetMarketing *(http://www.netb2b.com/wpi/index.html)*, a division of Advertising Age, has been monitoring the cost of creating Web sites for several years. The current national median costs for a small e-commerce site were shown in Chapter 2: $25,000 for a small (20-page) site, $33,000 for a medium site (20–100 pages), $78,000 for a large site (over 100 pages), each with increasingly complex features. Sites that are database driven or include transaction processing cost more than a standard marketing site.

Costs are rising rapidly as developers become more familiar with the scope of work involved. The price for a small site is about twice what it was in July 1997, while the medium site runs about 50 percent more and the large site has increased by about 25 percent. These prices include only development and hosting, not the additional costs of internal labor, maintenance, infrastructure, or site promotion.

You can create cut-rate Web pages using free, off-the-shelf features, as you'll see in the last section of this chapter. A well-organized, simple site that offers value and is well promoted may suffice to make sales or draw people to your business. In spite of the median numbers given here, most small businesses can put up a static, nontransaction site for $1,500 to $2,500 plus labor and equipment, if needed.

The table in Figure 4.13 provides some rough estimates of startup and annual maintenance costs for mini, small, medium, and large sites. Use these numbers as a guide and these categories as a template to create your own spreadsheet. Fill out your cost estimates as you proceed through the development process. Be careful: A 1999 Gartner Group study found that most companies had budgeted only 50% to 75% of what their site eventually cost. The most often ignored factor—labor, which accounted for 79% of total site expenses.

Except for the mini site, which is done by modifying a template offered by a Web hosting service, the table assumes contracting with a Web designer to build and maintain the site. The mini, small, and medium sites use a Web hosting service, while the large site is self-hosted. Both the mini and small sites are text and graphics only. The medium site adds multimedia in the form of limited animation and sound, while the large site budget includes some streaming media.

Item	Mini Site Setup/Annual	Small Site Setup/Annual	Medium Site Setup/Annual	Large Site Setup/Annual
Hardware	$1,500 optional 1x	$3,000 optional 1x	$7,500 optional 1x	$15,000 optional 1x
Software	$200	$600	$2,000	$5,000
Register Domain	$70/$35	$70/$35	$140/$70 (2 names)	$140/$70 (2 names)
ISP	$25/$300	$25/$300	$25/$480	$25/$480
WHISP	$25/$200	$50/$360	$50/$720	Self-host
Web Design inc. 1 yr updates	5-8 pages free template	20 Pages $1,800	50 Pages $5,000	100 Pages $10,000
Telecomm	$0/$600 @ $50/mo POTS 56K	$60/$480 @ $40/mo POTS 56K; new line	$275/$3,300 ISDN @ $275/mo	$1,300/ $6,000 partial T1 @ $500/ mo
Multimedia and extras	None	cgi-script $25/included	audio/animation $4,000	streaming media $12,000
Shopping Support	None	inc. by WHISP +$120 for secure server @ $10/mo	$150/$1,200	$6,000 (software)/NA
Monitoring	From WHISP	From WHISP	$700 software	$700 software
Create Banner Advertising	Free	$300 for 6 ads @ $50/ad	$600 for 12 ads @ $50/ad	$2,400 for 24 ads @ $100/ad
SET-UP COSTS				
Annual OUTSIDE COST				
In House Labor	$10K /yr	$25K /yr	$40K-70K /yr	$70K–120K /yr
TOTAL COST				
Estimated # Visitors				
Estimated CPM				
Estimated Sales (#/$)				
Cost of Sales				

Figure 4.13. Web site budget worksheet.

All except the mini site do some form of on-line sales. The small site starts selling online, adding a small, free catalog and shopping cart from its WHISP, and paying for access to a secure server. The medium site adds online payment processing and a merchant card account. Note the oft-ignored line item for in-house labor to service the site, from providing content updates to communicating with the Webmaster and customers.

After estimating how much you're willing to spend, fill in all the rows on your own spreadsheet. Think long and hard about how many visitors you expect on your site. Divide costs by anticipated unique viewers (in thousands) to estimate your CPM (cost per thousand). How does this CPM compare to your existing advertising, whether by newspaper, direct mail, or TV?

Perform a similar analysis if you're selling online or providing customer support. Estimate your cost per sale both per transaction (or per service inquiry) and per dollar (i.e., per average sale). How many online sales would be required to break even on the Web site? How does your cost per sale online compare to other means of selling? How many people do you expect to obtain customer support from your site instead of from telephone or in-store service? How much traffic needs to shift to the Web to save money on support staffing?

Timeline

You must establish the initial timeline, just as you do the budget. If you don't set a deadline and a schedule for achieving it, your Web project will never be done! Obviously, a timeline will vary with your situation and with the complexity of your site. One criterion for selecting Web designers will be their availability to work to your timetable. For instance, you may require an introductory site in conjunction with a scheduled event or product launch.

Spend about half the time available in the planning and design phase. The remaining half will be split almost equally between development and testing. These ratios, which are typical for both media production and programming, may seem excessive on the front end. They aren't. The time you spend planning will save you dollars in the end.

Don't try to launch all the pages on your site at once. Since it is difficult to recover from a botched launch, establish a small site with core products and features first. Continue to build, test, and add pages over time. Sequencing development not only spreads out the costs, it also enables you to see how well a specific page works. If you're not sure how to accomplish this, prioritize goals in your business plan. Develop first by audience, then by page or feature within that goal. You may want to delay all multimedia until the basic site is up.

Also create a timeline for additions, monitoring, and updates. Depending on the purpose of your site and the nature of your business, some element of your site should probably change at least once a month. New content might be a press release, a product announcement, a special offer, or simply different graphics. Unless your business is completely static, your Web site won't be either. There is a fine line between adding new information to draw repeat visitors and making changes for the sake of change. If your site successfully provides service to repeat customers, you may want to leave well enough alone.

As you'll learn in Chapter 6, changes on a site offer opportunities for promotion. By spreading out development and updates, you'll also generate multiple promotional announcements, drawing new or repeat viewers each time. The timeline in Figure 4.14 provides a sense of the relative time needed for various parts of the Web design process.

Set Up a Team

Developing a Web site can be daunting. Leonardo da Vinci was probably the only person who could have done it all himself—from stunning graphic design to elegant code, from mastering the aesthetic vocabulary of six different media to computing bandwidth requirements. Ordinary mortals need to designate a team and team leader (unless that's you) to meet with the Web designer. The team will also evaluate and test designs, provide initial content and site structure, schedule material for updates, and coordinate with other business operations.

Besides those involved with information systems, the team should include representatives from any department that will provide content and/or is expected to interact with users. This may mean representatives from publications, human resources, customer service, or marketing. If you plan to generate revenue from your site, include staff from sales, order fulfillment, accounting, and catalog development.

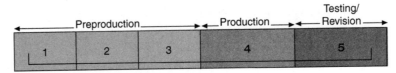

Preproduction
1. Establish needs, goals, objectives
   Setup team
   Establish budget and time frame
   Research other sites
   Survey internal resources
   Select providers
   Write treatment
2. Select and register domain name
   Prepare storyboards and flowchart
   Write script
   Create comp designs
3. Feedback cycle and design revision
   includes focus groups and internal review

Production
4. Collect and prepare content elements
   Write all text
   Produce all graphics
   Write Web site programming
   Produce any multimedia elements
   Research and create links
   Sell and obtain electronic art for ads and sponsors

Testing/Revision
5. Test programming, including syntax and links
   Test user interface/acceptability (internal)
   Review content for accuracy
   Test trial site with limited number of users (external)
   Launch

Figure 4.14. Development timeline.

Launching and publicizing your site when it is ready may be an in-house marketing responsibility, or it may be handled by your Web designer, Web host, PR firm, or advertising agency, depending on what you've decided. In any case, you'll want your marketing person to oversee the activities conducted by the contractors.

There are no fixed roles for participants in a Web project, nor are there rules saying what must be done in-house and what should be done by an outside provider. (The more you do in-house, the lower your costs, however.) Even the distribution of labor among outside providers is in flux. Both hosting services and designers, for example, may handle some initial promotion tasks such as submitting to search engines.

A Web site is not a one-time project. Like a river, it goes on forever. In your staffing plans, be sure to identify who will be responsible downstream for

- Managing the site

- Ensuring that users receive technical support

- Updating the site

- Responding to communications from users

- Monitoring and analyzing site traffic and providing feedback

Be sure to consider pre-existing workloads before tasking members of your team. What you think will be a one-time, 20-hour task completed within a month may easily turn into a task that takes 20 hours a week indefinitely.

Assess Infrastructure

As part of determining your budget and timeline, survey your internal resources. This is critical if you expect to host your own site, sell online, offer customer support, or receive a large number of new e-mail messages. (Remember that e-mail should be answered in 24 hours or less.) You may need to budget for new equipment or allow time to install additional phone lines or train staff on new software. Some of the items come with a substantial price tag—be sure they are included in your budget.

Hardware and Software In-House

Will you need more equipment if you bring on additional employees to handle demand generated by the site? Will you need to install plug-ins or other software to create content files or play back the contents of your Web page? If so, make sure your equipment has the capacity for them. (Of course, you will confirm that all your software and hardware is **Year 2000—Y2K—**compliant.) You may need to upgrade your computers to communicate with the server hosting your site. Before buying any additional equipment, check with the Web hosting service to make sure what hardware, software, and operating system are compatible.

If you plan to host your own site, it's critical to select the correct **server,** a computer with the software and telecommunications capacity to act as a host. The operating system you use will affect other decisions downstream, including selection of Web server software, whose cost ranges from free to thousands of dollars. Your choice of Web design software and other application packages, such as security, catalog, or multimedia, will also be affected. Consult with your information systems manager about your plans.

The general guideline for buying hardware definitely holds with purchases designed for Internet use. As a top priority, maximize the speed at which you can access the Web. Get the fastest method that your infrastructure will support, such as ISDN, 56.6 Kbps, or cable. After that, buy the machine with the fastest processor and most memory that you can afford. Any VGA monitor will do, although larger screens make it easier to see Web images without scrolling.

Internal Telecommunication Needs

If your company is on a network, discuss your Web project with your system administrator to see if additional equipment will be needed. You may require additional routers, for instance, if many more people will be online at the same time. If you expect increased Internet traffic, also check the capacity of your Internet connection and its server to make sure that it can handle more simultaneous users without slowing down.

Especially if your server is located in-house, consider upgrading to a dedicated 33.6 Kbps line, a 56 Kbps frame relay line, ISDN, ADSL, or a T1 or T3 line instead of a regular telephone connection. The table in Figure 4.15 shows the different types of lines, with sample rates, setup fees, and purposes. The rates for these lines vary around

Type of Line	Typical Monthly Rate	Set Up Fee	Purpose
Dial Up 56K	$20-$40	none	low volume, one-person, dial up connection, unlimited time, e-mail
Dedicated ISDN 64Kbps	$275	$275	Permanent Internet connection for LAN, e-mail, and/or low-volume server
Dedicated 128 Kpbs	$450	$400	average sized business, allows security, free access
Burstable T1	$1300-$2100 depending on speed	$1500	average-to-large business using multimedia, point-to-point access
Full T1	$1000-$1295	$1595	Large, high volume business, full time access, fastest

Figure 4.15. Telecommunication rates.

the country. They may run anywhere from tens to several thousand dollars per month, depending on your needs and usage.

Establish User Hardware/Software Requirements

You rarely have a guarantee about your potential users' computer skills, equipment, software, or navigational savvy on the Web. It may be helpful to include several questions about such matters on the survey you use to build your audience profile. Will your viewers have the latest version of a browser? Will your site be compatible with multiple browsers? Be sure to discuss your expectations with your Web designer. Plan to have in-house whatever hardware and software you expect your customers to have.

Remember that the more multimedia you put on your site, the more sophisticated the user software and hardware required, and the more likely some viewers will be shut out. Is your audience really likely to download and install plug-ins for multimedia? Too much animation, too much Java programming for scrolling or movie clips, and your viewers will click away to another site. Although the majority of testing will be the responsibility of your Web designer, you should duplicate a typical viewer's experience before signing off and accepting the work.

At this point, you're ready to locate service providers. Put the planning worksheets and budgets into your Web notebook—it will soon be filled with detailed schedules, cost estimates, task lists, RFQs, bid responses, contracts, design documents, and written sign-offs.

Selecting Service Providers: ISP, Web Host, and Designer

The first decision is whether to handle your site in-house or to hire others. It is certainly possible for a large company, with the right resources and skilled personnel on staff, to become its own ISP, host its own site, and handle all design and promotion internally. Many do. Some corporations staff their Web unit with 6 to 12 people; others create an entire online division as an independent profit center to market and sell products on the Web.

Even small, high-tech companies may have the in-house skills to create, maintain, and host a modest site, growing staff as the need arises. They may contract out only for Internet access and graphic design support. Some small companies decide their Web plans are so modest that they hire an owner's teenager or send an administrative assistant to take a class in Web design, locate a WHISP, and decide they're finished. Sometimes the results are great; sometimes the Web sites resemble the early newsletters produced when people decided they were skilled with desktop publishing software.

Most small companies don't have people with necessary Web skills in-house, and their staff is often stretched thin. Their options are to hire a Webmaster to manage the process or to outsource the entire project. Even then, the project will require an internal coordinator and draw on staff resources.

Someone who has learned Web site software or decides to use the site-building template on an online service may decide to start a one-person, Web-based, home business. (Many such companies skip the business plan step, to their later dismay.)

There is no one right solution. In business you usually have to spend money to make money. That may mean going with a pro, either in-house or outside. The more complex your site in terms of transactions, multimedia, or size, the more you need professional guidance. Web sites are subject to a truism that affects all other forms of media production: "You can have it good; you can have it fast; you can have it cheap. Pick any two."

If you are serious about the Web, it is worth an investment to make the site easy to use, graphically appealing, and effective for marketing and sales. Otherwise, it may turn out to be an expense that never returns cost savings or increased revenue. Your business and Web plan are your best tools for making the do-it-yourself decision.

Selecting an Internet Service Provider (ISP)

Chances are you long ago selected an ISP to connect your business or home to the Internet. How else could you have done all this research? You may also have established accounts with one or more commercial online services that you want to keep for marketing reasons.

Criteria for ISP selection are a subset of those used to select a Web hosting service. To obtain Internet access for your company, you probably looked at such factors as

- Rates for connect time; unlimited service is best for a business.

- Free local access numbers and cost-free access from out of town (most places should support Internet mail access at the very least). Many ISPs charge for access when you use a toll-free number; this can add up if you travel a great deal.

- Reliability and speed of access to the Internet and to your office. POTS (Plain Old Telephone Service) may be a limiting factor. Not all ISPs can bring you in on leased lines, T1, or ADSL service. Other limitations include the number of customers (the average ISP has several thousand) and the connection speed between the ISP and the Internet backbone.

- Number of e-mail boxes provided under one account.

- Security and backup procedures.

- Compatibility with your existing and planned hardware and telecommunications capabilities.

The graph in Figure 4.16 from *http://cyberatlas.internet.com/big_picture/hardware/reasons.html* shows what factors influenced ISP choice by over 1,000 businesses and 6,000 business users in 1999.

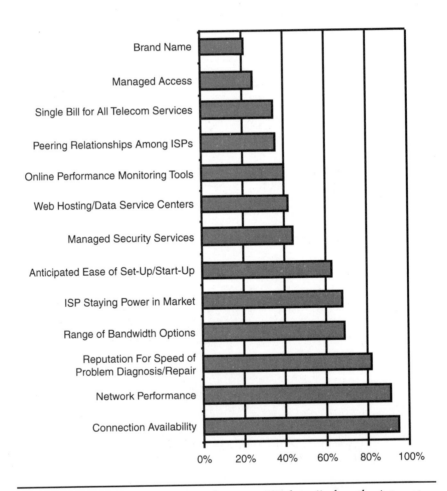

Figure 4.16. Reasons customers choose an ISP, *http://cyberatlas.internet.com/big_picture/hardware/reasons.html*. Reprinted with permission. © 1999 Internet.com, LLC. All rights reserved.

On the other side of the coin, the most frequent complaints about ISPs were

- Slow log-ins, 45%

- Busy signals, 26%

- Too expensive, 26%

For references, check customer ratings of ISPs in your area at *http://www.cnet.com/Content/Reports/Special/ISP/index.html? tag=st.cn.sr1.dir.* Nationwide providers like Sprint or MCI and regional suppliers have begun to displace mom-and-pop ISPs as the Internet service business moves into an era of commodity pricing similar to that of long distance. Figure 4.17 *(http://www.internet.org/cgi-bin/genobject/connectivity)* shows the market share of the largest ISPs in the United States.

Most ISPs now offer unlimited Internet access for $25 or less per month, with additional names on the same account for about $5 per month each. However, they vary widely in the availability of free

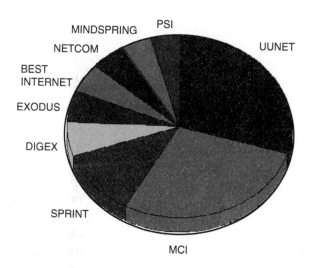

Figure 4.17.   ISP market share, *http://www.internet.org/cgi-bin/genobject/ connectivity.* Courtesy Michael Bauer, Internet.org.

local access numbers, the number of calls they can handle at any one time, the nature of their own connection to the Internet, and the space for personal home pages.

For serious marketing, look for an ISP that can provide mailing list programs (listservers), mailbots, news group access, and **FTP (file transfer protocol)**. The provider must give you a **SLIP/PPP** account (Serial Line Internet Protocol/Point-to-Point Protocol—the Internet protocols that support Web and FTP servers). If an ISP can't provide all or most of these functions, keep shopping.

Some ISPs have a startup fee; others offer a discount for year-long contracts; some charge extra for services like mailbots and listservers. Compare costs for startup, first year, and subsequent years of service, as well as connection track record, business history, and customer rating. The lowest-priced service may not be the best bargain; sometimes you get what you pay for.

Figure 4.18 provides an ISP selection checklist. Based on your online marketing plan, decide on the services you will need, customize this checklist, and request bids from several providers based on the same set of services.

Selecting a Web Hosting Service Provider (WHISP)

Not all ISPs host Web sites and not all Web hosts provide Internet access service. Depending on your choices, you may end up with two different providers or you may find one, such as Planet Systems Network *(http://psn.net/business)*, that offers an integrated business package encompassing both. In this virtual world, a WHISP with a server located thousands of miles away may host your site, but a local ISP with a free access number may be used for e-mail and Internet searching. If your ISP and WHISP are different companies, decide whether you want the WHISP to forward mail received at your site address to another e-mail name (called an alias). Figure 4.19 *(http://www.internet. org/cgi-bin/genobject/hosting)* shows the market share for the 13 largest Web hosting companies in the United States.

You will need to communicate directly to your site, often via FTP, for uploading new content files, downloading transaction records, or checking statistics. Your WHISP should provide you with directions for doing this. Some of the statistical analyses discussed in Chapter 5

ISP Name _____ Date _____

Item	Y/N	Description	Cost
General			
Length of time in business?			
Staff qualifications/turnover?			
Client references? (get 3)			
System			
Local access numbers?			
Access numbers nationally?			
800-number access? Surcharge?			
Type of Internet connection?			
What connection speeds does the ISP cater to/handle?			
How much traffic at once?			
Security, e.g. firewalls?			
What % of time was server available during past 3 months?			
Server/connection redundancy?			
Back-up policy?			
Pricing			
What is the pricing structure?			
Monthly Flat Rate?			
Hourly?			
Add-on and over-quota rates?			
Long-term discounts?			
On/off connection fees?			
Technical Services			
Software pre-configured for use on your end?			
Will they support reconfiguration of your existing set-up, if needed?			
Can they support mailing lists? News groups? Mailbots?			
What level/hours is technical support provided?			
What are the charges for technical support? Set-up? Troubleshooting?			
Other			
Free personal Web space? Size?			
How many free mailboxes with account? Cost for additional?			

Figure 4.18. ISP selection checklist.

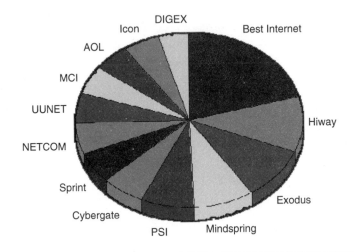

Figure 4.19. Web hosting market share, *http://www.internet.org/cgi-bin/ genobject/hosting.* Courtesy Michael Bauer, Internet.org.

should come with your hosting contract at no additional charge. Hosting services may not support all Web development packages equally. If a certain development package is critical, it, too, must become a selection criterion.

Depending on your needs, there will be additional technical questions, such as

- The bandwidth available, which determines the number of hits your site can handle at once. Approximately 1500 Kbps bandwidth (a T1 line) will handle 50K hits per month, assuming traffic is spread evenly. Remember, though, that traffic spikes may occur with special offers or events and other forms of site promotion.

- The connection between the host server and the Internet backbone, especially if you need high speed and wide bandwidth for multimedia.

- Whether the WHISP has redundant equipment in case a server goes down.

- The WHISP's provisions for backups and data security.

- Which catalog, shopping cart, and checkstand packages are supported, and what provisions exist for secure credit card processing (see Chapter 8).

- Whether the site supports **CGI** (Common Gateway Interface) programs that allow non-Web information to be turned into a Web document on the fly. This is frequently used for on-site registration, electronic order forms, and surveys.

- What other services are offered, such as Web design, Web mall operation, site promotion, or audited statistics for advertising traffic.

Most companies have an initial setup fee plus monthly charges and add fees for special services, such as automated fax-back. Most offer discounts for long-term contracts. Prices vary widely—from tens to hundreds of dollars per month. Identify several WHISPs that can provide the services and space you need, then compare prices on a spreadsheet. Web hosting fees may be based on

- The amount of space needed on the server (estimate 10 KB per page of Web text; graphics or multimedia will take more space)

- The amount of traffic you receive per month

- The frequency and size of data transfers

- Support for specialized programs, such as streaming video or databases

- Support for specialized electronic commerce services, including access to a secure server; some WHISPs specialize in transaction-intensive sites, with prices based on catalog size

- Additional statistical analysis

As with ISP selection, analyze startup, first year total, and subsequent year costs independently. A small business should be able to find a solution between $10 and $250 per month, depending on the size and complexity of its site. Cost will be only one factor in your decision. Pay particular attention to business history, performance history, technical support, and customer service. Almost all WHISPs provide a list of customers on their own site. For references, e-mail the Webmasters of several sites similar in scope to yours, or check the monthly ratings of the Top 25 Web Hosts at *http://webhostlist. internetlist.com/*.

The checklist in Figure 4.20 summarizes selection criteria for a WHISP. Before you start the process, check off the items you need and estimate quantitative entries, such as the number of expected hits per month (average and maximum) and the total space needed in megabytes. You may need assistance from your Web designer to fill in some of these blanks.

The Mall Alternative

Malls are virtual shopping areas on a server or online service that host or link to related commercial sites. Some WHISPs define their own mall as a package of services that includes hosting, design, store building, transaction processing, and promotion.

Like every other Web service, rates vary widely depending on the mall and the benefits it provides. For example, The Great Internet Mall of the Americas at *http://www.intermallamerica.com* shown in Figure 4.21 offers a turnkey solution including hosting, template-based store building, transaction processing, banner advertising on the mall, and assistance establishing a merchant card account through *http://www.ccnow.com*, an online reseller. (As you'll see in Chapter 8, the last option can be helpful if you have a new, small business.)

Another Internet mall, *http://www.internetmall.com/merchant_ center/service_maintenance.html*, prices more like advertisers. Its services consist of home page links with promotional and merchandising opportunities. Rates start at $99 per year for an "entry tenant" with a 20-word directory listing and a link. Other tenant levels, from "standard" to "anchor," range from $449 to $999 per year or more for a longer description, keywords in a search engine, and other features. This mall offers additional on-site advertising, ranging from $9 to $30 CPM based on location within the site.

WHISP Name _____   Date _____

Item	Y/N	Description	Cost
General			
Length of time in business?			
Staff qualifications/turnover?			
Client references? (get 3, preferably on the Web)			
System			
Type of connection to the Internet?			
What connection speeds does the WHISP cater to?			
How much traffic can they handle at a time?			
What provisions do they have for security, e.g. firewalls?			
What % of time was server available during past 3 months?			
Server/connection redundancy?			
Back-up policy?			
Pricing			
What is the pricing structure?			
Monthly flat rate? for space in MB? Hits in K?			
Add-on and over-quota rates for space or hits?			
Long-term discounts?			
On/off connection fees?			
Technical Services			
Predominantly UNIX or NT shop?			
What level/hours is technical support provided?			
What are the charges for technical support? Setup? Trouble shooting?			
Can they handle streaming media, if applicable?			
What kinds of monitoring/server and site reports are available? How often?			

Figure 4.20. Web host selection checklist (continued on next page).

WHISP Name _____ Date _____

Item	Y/N	Description	Cost
Do they do routine link verification? Syntax checking?			
What Web development packages do they support?			
How easy will it be to make changes to the Web site?			
Frequency and fees for updating?			
Web Development Services			
Do they provide design support? Custom or template?			
Do they bill by hour or by job?			
What kinds of multimedia can they create/support?			
Do they develop/support interactive pages? CGI? or perl?			
Do they handle SQL or other database programming?			
Do they have in-house copywriters?			
Web Promotion Services			
Do they offer Web marketing consulting? (by hour or job?)			
What kind of Web promotion is available/included? (e.g. submissions, What's New?)			
Transaction Support			
Catalog, shopping cart, and/or checkstand software?			
Secure server (SSL minimum)			
Real-time transaction processing? (e.g. Cybercash)			
Digital ID and/or encryption?			
Are they tied to any specific providers? If so, which ones?			

Figure 4.20. Web host selection checklist (continued from previous page).

Selecting a Web Designer

Web design has become the latest career fad for computer whiz kids, hackers, and underemployed artists, but a business site requires a great deal more skill and sophistication than a personal home page does. Not all Web designers are created equal. Highly skilled programming houses don't always have graphics and marketing know-how and vice versa.

Not all designers have the knowledge to build effective order-taking mechanisms; not all are familiar with specific feature modules; not all have business experience. You are likely to find people with excellent technical and/or graphic skills, but few come to the process with a marketing background. You must add that insight to

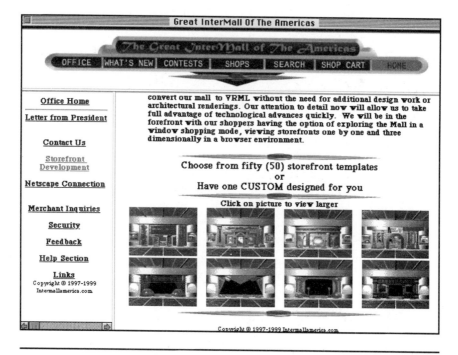

Figure 4.21. Turnkey mall site, *http://www.intermallamerica.com/flowbar/office/start.html*. Courtesy of Intermallamerica.com.

the process. You need to be sure that the designer you hire has

- References and a portfolio of existing sites

  - A reasonable business history

  - The skills and experience to do the job you need

  - The time and staff to produce the work according to your timeline

  - The flexibility to work within your budget

  - The willingness to contract for site updates on a regular basis

  - Experience with standard business and programming practices, from business contracts to commenting code

An ISP, WHISP, or advertising agency may offer design services, or you can check for Web designers in your city's creative directory or with an Internet professional association. You may search for design companies online or look for the designer's name at the bottom of a home page or About Us page on sites you like. You can always ask for a referral from a business whose site you want to emulate.

Always, always, always look at designers' work online; almost all have a portfolio of links on their own site. (If they don't, ask yourself, "Why not?") Call or e-mail several of their clients to check references. (E-mail addressed to Webmaster often forwards to the designer, so contact the clients' marketing or communications departments directly.) While a WHISP may be located anywhere, a local Web designer may be more convenient for face-to-face meetings if you want a custom design. Design costs may be lower if you select someone away from either coast; only you can weigh the factor of convenience versus cost.

If you're satisfied with a basic site, you can short-circuit the design process by signing up with a WHISP such as Hiway Technologies (see Figure 4.22, *http://hiway.com/expresstart*) that offers a template tool for Web design. For a low-cost, high-quality compromise, identify a local graphic artist with the skills to customize a template. (See the Freebies section at the end of this chapter for other templates.) An experienced eye can quickly select colors, typefaces, and buttons that add a sophisticated veneer to an otherwise pedestrian design.

Your needs, as well the designer's rates, skills, and availability, will determine the best provider for you. Selecting that Web designer is a multistep process. First, assemble a list of 8 to 12 potential providers based on referrals, sites you've collected, and/or local directories. After looking at their on-site portfolios, select no more than 6 whose work you like. Then use the worksheet in Figure 4.23, modified according to your Web plan, to prequalify potential Web designers by phone or e-mail. At this point, narrow your list to 3 or so that you will ask for specific bids.

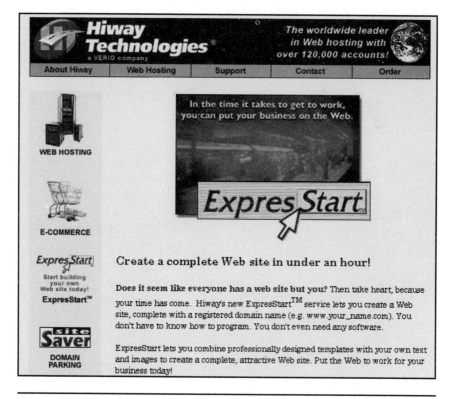

Figure 4.22. Templates for Web design, *http://hiway.com/expresstart.* Courtesy Verio, Inc.

Web Designer Questionnaire

1. How long have you been in business?
   How long have you been designing Web sites?
2. If not already available, please provide the URLs and client references for at least three sites you have designed, preferably ones similar to ours. Describe what services you performed for each of these sites.
3. Which Web services do you offer?
   a. Graphic design and page layout?
   b. Copywriting?
   c. Basic HTML programming? (What software/package do you use?)
   d. CGI scripting?
   e. Java/Shockwave (for animations)?
   f. Database programming?
   g. Other (e.g. Perl)?
   h. Site updates? Frequency and cost?
4. Do you design banner ads? Cost?
5. What is your policy on site updates?
6. Do you perform site testing? If so, on which browsers, which versions, which platforms?
7. Will you do site verification, e.g. code, dead links, spelling etc.? How often?
8. Do you offer any promotional services? Are they included in fees? Cost?
9. Do you work with a team or alone? If a team, who would be our contact? Who are the other members of the team?
10. What is your process for working with clients? e.g. comps? Review stages? Testing?
11. Our development schedule is:_____. What is your availability?
12. Do you price by job, page, or hour? What are your basic rates and/or rates for each service you offer?
13. What are your estimates for the following site outline? Rates for updates and future services? By hour? Page? Site?

If applicable, add:
14. We are thinking of adding multimedia (specify type) in the future. What relevant multimedia production experience do you have? (Get URL and reference)
15. We are thinking of adding a special feature (e.g. chat line, forum) in the future. Have you done this before? (Get URL and reference)
16. This will be a transaction site, with X (number of) products that are paid for by (Y) payment processes. We expect X (number of) purchases per week. What access to and experience with storebuilding, checkstand and payment software modules do you have? Are you tied to development and/or support of particular products? Confirm that we will own the copyright and that we will receive physical owner-ship (i.e. backup disk and/or download of code) for the site. Ask to see a sample contract.

Figure 4.23.   Web designer questionnaire.

If you haven't already done so, try to meet finalists at their office to discuss your actual RFQ. You need to confirm the designers have the equipment you'd expect and that the personal chemistry exists. An RFQ may consist of

- A cover letter requesting a bid and the due date for a response

- A brief description of how you envision the site

- A list of features

- A tentative site index

- A timeline for development

The more detailed your RFQ, the more accurate the bids you will receive. Three fictional RFQs, shown in Figures 4.24 through 4.26, will give you an idea. Unless you use a standard RFQ for your site, it

> **Old McDonald Web Site**
> This site will be Soybean Brothers' informational tool for farmers and ranchers with small-to-medium holdings. The objectives are to record 7,000 hits per week, with a minimum of 25% of the visitors returning at least four times within a three-month period. The site will provide real-time commodity and livestock prices direct from the Chicago Board of Trade; farm news; weather reports by region; live chat "Ask the Aggie" discussion sessions; and a bulletin board for farmers to seek advice from one another. Support for this project will be required from the MIS, sales, and marketing departments. Formal content sources, such as commodity prices and weather reports are available on a contractual basis; members of the School of Agriculture at Landgrant U. and employees of County Extension have agreed to participate in "Ask the Aggie" discussion sessions. Initial development costs of $20,000 and $2,000 per month mainte- nance costs will be supported by paid advertising and online sales of soy additives. The site is expected to generate $4,000 per month in revenues, breaking even after 11 months and earning a profit thereafter.

Figure 4.24. Fictional RFQ: Old MacDonald.

Humble Pie W eb Site

The Humble Pie Web site will be established to create a corporate Web presence while allowing customers to place pie orders for delivery or pickup at any of our 234 nationwide franchise locations. The site will incorporate contests, games, and client-printed promotional coupons. The objectives are to generate 20,000 hits in the first two months after launch, with purchases by 3% of the viewers.

This first module will later be augmented with an **Extranet** (a Wide Area Network with Weblike operations) to facilitate franchisee communication with headquarters for such purposes as ordering supplies, learning about new promotional campaigns, and training.

The advertising agency for Humble Pie will handle site construction and maintenance with input from our own marketing department. The $30,000 development expense and $6,000 monthly expenses will be offset by cost savings in training and order processing after one year of operation.

Figure 4.25. Fictional RFQ: Humble Pie.

My Favorite Guru W eb Site

My Favorite Guru will be an infotainment Web site constructed as a psychic mall for alternative religions. The objective is to generate 60,000 hits per month, with each visitor linking to at least three sites in the mall per visit.

To attract visitors to mall sites, My Favorite Guru will offer streaming audio of new age music, streaming video of blessings by religious leaders such as the Maharishi Maheesh Yogi and Baba Ram Dass, audio clips of mantras, and downloadable video clips of ever-changing Sufi patterns. When their psychic energy is low, users can communicate with one another through text and audio chat rooms. Response levels will be monitored for each mall tenant and for each multimedia activity. If an activity generates fewer than 2500 hits per month, it will be replaced.

Sixteen organizations have expressed preliminary interest in the mall. We will need to hire a programmer/Webmaster to program and maintain the site, with additional specialty work contracted out under supervision of the sales and marketing department. Mall lessees will pay a monthly fee of $1,000, 50¢ per hit, or 5% commission on sales referrals from this mall, whichever is greater, to cover development and maintenance costs.

Figure 4.26. Fictional RFQ: My Favorite Guru.

may be impossible to compare prices and services from different designers. With above answers and bids in hand, you should have the information to make a selection.

Before signing with your design choice, ask to see a sample contract. Confirm that your company will own the copyright and that you will have physical ownership (i.e., backup disk or download and hard copy) of commented programming code for the site. Having the code will make it easy to move your site or its maintenance to another provider, if necessary. This is particularly important if your designer is also your WHISP. A contract may include as attachments the design description from your RFQ, a schedule of interim deliveries and review points, and a schedule of payments.

Some companies offer an introductory package of $1500 to $2000 for a basic 12- to 20-page site. Others price by the page ($150 to $300 for roughly an 8.5" x 11" page), with add-on fees for custom design and multimedia. Still others charge only by the hour, though you can set a limit on the number of hours, prioritizing what will be eliminated if you run out of money.

Don't be surprised to find that hourly rates vary not only by region of the country ($50–$150/hour), but also by task complexity. Basic HTML programming is at the low end of the scale, with Java, database programming, and strategic planning at the high end.

As we've discussed, costs for design services range from free (see "Freebies and Features") to tens of thousands of dollars. As you can tell by looking at some of the sites in this book, there is no upper limit. A Fortune 500 company may spend anywhere from $500,000 to more than $5 million to create a transaction-intensive, electronic commerce site!

The Design Process

We're almost ready for the fun part. One more step remains, however: You must select and register a domain name, which usually ends in *.com* for a business. As you can tell from their presence in all advertising media, URLs have become ubiquitous. They have become more important to brand imaging than toll-free phone numbers.

Once it has been assigned, no one else may use your domain name. The name is actually converted into a numerical Internet Protocol address. All computers on the Internet are instructed that this address is found on the server where your domain resides.

Many Web hosts will handle domain name registration and pass along only the registration costs; some charge an additional service fee ranging from $10 to $50. If you are hosting your own site, you will need to register your server first and then your name.

If you want to reserve several names until you make a final decision, you can "park" a name on someone's server temporarily. Some WHISPs will "park" names for free (e.g., *http://www.domainsave.com at WebHosting.Com*) or a modest fee (*e.g., http://www.abiding web.com)* until you are ready to go online. This is an enticement to use their service, but you can usually transfer the name elsewhere without a charge. If you've pay a "parking fee," the WHISP will often apply the amount to your account if you select it as your host. A "parked" name is reserved until the payment period expires, 30 days after the date on the invoice you receive from InterNIC.

Register a Domain Name

To reserve a name, registrants previously had to use Network Solutions, Inc. at *http://networksolutions.com*, which had an exclusive, five-year contract with the U.S. government to manage domain name registration. In late April 1999, five additional vendors began testing an expanded Shared Registry System for *.com*, *.net*, and *.org* domains:

1. America Online

2. Core (Internet Council of Registrars)

3. France Telecom/Oleane

4. Melbourne IT

5. Register.com

By July 1999, another 29 accredited companies will be able to register names, and the list will then be open to any company accredited as a registrar by ICANN (Internet Corporation for Assigned Names and Numbers). For a list and more information on these companies, go to *http://www.icann.org/*.

At Network Solutions, domain registration cost $70 for the first two years, with an annual $35 renewal fee thereafter. Now that competing firms are providing domain registration, these rates are expected to drop. Different companies may offer reduced registration rates as a loss leader to win clients for other services, such as hosting, design, or promotion. Competition is also likely to counter such behaviors as Network Solutions' attempt to steer registrants to its private commercial site, where they charged an additional $49 fee for registration. On the other hand, ICANN has also received criticism for some of its plans and operating methods.

In the meantime, just follow standard procedures. To see if a name is available, search the InterNIC (Internet Network Information Center) WhoIs database at *http://whois.internic.net/* or similar databases available on the other registration sites. After you have selected an available name (as long as it doesn't use anyone else's trademark), submit an application online to any of the registration services.

How important are names? Very! Self-promotion starts with your domain name. Be as careful choosing it as you were selecting your business name. Make the domain name easy to remember, easy to type, and/or self-descriptive for easy searching. Most names are company names, which work particularly well if you already have brand recognition (e.g., Sony.com) or a pre-existing customer base. Sometimes you can be clever. A name like www.eat.com, which Lipton Inc. uses on its Ragu Sauces site, draws attention from the curious. Portals aim for short, easy to remember names like go.com or snap.com.

Names are important enough that some companies try to buy up any possible spellings (and misspellings) of their name, as well as any derogatory terms that could refer to them. Businesses may find themselves paying to reclaim their own brand names unless they have reserved them through trademark. (Courts have held that it's illegal to use trademarks within a domain name.) This happened to Compaq, owner of search engine AltaVista, which paid $3.35 million to reclaim altavista.com in 1998. If your desired name is taken, you may be able to negotiate a purchase with the owner, whose name you will find in the InterNIC database. If a site is already active, the price may be higher.

Some companies and individuals have simply gone into the name game, buying up as many names as they can think of and then licensing or selling them. The name *wallstreet.com* was auctioned in April 1999 to a Venezuelan company for over $1 million. Most names sell for much less; even popular ones like *tv.com* or *internet.com* sold in the $15,000 to $150,000 range.

Design Overview

While it may vary according to circumstances, the design process for a Web site generally incorporates the following steps:

1. Initial design conference and review schedule

2. Design "comps" for you to choose from

3. Storyboards and prototypes done by the Web designer

4. Element creation

5. Programming and integration

6. Testing and corrections

As described in the timeline section earlier, the first three steps, along with your other preplanning, will absorb about half the time before launch. Steps 5 and 6 will each take roughly one quarter of the time. Even while these two steps are underway, you will be working on the promotion plan described in Chapter 6!

Initial Design Conference and Review Schedule

Your RFQ provides the designer with an excellent starting point for discussion at your initial design conference. Bring your collection of printouts and URLs of sites you like and dislike. It will also be helpful if you identify desired internal and external links and where they belong. The more information you provide, the more likely it is you will be satisfied with the results and the less expensive the design process will be.

Although it may seem like a nuisance, the earlier and more often you seek internal and external review, the less difficulty you will have with implementation and operation. Ensure that all appropriate members of your team (and others if necessary) have an opportunity to sign off on decisions before major funds are committed.

A review cycle is also an opportunity to confirm that content is ready and accurate. This is particularly true if others are providing technical information, bibliographical references, or up-to-date databases. Checking content from internal sources is just as important. You might discover that the Human Resources Department updates the Job Openings database daily, but the Web designer expected updates weekly.

As part of the review cycle, you may want to conduct focus groups with potential users of the site. Try to find people who match your expected audience profile closely and who have a range of computer or content knowledge. Don't wait until the testing stage of development to find out that users haven't got a clue how to navigate the site. Use focus groups to read the content for comprehensibility. If you are aiming a site toward children, you might want to assess readability level as well. If it's not already specified in your design contract, establish a review schedule now. Indicate clearly at what points you want to see material and how long you will need for review.

Design Comps

As with print, a designer will generally try to provide several different graphic approaches to your Web site. These may consist of a block diagram of screen elements (see Figure 4.27), as well as suggested colors, fonts, and decorative items. Generally, after you select one approach and make suggestions, the designer will provide a final comp to confirm the look and feel of the site. If the site is large, the lead designer or project manager should establish a standards book for the creative team to follow, especially if multiple contractors will be involved. A standards book establishes consistency in icons, layout, typography, colors, graphics size, tone, style, and ad placement.

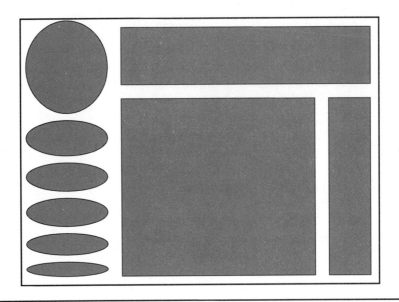

Figure 4.27. Block diagram of sample screen layout.

Storyboards and Prototypes

Your Web designer will present the navigational elements of your site as a storyboard and/or a flowchart for your approval. A storyboard, which looks like the cels from a cartoon, depicts activity using pictures of each page. The designer may use presentation software, such as the Slide Sorter view or Notes printout in Microsoft PowerPoint, to generate individual screen layouts for draft storyboards, or just draw them on half sheets of paper.

You can easily rearrange these individual pages on a wall or table to experiment with different ways of moving through a site. Try to imagine how different visitors might experience it. Would navigation be obvious to someone who stumbled on the site by accident? Would an experienced, repeat visitor get frustrated at information buried too deeply? Will links keep visitors on the site or take them away?

Most people don't want to play an adventure game on your site, hunting high and low for information. Strong visual cues help viewers find information and orient them in virtual space. Good structure is obvious and intuitive, such as in the Epicurious site at *http://food.epicurious.com/c_play/c00_home/play.html*, shown in Figure 4.28.

Make sure the site organization is optimized for marketing, too. You may want the site divided so that different pages use different keywords, giving you better exposure in search engines. You might want a splash page designed with specific keywords in mind. If there are messages you want to reinforce with a click action, be sure the page with that call to action and the result are separated.

Many Web development packages include a navigation flowchart that summarizes the final result. The flowchart provides context, showing where users are, where they might have been, and where they are able to go. Depending on the complexity of the site, your designer may want to build a prototype or shell before proceeding to actual programming. This is a good time to bring in members of a focus

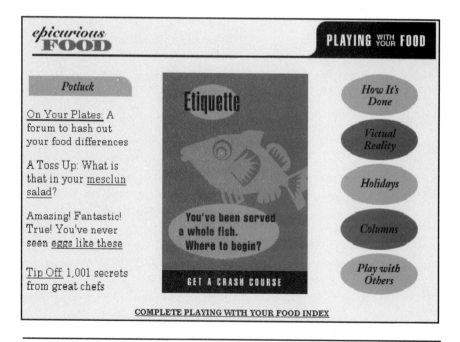

Figure 4.28. Visual navigation cues, *http://food.epicurious.com/c_play/c00_home/play.html*. Courtesy Epicurious Food © 1999 Conde Nast Inc. All rights reserved.

group for comment. You can also check the proposed structure against the suggestions listed in "Navigation." If a designer asks you to sign off on the Web plan at this stage, recognize that any changes you request in structure after signing will probably incur additional charge.

Element Production

Some of the elements for the site can be collected from company files; others will be created fresh. The less the designer has to do from scratch, the lower your cost. Perhaps someone in your company can write, edit, and/or proof the copy. Whoever handles the copywriting must optimize it for marketing purposes, with calls to action placed at strategic locations. On pages intended for search engine submission, the copywriter should consider the precepts discussed in Chapter 6 for improving search engine placement, particularly the ratio between keyword occurrence and the number of words on the page.

Since poorly written, ungrammatical text is a turnoff to readers and a putdown of your company, proofread all content and check the spelling. Do you have staff who could collect and digitize existing photographs, art, or database material, or review some of the free sources for line art, sprites, or digital images? Will some content be contributed by other departments?

The designer should have budgeted for the creation of any new material, such as animation or audio files, unless it was clear from the RFQ that material would be provided independently. Depending on the project, either you or the lead designer will be responsible for making sure those pieces are created on time and in the required format. A good Web designer will bring to this project his or her knowledge of how to optimize the various pieces to get the best quality in the fastest download time. The designer usually is also responsible for establishing file naming and version numbering conventions and backing up all the various elements.

Remember to provide the designer with a list of proposed links to other sites and where on your site they should be placed. Keep the list of external links short—every time you link outside your site, you risk losing your viewer. Since it will also help the designer to know who might be linking to your site, provide the list you will have researched in Chapter 6.

Programming and Integration

A Web designer decides how to code your site based on his or her familiarity with different development packages, which tools will be supported by your selected WHISP, and the skills, available Web time, and equipment capabilities of your target audience. It is sometimes tricky to put all the different elements together in a way that will be compatible with various versions of browsers, plug-ins, and computers.

Don't be surprised if your Web designer first programs your site with standard elements, such as pre-existing video clips or photos, instead of using your specific material. Often, it is easier to debug the programming portion of the site independent of actual images and content.

Finally, elements will be inserted into the program structure and you will be able to see your Web site. Generally, one page or type of program element comes up at a time.

Testing and Corrections

Through internal testing and debugging, the designer should catch any obvious problems, such as images that don't fully download or pages that don't appear. Ask your designer to run a **syntax checker,** which confirms there are no errors in the code, and a link verifier to confirm that links on your site remain valid. (See Chapter 5 for more on testing and analysis tools.)

The designer's next task should include testing the site (still on local drives) on an assortment of equipment, with various plug-ins installed. Make sure that the site is tested on equipment with the minimal configuration your viewers might have: perhaps Windows 95, a 486 processor, a 28.8 modem, and 24 MB of RAM. Test on a Macintosh or when running on a local area network under Windows NT.

Test the appearance of the site under several versions of Netscape and Microsoft Internet Explorer browsers. Each browser operates slightly differently, so what looks great in Internet Explorer may not look right in Netscape and vice versa. (Check the appearance of your site whenever a new browser version is released by one of these two major companies.) You many find support for compatibility testing at *http://www.cast.org/bobby* or *http://www.AnyBrowser.com.*

At this point, request testing from both those who are new to the site and those who provided feedback during the design stage. If you have a complex site, it is particularly important to see what happens in terms of user interface, site navigation, and content accuracy. Once again, check all content for accuracy and correct placement. Reproof content that may have been edited to fit on the page or around an image. Each round of corrections should be followed by a round of testing.

Finally, upload the site to the Web host's server, but don't post it yet for the world to view. Test again with different hardware, plug-ins, and browsers, running on modems at different speeds. It's impossible to check all the permutations, but keep a careful record of the configurations used for each test.

To pre-test the site in actual operation, you can ask small audiences of existing customers, members of news groups, mailing list subscribers, or a professional society to help test your site. Although they may be more knowledgeable than a naive user who visits your site, these users can be very helpful. Post a notice with a password or special extension, asking for testing assistance and feedback. You might offer a small freebie or discount to those who fill out an online survey about the site and something larger if they catch a serious bug or make a suggestion you use. Ask testers to

- Confirm that the directions, index, and structure are clear.

- Assess the value of the links and suggest others.

- Exercise any contest or user-response mechanism.

- See if there are problems with multimedia or plug-ins on any platforms.

- Check for errors in content, from spelling to facts.

If you're confident of basic operations, but need to test the site under a heavy viewer load, run a beta site like *http://www.jump.com*, shown in Figure 4.29. Once the site is up and running, you or the Webmaster should check basic operations daily, and run an online checker like Site Inspector *(http://siteinspector.linkexchange.com)* at least monthly.

If the site runs too slowly, you may need to scale down or eliminate some images or multimedia. In the worst case, the designer may

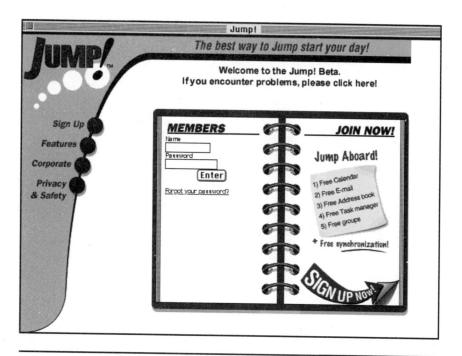

Figure 4.29. Beta test site, *http://www.jump.com*. Screenshot reprinted by permission from Microsoft Corporation.

create a stripped-down version of the site as an option for those with less-capable equipment. Only when you're sure the site is stable should it site be posted at your URL and announced to the Internet universe.

One advantage of template-based sites is that much of this testing has already taken place. Minimum hardware configurations, plug-in versions, and software incompatibilities are well known; existing problems are usually documented. With a template, errors usually result from problems during the process of creating or integrating the elements, not from the program.

Helpful Hints for a Successful Site

What draws visitors to a site again and again? What enables you to build a relationship on the Web that turns a prospect into a customer? An existing customer into a repeat customer? An investor into a holder of your stock? According to a Forrester Research poll, seen in Figure 4.30, high-quality content and ease of use are the biggest factors, but speedy downloads and frequent updates are important as well.

While this chapter focuses on the Web site itself, don't forget that the user's view of your site is often colored by the after-the-Web experience. Make sure that all your business operations can support the expectations for speed, service, convenience, and delivery that the Web creates. With that in mind, let's look at a few ideas for optimizing Web site design and operation. You might want to check your Web designer's work against the list that follows. Keep a running list of ideas as you research other sites.

Splash Screens

A **splash screen** is often displayed as a distraction while a Web site loads. It sometimes lists the browser version for which the site is optimized or includes information about what plug-ins are needed to run special features. Links to plug-ins or suggestions about how to speed up the Web site if you have a slow computer are often included.

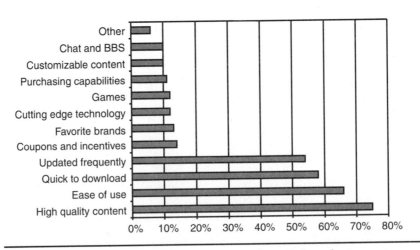

Figure 4.30. Factors driving repeat visitors, *http://cyberatlas.internet. com/big_picture/traffic_patterns/repeat.html*. Reprinted with permission. © 1999 Internet.com, LLC. All rights reserved.

A splash screen might dissolve into the home page or ask the user to click for entry. Multiple splash screens can be customized according to source link, providing visitors from that link with a submenu of choices appropriate to their interests. Different splash "doorways" make it easy to track the effectiveness of promotional activities by counting how many viewers arrive via each entry point.

Splash screens, like the one in Figure 4.31 *(http://www. pathfinder.com)* from Time Inc. New Media are an opportunity to make a first impression or establish a creative theme. Time uses theirs for a call to action.

Home Page

Your **home page** is a welcome mat, main menu, and advertisement rolled into one. Whether your viewers consist of customers, suppliers, potential employees, or just casual visitors, your Web site makes

Figure 4.31. Splash screen / doorway page, *http://www.pathfinder.com*.
© 1999 Time Inc. New Media. All rights reserved. Reproduction in whole or in part without permission is prohibited. Pathfinder is a registered trademark of Time Inc. New Media.

a critical statement about your company. You have only one chance to make a first impression, whether it is your lobby, window display, telephone receptionist, brochure cover, splash screen, or home page.

The best home pages arrange pictures and text artistically to catch the eye of the viewer and entice him or her to explore further, like that shown in Figure 4.32 *(http://www.vivid.com/home.phtml)*. Complex, yet simple, this site intrigues with a mysterious image of an eye floating within an oval. The oval itself is defined by contrasting color, not by a hard edge. The lack of clutter leads the eye to what's important.

Requiring the viewer to scroll to see a complete image or description can be very distracting. In particular, try to avoid horizontal scrolling unless there is a valid aesthetic or display reason for doing so. The dinosaur home page at National Geographic *(http://national geographic.com/dinorama/)* is a good example of horizontal scrolling. Check out the Open Site client page *(http://www.opensite.com/ clients/index.html)* in Fig. 4.33 for a good example of vertical scrolling. The alphabetical list of 25 clients for this auction software makes

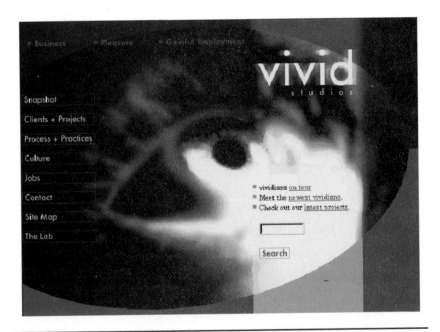

Figure 4.32. Artistic homepage, *http://www.vivid.com/home.phtml*. *Courtesy* vividstudios.

Figure 4.33. Good example of vertical scrolling, *http://www.opensite.com/clients/index.html.* Courtesy Opensite.

the scrolling obvious. If scrolling is unavoidable, try not to wrap text before and after an image. Instead, group text together so it will fit on one screen, with the picture on the next.

If it's too daunting to remember all this, use a WHISP that offers a gallery of templates you can customize, such as those from Marketing & Computer Solutions at *http://www.custom-web-sites.com/products.html#sbb* (shown in Figure 4.34). Additional template sources may be found in the Freebies section.

Multimedia Beware

Although we will discuss multimedia in detail in Chapter 7, the hard truth is that only some viewers have the hardware, software, and patience to enjoy animation and sound, let alone video. Although this will change in the future, be cautious in the near term about

Figure 4.34. Template options, *http://www.custom-web-sites.com/products.html#sbbs*. Courtesy Marketing & Computer Solutions.

including multimedia-intensive activities unless you also include an optional way for viewers to obtain information.

The easiest way to deliver video and sound is to download files for future playback. The alternative, streaming media, sends out video and audio signals while viewers are online. Since it would take about two hours to download an uncompressed 60-second AVI (Video for Windows) file with a 28.8 Kbps modem, most online video is compressed, even though it makes playback somewhat jerky. Multimedia needs to be used with caution. It can generate more oops! than aahs!

Avoid Causes for Complaint

According to a 1998 Georgia Tech survey, the most common complaints from Web users are

1. Slow downloads, 66%

2. Broken links, 50%

3. Finding known information, 30%

4. Organizing what is found, 28%

You can avoid all four concerns in your Web design. One bad Web experience can turn a viewer off your site forever.

First, reduce download time. As a rule of thumb, estimate one second per kilobyte of information for most downloads with a 28.8 modem. Try to keep each image or file below 25 KB. If it's more than that, decide whether the image or information is really necessary. If so, compress large files, even if it means sacrificing resolution for speed.

For instance, a high-contrast, print-quality photograph may take as long as two minutes to transfer across phone lines. This could be converted to a much smaller, low-resolution JPEG file that down loads in less than 30 seconds. Tools like Photoshop's WebVise further optimize JPEG and GIF files for the Web. Or consider using a series of thumbnail images, allowing viewers to select only the one or two pictures they would like to see in detail. Sometimes it is more effective to display an image unfolding as it downloads, instead of waiting for it to finish and pop on. As alternatives, consider line drawings or illustrations, which download much more quickly than photographs. Keep in mind that a plain white background will download faster than a colored or printed one.

Some 15 to 20 percent of users still turn off Web graphics so pages will download more quickly, clicking on an image only if it interests them. Be sure that your text entices viewers to watch the image and that your layout and information flow works well without photos.

Since people can easily abort an image transfer and move to another site, try following Tetra's lead in Figure 4.35 at *http://www.tetra-fish.com.* Viewers build their own virtual aquarium on this site one fish at a time. By occupying viewers with decision making while an image downloads, Tetra makes the wait almost imperceptible.

The broken link problem is easy to solve with good maintenance. **Links** (internal and external) are enormously powerful because they lead users through a chain of related information with the simple click of a mouse button. No wonder viewers get annoyed when a broken link turns up one of those infamous 404 errors!

Figure 4.35. Virtual Aquarium, *http://www.tetra-fish.com.* Courtesy Tetra/
Second Nature.

This problem is easily avoided by running verification software
at least monthly to monitor links for valid connections and obtain
referrals to a new address. (See Chapter 5 for details.) On a site that
is link-heavy, a Webmaster should run this program weekly. If you
can't be this religious about maintenance, ask yourself whether you
really need all those links. Could you reduce the number to a few
stable sites?

Don't forget that internal links (to other pages on your own site)
can generate a similar problem if a page has been removed or re-
named. This happens frequently on large sites with many stored documents. Be sure to search your own site for any links to an altered
page whenever you update content.

Visitors might also become frustrated if they can't use your link
to a popular URL, such as the Mars Pathfinder images at NASA,
because the destination site is busy. Instead, obtain permission to
mirror the information on your own site with appropriate credit, in-

stead of linking. You can use mirroring creatively to draw visitors to your site and away from a jammed site. In fact, a mirrored site closer to a viewer's physical location is often faster for them to access.

Problems finding known information and organizing what is found can be addressed in several ways. First, return to the principles of good navigation described earlier. The complexity of your navigation scheme will suggest presentation needs for your pages. For instance, secondary pop-up or pull-down menus may keep pages from getting too cluttered and offer more choices to those who need them.

Since viewers linking to your site may enter on pages other than your home page, maintain consistent access to a menu and site index on every page, as Epicurious did in Figure 4.28. Implement an on-site search engine if your site is large, and make sure that your site index contains active internal links.

Your page-naming conventions can help users organize information they collect. Use similar page names for similar information. Consider a call to action that reminds users to create an electronic folder for information they have gathered. Use another call to bookmark separate pages, not just your site overall. Test that your pages will print out and offer the option of reverse printing (black text on white) if your site uses a dark background. Web or no Web, many people still prefer tangible sheets of paper in a manila folder stuck in a filing drawer.

Forget-Me-Nots

Check your design against this compilation of pointers and reminders.

- Use many calls to action. In classic marketing terms, a call to action is the closing step in a sale. You ask people to buy. You can also ask them to demonstrate interest with smaller calls to action, moving them ever closer to a sale. On the Web, internal calls to action are almost always active intra-site links that ask users to take an action online, such as subscribing to an extended service, signing a register, or bookmarking a page. They can also be used simply to move people through your site. External calls to action ask people to take an action off the site.

Calls to action often use an active verb in the imperative: Save money, Get a Free... Learn About..., Check out our new..., Try..., Test drive..., For more information contact.... Be specific, but gentle, if you want users to take action. Don't bury a call to action three levels down. Make different opportunities visible at the highest level and on every page. Whatever the call to action, it should be tied to marketing goals and objectives.

Take a look at the clever calls to action on Ragu's home page in Figure 4.36 at *http://www.eat.com*. This site is loaded! Three external calls are found on the right: "Free" (an implicit call to action), "Fix Your Kitchen Up" and "Try Our Mac & Cheese Recipe." Can you find at least four internal calls to action on this page? (There are more than that). If you click through this site, you 'll find dozens of calls to action, both external ("Don't forget to look under the Ragu Label...") and internal ("Go Peek!"). Keep a list of URLs or printouts in

Figure 4.36.   Subtle calls to action, *http://www.eat.com*. Courtesy Lipton Investments, Inc. and Unilever USA, Inc.

your Web notebook with great calls to action like these. We'll talk more in Chapter 6 about using internal calls to action as a method of promotion.

- Include at least one e-mail address and point of human contact on your site, preferably on every page. If there are multiple points of contact, try to put the specific, relevant e-mail address on the page instead of using a generic *info@your company.com*. It will shorten the time for response, making it more likely that you can stay within a 24-hour window. It's a mistake to show an e-mail address only for your Webmaster, who may not know enough about your business and staff to forward mail appropriately or promptly.

- Even if your site includes a corporate phone directory, don't forget street address, telephone, and fax number. If you are selling goods or services, be sure to include a toll-free number for those who do not want to enter credit card numbers online.

- For your own benefit show the date of last modification, the name of the person who made it, and the e-mail address of the person who has overall responsibility for the site (Webmaster).

- If appropriate for enrollment or payment purposes, make provision for passwords. Keep abreast of developments for protecting credit card numbers. (See Chapter 8 for more information on security protection.)

- A What's New section directs repeat visitors immediately to new content on your site. Note the kitten icon on the lower left of The Electronic Zoo at the Washington University St. Louis veterinary site shown in Figure 4.37 *(http://netvet.wustl. edu/e-zoo.html)*.

- Watch This Space. If you must remove content and can't delete references to a page, post a construction icon. This may frustrate viewers, but it's better than an error message. Avoid posting frequent messages about coming pages that may never get built. To generate user interest in a return visit, announce

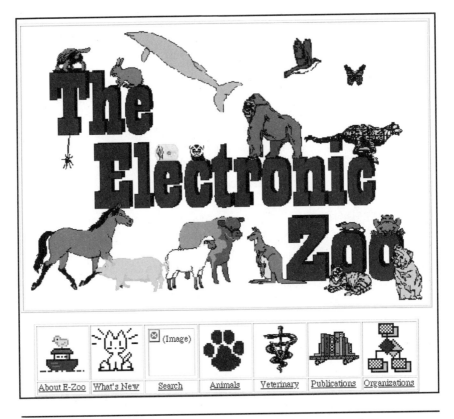

Figure 4.37.   What's New, *http://netvet.wustl.edu/e-zoo.html*. Courtesy
Washington University (*www.netvet.com/e-zoo.htm*).

an opening day for the page and include a call to action to
bookmark the site for a return visit, perhaps with a chance to
win something. If you use a site reminder service, as described
in Chapter 6, encourage people to register so you can notify
them when the new page is available.

For more advice on site building, try

http://www.cnetbuilder.com

http://www.lcc.gatech.edu/

http://www.webpagesthatsuck.com

Freebies and Features

As you've learned, developing a good site is a detailed and time-consuming process. The more you can acquire elsewhere, the shorter and less expensive your development cycle will be. Features that required custom programming several years ago are now easy to add to your site as links or downloadable code. You'll find sources for such site improvements such as maps and search engines in Figure 4.38. Figure 4.39 offers sources for free Web and Internet services, and Figure 4.40 provides places to obtain decorative items like backgrounds, buttons, and bars. Additional sites for free tools may be found in Chapter 5, for free promotional options in Chapter 6, for multimedia plug-ins in Chapter 7, and for e-commerce software in Chapter 8.

Features and Site Amenities

Use the added features and site amenities shown in Figure 4.38 only when appropriate as a way to encourage visitors to linger on your site. For instance, a contractor or architect might include a map and direction service linked to photos of their buildings so potential clients can drive by their projects. A children's site might encourage youngsters to create and send free greeting cards. A company that offers hundreds of products or documents would benefit from a site-based search engine. A tourist-oriented company in San Diego or Puerto Rico might want to tout local weather, while one that sponsors conferences might create online forums for past participants. If you add features randomly, it will only detract from your marketing message and dilute the impact of your site.

Affiliate programs offer a commission on viewer click-throughs (prospects), qualified leads, or sales referred from your site. While bookstore programs from sites like barnesandnoble.com and Amazon.com probably are the best known, hundreds of such programs are now available. Affiliate programs link viewers away from your site to make a purchase, but usually provide a Back button to increase the likelihood that viewers will return. Most affiliates provide code to "cut and paste" onto your page and allow you to select certain items to highlight or sell.

Commissions usually run 5%, but a few go as high as 15%. Usually, you'll receive a monthly statement with payment made when

Type of Resource	URL	Free (✔)
Affiliate program (established on your site)	http://www.clicktrade.com	✔
Catalog and shopping cart	http://www.yahoo.com	✔ up to 50 items
Catalog and shopping cart	http://www.icat.com	✔ up to 12 items
Catalog and shopping cart	http://www.openmarket.com	✔ up to 12 items
E-mail (offer on your site)	http://www.zzn.com/informail/signup.asp	✔
Games (trivia)	http://www.uproar.com/webdevelopers/	✔
Greeting cards	http://www.regards.com	✔
Guestbook	http://www.guestbooks4free.com	✔
Guestbook	http://freeguestbooks.com	✔
Guestbook	http://www.miatrade.com	✔
Hub (search engine) for affiliate programs	http://www.refer-it.com/main.cfm	✔
Hub for affiliate programs	http://www.associateprograms.com/main.cfm	✔
Hub for other free resources	http://bizwizard.virtuallave.net/webres.html	✔
Hub for other free resources	http://www.totallyfreestuff.com	✔
Listbot	http://www.linkexchange.com/index.html	✔
Map & direction service	http://www.aaa.com	✔
Map & direction service	http://www.vicinity.com	✔
Map & direction service	http://www.infospace.com/info/cbsite.htm OR specific map link at: http://www.in-100.infospace.com/info/keymap/linktomap.htm	(✔ with link; $ for co branding)
Mutiple: chat room, message board, search engine	http://freecenter.digiweb.com/index. cgi?action=FreeSearch	✔
Multiple: banner ads, statistics, e-mail counter, intra-site, polls, more	http://www.hyperbanner.com	✔

Figure 4.38. Free features and site amenities (continued on next page).

Type of Resource	URL	Free (✔)
Multiple: cartoons, classifieds, counters, e-mail form processing, forum, greeting cards, guestbook, mail list, polls, search engines, Web announcements, free links	http://www.bravenet.com	✔
Multiple: chat room, counters, e-mail list, guestbook, message boards, quizlet, search box, site submission, Web e-mail	http://www.beseen.com	
Multiple: games, greeting cards, screensavers, Web e-mail	http://www.maxpatch.com	✔
Personalized event & calendar service	http://www.when.com	✔ with link
Personalized event & calendar service	http://calendar.yahoo.com	✔
Polls	http://www.pollit.com	✔
Real Name Service Link	http://company.realnames.com	✔ for community
Search engines, other search tools, scroll-able menus	http://www.smartlinks.looksmart.com/smartlinks?chan=home	✔
Tools	http://hyperbanner.com	✔
Tools: Autoresponder	http://www.web-source.net/links/	✔
Tools: Site statistical tracker	http://www.extreme-dm.com/tracking/?home	✔
Tools: spell checking, link verifier, syntax	http://www.siteowner.com OR http://siteins pector.linkexchange.com	✔
Topical search engine	http://abcparenting.com	✔
Weather	http://www.weatherlabs.com	✔ with link
Weather	http://www.accuweather.com/wx/company/link.htm	✔ with link, selected cities
Weather (local stickers)	http://www.wunderground.com/geo/BannerPromo/	✔
Yellow Pages	http://www.superpages.com/prom/linktous.html	✔ link and/or search

Figure 4.38. Free features and site amenities (continued from previous page).

commissions reach a certain level. Unless you spend a lot of time and effort driving traffic to your site, don't expect to make a fortune. However, the right affiliation can be a convenient, value-added service for your visitors. Again, be selective. Choose no more than one or two affiliate programs, unless you want to be a virtual flea market!

Free Web and Internet Services

If you're really strapped for cash, the resources in Figure 4.39 may be a reasonable alternative. They are certainly better than putting up a free site without your own domain name on a portal like *http://www.geocities.com* or *http://www.tripod.com*. Supposedly these portals make some free domain name space available as long as you are willing to allow their advertisers to appear on your pages.

As an alternative, many ISPs now include 2 to 10 MB of Web space in their monthly fee. Check to see if they will allow you to use your own domain name, or if they permit only an extension (yourcompany.ISPname.net or ISPname.net/yourcompany). Many search engines no longer index sites with such names.

Decorative Doo-Dahs

You'll have to decide whether the time it takes to search through the decorative resources in Figure 4.40 is worth it. You'll find many additional resources for free clip art and digital photos on commercial online services or by using a search engine.

In the next three chapters we'll cover the remaining steps to Internet marketing success. Chapter 5 deals with maintaining and monitoring your site, and Chapter 6 discusses promoting it online and off. In Chapter 7, we'll explore multimedia in greater detail.

Type of Resource	URL	Free (✓)
Brand naming guide	http://www.namestormers.com	✓
Domain Name Parking	http://www.9netave.com/park/uuuhl	✓
Domain Name Parking	http://wyattweb.com/wyattweb/domainparking.html	✓
Domain Name Parking	http://www.domainsave.com	✓
Domain Name Parking	http://www.verio.com	✓
Fax Service	http://fax4free.com	✓ with link
Hosting and domain registration	http://www.webjump.com	✓ with banner ad
Hub for free Internet access sites	http://www.lights.com/freenet	✓
Internet access	http://www.tritium.com	✓ with ads
Site design and domain registration	http://www.worldwidewebinstitute.net	✓ 6 pages with paid hosting service for 1 yr
Site design, hosting, and registration	http://www.virtualave.net/	✓ 20 Mb
Site design, limited free hosting	http://www.vr-mall.com/index3.html	✓ 1 month
Site design, hosting, domain registration, search engine submission	http://www.prosperitypromo.com	✓ 5 pages
Template design (site builder)	http://www.smartage.com/site_creator/index.html	✓ with hosting service
Template design (site builder)	http://desktoppublishing.com/template/web/sitekits.html	✓ for non-commercial only

Figure 4.39. Free Web and Internet services.

Type of Resource	URL	Free (✔)
Animated GIFs, e.g. balls, buttons, bullets	http://www.beseen.com/beseen/free/	✔
Animated GIFs	http://www.vr-mall.com/anigifpd/anigifpd.html	✔
Animated sprites	http://www.top100.net/Animations.htm	✔
Animated sprites	http://www.atnet.net/~mlosborn/	✔
Backgrounds, buttons, icons, rules, design tips	http://dspace.deal.pipex.com/leubusen/index.shtml	✔
Background patterns	http://www.netcreations.com/patternland	✔
Clip art, sounds	http://www.maxpatch.com	✔
Graphics (non-professional)	http://members.tripod.com/~GIFPRO/index.html	✔ CD $10
Graphics, clip art	http://www.arttoday.com/PD-0025148/newfree/main.html	✔
Graphics, clip art, Web sets, toon-a-day, and more	http://desktoppublishing.com/free.html	✔
Graphics, design sets, fonts, design tips	http://www.geocities.com/siliconvalley/heights/1288/index.html	✔
Graphics generator for logos, buttons, and bullets	http://www.cooltext.com	✔
Multimedia creation tool simplified for drag & drop	http://geocities.yahoo.com/addons world/thingmaker.html	✔ for Geocities members only
Sound effects	http://soundamerica.com	✔
Sprites, home page template, other graphics	http://www.geocities.com/SiliconValley/Horizon/1501	✔

Figure 4.40. Free decorative doo-dahs.

5

Maintenance and Monitoring Results

Unlike a videotape or music CD, your Web site is not "over when it's over." Your site is an ever-changing marketing tool. Art goes "stale" quickly online; good links appear and disappear; unexpected errors crop up when developers release new versions of plug-ins or browsers; your product line grows. As your business and cyberspace change, your Web site must change with them.

In this chapter, we'll explore Step 6 for Internet success: maintaining and monitoring your Web site. You'll want to determine how well your site fulfills the objectives you set for it. Is it attracting as many visitors as projected? Are they clicking away as soon as they arrive on your home page, or do they continue to view additional pages? Does your newest call to action draw more or less response than the prior one? Instincts and anecdotal evidence, although critical, can be deceptive. Let statistical data cushion your decision making.

Planning for a Web site must take into account the budget and personnel needed for ongoing maintenance, updates, and monitoring. If you are working with an outside Web designer and/or Web host, include questions in your selection survey about update frequency and available tools for analysis. In this chapter you'll learn about

- A site maintenance schedule to keep your Web site at its peak

- Site statistics

- Analyzing statistical reports provided by a Web host

- Available statistical tools

- Using results effectively

Maintenance Basics

Include a regular maintenance schedule in the Site Maintenance section of your Web notebook. Identify the people both in-house and outside who will be responsible for each maintenance activity. Designate the frequency with which it will occur, and coordinate these activities with your Webmaster and/or Web host. Your schedule should cover at least three types of checking:

1. Operational errors

2. Links

3. Content

Maintenance Schedule

Schedules for maintenance depend on the type of site you run. A complex multimedia site that relies on plug-ins for accessibility needs to be checked more often than a simple, static site. One with dozens of links, particularly to sites that are new themselves, will need more monitoring than a site with a few links to well-established databases at educational institutions. A site that updates price lists or inventory should be verified independently every time a change is uploaded to confirm that the right data appear.

As obvious as it sounds, check that your site is up and running properly every day. You might keep a running list of priority applications or pages to add, based on customer requests or internal marketing needs. Run a wish list of less important but attractive options as well. Then develop a schedule to add one item every month or quarter, or as time and budget permit. At a minimum, plan on monthly additions or changes to your page.

Some of your most useful feedback will come from users who e-mail messages and queries to the Webmaster. Be sure you receive copies of all those messages, good and bad; you can always include a "copy to" option on the e-mail form so both you and the Webmaster receive complaints and praise. Keep these e-mails in the Site Feedback section of your notebook, along with the results of user testing conducted in Chapter 4.

Check Syntax

Confirm that your Web designer uses a syntax checking program to catch the inevitable typos and errors in his or her code. This may be done in the form of an HTML editor, such as the free program HoTMetaL *(ftp://ftp.ncsa.uiuc.edu/Web/html/hotmetal),* which checks code as it is written. Syntax review can also be done with after-the-fact checkers, such as those available at the following sites:

- Dr. Watson: *http://watson.addy.com* (shown in Figure 5.1)

- Weblint: *http://www.weblint.com*

- Site Inspector: *http://siteinspector.linkexchange.com/*

- Imagiware: *http://www2.imagiware.com/RxHTML*

- Web Site Garage: *http://www.WebsiteGarage.com*

- *HTML Online Validation Service: http://val.svc.webtechs.com/ index.htm*

Since these free services check programs online, the site must be up and running before it can be tested. If your designers use one of these,

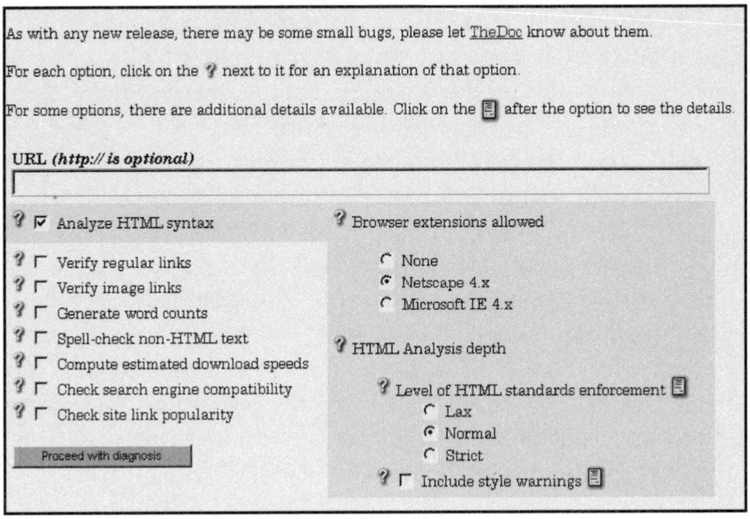

Figure 5.1. Syntax error checker, *http://watson.addy.com.* Courtesy Cliff Addy, Addy & Associates, Inc.

consider publishing your page with limited password access until it has been validated, or have them check it on their server. Different checkers offer different features, so compare them carefully. For instance, Site Inspector checks for browser compatibility, while Dr. Watson generates word counts.

Verify Links

Web surfers complain frequently about dead links that yield the frustrating message "404 Not Found" or "URL unknown." Once you have more than a few links, verifying becomes a painstaking and tedious task. Let a computer do it! Software is available to check all links automatically on a regular basis. Generally you will need to ask your Web designer:

- Whether they have such software
- How often they run it (weekly would be good for links!)

- If there's a charge

If the designer doesn't have these capabilities, see if your Web host will run a link verifier for you. You (or they) might try Linklint 2.1 for automatic link-checking software *http://goldwarp.com/bowlin/ linklint/* (shown in Figure 5.2). It has a one-time shareware fee of $10 for individual use or $100 for commercial use.

A talented Web programmer can arrange for a dead link to generate an e-mail notification to the Webmaster so that the link can be removed even before a routine verification check occurs. A copy of the e-mail can be sent to viewers so that they know the problem is being handled—a nice touch.

MOMspider (Multi-Owner Maintenance Spider)

It's helpful to receive notification about links that have changed so that you can be sure their content remains relevant to your site. As

---

Linklint 2.1 - Fast html link checker
Version 2.1.0 July 24, 1997 (recent changes)

Other pages:
Linklint Home | Inputs | Instructions | Specifications | Ordering

Linklint is a Perl shareware program that checks all local and remote links on a web site. It works with Perl 4 or Perl 5 on Windows and Unix platforms. Ftp sites for Perl can be found at http://www.perl.com/perl/.

Linklint has earned high praise from many users, including these comments:

... kudos on a fantastic application ... I'm definitely going to use your software from now on. It beats every other link checker I've tried, hands down.

Mike Simpson, Web Manager
University of Pennsylvania's Library
20,000 HTML pages, 2 gigabytes of content

Three Modes of Operation

Local Site Check:
Checks links on your site locally, looking for files on the local file system. This mode is ideal if you are developing on a system that does't have a web server, or to check a group of pages before posting them on your server.
input examples | output example

Figure 5.2. Link checking software, *http://goldwarp.com/bowlin/linklint.* Courtesy Bowlin Software.

you may recall, a spider is a program that automatically searches the Web. MOMspider not only finds broken links, it also finds ones that have moved, changed, or expired. It is free at *http://www. ics.uci.edu/pub/websoft/MOMspider.*

Make Corrections and Fixes

Some people like to make and test changes off-line and publish a finished page. Others like to work on pages in real time, allowing viewers to watch their progress. Most contractors prefer a structured, off-line approach, which is probably better for you. A structured release of fixed, updated, or new pages allows your team to plan its work, at the same time providing a clear way to assess whether your designer is meeting contractual terms.

In response to feedback from users or your own review process, you may have a collection of fixes that have been programmed and tested. Except for critical errors that must be repaired immediately, it is better to collect a batch of changes and make them part of a scheduled maintenance activity. Every time you go into your site, you risk introducing an error.

Be especially careful when more than one person makes changes. It is common in the software world to develop and test new modules independently and then integrate them into the existing structure. (A module can be a page, a database, or a function such as sound playback.) Your Web designer should enforce some form of version management so that all developers work from the same base. A systematic approach tests each new module with all the other revised modules in place to avoid negative interactions, particularly when the navigational structure changes.

Update Content

Updating a site maintains interest and draws repeat users. It keeps your site fresh and, as we'll see in the next chapter, provides a reason for past viewers to return to your site. Your update strategy will depend on the goals for your site. An online archival database needs less frequent updating than one pushing audio for a recording company's new releases. A sales site, on the other hand, may constantly offer new promotions, quizzes, or contests.

You may be able to automate some content changes by referencing or uploading a file that is regularly updated by others or is dynamically modified (e.g., an inventory of auto parts). Real-time information feeds are an obvious form of content updates. If you are carrying advertisements, a schedule for ad replacement will be negotiated in the advertising contract.

Some event-driven updates, such as product announcements from a supplier, can't be prescheduled. Even if content updating doesn't apply to your site, schedule at least a monthly review to confirm that the information on your site is still correct. At this time, you can also decide whether you want to incorporate any new links.

Moving Your Site or Pages

Your URL may change if

- You change Web hosts and don't have your own domain name

- Information is moved from one part of a server to another

- Your company or Web host sets up a new server

You may also decide to move information from one page extension to another, or even to another one of your URLs. As a result, links to your former address or bookmarks in user files will be incorrect. Be sure your Web host sets up redirection information in such circumstances.

Take a few other steps as well:

- Notify everyone with whom you have established a reciprocal link.

- Notify visitors who have registered on your site via e-mail.

- Notify everyone who has established a link to your site, using the referrer log described later.

- Use the announcement, submit-it, and indexing services described in Chapter 6 to post your "moved" URL.

Monitor Results

In Chapter 2, we talked about writing quantifiable objectives. To see if those objectives are met, you will need to specify ways to measure progress and decide how often data will be collected. In your selection survey for Web hosts, be sure to find out what statistical analysis tools they have and the types and frequency of reports you can expect.

Most hosting services offer a limited set of Web site statistics for free but charge for more extensive analysis, on the order of $200 to $350 per quarter. Statistics may be available daily, weekly, and/or monthly. Don't be shy about asking your Web host to change the parameters in a report if that would make it more useful to you. The worst they can say is "no."

What you are trying to accomplish with your site will determine what you need to measure and how you measure it. Various hit counts are valuable for determining the percentage of visits that convert to sales, for assessing whether your strategy for launch publicity met expectations, and for measuring the advertising value of your Web site compared to other media. However, a high hit count does not always mean success. For instance, if your goal is to sell clear plastic lunch boxes online, the number of hits on your site is not the ultimate measurement—sales volume and profit margin are. Web site statistics can't give you those answers.

Hit Rate: Fact and Myth

Not all hits are created equal. The number of **raw hits** or visits to your site may be quite misleading. Detailed analysis will yield greater marketing value. On the one hand, raw hit counts dramatically overstate the number of visitors because each separate text, sound, image, or CGI file on a page is counted as a separate hit. A page with four images and a menu bar generates six hits; one for the link to the page, one for the menu bar, and four for the pictures. Often, those selling ad space on their sites will quote the raw hit number because it's the highest one available.

On the other hand, actual usage may be undercounted, because a page may be downloaded to a user's computer or LAN and then viewed multiple times by the same person or others. If you can't get the number of unique visits from your statistical reports, you can estimate it roughly by (a) dividing the total hit count by the number of images, (b) looking at the number of requests for the home page, or (c) totaling the number of referrals by either URL or ISP.

To measure the frequency with which pages are **cached** (saved in memory on a local computer or server), conduct a quick survey of site users to see how often this occurs and then adjust your numbers upward accordingly.

Even with adjustments, the raw hit rate alone misses much valuable information, such as

- Browser: Estimated number of computers that visited site or page

- Click Rate: Specific images or files requested by clicking on a link

- E-mail: Feedback from users sorted into categories

- File: Number of times a particular file is accessed

- Impressions: Number of times a logo or sponsorship was viewed

- Number and Demographics: User registration compiled automatically into a database

- Page Count: How often whole pages were requested; estimate of click count

- Path: Page sequence followed by viewer

- Repeat Visitors: Number of repeat visits from the same address

- Sales: By frequency, volume, revenue item, buyer, or category

- Sessions: Count of all the times the site is accessed by one user

- Time: Time users spend on site and/or on a page

- Unique Home Page Hits: Only one hit to home page per session counted

- User Survey: Data compiled automatically into a database and/or report

- Visitors: Number of unique addresses from which calls were made

All these numbers are somewhat inaccurate. Browser numbers don't tell you whether several people share a computer or whether the same person has called several times from an online service that generates multiple source addresses. Although you can determine how much time users spend on a page, you can't guarantee that they were actually looking at that page. They could have been chatting with a co-worker or talking on the phone. However, you can get a sense of relative use.

You can also follow the paths users travel through your site. Perhaps you'll detect patterns that show which pages or links within your site are least or most effective. Compare usage before and after a page is updated. Instead of just raw numbers, look at access rates by date to correlate what happens after you have reworded a call to action, changed a headline, or substituted a new photo. Did any of these make a difference in number of visits, length of time spent, or how often visitors proceeded to an order page? Careful analysis can help you decide which parts of your site to delete, modify, or expand.

Remember, too, that the number of hits on a counter or in a log doesn't indicate how many of those hits came from the same person. Did you give your mother your new Web address? Statistics showing which "visitors" accessed your page really tell you only which computers called your server, not which people. Was it the 10-year-old surfing after school or the parent with purchasing authority?

It is especially important to check how your visitors reach your site (referrals). You want to see if you are getting visits based on a link from someone else's site or as the result of a search engine listing. You want to see which of your promotional activities, described in Chapter 6, result in hits. Try to correlate referrals with the date that a new link went up. If you don't usually obtain daily or weekly statistics, ask your Web host to provide them for several days or weeks following such events as new links, keyword changes, or the appearance of your site on a Cool Link list.

On-Site Page Counters

Some companies like to install simple counters on their home page, or on every page, to track the number of visitors. You can obtain free counters from many sources, sometimes in exchange for putting the supplier's icon on your site. If you use one, be sure to note the date you started counting, at least internally! Or you can try a free service like The Counter.com (shown in Figure 5.3), where the counter is invisible; you log onto The Counter.com at *http://www.TheCounter.com* to see your statistics privately.

Before you implement an on-screen counter, however, consider its implications from a marketing perspective. First, it should not be used in lieu of statistical analysis; a page counter is much more like a raw hit count. Second, think how it will look to your viewers. Really low numbers may reduce the confidence of potential customers. Do you really want to advertise a lack of success? On the other hand, if you're selling advertising online and your numbers are really high, an on-screen page counter may be a selling point for an advertiser who wants a quick way to monitor impressions.

Analyzing Statistical Reports

Besides showing activity on your site, statistical reports can provide operational information about the computer that hosts your site, whether it's on your premises or at your Web host's. These reports often include such things as overall usage by hour, day, and week, which documents and sites are most heavily used, where errors were encountered, and comparative historical data. They can help you judge the relative popularity of various pages, whether a site is so popular

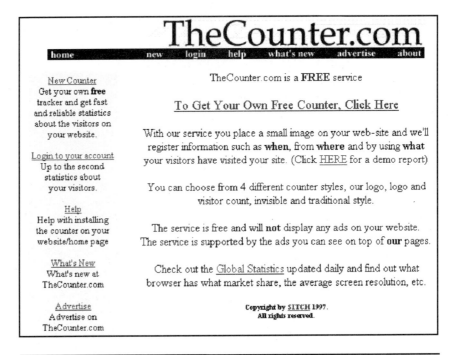

Figure 5.3. Free counter, *http://www.TheCounter.com.* Courtesy SITCH Stockholm, Sweden.

that access has become a problem, or whether some part of your site is generating many errors.

Statistical tools analyze detailed access logs from the server to provide precise information for your Web site. If your Web host does not provide this service, you may need to look for another host. Before you select a Web hosting service, be sure to check out their sample reports! Generally, at least the basic statistical reports will be free with your account. You usually access your reports either on a special, hidden page of your site or by retrieving the files with FTP. You can always download the data as a text file and search through it using the Find command in your word processor.

An **agent log** tells which programs have accessed a server, that is, which browsers, spiders, or link verifiers have been used. A **referrer log** shows how users reached a specific document on the server, that is, which URLs linked to your site. From a marketing perspective, it's extremely valuable to know which search engines were used to find your site, what keywords were used, and what other URLs the viewer came from. As you will see in the next chapter, this will enable you to track the relative value of your reciprocal links.

Reports from a good hosting service will also tell you which pages viewers arrived at first. Exceptional reports, for which there may be an extra charge, could include path through the site, time spent on each page, and graphical presentation of data.

In a pinch, you can download raw data files as text, use the Find command in your word processor to search through it, and create your own reports. If the data seem incomprehensible, watch for a few key items in a long string of characters:

- A phrase that starts with "GET/..." This indicates the name of the first file requested by the browser.

- The referral source, in the usual *http://* format. If this is a search engine name, it might be followed by the keywords used to locate your site.

- The browser information, preferably including version number so you can see if most of your viewers are using current or out-of-date technology.

- The acronym "**cgi**" (**common gateway interface**), which often indicates a search engine address, since it means something was typed in by the user. Use the Find command in your word processor to search for that term, the names of search engines, keywords, or browser names.

Let's compare the reports provided by two different Web hosts seen in Figures 5.4 and 5.5. The extract of the server report for the host in Figure 5.4 analyzes server access by day, hour, and domain, but provides only the inflated number of requests or hits. The server report in Figure 5.5 offers a more useful total that counts unique referring hosts, but doesn't offer the hourly server analysis. The report shown in Figure 5.4 analyzes accesses by domain, while the report shown in Figure 5.5 analyzes accesses by server address ("accesses per host"). Both companies provide accesses broken down by files requested and by referrer URLs (same as "reversed subdomain"), but only the re-

World-Wide Web Access Statistics
Last updated: Fri, 01 Jan 1999 05:13:31 (GMT -0700)

Totals for Summary Period: Dec 1 1998 to Dec 31 1998

Files Transmitted During Summary Period	765
KBytes Transmitted During Summary Period	36977.7
Average Files Transmitted Daily	26
Average KBytes Transmitted Daily	1275.1

Daily Transmission Statistics **Hourly Transmission Statistics**

%Reqs	%KB	KB Sent	Requests	Date	%Reqs	%KB	KB Sent	Requests	Time
24.58	56.84	21018.4	188	12/1/98	6.01	8.61	3182.4	46	10
5.75	0.35	131.0	44	12/2/98	4.31	8.62	3188.3	33	11
1.05	0.14	53.0	8	12/3/98	11.11	21.02	7773.4	85	12
5.36	8.66	3201.6	41	12/4/98					

Total Transfers by Client Domain

%Reqs	%KB	KB Sent	# Reqs	Domain	Domain Name
1.70	0.94	346.2	13	cz	Czech Republic
0.39	0.13	47.2	3	nl	Netherlands
0.13	0.00	0.2	1	uk	United Kingdom
0.78	0.20	73.6	6	us	United States
48.37	60.06	22209.4	370	com	US Commercial
31.24	28.25	10447.6	239	net	Network
3.79	8.60	3178.6	29	org	Non-Profit Organization
13.59	1.82	674.6	104	unresolved	

Total Transfers by Reversed Subdomain

%Reqs	%KB	KB Sent	# Reqs	Reversed Subdomain
19.08	24.75	9152.1	146	com.aol.proxy
13.59	1.82	674.6	104	Unresolved
9.28	16.77	6202.6	71	com.nabisco
5.62	6.46	2387.4	43	net.psi.pub-ip.md.laurel
3.53	4.30	1591.8	27	net.flash.abq1.dialup.utc2
2.88	8.45	3126.3	22	org.frb
2.88	8.44	3120.2	22	net.uu.da.bos1.tnt3
1.96	0.33	120.5	15	com.intel.rr
1.96	0.21	77.3	15	com.aol.ipt

Total Transfers from each Archive Section

%Reqs	%KB	KB Sent	# Reqs	Archive Section
12.16	1.18	434.5	93	/
6.41	0.04	13.0	49	/blue_swirl3343.gif
8.24	4.18	1545.6	63	/chinapat.jpg
2.88	0.27	101.2	22	/client.htm
2.75	0.42	154.1	21	/open.htm
1.44	0.24	86.9	11	/ourstory.htm
2.09	0.27	98.8	16	/partner.htm
1.96	0.11	39.0	15	/philos.htm
7.06	0.05	16.9	54	/red_swirl12350.gif
1.70	0.06	22.1	13	/service.htm
6.54	0.32	119.8	50	/speckled_gradient1e3.gif
2.09	0.03	10.3	16	Code 404 Not Found Requests

Figure 5.4. Extract server report host 1. Courtesy ProcessWorks.

Monthly Report
Date: Friday, January 01, 1999 7:16 AM

<u>WWW Server Statistics</u>

date YYYYMMDD	total accesses	unique hosts	unique files	bytes sent
19981201	583	58	44	4404774
19981202	521	59	46	3580891
19981203	447	56	45	3124989
19981204	244	49	45	1662158
19981205	155	29	43	1019935
19981206	252	37	36	1689431
==
summary 9085	924	47	63654000	

<u>Number of accesses per file (top 1000):</u>

842 index.htm
775 dbl_rck-gif.gif
683 welcomeanim.gif
679 logo.gif
396 products.htm
367 prod-botm.gif
366 prod-top.gif
313 stickers.gif
293 calinfo.htm
265 calendar.gif
203 cal1page.htm

<u>Number of accesses per host (top 1000):</u>

71 140.90.239.72
49 proxy-gw.fs.lmco.com
47 bmmst.com
46 proxy3b.lmco.com
44 ppp23.parlorcity.com
44 194.93.3.1
43 groton4-a36.nvc.net
43 146.135.123.176

<u>Number of referrer URLs (top 100):</u>

125 http://dir.yahoo.com/Business_and_Economy/Companies/Office_Supplies_and_Services/
Calendars_and_Personal_Organizers/Personalized_Calendars/
64 http://www.4calendars.com/
23 http://www.nucleus.com/~jlassali/kids.html
13 http://www.nucleus.com/~jlassali/links.html
11 http://members.tripod.com/~GinCarb/KidsPage.html
(Note the queries showing keywords entered for a search)
2 http://www.altavista.com/cgi-bin/query?pg=q&q=divorce&stq=80&c9k
2 http://search.yahoo.com/search?p=single+parent+children
2 http://search.yahoo.com/search?p=custody&hc=0&hs=191&h=s&b=61
2 http://search.yahoo.com/bin/search?p=visitation+schedule
2 http://ink.yahoo.com/bin/query?p=valentine+stickers&hc=0&hs=0
2 http://ink.yahoo.com/bin/query?p=Christmas+stickers&z=2&hc=0&hs=0
1 http://www.webcrawler.com/cgi-bin/WebQuery?src=att-search&text=Divorce+ kids

---

Figure 5.5. Extract server report host 2. Courtesy LadyBug Press.

port in Figure 5.5 shows search words entered by the user. In other words, "you pays your money and you takes your choice." Knowing what reports you need and what various hosts provide may help you select the appropriate hosting service.

Available Statistical Tools

The results of these statistical tools are useful not only to the Web host but to you, since you also should monitor the performance of your Web host. Has the server been down? Is it able to handle the volume of hits? Are visitors being turned away? If your Web host can't provide the custom analysis you want, or can't do it for a reasonable price, request the access logs for your site. Then apply one of the following statistical tools to analyze the data yourself.

- Two free log analysis tools can be found at The Netstore at *http://www.netstore.de/Supply/http-analyze/findex.html*. Http-analyze 2.0 analyzes server logs in graphs and tables, while 3dstats 2.1 (freestanding or incorporated with http-analyze) provides a three-dimensional representation of statistics as seen in Figure 5.6.

- WebTrends at *http://www.webtrends.com/* offers a comprehensive package of server tools including traffic, link, streaming media, and proxy server analysis, as well as monitoring and alerts.

- NetCount software from Price Waterhouse at *http://www.netcount.com* is one of the more detailed traffic analysis tools, tracking such things as a viewer's path through the site and length of time on a page.

- WebTechs at *http://valsvc.webtechs.com/stats.htm*.

- RefStats (freeware) summarizes the URLs from which users access your site. You can tell whether the user located you from a search engine, a sponsorship, an ad, or a link from another page. It is available at *http://www.netimages. com/~snowhare/utilities/refstats.html*.

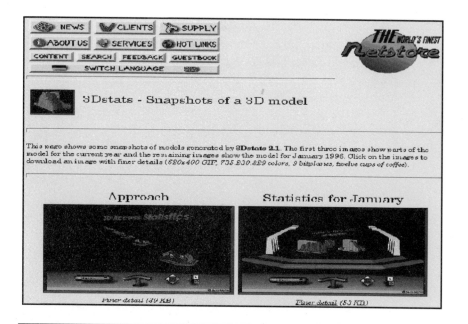

Figure 5.6. 3D statistical representation, *http://www.netstore.de/Supply/3Dstats/snapshots.html.* © 1999 Rent-a-Guru Æ, Heidelberg, Germany.

- Getstats (C language for multiple platforms) offers hourly, daily, weekly, and monthly summaries of use, sorted in a variety of ways. This is great for specific analysis. Documentation and directions for file access are available at *http://www.eit.com/software/getstats/getstats.html.* Graphing software for Getstats may be found at *http://infopad. eecs.berkeley.edu/stats/* or *http://www.tcp.chem.tue.nl/stats/ script/.*

- AccessWatch (UNIX; free for individuals, $400 per server for service providers, discount program) generates statistics of server use by hour or day and computes access by page, domain, host, browser, platform, and referral source. For information, go to *http://www.accesswatch.com/license.* A sample report from this program can be found by a link or at *http://netpressence.com/aw-sample/.*

- VBStats 3.1 (Windows freeware) offers standard reports and will build Top 10 lists, such as most-requested pages. It can be found at *http://www.tech.west.ora.com/win_httpd.*

- Accrue Insight *(http://www.gauge.com),* provides detailed user analysis software to assess purchase behavior and marketing effectiveness. The cost is based on network configuration and traffic levels. (See Figure 5.7)

- Finally, WWWstat at *http://www.ics.uci.edu/pub/websoft/ wwwstat* is another university freebie, offering basic log analysis, including graphics. Gwstat, a companion site at *http://dis.cs.umass.edu/stats/gwstat.html,* creates GIF graphs from the output of WWWstat.

For an up-to-date list of various log analysis tools, check Yahoo's list at *http://www.yahoo.com/Computers_and_Internet/Software/*

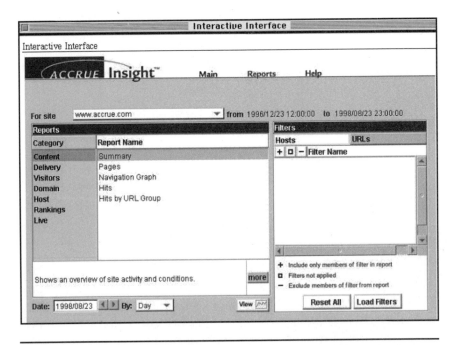

Figure 5.7. Detailed user analysis, *http://www.gauge.com/overview/ aimain400.html.* Courtesy Accrue Software, Inc.

*Internet/World_Wide_Web/Servers/Log_Analysis_Tools/*or Ziff-Davis's tool review at *http://www.zdnet.com/yil/content/profit/soho/web1.html.*

Counting What Really Counts

Statistical analysis packages can't track where someone saw your URL off-line and used that source to type it in. You can adapt a trick from direct marketing to analyze this yourself. Create a new page for each of your advertising campaigns and run a slightly different URL extension, such as *www.maxpress.com/catalog/marketing.html* or *www.maxpress.com/Marketing3e,* as a lead-in to your home page. Then you can use a standard package to monitor traffic on the lead-in pages.

Because these addresses might be temporary, be sure to include an automatic "forward" to your real home page if you take them down. Alternately, you could use your main URL but include directions to search on different words in each promotional campaign. Then track the search words used to reach the product page. By comparing the number of times each search word was used, you can estimate the effectiveness of different promotional campaigns.

Tracking Advertisements

Several companies now offer tools for advertising purposes that go beyond analyzing server logs. You may need to install such third-party auditing software to confirm viewership for advertisers or sponsors.

I/PRO software from Internet Profiles Corporation, in Figure 5.8, at *http://www.ipro.com,* monitors what percentage of visitors click on a banner. With click-through rates now down below 1.5% by some reports, advertisers want to know whether those "clicks" are from their target audience or from general cruisers.

According to I/PRO's site, their "Nielsen I/PRO Audited reports account for over 90% of all audited reports issued for the Web." Prices start at $1250 a month based on the number of hits received. For Web site measurement and analysis, I/PRO offers Netline for both sites and Web hosts, starting at $750 a month.

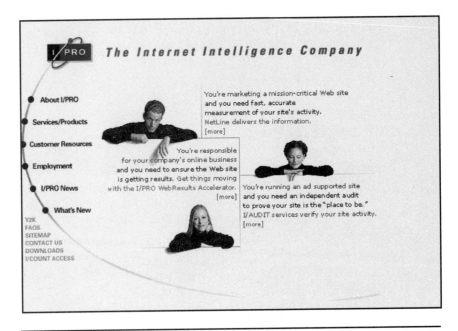

Figure 5.8. Audited ad statistics, *http://www.ipro.com*. Courtesy I/PRO.

Webwide comparisons of raw hits are performed by software such as PC Meter from the National Purchase Diary (NPD) at *http://www.npd.com*. This software, similar to Nielsen's TV rating box, is installed on 10,000 home computers to monitor the habits of Web surfers. The program extrapolates data to establish demographics and hit rates for top-rated Web sites. Sites that are used by a high percentage of computer viewers within a month, such as portals and search engines, draw the most impressions and thus charge the highest rates for advertising.

Using Results Effectively

To make the most of the data you gather, use the information from registrations to establish a demographic profile and match that to usage profiles. Do younger viewers spend more time on one page than another? Which viewers are most likely to buy? Be aware that registration information is not always accurate and that optional registration may inaccurately represent your audience. Freeware for registration guestbooks is available at *http://www.toolzone.com*, as seen in Figure 5.9.

If you hope to derive income from your site, whether by selling product, leasing space in a mall, charging subscription fees, or carrying advertising, defining the visiting audience is critical. Without a demographic analysis and a reasonable estimate for the number of impressions you or your advertisers can expect, it may be hard to attract advertisers or set reasonable subscription rates.

By structuring pages on your site carefully, you can discriminate among types of buyers, such as those more interested in a possible purchase than in the information presented. For example, requiring an additional click to obtain price information or print out a coupon could distinguish between those interested in incidental products, such as an online game, and those interested in buying your real product.

Figure 5.9. Free registration guestbooks, *http://www.toolzone.com*. Courtesy Urbanite Information Systems Inc.

Some things you can measure only off-line. For instance, how much coverage did you get in other media when introducing your Web site? Does your sales staff find a difference in the e-mail it receives from the Web versus calls generated from print or other media? Comparing online sales to off-line ones is easy. If you're not selling online, it's more difficult, but worth the effort, to track the results of Web versus non-Web promotions.

Statistics, like your site itself, are a means, not an end. You must close the feedback loop by using the information to hone your online marketing efforts. Use the data you gather to improve your

- Web site

- Marketing strategies

- Products or services

- Customer service

For more information, check out the Internet Marketing Discussion List at *http://www.o-a.com*. The discussion group covers many topics, including the one addressed in Chapter 6, promoting your Web site.

6

Marketing Your Internet Presence

The Web is not a field of dreams. You can build a site, but visitors may not come: They must know where to find you and why to look. Just as you reviewed long-term strategy before you began to design your Web site, you need to have a clear sense of where you're going before you start promoting it. Be sure to bring the right people into this decision-making process. You wouldn't ask marketing people to write HTML code; don't ask programmers to figure out advertising. Some Web designers can do both, but many can't. If you don't have the time or staff in-house to handle Web promotion tasks, consider hiring outside help.

This chapter will review methods for promoting your Web site, as opposed to promoting your business. Unless you have an advertising site (which means the product is the audience), your goal is more than the greatest number of hits. You want to bring your target audience(s) to your site and to ensure they "get what they came for." Achieving these goals should ultimately improve your bottom line. In this chapter, you'll learn how to

- Research and write a Web promotion plan

- Evaluate the effectiveness of promotional activities

- Launch a Web site

- Find marketing assistance

- Submit your site to search engines and directories

- Improve search engine ranking

- Promote your site in the cheapest place of all—itself

- Promote your site elsewhere on the Web

- Advertise on other sites or have others advertise on yours

- Use other Internet-based communications to draw people to your site

- Amplify your message with off-line promotion

Remember one of the basic laws of marketing: *When you find something that works, don't fix it!*

A Web Promotion Plan

Site promotion is no different from other online activities already discussed. You'll follow the by now familiar drill for Internet success: research, plan, execute, evaluate. You'll be adding many items to the Site Promotion and Advertising sections of your Web notebook. You may also want to create an electronic Promotion subfolder for bookmarked sites. Save sites for potential links, announcements, and advertising, as well as sites whose techniques or ads you'd like to emulate.

Promotional Research

Go back online, ladies and gentlemen. Start researching the Web for examples of the advertising and promotional methods described in this chapter. Analyze lists of What's New, award-winning, and recommended Hot Sites/Cool Links, which often drive a brief but intense flurry of activity to a site. Save examples of internal calls to action and banner ads. Check complementary sites for existing links. See where your competitors place their links and who links to them. Collect promotional e-mail to see what others are doing. Research advertising rates and record the locations of your competitors' ads. For ideas on generating traffic on your site, check out locations such as

- Traffic Tribune at Submit It! (*http://www.submit-it.com*)

- Links:2000 Marketing and Advertising on the Net (*http:// www.2000.ogsm.vanderbilt.edu*)

Writing the Plan

Unless you have a photographic memory, it will be impossible to track all the details of your promotional plan without a written schedule and record. A written plan helps you

- Communicate your objectives clearly to others

- Delegate responsibility for implementation and monitoring

- Outline related activities

- Avoid repeating what has already been tried

- Compare the results of different promotional methods

- Have a basis for future changes

- Recognize when you have achieved your objectives

Your Web promotion plan should include all the standard elements of other plans:

- Goals and objectives, including target audience

- Implementation methods

- Budgets for time and dollars

- Required personnel

- Schedule of activities from prelaunch to at least six months post-launch

Goals and objectives for a promotion plan require a clear definition of the target audience(s) for your site and for each promotional activity. Your audience may include press, stockholders, and potential employees, as well as customers and prospects. It may be as narrow as 100 current business customers, if your new password-keyed pages are intended to shift them to electronic catalog ordering. Or perhaps you want to inform only owners of a particular product about a page that supplies warranty information, product upgrades, add-ons, customer feedback, and service data.

Different pages with different purposes need to reach different audiences, so it's no surprise that they need different promotional techniques. Plan to repeat promotional activities whenever you add a new page or function to your site. After deciding on implementation methods, create separate logs to schedule and track each promotional activity. Such a log might look like the worksheet in Figure 6.1. The promotion plan, especially the timeline, should be in place before launching your site.

Evaluating Results

You may already track the results of off-line advertising and promotional activities by coding that identifies the source of inquiries or sales. You should do the same online. By varying text, graphics, special offers, or placement, you can determine which ads have the greatest pull. You may track results to see whether traffic builds and then drops off, whether it increases steadily, or whether there is no difference. Advertising and promoting your site may become expensive in both time and money, so you'll want to ensure that expenditures bring results.

Submitted to: Name & URL	Date Submitted	Appeared From/To	Cost $ & CPM	Results (if known)
Search Engines & Directories				
http://www.				
http://www.				
What's New Announcements				
http://www.				
http://www.				
News Group Announcements				
http://www.				
http://www				
Mailing List Announcements				
http://www.				
http://www.				
Hot Site/Cool Link Submissions				
http://www.				
http://www.				
Links (Specify Reciprocal, in-or Outbound)				
http://www.				
http://www.				
Link Exchanges				
http://www.				
http://www.				
Banner Ad Exchanges				
http://www.				
http://www.				
Paid Advertisements				
http://www.				
http://www.				
Sponsorships				
http://www.				
http://www.				
E-mail Promotions				
http://www.				
http://www.				
Off-line promotional activities				

Figure 6.1. Web promotion log.

Try to correlate Web promotional activities with the traffic statistics described in Chapter 5. See whether sites carrying your ads can report click-through rates as well as impressions. Confirm that your own WHISP can provide referral page statistics and identify initial files accessed. You may want to create an ad response number or different **doorway** pages that act as special "ports of entry" for viewers who click through from different links. Like tracking return address codes on direct mail flyers, tracking ad response numbers or doorways tells you which links and ads are most successful.

Launching a Web Site

If you've invested a lot of money developing a Web site, treat its launch as you would the opening of a new storefront. The launch need not correspond with the day the site first becomes available to the public. In fact, it's probably better that the site be running solidly for several weeks before you launch activities that will drive traffic to it.

You may want to piggyback your site launch on another event, such as a trade show, a sales or stockholder meeting, a holiday promotion, or the introduction of a new product. Your goal for the launch is to create enough word-of-mouth advertising to generate good baseline traffic. You will need to build a sense of anticipation and excitement. Here are some ideas drawn from the promotional concepts described in detail later:

- Announce special "opening day" or "inaugural week" site offers, whether these are deep discounts, free gifts for every order placed online that day, or special contest drawings. Do these announcements on the Web, through other Internet venues, and off-line.

- Offer a premium above your normal registration payoff (e.g., a discount coupon redeemable for several months) for those who register on your site before or during the first week or month. For an example see the Folgers site shown in Figure 6.2 at *http://www.folgers.com/cgi-bin/coupon.cgi*.

- Plan a live event for that day (practice first), such as a chat with a well-known person; promote that event online and off-line.

- Do several sequenced direct mailings and e-mails to an audience of customers, clients, suppliers, sales reps, and employees to announce your plans in advance of "opening" day.

Figure 6.2. Coupon promotion, *http://www.folgers.com/cgi-bin/coupon.cgi.* Courtesy Procter & Gamble.

- You can't control when your site will appear on a search engine, but you may be able to time postings on What's New sites, as well as on appropriate news groups and mailing list announcement services.

- If you have a storefront, put computers running your Web site on the show floor.

- Your formal inaugural week may be worth an advertising buy for a well-targeted audience; it might even be worth creating a special banner ad.

- If you are selling from the site, provide an incentive for both customers and sales reps who book orders online. (Be careful how you handle this; you don't want buyers holding orders while they wait for the big event.)

- Coordinate off-line press releases and publicity events. Host a special event with a school or perform some community service that draws local or trade press.

- Partner with a not-for-profit to make a contribution for each site visitor, thus encouraging the not-for-profit to help with promotional activities.

- Partner with a supplier or manufacturer for the event, asking them to assist with online promotion from their own site.

There are no rules for a launch, but stealth won't help if you're counting on the Web to drive traffic. Don't be shy.

Help Available

When there is a need, someone on the Internet pops up to fill it. Your existing Web site designer, WHISP, advertising agency, or PR firm may already provide promotional services. The Web has spawned an industry of online promotional consultants, online agencies, and specialized Web marketing services. Such service providers can

- Submit your site to multiple directories, search engines, and lists on a regular basis.

- Place your advertisements. (These people are called media buyers).

- Coordinate Web and other Internet announcements with a total PR or ad campaign.

- Plan and implement long-term strategic Web marketing.

For this type of vendor, you might try sources such as those shown in Figure 6.3. One of these, Go Beyond at *http://www.gobeyond.com*, is seen in Figure 6.4. Lists of other Net marketing companies may be found at *http://www.lib.ua.edu/smr/ad0.html*.

Beyond Interactive	*http://www.gobeyond.com/*
Interactive Traffic	*http://www.i-traffic.com*
Media Associates	*http://www.mediaassociates.com/*
NetCreations	*http://www.netcreations.com/*
Online Ad Agency	*http://www.postmasterdirect.com*
Webtastic	*http://www.webtastic.com*

Figure 6.3. Net marketing service providers.

Figure 6.4. Sample Web promotion provider, *http://www.gobeyond.com.* Courtesy Beyond Interactive.

If you are planning a major site with a large advertising budget, you might need the services of a major ad agency, such as DoubleClick at *http://www.doubleclick.net*, seen in Figure 6.5. Other large agencies are found in Figure 6.6.

Marketing services aren't cheap. Hourly rates range from $50 to $250 an hour depending on the nature of the service, the size of the agency, and the type of contract you have. In the section about on-

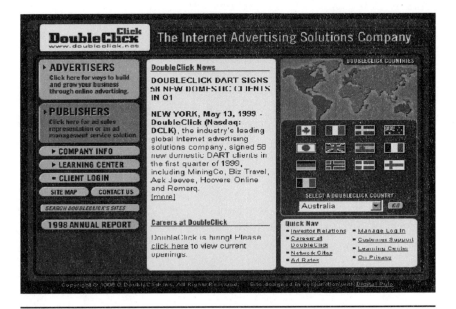

Figure 6.5.   An Internet ad agency, *http://www.doubleclick.net*. Courtesy DoubleClick.

AdSmart	*http://www.adsmart.net*
Agency.com	*http://www.agency.com/irm.html*
DoubleClick	*http://www.doubleclick.net*
Razorfish	*http://www.razorfish.com*
24-7 Media	*http://www/24-7media.com*

Figure 6.6.   Large online advertising agencies.

the-Web promotions, we'll discuss free and do-it-yourself promotional options. In many cases, the trade-off is between your money and your time. Online guerrilla marketing can be inexpensive, but you will need to commit the time of someone in your organization to plan, execute, and track the tasks.

If you elect to use a Web marketing provider, don't be reluctant to ask for references from other clients. Evaluate those clients' sites and contact the companies to see if they are satisfied. Besides rates and the number of submissions a provider guarantees, ask such questions as

- How broad is the promotion service? Just search engines? Or does it include cool lists, news groups, mailing lists, press lists, banner and link exchanges, and/or individualized research?

- Are postings customized according to the requirements of various search engines and individually addressed? Automated and/or mass e-mails may not result in as many successful postings as you might expect.

- Do they customize postings according to your business needs, maximizing exposure to your target audience, or post all businesses the same way?

- Do they guarantee a certain number of postings? If so, where and how many? Will they submit to small, targeted directories and search engines, only the main ones, or both?

- What kinds of inbound and reciprocal links can they provide?

- Do they offer printed confirmation for every posting?

- Do they charge by the hour or by the service?

- Will they promote only one company per category (exclusivity), or will they also promote your competitors?

For additional research on marketing and advertising services, try *http://www.ad-guide.com* or *http://www.adresource.com/*.

Search Engines and Directories

Viewers come to your site in a variety of ways: Content searches, opportunistic links from other sites, bookmarks, and typing in known URLs are the most common sources on the Web itself. (See GVU'S survey site at *http://www.gvu.gatech.edu/user_surveys/* for updates on browsing strategies.)

Figure 6.7 compares the value of banner ads and offline strategies to content searches conducted through search engines and directories. The terms *search engine* and *directory* are often used interchangeably, but actually they are quite different. A directory, such as the Yellow Pages, is an hierarchically organized database arranged by categories and subcategories. A directory may index and link only to a site's home page.

Search engines, on the other hand, use intelligent indexing agents called **spiders** (also known as robots, crawlers, or wanderers) that automatically explore the Web, visiting and revisiting URLs to collect links and pages of text that are eventually analyzed for **keywords.** Assuming there are internal links to every page on a site, search engines will ultimately review an entire site. Once the pages and URLs have been collected, search engines apply various logic **algorithms** (computer formulas) to check the relevance of keywords. From these results, engines rank sites in response to a search request.

There are about 20 major search engines (Figure 6.8) and directories (Figure 6.9) on the Net, and hundreds of lesser-known ones. Don't dismiss the latter out of hand. If they are specific to your busi-

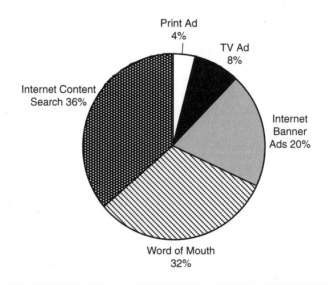

Figure 6.7. Vehicles driving traffic to new sites, *http://www.iconocast.com/whatis/whatis.html.* Courtesy Iconocast, Inc.

Name	Submission URL	Notes (optional)	Time to appearance
AltaVista	*http://www.altavista. com/av/content/addurl.htm*		1 day- 2 weeks
Excite/Netfind	*http://www.excite.com*		2-4 weeks
HotBot	*http://www.HotBot.com/ addurl.asp*		2 days- 2 weeks
InfoSeek	*http://www.infoseek.com*	commercial emphasis	2 hours- 2 weeks
Lycos	*http://www.lycos.com/ addasite.html*	can find pictures, accurate keywords	1-4 weeks
MSN Web Search	http://search,msn.com/addurl.asp		2-4 weeks
Northern Light	*http://www.northernlight.com*		3-6 weeks
PlanetSearch	*http://www.planetsearch.com/ ?a=19&flags=38count=10*		1-2 weeks
Web Crawler	*http://www.webcrawler.com/ mak/projects/robots/ robots.html*	Natural language spider, part of Excite group	2-4 weeks
What U Seek	*http://www.whatuseek.com/*		2-4 weeks

Figure 6.8. Major search engines.

ness area, smaller engines and directories may be the most likely to be searched by your target market. Among other sources, there's a list of search engines at *http://www.bizynet.com/web-srch.htm* and a list of business directories at *http://www.bizynet.com/web-dirs.htm.* Or look them up at *http://www.DirectoryGuide.com.*

The growth of the Web makes search engines' tasks nearly impossible; their indexing success has fallen in half in the past years. A 1999 study by the NEC Research Institute showed that 11 of the major search engines indexed no more than 16% of the estimated 800 million Web pages. Northern Light led the pack (16%), followed by Snap and AltaVista (15.5%), HotBot (11.3%), and MSN Search (8.5%); the others, including Infoseek, Yahoo!, Excite, and Lycos found 8% or less. Some engines no longer index sites without a registered domain name. In spite of the published time to appearance in Figure 6.8, the sutdy found that it takes more than six months on average for a new listing to appear.

Name	Submission URL	Notes (optional)	Time to appearance
AT&T	*http://www.att.com/ directory/website.html*	White Pages	Instant
Downtown Anywhere	*http://www.awa.com*	Virtual cities directory	
Galaxy	*http://galaxy.einet.net*	Search by subject	Guaranteed within 30 days only with $25 payment
Open Source (Newhoo)	*http://www.dmoz.org*	Reviewed for inclusion	
Pronet Directory	*http://www.pronet.com* or *http://pronet.ca*	International directory	
Wired	*http://www.wired.hot bot.com/addurl.asp/*	Computer-related directory	21-60 days
Yahoo!	*http://add.yahoo.com/ fast/add*	Hybrid; hierarchy with search engine; sites reviewed	6-8 weeks
Yellow Pages (GTE)	*http://customer.super pages:887/servlet/ Marketing/Listing*		Instant

Figure 6.9.   Major directories.

Submission

To promote your site on search engines and directories, you need to accomplish two things:

1. Your site must be found.

2. It must be ranked in the top 20 or 30 sites resulting from a search of likely keywords. Most Web surfers go only to the top few sites on a list.

Directories.   Sites can't be found by directories unless you submit your URL, usually with proposed keywords and categories, on a fairly lengthy submission form. Yahoo! and the Yellow Pages allow only a single URL per site, with a single description and title or keyword. Most other directories permit multiple pages from the same site, as long as each page has a different description, keyword list, and URL. (Change the extension name following your domain name, e.g., *http://www.yourdomain.com/extension*).

Search Engines. Theoretically, search engines eventually visit URLs whether or not a formal submission has been received, as long as enough links exist for the site to be identified. However, given that less than one third of all sites are usually found, submitting your URL to search engines will speed up the process. Search engine sites usually require only your URL for submission.

Submit to InfoSeek (*http://infoseek.go.com/AddUrl? pg=submit.html*, shown in Figure 6.10) or another fast-posting search

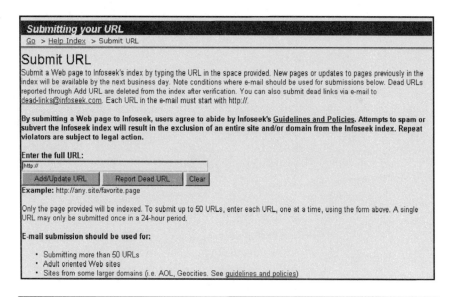

Figure 6.10. Infoseek submission, *http://infoseek.go.comAddUrl?pg= SubmitUrl.html.* "Reprinted by permission, Infoseek, Ultrasmart, Ultraseek, Ultraseek Server, Infoseek Desktop, Infoseek Ultra, iSeek, Quickseek, Imageseek, Ultrashop, the Infoseek logos, and the tagline "Once you know, you know", are trademarks of Infoseek Corporation which may be registered in certain jurisdictions. Other trademarks shown are trademarks of their respective owners. Go Network is a trademark of the Walt Disney Company, Infoseek Corporation authorized license. © 1998-1999 Infoseek Corporation. All rights reserved.

engine to see how well your keyword selection works. When you're satisfied with the results, submit at least to Yahoo!, AltaVista, and HotBot. Directory-wise, list in the AT&T White Pages and the GTE Yellow Pages *(https://customer.superpages.com:887/servlet/Marketing/listing)*, shown in Figure 6.11. Other companies also maintain free Yellow Page listings. Try *http://www.infospace.com*, *http://www.switchboard.com* or *http://www.four11.com*.

Every directory has a slightly different registration form and process, so you may want to individualize submissions, at least to critical sites; look at online forms and existing listings to see what's appropriate. In most cases, you simply fill out a Web-based form with the site name, the URL, and a brief descriptive paragraph that will appear with the URL in a list of search results. A few locations require that you e-mail your entry.

Yahoo! is unique among the search engines and directories because it shares the characteristics of both. Like a directory, it is hierarchically organized, uses categories, and requires the detailed

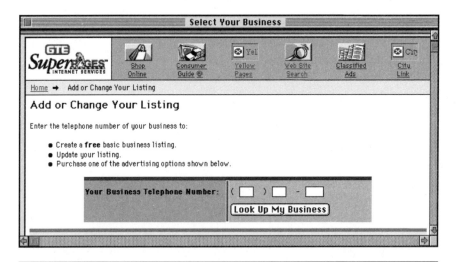

Figure 6.11. Yellow Pages submission, *https://customer.superpages.com:887/servlet/Marketing/Listing*. GTE Directory Superpages.com. Courtesy GTE Directories Corporation.

submission form found at *(http://add.yahoo.com/fast/add)*. Yahoo! also has a robot that searches announcement sites and other collection points on the Web, and rates your site for relevance.

To make sure your Yahoo! submission is successful (it will take several months to find out), note the following:

- Commercial sites must be placed in a Business and Economy subcategory.

- Locate up to two good subcategories by searching until you find businesses like yours, or by using a likely keyword and seeing where responsive sites have been placed.

- Since you can't suggest keywords for Yahoo!, the Title and Description fields are particularly important. The title can be a maximum of 50 characters; see if you can include keywords in that count. The description has a maximum of 20 words or 200 characters; try to create a complete sentence that includes the keywords you want while providing a good description of your company's products or services.

- Yahoo!s reviewers will check your categorization for appropriateness and your description for accuracy. If they aren't correct, your site won't be listed.

Depending on the engine or directory, it may take anywhere from two minutes to two months for your site to appear. Several days after its anticipated appearance (see Figures 6.8 and 6.9), start searching for your entry until you confirm it has been listed. If you don't find your listing within a week after the anticipated time, resubmit your site.

Check each search engine's or directory's FAQs if you have specific questions. For example, from the FAQs for MSN Web Search seen in Figure 6.12 *(http://search.msn.com/helpS_FAQ.asp#web page2)* you learn that your entire site will be crawled from a one-page submission.

As tempting as it may be to submit your URL to search engines as soon as you decide to have a Web site, wait until the site is up and running before you do. Many things can change or go wrong. You could easily turn off a future customer or directory researcher who

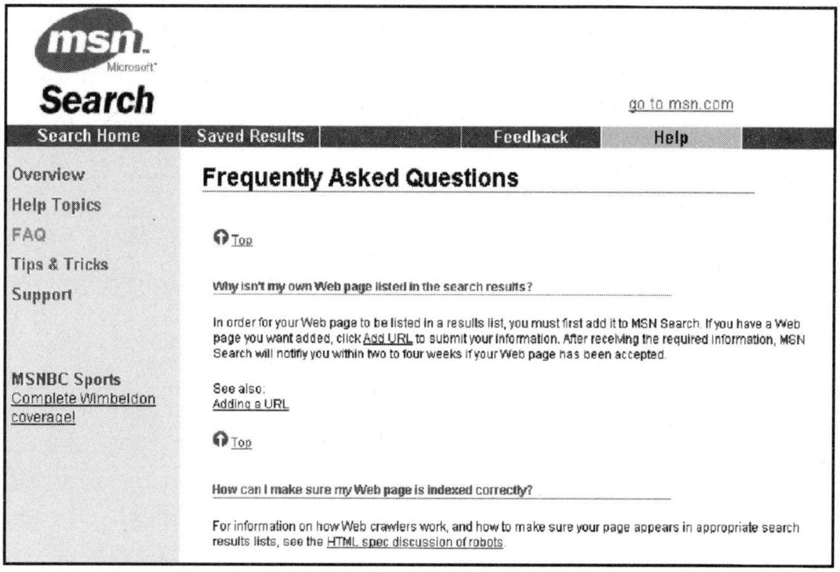

Figure 6.12. Search engine FAQs, *http://search.msn.com/helps_FAQ.asp.*
Screenshot reprinted by permission from Microsoft Corporation.

reaches a page under construction or a page whose content has nothing to do with the keywords you anticipated using.

You can list your site in each engine and directory one by one, or point to a free, one-stop interface to the most popular engines. There are dozens of free submission sites, but Submit It!, at *http://www.submit-it.com,* shown in Figure 6.13, and NetCreations, at *http://www.netcreations.com,* shown in Figure 6.14, are two of the largest. You might also want to try *http://www.register-it.com* or *http://www.netpost.com.* After you enter your information at one of these sites, it automatically registers your site with the top 10 to 20 search engines and directories on the Web.

For submission to over 400 engines and directories, Submit It! Online charges a fee of $59 for two URLs and up to $300 for 20 URLs. Submit It! offers a number of other services, from a free mailbot (automated e-mail response) to fee-based monthly services. NetCreations also charges for more extensive submissions. Like Submit It!, other specialized search engine announcement services charge for regular monthly submissions of multiple URLs to multiple search

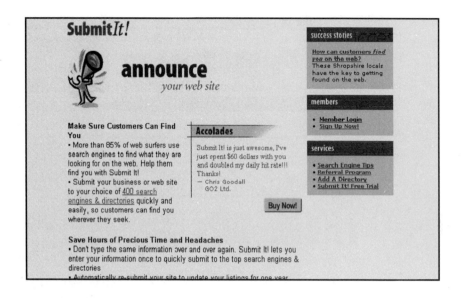

Figure 6.13. Multiple submission site, *http://www.submit-it.com.* Screenshot reprinted by permission from Microsoft Corporation.

engines, e.g. SearchTrends (*http://www.searchtrends.com*) or Position Agent (*http://positionagent.linkexchange.com*). Most of these services consider each page to be a separate URL.

Improving Search Engine Ranking

Frequently thousands, sometimes hundreds of thousands, of matches are found in response to a search on a particular topic. Most directories present results of a search in alphabetical order, compared to search engines, most of which rank by relevance.

Combined, these search engines and directories have literally millions of entries and receive tens of thousands of submissions a day. The search engine world has become so competitive that at least one engine, AltaVista, now lets advertisers pay to have their sites listed at the top of search results on 500 of the most commonly used keywords, such as computer. Although "paid" results are bracketed, it remains to be seen how users will react. If more engines adopt this

Figure 6.14. Multiple submission site, *http://www.netcreations.com/post master.* Courtesy Net Creations.

policy, search engines will become more expensive and less accessible to small businesses seeking to enhance their online presence.

Given the delay in appearance on many engines, it can be frustrating to realize that you didn't optimize your submission, resubmit, and wait again to see what happens. To avoid this, you can purchase software like WebPosition at *http://www.webposition.com* to test your keywords on the major search engines before submission. Some vendors allow you to download trial positioning software from their sites.

Web marketing consultants like those listed here now use one of these packages or proprietary tools to improve their clients' placement and/or provide an optimization service on a per page basis. Before you go with a consultant, read the fine print in their contract regarding guaranteed results, which may be a myth, and ask for references from other customers. Some of these sites say that you pay only for rankings achieved, but require a minimum purchase.

http://www.macor.com/faq.htm

http://www.coastsites.com

http://www.searchtrends.com

http://www.searchenginegeeks.com/faq_geeks.htm

Many sites offer search engine tips online or through e-mailed newsletters. Look at

http://www.submitit.linkexchange.com/subopt.htm

http://www.webposition.com (as seen in Figure 6.15)

http://www.searchsecrets.com

The BEST tips to improve your rankings:

1. **TITLE:** Include and repeat keywords that people might search for to find you in the TITLE of all your pages. This is very important. Keep common word groups or phrases that people might search on *together* if you can. The TITLE is EXTREMELY important to achieving good rankings.

2. **PROMINENCY:** Keywords that are more prominent will be weighted much higher with the search engines. Most engines rank you higher if the keyword or phrase is near the beginning of the title and as close to the beginning of the page as possible.

3. **LENGTH OF PAGE:** Keep your pages short while including and repeating keywords frequently, particularly in the first 3-5 lines of the pages. Some engines ignore or largely ignore wording beyond the first paragraph or two. Having a short page goes much farther to improve your rankings with many engines than you might think, even if the keywords are not repeated very many times.

4. **"DOORWAY" PAGES:** Unfortunately, what is appealing to the search engines is not always the best way to display the content for you Web site. Therefore, strongly consider creating a secondary page for each product or service you offer designed for the search engines. Describe the product/service clearly but make sure you make generous use of keywords in your sentences. At the bottom of this short paragraph, put a link to your primary page such as "For more information on XYZ click here".

The reason this works, and generally works better than most methods, is that engines often take the keywords being searched and divide it by the total number of words in the page or in the first portion of the page. Therefore, you may only have the keyword on the page a couple of times, but if there's not a lot of other words, those keywords appear to be much more "significant" to the page's overall content.

You don't have to have links to these secondary pages from your home page. They simply act as a "doorway" to the appropriate page on your Web site so are not seen by other visitors. If you don't link to them though from your home page or a close secondary page, you'll need to submit each of these pages manually for the search engines to find and index them. Be sure to review the warnings in Submitting Your Pages before doing this though.

5. **REPEATING KEYWORDS:** Experiment with repeating keywords up to six times and more on some engines. If this makes your page look bad, consider putting the keywords at the top of the page preferably in the same color as the background. That way nobody can see them but they should still get indexed. **Warning:** Some engines are now detecting wording in the same color as the background and either ignoring such text or leaving the page out of the index altogether! We'll try to update you on these kind of specifics in our MarketPosition Newsletter. Proper "netique" discourages blatant "spamming" of keywords. You should not try to go overboard repeating the same keyword or using keywords that don't apply to your site.

Figure 6.15. Search engine tips, *http://www.webposition.com/userguide howtoprepareyourpagesforsubmission.htm.* Courtesy *www.Firstplacesoftware .com,* developers of WebPosition Gold.

The reports just listed usually provide suggestions to improve ranking according to the approach used by each engine. The engines change their algorithms over time, partly to increase accuracy, partly to outwit people who are trying to outwit them, and partly to distribute visibility among indexed pages. If you want to get really fancy, you can optimize splash or **doorway** pages (special entry pages) based on different search engine techniques. In spite of this, there are some general principles about the way most search engines determine relevance.

Keyword Weighting. This is a ratio between the occurrence of a keyword and the total number of words on a page. Try to keep your total word count per page to 350–450 words. Look at what percentage of the total words on the page are keywords, counting all occurrences of all keywords on that page. Keywords should represent somewhere between 3 and 10% percent of total words. Instead of trying to get the maximum number of different keywords on a page, try to focus your pages so that different keywords pop out as the most relevant on different pages.

Ease of Finding Your Site. Many engines judge your value to the world by the number of inbound links to your site. This increases the importance of reciprocal and inbound links, described in "Promoting Your Site on the Web." Not only do inbound links boost your rankings, they also represent your most likely target audience. Several search engines have ways to let you know who's "voted" your site "most popular" with links. At AltaVista and Excite, simply type your URL on the screen without *www*. *HotBot* requires the full URL, but you change the default setting to a search.

Keyword Emphasis. Think newspaper article, not essay. Write in the inverted pyramid style of classic journalism. The lead—the first sentence or paragraph—answers all the essential questions (who, what, why, where, when, and how) in case a reader doesn't have time to complete the story. Don't save the best till last: Make your title and the first 25 words of your page keyword-rich. Most search algorithms expect keywords specific to a page to be located near the top, relatively close to each other (as in an abstract), and then scattered in various places around the page. Each search engine has a unique, proprietary set of criteria to determine keyword emphasis.

Keyword Density. Sophisticated algorithms not only count how often a keyword is used on a page, they watch where keywords appear with high frequency. Some engines will bounce sites that try to boost their ratings by repeating keywords over and over behind a graphic or hidden in one section of the background. Draw a delicate balance between good repetition of a keyword (6 to 10 times each per page), and overuse.

Search engines are not static. To increase the likelihood of getting your Web site ranked highly, submit multiple pages with different URLs whenever possible, optimizing them for different keywords. If you use multiple doorway pages, be sure to change the META tags (see "Optimizing Your Pages") for each one. Besides your home page, submit major topic pages, unique content, or pages describing a special product or service. Your Web designer should follow the principles outlined below such as using descriptive TITLE tags, on these sub-pages as well.

Finally, submit new pages as they are created and resubmit pages if their content changes significantly. Although these changes should eventually be caught on a revisit by a spider, submission will speed up the process. Schedule a resubmission of your entire site every 2 or 3 months to account for changing algorithms and random drop-offs from the search databases. Keep track of all your submissions and rankings in your Web notebook.

In the case of directories, consider carefully the categories to which your site belongs. Directories may define the same category names differently and divide up broad categories into subcategories on a unique basis, so this submission process can become quite cumbersome. Search each target directory until you find other companies like yours. If you can't find a subcategory that fits, suggest a new one. There is no point in going into a less appropriate category—your audience won't find you. Resubmit to directories if your URL, category classification, or description changes.

Schedule a monthly maintenance visit to all your directory and search engine listings to confirm your presence, check your rankings, and see whether there have been any changes to the site.

A Few Words about Keywords

Since search engines operate by using keywords to rank relevant sites or articles, an accurate and extensive list of keywords is important to improve your ranking. An online florist who stops with the obvious keywords *flowers, bouquets,* and *florist,* will lose anyone who searches for *gifts, weddings, houseplants, funerals,* or *floral arrangements.*

Brainstorm as many keywords as you can—at least 50. Since some engines restrict the number of keyword entries, you might not be able to use them all. However, spreading keywords around to different engines and assigning them to different pages will improve the likelihood of attaining a reasonable ranking somewhere.

Think like the audience you are trying to reach. What words or phrases might they type in? People looking for a small, intimate hotel in San Antonio don't type the word *hotels.* They type *bed-and-breakfast San Antonio.* The more narrowly focused the phrase or keywords used, the smaller the list of search results, and the higher in the rankings you are likely to be. For instance, instead of the word *gifts* above, try *women birthday presents, fresh flowers $30,* or *office-warming plants.* Try *electronic funds transfer software,* not just *software program.*

Most of all, test your keywords. Create a spreadsheet or table with a proposed list of keywords and the list of search engines and directories in Figures 6.8 and 6.9 seen earlier. See what other sites and how many sites result from a search on those words. Are the results similar to your company? If so, you're on the right track. How do the results differ among the search engines?

If you find a phrase that returns a reasonable number of results (say less than a thousand instead of several hundred thousand), optimize your page for that phrase: You're more likely to end up at the top of the list. Of course, you can't choose words just because they return a good result—it's a meaningless victory to rank first if no one in your target audience would type that keyword or phrase.

If you are already listed in the search engines, be honest with yourself: Type in your existing keywords and see where you rank. If you are not in the top 30 sites for at least one page in each engine, start revising your keywords. Ask potential viewers, either now or in your testing cycle, what keywords they would use to find your site. Everybody's brain works differently—you might be surprised. You can improve your keywords by working backward as well. Go to a site that is like yours and that consistently ranks well in search engines. Look at their source code to view their keywords and META tags.

The following list of tips may come in handy:

- Your company name should be one of your keywords, especially if it is not obvious in your domain name or if it could be spelled or abbreviated several ways. (Note: If your company name isn't obvious within your domain name, you may want to arrange for your brand name, trademark, or slogan to map to your Web site. The charge is $100 per year per name. Go to *http://realnames.com/Frontpage/RealNamesHome page.html*.)

- Use only keywords that apply to your site. In the end, any other choice of words will be self-defeating for a business presence.

- In general, use two- to three-word phrases instead of individual keywords.

- Make sure your keywords are spelled correctly.

- You might want to target commonly misspelled words deliberately, perhaps creating a doorway page with a keyword slightly misspelled (e.g., *Caribean* for *Caribbean*).

- Don't use *stop words*, common words that search engines skip (e.g., a, an, the, and, but, or, of, that, *Web*). Try to avoid the as the first word in a title, since it might reduce the prominence of keywords in the TITLE tag. If you must use a stop word, put it in quotes.

- If you have purchased banner ads (discussed later), coordinate keywords with words in the ad.

- Don't be afraid to include regional words or phrases to target your audience, (e.g., Appalachian).

- Use long versions of words, such as photographer instead of photo. The short "root word" will usually be derived by the engine.

As described earlier, some sites try to increase keyword frequency by hiding the words behind graphics or in a text color that matches their background. This technique, called **keyword stuffing**, may increase the ranking if that is based on absolute numbers or on the ratio of keywords to text, but not for long. Most search engines now set a limit on the number of occurrences per word they will accept. "Web watchers" like CNet also review the Web for stuffing techniques and the use of keywords inappropriate to a site.

If you try to stuff the ballot box or "spam" an index by submitting too many pages, too many keywords (more than 6 to 10 uses per word per page), or use keywords unrelated to the content of the site, you may find your submission rejected. If you persist, many engines will permanently ban all your pages.

Optimizing Your Pages

By adjusting your Web pages slightly, you can increase the likelihood of a high ranking on a search engine for one or more of your pages. Here are some tips to share with your Web designer.

1. Include one or more descriptive keywords in the TITLE tag of the document. This TITLE tag is what a browser displays in the title bar of a page. (See Figure 6.16 from *http://www. finecoffee.com* for an excellent example of title bars for different keywords to distinguish pages on a site.) A good title helps your viewers find your site again in their bookmark list as well.

2. Use META tags to define what will appear as the summary of your site in an index listing instead of a sentence fragment from your first paragraph of text. META tags are especially important when a site uses Netscape frames or Javascript at the top of the page. Your Web designer will know the syntax and location of META tags (see the comprehensive example in Figure 6.17 from *http://www.phs.org*), but you need to provide the content, preferably from a marketing perspective. META tags can encompass keywords that appear on other pages and incorporate singular, plural, and other forms of keywords (e.g., clothes, clothing, shop, shopping).

   Not all search engines score on META tags, so be sure to utilize META keywords within page content as well. Repeating the same word too many times in a META tag can get a site bounced from an index.

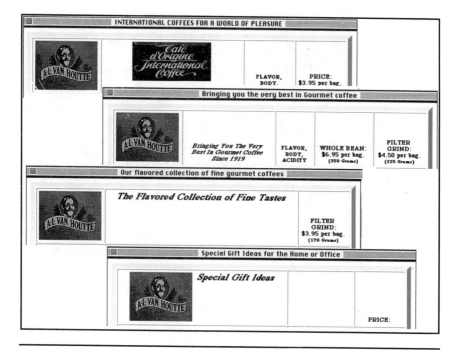

Figure 6.16. Good title bars with different keywords, *http://www.fine coffee.com.* Courtesy Fruba, Inc. dba College Hill Coffee Shop.

3. Provide keywords in a comment tag in the first few lines of HTML code, as well as in a header tag.

4. Since the top of a page is assigned greater relevance, a graphic near the top should have text immediately beneath or next to it.

5. If the site uses multiple photos or graphics, use text within ALT tags to give search engines a basis for determining keywords. The 20 to 40% of viewers who download pages with graphics turned off also find this helpful in deciding whether they want to see a specific image.

6. After indexing a home page, search engines return at a later time to index internal links. In a frame-based site, frames are treated as internal links, delaying a correct analysis of the home page. Since this may result in a poor ranking initially, include descriptive text between the <noframes> and

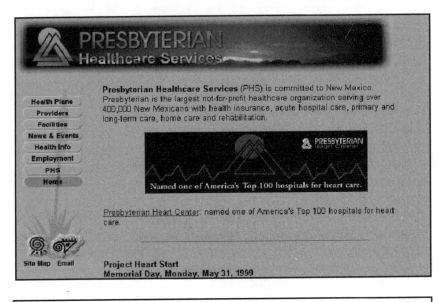

```
<head>
<meta http-equiv="Content-Type" content="text/html; charset=
iso-8859-1">
<meta name="description" content="Presbyterian Healthcare
Services in Albuquerque, NM provides managed care and tradi-
tional health plans for employers of all sizes, groups and
individuals.">
<meta name="keyword" content="PHS, Presbyterian, healthcare,
homecare, medical, medicine, family practice, integrated
delivery system, IDS, hospital, Albuquerque, medical prac-
tice, primary care, doctor referral service, ambulatory
care, day surgery, outpatient care, tertiary care, urgent
care, emergency care, managed care, health insurance, New
Mexico, health maintenance organization, HMO, preferred
provider organization, PPO, Medicare, Medicaid, Medicare
risk plan, air ambulance, women's programs, children's
programs, heart, home health foundation, acute care, long
term care, managed care organization, MCO, salud, PHS foun-
dation, foundation, southwest, outpatient, emergency room,
rheumatology, endocrinology, specialists, practice opportu-
nities, internal medicine, ob/gyn, obstetrics, gynecology,
provider, nurse practitioner, urgent care, locum tenens">
<meta name="GENERATOR" content="Microsoft FrontPage 3.0">
<title>Presbyterian Healthcare Services</title>
<base target="_top">
</head>
```

Figure 6.17. META tags for a site, *http://www.phs.org.* Courtesy Presbyterian Healthcare Services, New Mexico.

</noframes> tags of the source code. This gives the search engine something to work with.

7. Use keywords in internal links.

8. Substitute keywords in URL extensions for a page instead of a generic word like *index*.

9. If a particular page is likely to generate a flood of responses, consider asking users to do one of the following:

   • Select one of several buttons to sort the responses.

   • Require a second click-through to weed out some of the looky-loos.

   • Use a mailbot to respond automatically.

Promoting Your Site on Your Site

The following sections discuss ways to use your Web site itself as a promotional tool. Some of the techniques are designed to encourage people to remain on your site for a longer period of time, thus allowing you to reinforce your company name and increase perceived value. Others are designed to encourage repeat visits, gradually building a relationship with self-qualified prospects and preparing them to buy from you.

If viewers are current customers, so much the better: It's easier to make repeat sales to satisfied customers than to develop new customers. Existing customers have eliminated the risk of dealing with an unknown company online. They already know the quality of your products, the guarantees you offer, and the excellent service you provide.

Registration on Site

Use the registration tools in Chapter 5 to build an e-mail list of self-qualified prospects. This is also an inexpensive way to establish a circulation figure, which can be useful when negotiating reciprocal links, bartering an ad exchange, accepting paid advertising, or recruiting sponsors.

On-site registration invites you to provide targeted e-mail to your viewers, such as the one in Figure 6.18 from Making Lemonade at *http://www.makinglemonade.com.* You can also notify them of changes to your Web site, thus encouraging a repeat visit. You can even ask viewers on your list to test changes to your site before you unveil them publicly.

Registration is probably the most important call to action in terms of self-promotion. Use registration as more than a guestbook. Collect some brief information about the user, as Federal Express does in Figure 6.19. Note that FedEx describes how the information will be used and directs viewers to the company's privacy policy.

You might want to offer something in exchange for registration, such as

- Entry in a drawing with an online announcement of the winners. See ParentTime at *http://www.pathfinder.com/ ParentTime/fpcontest*, shown in Figure 6.20, for an example. If a minimum number of entries is required, provide a registration counter that shows how close you are.

- A free e-mailed report.

- A print-out discount coupon for use online or off-line.

- A subscription to your free e-mail newsletter or information service.

- A small sample of your product.

- The ability to download free software, from demo software to an animated greeting or a screensaver. You may be able to negotiate something with shareware developers who would like to attract customers to their products as well.

- Donation to a not-for-profit organization that your viewers care about.

Subj: Making Lemonade Picks to Click

Date: Thursday, March 25, 1999 7:00:10 PM

From: *http://www.makinglemonade.com*

Dear Lemonaders....

Over the next few weeks you'll be seeing a lot of additions and changes on Making Lemonade. In the Creative/articles section, our current theme is "Anger and Forgiveness"....Also in this section you'll find our Single Dad's section... and our famous "And you thought you had it bad" stories....

Find fun links for your children in our children's section, along with articles and a children's astrological guide. We also have a child support calculator in our children's section next to the yellow ribbon. If you have any ideas or requests - please feel free to send them along....In the Creative/Stories section, you'll find articles on starting your own support group and my story in "Sam's Single Mom".

Our Resource Guide is getting under way and we're ready to bring you all the resources you'll need to make it through each day. Tip: When you sign up on the site to receive the newsletter it is helpful to fill in your location - so I know where to target my research for childcare and other resources....

Here's our list of Picks to Click....Making Lemonade's Top Books of the Month...just point and click to check them out and order them right from here!....Also, on the Making Lemonade Hits to Click List is our shopping guide....

Your lemonade maven,

Jody

Figure 6.18. Targeted e-mail, *http://www.makinglemonade.com*. © Making Lemonade.com 1997, *Making Lemonade: The Single Parent Network*.

- Automatic notification when your site is updated. Services like Mind-It (*http://www.mind-it.com*) and NetMind (*http://www.netmind.com/html/webmaster.html*), shown in Figure 6.21, allow any visitor, whether or not otherwise registered, to request e-mail when site changes occur. (Individual users can configure their own reminder systems for multiple sites by going to *http://minder.netmind.com/mindit.shtml*.)

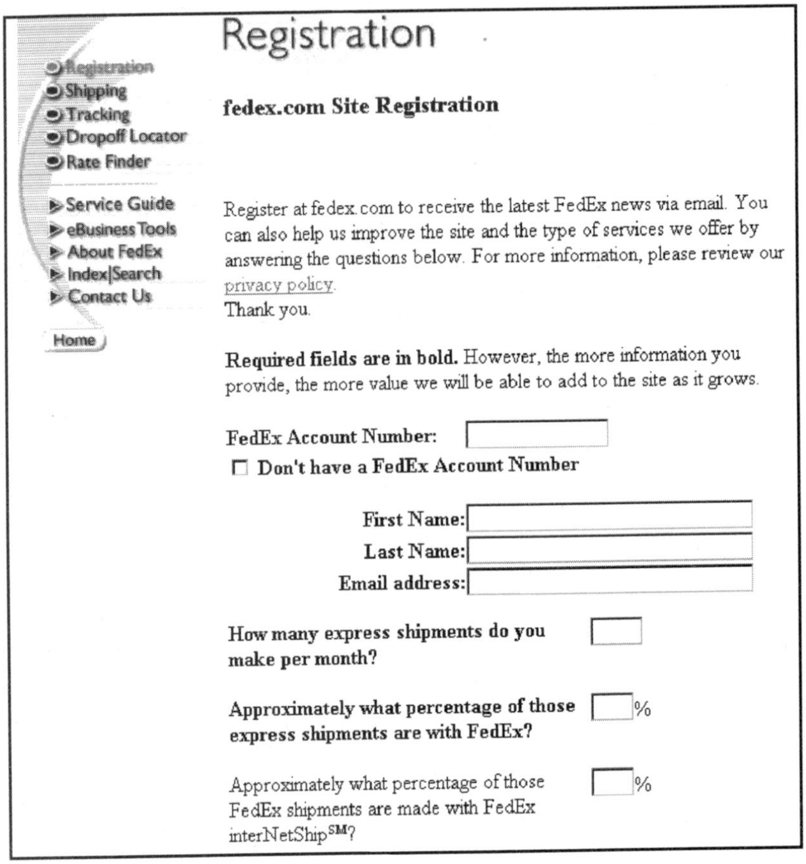

Figure 6.19. Site registration with questions, *http://www.fedex.com/ registration.site.html.* © 1995-1999 Federal Express Corporation. All rights reserved.

Internal Calls to Action

If you don't suggest that viewers take an action, they may not think of it themselves. In Chapter 4, we described external calls to action that move the visitor toward a sale, and we've talked about site registration as a powerful call to action. You can also move a visitor through or back to your site by using such internal calls to action as

* Bookmark this site/page.

Figure 6.20. Registration sweepstakes promotion, *http://www.pathfinder com/ParentTime/fpcontest.* © 1999 Time Inc. New Media. All rights reserved. Reproduction in whole or in part without permission is prohibited. Pathfinder is a registered trademark of Time Inc. New Media.

- Make this site your browser home page. The Discovery Channel does this in Figure 6.22 at *http://www.discovery. com/mydcol/yourhome.html.*

- See What's New as NetVet does in Figure 4.37.

- Sign up for e-mail reminder service or newsletters.

- Return for a scheduled special event, such as a chat.

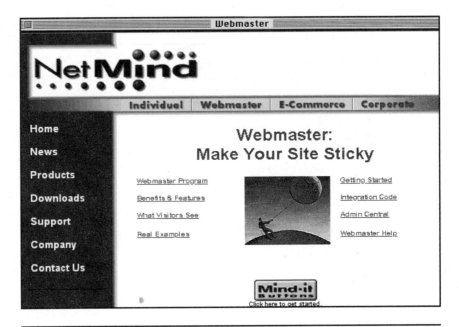

Figure 6.21. Site reminder service, *http://netmind.com/html/webmaster. html.* Courtesy Netmind Services, Inc.

Clever internal calls to action can be camouflaged as a poll or teaser. America Online is particularly good at this, as you can see by the example in Figure 6.23. Clicking on the Y2K box takes you to the Millenium Store. Internal calls to action can also look like banner ads, as you can see from the examples shown on one of Ragu's pages in Figure 6.24 from *http://www.eat.com.* The three banner ads, "Mama's Soap Opera," "Learn Italian," and "Play," actually rotate on this screen. Each one takes you to a different page on the site: funny stories, a RealAudio language lesson, or a glossary of Italian cuisine, respectively. (Besides the banners, there are at least six internal calls to action and three external ones on this page. Can you find them all?)

What's New With You?

In Chapter 5 we talked about the importance of changing content to draw return visitors to your site. You've even drawn up a schedule

Figure 6.22.   A unique call to action, *http://www.discovery.com/mydcol/ yourhome.html.* © 1999 Discovery Channel Online. Source: discovery.com.

for content updates and expansions. Every time you change your site, repeat the announcement and publicity processes described here.

Make it easy for repeat viewers to find new information quickly. A What's New icon on the menu, as seen in Figure 4.37, is one of the most effective ways to do this. No returning visitor wants to link through eight pages to find new material. The icon should link to the new page or information, or to a submenu (maybe one that pops up or pulls down) of new material on a variety of pages.

By placing new information on a new page, you may be able to generate another search engine submission with a new extension name and keywords. Some directories and engines will accept an additional page as a new listing, even if the "new" part of the URL is just an extension (use a keyword) after the domain name.

What's New announcement sites also accept changes in content on an existing page. Use any of these changes as an excuse for a press release, sending notification to news groups and mailing lists. You can certainly inform your e-mail registrants or use NetMind.

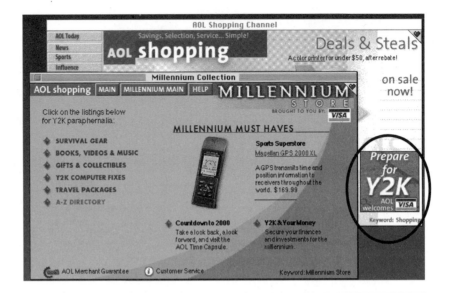

Figure 6.23. The Y2K box acts as a "teaser" call to action on AOL. Clicking on it takes you to the Millenium Store. "America Online", "AOL" and the Logo design are registered trademarks of America Online, Inc. © 1997-1999 America Online, Inc.

Figure 6.24. Internal calls to action on Ragu. The three oblong internal banners alternate in the lower left hand corner. (*http://www.eat.com/good ies/index.html*). Courtesy Lipton Investments, Inc. and Unilever USA, Inc.

Pat Yourself on the Back

Is your site on a list of Hot Sites or Cool Links? Did it win an award from one of the many organizations that recognize good Web sites? Shout it from your cybertop! Besides putting out a press release in traditional and Web media, incorporate a notice on your page. Award postings not only keep a record of your site, they act as a testimonial to your talent and will help draw new and repeat visitors. Take a look at all the awards won by Ragu in Figure 6.25 at *http://www. eat.com/trophy-room.html*. (This screen shows only a fraction of their awards.)

Think of awards as part of a press kit. A press kit would include a list of magazines, online and off, that have reviewed your site or mentioned your product or service. Preferably a kit would include copies of the actual reviews. (Ask the original publisher for permission to reproduce their reviews on your site; reviews and articles are usually copyrighted.)

There are dozens of awards for Web prowess. They range from serious (the Golden Tag Award for excellence in HTML design or the IPPA Award for Design Excellence for commercial sites), to sarcastic (The Dancing Finger O'Sarcasm Award), to silly (The Cow Pie Awards). Some awards are designed for specific enterprises (Golden Tin Award for law enforcement sites) or features (Red Eye Award for best use of plug-ins or Digital Media Awards for multimedia). Usually, sites must be nominated for awards, with the submission sometimes requiring a brief description as well as the URL. Review previous winners before nominating your site to ensure that your site will fit well with the nature of the award. The creators of the SpunkyMunky Awards probably have very different criteria than the people who compile Lycos Top 5%.

Try one of the sites listed in Figure 6.26 or use a search engine for a more complete list of award URLs and links. Several sites, like Award-It, offer the opportunity to submit to multiple award sites, usually a few at a time. Spacing award submissions makes sense; every new award or listing gives you a reason for a Web announcement and an addition to your What's New feature. You will probably want to maintain a spreadsheet or table in your notebook for award submissions, showing name of award, URL, date submitted, date of response, date notice appeared on the award site, and date you posted the award icon on your site.

Figure 6.25. Award page, *http://www.eat.com/trophy-room.html.* Courtesy Lipton Investments, Inc. and Unilever USA, Inc.

The Webby, from the International Academy of Digital Arts and Sciences (IADAS), is one of the premier awards for Web designers and advertisers. Webbies, judged by professionals in the field are given annually in 22 categories, along with a People's Voice Award for a site chosen by the online community. For more information on nomination criteria, go to *http://www.iadas.net.* For current and past winners, check out *http://www.webbyawards.com*, a great place to seek inspiration during your Web research forays.

Promotional Giveaways, Contests, and Games

Promoting your site with giveaways, contests, and games is no different from off-line promotions that keep your name or brand in front of your audience. These activities give viewers a reason to return. You can further entice repeat visits by highlighting future promotions.

Use your mailing list to tell people when a new game has been placed online or remind them to visit your Web site to see if they have won in a drawing. Give away one of your products, a related item, or something with your name on it. Make it attractive enough that people will talk about your promotion online and off.

For example, a travel agency could enter people who leave their e-mail addresses in a drawing for a free trip to Hawaii. It could pick a winner every time it reached some preset number of registrations,

```
http://point.lycos.com/categories (Lycos Top 5%)
http://www. award-it.com
http://www.bizbotweekly.com/awards.html
http://www.bizwizard.virtualave.net/award.html
http://www.contestnetwork.com
http://www.coolgraphics.com/award.html
http://www.happymall.com/awards.htm (on-line shopping sites)
http://www.mastersites.com/spunkymunky
http://www.mel.addr.com/winthe.htm
http://www.netprobe.net/body_submit.html
http://www.register-it.com/O-register/plus/index.html
http://www.smartbiz.org/submissi.htm
http://www.webflier.com/addasite.html
http://www.yahoo.com/picks
```

Figure 6.26. Award submission sites, *http://www.bizbotweekly.com/awards.html*. Courtesy BizBot Weekly.

say 50,000. It could use a free piece of carry-on luggage for every 10,000 names and a luggage tag for every 100th e-mail registration. Figure 6.27 (*http://www.krxo.com/game.html*) shows a site that pulls repeat visitors by posting four new contests every week. For a list of contest sites, see *http://www.korax.net/~quest/shtml*. The site *http://www.sweepsadvantage.com* offers a list of online sweepstakes.

Chat Lines, Forums/Boards, and Events

Consider scheduling a moderated live chat with a professional or well-known figure, or offering opportunities for viewers to consult with business experts through a forum or **message board** (nonsimultaneous chats in which messages are posted for others to read). Free software

Figure 6.27. Online contest draws repeat visitors, *http://www.krxofm.com/games.html.* KRXO-FM Courtesy Bryan Kerr, Oklahoma Internet Consulting, Inc.

for both these features was listed in Chapter 4. Forums are an ongoing feature available at any time, while chats are booked and promoted on the site (and sometimes off) well in advance. For example, see how Third Age handles on-site promotion for its chats and forums in Figures 6.28 and 6.29, from *http://www.thirdage.com.*

You could also host a special online event, as simple as a chat or as elaborate as a live **sitecast,** that incorporates multimedia and live audio or video. Collaborate with some complementary businesses to share the cost, help with publicity, and bring in participants through their own sites. For example, a company that makes monogrammed athletic uniforms could team with a manufacturer of soccer balls and the local soccer association for a real-time event that includes a coach or player from a professional or local team. Use the event to discuss contemporary soccer issues, from its popularity as an intramural sport to rules changes or the need for more sponsors for local teams.

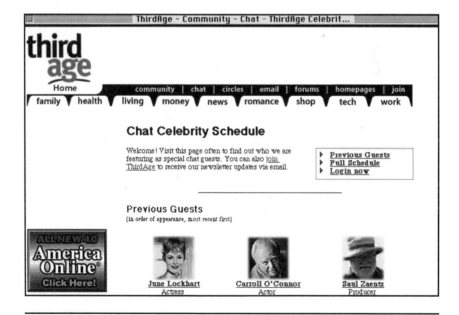

Figure 6.28. Chat promotion onsite, *http://www.thirdage.com/chat/ stars.html.* © 1997, 1999 Third Age Media, Inc. All rights reserved.

Figure 6.29. Forum promotion onsite, *http://www.thirdage.com/WebX.*
© 1997, 1999 Third Age Media, Inc. All rights reserved.

Each company's site promotion can be subtle—a logo link at the bottom of the sitecast page. Drawing the right visitors is ample reward. Once again, promote the event both online and off, especially on your own site. (See *http://www.local.com,* shown in Figure 6.30.) It's no different from what you would do if you had a star athlete come to your store to autograph sports caps.

More Ideas

For a unique way to drive traffic to your site, distribute a browser preset to have your home page appear whenever a user boots it up. You could collaborate on this promotion with a local ISP or online service that offers a free trial period. An excellent Web site announcement, this off-line promotion can be mailed out to current customers with an invitation to visit your new site or given away free at your physical location. Of course, you know your customers well enough

Figure 6.30. Live event promotion onsite, *http://www.local.com*. Courtesy Local.com.

to assess whether they have a computer, whether or not they are already online, and whether they are likely to buy online if they buy from you in person. You can distribute a customized Netscape browser for free, in exchange for filing a quarterly report on distribution, by going to *http://www.home.netscape.com/partners/distribution/ index.html?cp=leb21hig4*.

Many portals, ISPs, and other sites offer free, small (2–5 MB) Web sites to viewers and clients, usually without a domain name. These sites, which often aren't indexed by search engines, may not work as a full-fledged business site, but they can become an effective place for a splash page or subset of your site with a link to your URL. If your target audience uses the host service, they might well stumble on your site through the host's directory.

An expanded listing in a directory is another variation on this theme. For instance, Women's Work offers free, multiple directory listings to businesses in their marketplace at *http://wwork. com/ServiceCenter/bizdir.htm*, shown in Figure 6.31. This is some-

Figure 6.31. Business directory listing, *http://wwork.com/ServiceCenter/ bizdir.htm.* Courtesy Numont Enterprises.

what akin to a business card ad in a mini–telephone directory of local businesses, but it draws focused traffic instead of a general audience. Finally, encourage viewers to send a friend a link to your site, as done by the resource site, HitBox (*http://w21.hitbox.com/world/ page.cgi?tellafriend*), shown in Figure 6.32).

Promoting Your Site on the Web

The opportunities for on-the-Web promotion are many, whether free or paid. You'll run out of time—or money—long before you run out of ideas.

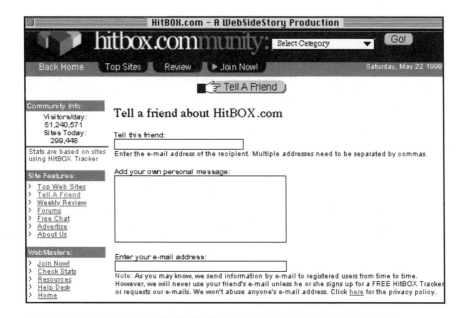

Figure 6.32. Send a friend a link, *http://w21.hitbox.com/world/page.cgi? tellafriend. Courtesy WebSide Story.*

What's New Listings

These free announcement sites, easily found by browsers, are an excellent place to pick up new "eyeballs." What's New listings, which remain up for about a week, announce a new site, a new page, or simply new content. Expect a brief flurry of 5,000 to 10,000 additional visitors (mostly looky-loos) to your Web site as a direct result of these announcements. Be sure that your ISP knows that you plan to make such postings and that it will be able to handle the traffic generated without overloading your site. As mentioned earlier, a What's New posting is an occasion for a NetMind notice to past visitors.

What's New facilitators are overwhelmed with announcements. Each list generally posts 400 to 600 What's New items per day. As with directory and search engine registrations, you may need to customize your submission. In general, you submit by clicking on each site's "submit" page. A typical listing appears on the What's New Too site, *http://www.nu2.com/index.html*, in Figure 6.33. As with search engines, check the postings every several days to see if you've been listed. Resubmit if you haven't appeared after a week.

Hits from What's New announcements follow a pattern: a rapid, straight-up peak right after publication; a less rapid, but still steep decline; and finally a plateau slightly higher than the base level of hits. To keep the hit rate high and more balanced, make announcements on each What's New list as often as possible. Instead of making submissions to all the What's New sites at once, space them out to a different one every day or so. Add to your content regularly so that every several weeks you have something new to announce.

There are many What's New pages. The table in Figure 6.34 provides a list of some popular ones. You can find a directory of more What's New pages at *http://www.stpt.com*, at *http://www.yahoo.com*, or on most of the other search engines. As with awards, make a spreadsheet or table to keep a record of the What's New site location, submission date, and appearance. See if you can correlate appearance with traffic statistics for your site.

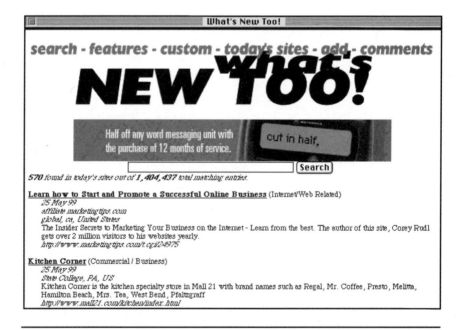

Figure 6.33. Sample What's New listing, *http://www.nu2.com/index.html*. Courtesy Manifest Information Services.

```
http://dir.yahoo.com/new/
http://home.netscape.com/netcenter/new.html
http://stpt.com/default.asp
http://web66.coled.umn.edu/new/new.html
http://www.icsa.net/news/whatsnew.shtml
http://www.netcreations.com/postmaster/whatsnew.html
http://www.netpost.com
http://www.newtoo.com/index.html
http://www.whatsnew.com/
http://www.yahooligans.com/new
```

Figure 6.34.   Some popular What's New sites.

Hot Sites and Cool Links

Unlike What's New pages, which publish all the announcements they receive, Hot Sites or Cool Links lists are discretionary. The compilers of these lists use their own intensely personal criteria to sift through sites, just as film critics and restaurant reviewers do. Cool Links lists range from a site of the day maintained by an individual, to rankings from USA Today, the San Jose Mercury News, Netscape, and Yahoo! A number of sites are shown in Figure 6.35. For a list of more sites that post their own hot sites and cool links, check *http://www. bizbotweekly.com/awards.html.*

If criteria for a list are unpublished or too vague to determine if your site is qualified, evaluate the sites recommended on the list. Nominate your site only for lists that endorse sites similar to yours. As before, record your submissions and appearance on a table so you can determine if there is a correlation with traffic to your site. Sites like NetGuide at *http://www.netguide.com* review useful sites organized by category, much like an annotated bibliography, for their members. You'll need to search out such opportunities individually based on your business needs and target audiences.

Because appearing on one of these recommended lists can result in thousands of additional hits, competition for placement has become intense. An appearance on a Hot Site or Cool Link list, which lasts between a day and a week, generates a brief but predictable flurry of

```
http://cool.com/way/cool/submit1.html
http://www.usatoday.com/leadpage/usanew.htm
http://www.ala.org/alsc/children_links.html
http://www.coolcentral.com
http://www.coolsiteoftheday.com
http://www.mediacom.it/siti2/hotsite.htm
http://www.netscape.com/escapes/whats_cool.html
http://www.shsu.edu/shsu/Internet.html
http://www.ten-tenths.com/links/Cool/
http://www.yahooligans.com/docs/cool/index.html
```

Figure 6.35. Hot sites and cool links: A sample list.

hits. At the same time, the number of such sites has multiplied like bunny rabbits, saturating the Hot Site/Cool Link field itself.

Create your own list with a unique, topical twist and accept nominations or allow viewers to vote. It's another way to generate repeat visits. Or exchange nominations with a complementary business that also maintains a Hot Site list.

Some agencies and service providers specialize in getting your site listed as a Hot Site or Cool Link, just as some PR firms specialize in getting articles placed in the Wall Street Journal or local business magazines. The application process for most sites involves sending an e-mail with your URL and a short description (with style and verve) of your site, its features, and its value to the user. You must decide whether appearing on this list, or on any other award list, will draw the audience you are looking for.

Links with Other Sites

Links can be a reciprocal exchange with another site, one-way outbound, or one-way inbound. **Reciprocal** linking with other sites is one of the most effective and least expensive ways to attain greater visibility for your own. Be sure to visit the other site to confirm that it attracts the same people you want to attract. Figures 6.36 and 6.37 show two sites, My Two Homes and Making Lemonade, with reciprocal links.

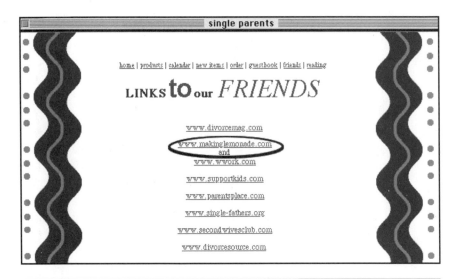

Figure 6.36. Reciprocal link, *http://www.mytwohomes.com/friends.htm.* Courtesy LadyBug Press.

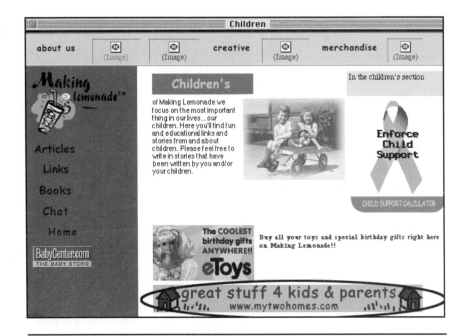

Figure 6.37. Reciprocal Link , *http://www.makinglemonade.com/ newchildren/children.htm.* © Making Lemonade.com 1997 Making Lemonade: The Single Parent Network.

To establish an individual reciprocal link, e-mail a request to the other business. Attach a digital logo, in case the other site will let you have something more elaborate than straight text for your link. You might generate some goodwill by creating a link to the other site's home page first. Try to find sites with more traffic than yours. Generally, a link from their home page is preferable to one from a page further down, but that will vary according to your needs, the structure of the other site, and the willingness of the site owner. You might want to direct the inbound half of the link to a page other than your home page, bringing visitors directly to relevant information based on the referring source.

Free link matchmaking services (also called banner exhanges) are available at many places such as *http://www.exchange-it.com* or *http://adnetwork.linkexchange.com* shown in Figure 6.38. You can

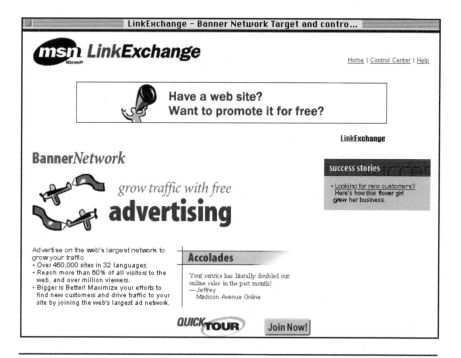

Figure 6.38. Link Exchange Service, *http://adnetwork.linkexchange.com/.* Screenshot reprinted by permission from Microsoft Corporation.

specify categories of sites that would be a good fit for your business, but will usually be asked to provide more links than you receive.

Outbound links to complementary, informative sites add value for your user. Think of linking to your business customers, subsidiaries, suppliers, reps, or manufacturers of products you carry. These links expand your virtual presence because the link title can be topical, using a keyword rather than the destination name. For instance, your veterinary hospital site might have a link reading "Learn more about hay and oats," instead of "Burley's Feedstore." The biggest disadvantage of outbound links is that users must know how to take advantage of the "back" function on their browser to return to your site.

Think strategically about how many links to include. You want to hold your visitors as long as possible. If you provide too many links early in your site, viewers may jump away and never return. Instead of placing links in context throughout a site, some organizations collect links on a page fairly far down in the site structure.

Finding **inbound** links is a matter of good Web research. The trick is to identify places where your target audience is likely to be found online and encourage them to link to you from those sites. (The same process will work for banner ads.) Certain types of sites are more likely to support an in-bound or one-way link link from their site to yours:

- Professional, business, and trade associations to which you, your company, or your target audience belong.

- Online sites for any magazine or other places where you advertise; often a link is included in advertising contracts for other media.

- Sites that offer directories of service providers or distributors.

- Web sites with search engines that provide Web company references and sources for their viewers (your audience), such as *http://www.abcparenting.com* in Figure 6.39.

- Home pages owned by satisfied clients or customers for whom you've provided service (e.g., Web designers often put a link from their clients' sites back to their own home page).

- News group announcement sites.

Some of these sites may charge a modest amount for a link, some may have a routine submission form, and some may need an individual e-mail contact. To track the status of all three types of link requests, you'll need another table in your Web notebook. Columns could include name of the site, URL, contact person, e-mail address, contact date, response date, and nature of the link. Add columns for verification that the link has been established, and regularly scheduled confirmations that the link (and the referral site) still exist. It's well worth the effort to get inbound links. Not only are links one of the most common ways for viewers to find new sites, they also increase your ranking on search engines.

Web Rings

Web rings (also called alliances) are multisite, reciprocal links connecting a group of sites, usually with similar content. Viewers click

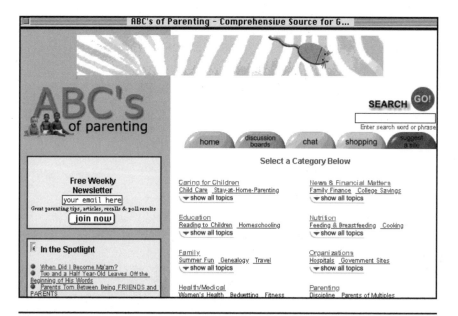

Figure 6.39. Links from a reference site, *http://www.abcparenting.com.* Courtesy Parenthood Web (*www.parenthoodweb.com*).

on a next, previous, random, or selected link to go to another site on the ring, eventually returning to their starting point. For an example, try the Women-Owned Business Web Ring, which is part of the wwwomen.com Web ring shown in Figure 6.40 (*http://www.wwwomen.com/webring.shtml*).

To join a ring, you copy HTML code provided by the ring onto your site. A **ringmaster,** who maintains the ring database, may review each application for inclusion. Some rings have specific criteria; others may consist solely of personal pages or might include a number of competitors. Check out all the sites on a ring before you join.

You can obtain a list of rings on the Web by going to a RingWorld directory at *http://www.owt.com/arts/webring/ringinfo.html* or Ring Managers at *http://www.webring.org/#ringworld* or *http://www.daytaless.com/webring/webring.shtml*. Of course, if the Star Wars, fashion, personal coach, or any of the hundreds of other rings don't meet your needs, you can always start a ring of your own.

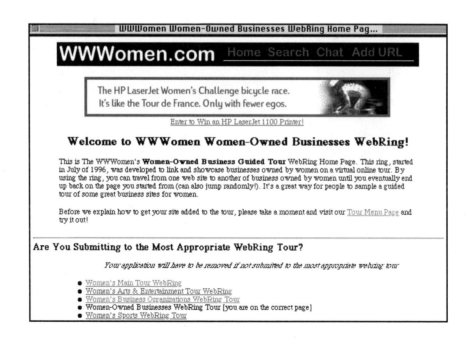

Figure 6.40. A Web ring, *http://www.wwwomen.com/webring_biz2.shtml*. Courtesy WWWomen, Inc.

Online Sponsorships

Sponsoring is similar to advertising, but it generally carries a lower price tag, a smaller link to your site, and lower placement on a page than a full advertisement. Sponsorships are more comparable to the corporate ads on public radio or TV than to the 30-second spots on daily soap operas. As with links, be sure the sites you sponsor are related to your field of business and that they draw your target audience. For example, look at the four linkable buttons from sponsors on *http://wwwomen.com,* which reserves the bottom of its pages for sponsorships. (See Figure 6.41).

Like advertisements, sponsorship rates are usually determined by a Web site's circulation and the number of impressions purchased. Sponsorships now account for about 30% of Web advertising purchases, compared to 53% for banner ads and 6% for interstitials.

If you are creative with your selection of sites, you may find ways to locate your target market at a low cost or perhaps establish a bar-

Figure 6.41. Linkable sponsor logos, *http://www.wwwomen.com.* An example of sponsorship buttons. These images reside at the bottom of wwwomen.com's pages. Courtesy WWWomen, Inc.

ter arrangement. For instance, a CD store in a college town might sponsor student sites around the country to reach its target market for world music.

Popular student-created sites might trade a sponsor ad in exchange for space on your server. (Student pages with heavy hit rates are often removed from university servers because they slow down the system.) You can find student sites by posting in news groups, advertising in college papers, or asking your part-time, student employees what sites are hot around campus. Students often put up highly creative sites, heavy in multimedia or pop culture. It's certainly easier to sponsor a student's e-zine than to create your own (unless it's your ordinary newsletter).

Consider sponsoring a not-for-profit site that's related to your business. For instance, a nursery specializing in native plants could sponsor some of the costs associated with a Web site for a local chapter of Tree People. A not-for-profit might agree to take a donation for every hit or registrant you receive from their site, instead of asking you to pay up front. Figure 6.42 shows a unique program at *GreaterGood.com* that allows not-for-profits dozens of shopping affiliate programs. GreaterGood splits the affiliate fees it receives with not-for-profits on its list or others you suggest.

Advertising on Other Sites

It's amazing how quickly the advertising industry has found ways to sell the Web audience as product. Both space and time have been carved up multiple ways, creating the online equivalent of every form of advertising and promotion that exists off-line: classifieds, display ads, event sponsorships, product placement in movies, and logos, logos everywhere. We'll look at both paid advertising and free banner ads, which are generally handled through an exchange service. Ads are really hyperlinks dressed up with graphics and other media to draw attention to the advertiser's message. Different ads may rotate in the same position on different content pages or rotate after a fixed time on a frame-based site.

Paid display advertisements on the Web, like the ones on the Internet Mall at *http://www.shopnow.com*, shown in Figure 6.43, generally take one of the forms shown in Figure 6.44. Sizes for ads have

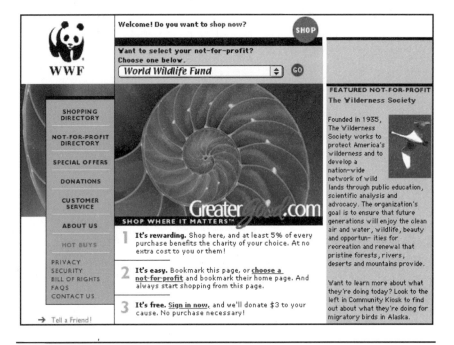

Figure 6.42. An interesting way to sponsor not-for-profits, *http://www. greatergood.com.* © Greatergood.com 1999.

begun to standardize, but they may vary from site to site. Most ads are supplied in GIF or JPEG format. Check both the size and format before you submit an ad.

Particular sites may have special advertising opportunities, such as a headline ad placed near the lead story on a newspaper site. Major advertising sites will have either a contact name and number or an online **media kit,** which usually includes online advertising rates, site demographics, ad dimensions, and graphics requirements. Most media kits spell out the submission process (ads can be placed on the site's server or called from yours), purchasing method, and special opportunities for media buyers.

If you carry brand items, see if the manufacturers will let you apply co-op marketing dollars (ad costs shared between the manufacturer and retailer) to online advertising. Manufacturers may require that their logos appear in your ad. You might also get them to

Figure 6.43.   Variety of dsplay ad sizes, *http://www.shopnow.com.* Courtesy ShopNowCom, Inc.

place a link from their site to yours, or pay you to place a link from your site to theirs.

Trends in Web Advertising

Surveys that track ad dollars show that advertisers are switching from print to online advertising, a category that didn't exist five years ago. Even some unlikely activities like political campaigns are shifting some of their ad spending from expensive television buys to much more reasonable banner ads on the Web. Online ad expenditures are not distributed evenly across all product categories, as Figure 6.45 shows.

Estimates of Web advertising revenues exceed $3 billion annually by the year 2000. As seen in Figure 6.46, that's a 50% increase from only $2 billion in 1998, $1 billion in 1997, and $37 million in 1995. By comparison, 1998 advertising expenditures on billboards were $1.5 billion.

Type	Description	Size in Pixels (if applicable)
Banner	most popular size; short, wide ad with link to advertiser's site	468 x 60, 460 x 55, 460 x60, 480 x 60
Box	a nearly square ad, with a link to the advertiser's site	125 x 125, 120 x 90
Display	usually quarter-, half-, or full-screen size, with a link to the advertiser's site; some full-screen ads appear between destination screens (interstitials)	
Ear	short banner, with a link to the advertiser's site, usually appears in a fixed corner position	120 x 60
Floating strip	medium size banner near bottom or middle of a page	392 x72
Logo	paid sponsorship with a link to the advertiser's site usually smaller and less expensive than a banner	
Mini	small, narrow banner, often just a boxed name	88 x 31
Nonlink	ad or sponsorship of any size without a link; less expensive than linked ads; often used for name recognition or brand imaging	

Figure 6.44. Typical online advertising sizes.

Predictions for advertising growth remain robust despite evidence that some Web users are tiring of commercial saturation. Internet Mate claims to have developed the Web equivalent of cable zappers to block ad windows, and one recent survey claimed 22% of Web users would pay extra to subscribe to sites without advertising. How many people would actually make such payments or buy such products remains to be seen. The majority of Internet users recognize that advertising is needed, to keep the content and many other online services free. For more information on advertising activities, check out the following sites.

- Online Advertising Index at *http://www.net creations.com/ipa/adindex.htm* tracks the rates requested by major sites accepting ads.

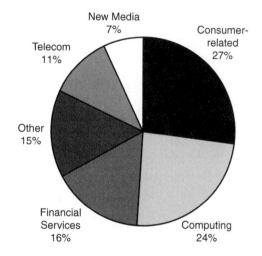

Figure 6.45. Top categories of online ad spending, *http://www.cyberatlas. com/segments/advertising/ad.index.html*. Reprinted with permission. ©1999 Internet.com, LCC. All rights reserved.

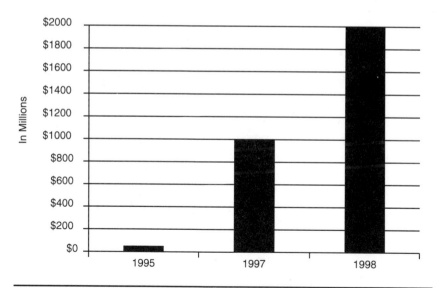

Figure 6.46. Estimated Web advertising revenue.

- WebTrack Information Services at *http://www.webtrack.com*, surveys how companies are placing their ads and what they pay.

- Ad Resource has an Ad Rate Guide at *http://www.adresource. com/html/new/rate.html* and offers an advertising primer at *http://www.adresource.com/html/new/adver tising_terminology.html*.

- The Online Advertising Report (OAR), issued quarterly by Adknowledge, provides useful information about advertising trends at *http://www.adknowledge.com/corporate/press/*.

- The Advertising section on Cyberatlas at *http:// cyberatlas. internet.com/segments/advertising/ad_index.html* offers multiple reports on ad rates and trends.

Online Advertising Rates

Web advertising on major sites, which can cost far more per month than Web design and hosting combined, is best used to reach a mass audience, promote well-known brands, or build name recognition. Given the sample ad rates seen in Figure 6.47, it's clear that advertising on such sites as portals, search engines, news organizations, and financial services is now a promotional playground only for rich corporations.

Only average rates are shown in this table. Many sites charge higher prices for premium location or offer different targeting options (e.g., appearance only when certain keywords are selected on a search engine). Others set a minimum on the number of impressions you must buy.

As you can see from the table in Figure 6.47, the more targeted the audience, the higher the CPM. Although a CPM rate may seem reasonable, the absolute cost on a major site is boggling. A portal site with 60 million visitors a week could easily guarantee 2 million impressions per month, costing over $40,000. E-mail newsletters are becoming a more attractive advertising venue given their relatively lower costs for space and the reasonable production cost of text ads. For a more complete table, go to *http://www.adresource. com/html/new/rate.html*.

Type of Site	Type of Count	#	(CPM/Month) Rate	$ Cost/Month
Newspaper	Impressions	<500K	$40	$20K
		>860K	$35	$30.1K
		>5M	$24	$120K
E-mail Newsletter	Impressions	<250K	$30	$7.5K
		>1M	$14	$14K
Search Engine/Portal	Run of Site*	<250K	$29	$7.25K
		>1M	$24	$24K
		>5M	$18	$90K
Financial News	Run of Site	<400K	$57	
		>1.2M	$51	$61.2K
Technology	Impressions	<250K	$70	$17.5K
		>1M	$56	$56K
Ad Network	Content Category	NA	$25	average
	Auto		$30	
	Entertainment		$20	
	News		$25	
	Sports		$20	
	Travel		$25	

*Run of Site (ROS): when an untargeted ad runs across the selected section and all other sections of the site that have available impressions

Figure 6.47. Sample online advertising rates in March 1999, *http://www. adresource.com/html/new/rate.html*. Reprinted with permission. ©1999 Internet.com, LCC. All rights reserved.

Ad agencies receive a 15% discount from these prices but pass along the full charge to you. Are ads worth this much, with average click-through rates down below 1%? That's obviously why some ad pricing is now based on click-throughs, with prices varying not only by site, but also by the nature of the audience drawn.

At an ad auction in late 1998, clicks sold for 20¢ each in the computers and technology category, but 16.2¢ for women's interest. Overall the average price for click-throughs at this auction was 10.6¢ per click. While the average price for click-throughs has been rising, the average online CPM (impression-based rates) has been dropping, down 6% between 1997 and 1998 to $35.13. This is partially due to an increased supply in ad space, as more sites seek advertisers.

If you decide to use paid advertising, set a dollar limit first, then decide how to distribute the funds. Keep your advertising expenses in line with the amount you spent on site development. It's not worth tens of thousands of dollars to promote a minimal site that visitors click away from because it lacks interest.

Even if your business exists only in cyberspace, don't spend all your advertising dollars on the Web. The 1998 Webcensus survey on *http://www.iconocast.com* in Figure 6.48 showed that Web users' time on the Internet exceeded time spent watching television, but still accounted for only one-third of their daily media exposure. Remember, the universe of Web users may not be identical to your universe of customers or other target audience.

Always test a handful of different ad locations to see which ones work best before you lock up your budget in long-term contracts. Ask for a 30-day trial. Remember, it may be cheaper to advertise on several smaller sites than on one premium site. Ten sites with 100,000 weekly hits each may cost less than one site with a million weekly hits, but yield the same total exposure with an audience better targeted to your needs. Look around for options. For instance, BannerWorks (*http://www.bannerworks.com*) sells ads for business

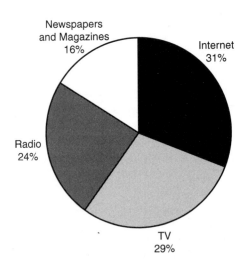

Figure 6.48. Web users' media time during the day, *http://www.iconocast .com/whatis/whatis.html.* Courtesy Iconocast.

audiences in packages as low as $75 for 10,000 impressions spread across multiple sites. Or negotiate your own ad with a site you'd really like to be on.

Once you've determined which places work, stay there, whether online or off-line: An advertising message repeated multiple times in one place is better than an ad that appears once in many places. You can change creative approach or content, but get viewers used to seeing your name in a particular location. Above all, don't overcommit your marketing resources to advertising; it isn't worth the anxiety. Do the best you can with what dollars you have available.

When making ad placement decisions, consider audience size, demographics, and CPM, as well as absolute cost. This is tough, because Web advertising can be priced by impressions (number of contacts to a site or page), exposures (ad files actually seen on a user's computer, i.e., the user didn't click away before the ad downloaded), or click-throughs (executed links to the advertiser's site). The following factors may affect the purchase price of an ad:

- Past history for the number of unique visitors to the site, hit rates on the page on which the ad appears, and/or number of click-throughs.

- Ad size, generally given in pixels.

- Placement on the screen.

- Frequency with which the ad runs. Most sites rotate ads in each screen location based on the relative number of impressions purchased. Ads are usually refreshed each time a page is requested, but some are now sold by fixed length of visible time. Confirm the length of time and the frequency with which your ad will appear.

- Specified time of appearance. You may want ads, such as those advertising a specific sitecast, to appear at a certain time or on a certain day. Late night placement might be available at a discount.

- The number of impressions, exposures, or click-throughs purchased.

- How many other advertisers share the same space.

- Demographics—usually the more targeted the audience, the higher the CPM.

In the end, sites charge what the market will bear. The ultimate proof of market pricing is an auction market for Internet advertising at sites like Adauction (*http://www.adauction.com*), shown in Figure 6.49). Some experts contend that banners are overpriced for what the advertiser receives. This may be true, given that many advertisers report negotiating significant reductions from published rate cards. It's worth a try.

How do you know whether you got what you paid for? Ask if the site is audited by an independent company like I/PRO (described in Chapter 5). I/PRO (*http://www.ipro.com*), which claims a 70% market share of audits, includes session length, daily statistics, compara-

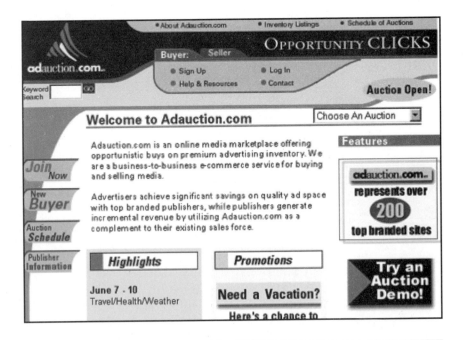

Figure 6.49. Advertising auction site, *http://www.adauction.com*. Courtesy Adauction.com.

tive reports, multimedia access counts, and site path analysis in its services. If you are planning to manage an extensive advertising campaign with multiple ads placed in multiple locations, you might want to purchase one of the very expensive software packages that tracks ad performance in real time. Accrue Software (*http://www.accrue.com*) and Straight Up! (*http://www.straightup.com*) track ads from impression to sale, so you can determine the cost of sale or cost of inquiry for each ad.

Try to avoid sites that count by ad hits or page hits, since that inflates the number of impressions. The number of unique visitors is apt to be lower than the number of impressions implies, since visitors may repeatedly visit the same site and often ask for more than one page of information. Or try using a service like *http://www.goto.com/d/about/advertisers* that charges only on click-throughs. Less-expensive ways to reach an audience include classified ads (discussed in Chapter 3), banner ad exchanges or a link from an electronic coupon site, such as *http://www.ecentives.com*. (Click on "partner stores" on that site for information about participating.)

Banner Ad Exchanges

Banner ad exchanges work like link exchanges. You register with the exchange, designating desired categories of sites, and provide your ad in the required format. Most banner exchange sites offer a 50% credit ratio: Your ad is placed once for every two ads from others that you display. You are usually required to place an ad near the top of a page. Check each exchange site listed in Figure 6.50 for details on ad size, credit ratio, and other services they offer. Credit ratios have become more competitive in the recent past. For a list of additional banner exchange services, go to *http://www.adresource.com*. To operate your own link partner program, check out ClickTrade at *http://www.clicktrade.com*.

Banner Ad Effectiveness

With click-through rates on ads now averaging less than 1%, it takes some effort to make a banner ad work for you. Give viewers a reason to click through to your site by providing an incentive in your ad: a

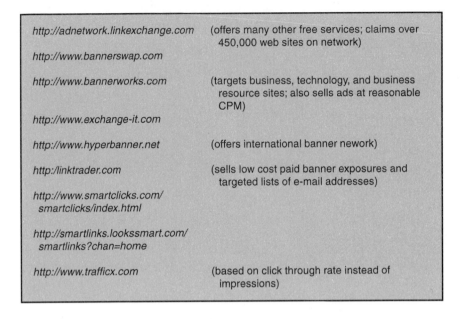

http://adnetwork.linkexchange.com	(offers many other free services; claims over 450,000 web sites on network)
http://www.bannerswap.com	
http://www.bannerworks.com	(targets business, technology, and business resource sites; also sells ads at reasonable CPM)
http://www.exchange-it.com	
http://www.hyperbanner.net	(offers international banner nework)
http://linktrader.com	(sells low cost paid banner exposures and targeted lists of e-mail addresses)
http://www.smartclicks.com/ smartclicks/index.html	
http://smartlinks.lookssmart.com/ smartlinks?chan=home	
http://www.trafficx.com	(based on click through rate instead of impressions)

Figure 6.50. Banner ad exchanges, *http://www.adresource.com*. Reprinted with permission. © 1999 Internet.com, LCC. All rights reserved.

call to action, a teaser, or a free offer. Banner ads also lose their punch after seven to ten viewings by the same user, so you may need to create multiple banners that are swapped on a regular basis.

Advertisers have found that **rich media** ads, those containing some type of animation, audio, video, or interactive programming, are more likely to generate click-throughs. Most rich media ads are done with HTML or Javascript.

At the high end of banner advertising, new technologies from companies like Narrative Communications (Enliven) or Thinking Media can be used to create **live banners**, which allow viewers to take action without clicking through to the advertiser's site. Besides being more expensive to develop, both rich media and live banners may download slowly on low-speed modems, clog heavily trafficked sites, or crash servers. (Not all places accept such ads, including AOL. Check first.) However, early results showing that rich media and live banners obtain much higher participation rates (10–30% click-throughs) have encouraged major advertisers to spend the extra dollars on development.

What can you do with a limited budget? Consider the responses to a recent Jupiter Communications survey shown in Figure 6.51. Let people viewing your banner ads know the benefits of clicking on your site. Tempt them with information, contests, awards, colorful graphics, and just plain fun.

If the purpose of your ad is brand imaging, the click-through rate is much less critical. Recent studies show that the immediate recall level for an online ad is about the same as that for a television ad. According to the research, 40% of those who view a static (non-click-through) online ad will remember it, compared to 41% who view a 30-second TV commercial. Since online advertising reaches an audience that is active and engaged, some might argue that online ads will ultimately prove even more effective at brand imaging than TV.

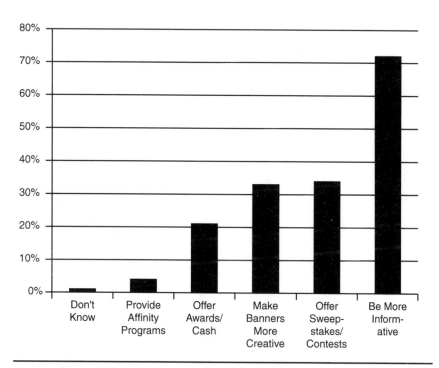

Figure 6.51. What makes users click more often? *http://www.iconocast.com/whatis/whatis.html.* Courtesy Iconocast, Inc.

The implications for your own advertising are obvious. First, if your concern is name recognition, less-expensive, nonlinking ads may be just as cost-effective as linkable ones. Second, standard brand-imaging techniques, such as logo reinforcement or repeating themes across advertising venues, can be effective on a static ad. Different techniques are required for a banner ad that generates a consumer click. Third, banner ads need strategic placement. For instance, image and message ads might be best on sites with huge audiences, while click-through ads appear on sites with more focused demographics. If you watch the ads being placed by major corporations or portal and search engine sites, you will see all these trends in action.

The top 10 banner ads for one week in May 1999, shown in Figure 6.52, represent a cross section of intriguing ads that encourage click-throughs or brand memory. The ads ranked 4th through 7th and the one ranked 9th are completely static. Numbers 2 and 3 use simple GIF animation to flash an element within the ad, while the others (1, 8 and 10) rotate several different banners for the same product in a planned sequence. Cyberatlas maintains archive files for each week's top banners at *http://209.249.142.16/nnpm/owa/ NRpublicreports.topbannerweekly*. It also displays the top 50 banner ads for the prior month.

Selling Advertising on Your Site

What if you want to reverse this process and sell advertising on your site? You're not alone. The number of sites accepting ads increased by 38% during 1998, with the fastest growth in ads coming among shopping/transaction and classifieds sites. Advertising is only a modest source of revenue for most sites as seen in a recent GVU survey (see Figure 6.53). If you're counting on major income, you'll need to plan a site that generates a great deal of traffic.

In preparation for selling ads, designate locations and sizes for ads in such a way that you can meet advertisers' demands for space **above the fold** (on the first half of the page so ads are visible before scrolling down) without disturbing the look of your site. Confirm the amount of traffic your site currently draws. Make sure you can obtain meaningful statistics from your WHISP. If its statistical package doesn't count unique users and requests for a specific file, supple-

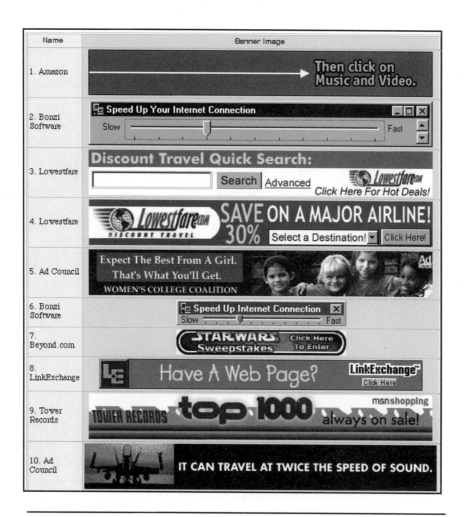

Figure 6.52.   Top banner ads, *http://209.249.142.16/nnpm/owa/
NRpublicreports.topbannerweekly.*   Courtesy Net Ratings, Inc.

ment your WHISP's statistics with WebTrends or some of the other
tools described in Chapter 5. Any demographic information from
user registration would help recruit advertisers.

Estimating charges for advertising on a small site is a bit tricky.
Start with a guesstimated CPM of $10 per month and adjust within a
$5 to $70 range based on your traffic and the specificity of your
demographics. If you're essentially a small local site, price yourself

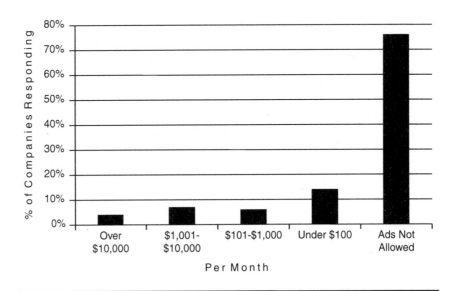

like one of the coupon advertisers, such as *http://www.nm coupons.com.*

You can research ad pricing information by e-mailing a request to similar, but noncompeting, sites that accept ads. Or try to do a brief survey of potential advertisers you've identified to see what they pay to advertise on other sites and what they pay (CPM) for other media. Set up a trial rate card (media kit) with the types, sizes, and prices of ads you are willing to sell. Unless you expect to be a truly major advertising link, don't worry about ad rotation. (Major ad servers use special software to rotate ads, track impressions, and change creative content for each advertiser on a regular basis.)

Assume that you will need to discount rates for early advertisers and for those who sign up for longer terms. Once you have an experience base and an established viewer rate, selling online advertising will be more straightforward. If the process of finding buyers for your ad space seems too daunting, list your site for free on WebConnect's W.I.S.E. database of sites that accept advertising at *http://www.webconnect.com*. WebConnect is one of the few "open network" agencies that will sell space on sites not owned by its clients. It will place ads on sites with relatively light traffic as long as the sites deliver their clients' target audience. By contrast, most big agencies look for sites drawing a minimum of 500,000 to one million impressions per month.

Congo's Money Maker at *http://www.globalserve.net/~bloemink/money/brokers.html* lists a number of other companies like Burst Media (*http://www.burstmedia.com*) or CyberLoft Hot Buttons (*http://www.cyberloft.com/buttons.html*) that promise similar efforts. To be sure these companies can successfully sell ads for your site, check with other clients before signing a long-term exclusive agreement. You could always try your own little ad auction on an open auction site like eBay.

Promoting Your Site Elsewhere on the Internet

In Chapter 3, we talked about using non-Web services on the Internet to promote your business. Use these same tools to promote recognition and repeat visits for your Web site.

News Groups

News groups and mailing lists offer a unique opportunity to reach a highly targeted, computer-savvy audience with information about your Web site. According to the GVU survey in October 1997, approximately 38% of users access news groups at least weekly, as seen in Figure 6.54. However, another 47% rarely or never access one, so make sure that your target market fits the news group profile. Females and people from 19 to 25 years old are the least likely to seek out a news group.

As we discussed in Chapter 3, moderating a news group, a forum on an online service, or a mailing list discussion provides an opportunity for you to leave your signature file and URL all over the place, but don't stop there. Some news groups and mailing lists now accept sponsors to defray the costs of maintenance and monitoring. Remem-

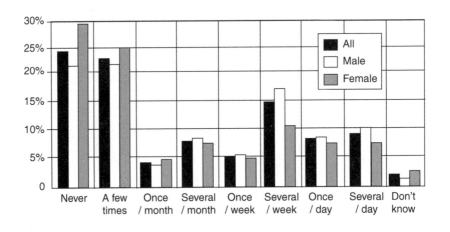

Figure 6.54. News group access by gender, *http://www.gvu.gatech.edu/ user_surveys/survery-1997-10/graphs/use/Newsgroups.html*. © 1994-1998 Georgia Tech Research Corporation. All rights reserved. Source: GVU's WWW User Survey at *www.gvu.gatech.edu/user_surveys*.

ber to follow the rules of Netiquette whenever you operate in this section of the Internet.

To find news groups that permit site announcements, check out the FAQ files of well-trafficked topical groups, such as

comp.internet.net.happenings

comp.infosys.www.announce

misc.news.inet.announce

Most moderated groups (e.g., misc.news.inet.announce) state that postings to the group are for new and revised Web site addresses only. Check the FAQ files if you are not sure. There are many regional, event-oriented, or industry-, company-, and product-specific news groups that might be appropriate, depending on the nature of your business. Search through the news groups on Liszt (*http:// www.liszt.com*) for names ending in .announce. Most of these sites allow you to post once for each unique URL.

Like What's New and Hot Site/Cool Link postings, news group announcements remain up for only a few days to a week. From a strategic point of view, spread out your announcements. Post to a different news group each week to increase traffic without overloading your server.

For this audience, your title, message, and form of announcement are all important. If you post a press release on one of these groups, try to include a photo, sound file, or video, unless the site accepts only text.

As mentioned in Chapter 4, news groups are a good place to recruit testers. Having tested your site, these viewers are likely to become repeat visitors because they have developed a "proprietary" interest in your site, and they'll want to see if you've implemented their suggestions.

Mailing Lists

Like news groups, some mailing lists now accept sponsors and Web announcements. The Internet Marketing Discussion List and news group, which supports itself with sponsorships, is a good one to try. To join this list, which has over 5,000 subscribers, go to *http://www.o-a.com*. It's a great list for companies that sell marketing-related products and services.

Use mailing lists selectively to promote your site. For instance, Online News, which has a number of readers in the press, is a good location to e-mail press releases. To subscribe, e-mail *major domo@marketplace.com*. In the body of your note, say subscribe online-news<your e-mail address>. Note that this mailing list does not accept ads, just press releases.

Promoting Your Site Off-Line

Take advantage of all existing off-line promotional methods to tell people about your Web site. Use the opportunity not only to provide your URL, but also to describe the benefits of visiting your site. You might tell customers "to see the flavor of the month," or "receive instant price quotes," or "place custom orders."

Coordinate Your Campaign

Use your current press release mailing lists, and advertise your new site on print, radio, and TV as your budget permits. Accept speaking engagements, attend conferences, run workshops. Take advantage of every opportunity to publicize your site. In addition to passively including your URL in an ad, consider creating ads specifically to increase awareness of your Web address. etown, an electronics distributor, tested its Web site promotion on billboards and radio. Although the print ads worked well, their best response was from radio. (*http://www.etown.com*) does a tantalizing job of this in its print ad seen in Figure 6.55. Its Web site appears in Figure 6.56.

Literature, Stationery, Packaging, and Promotional Items

Depending on your budget, you may want to update all your literature and stationery at once or replace the items as you run out. You may be able to add a designer-created label to existing brochures to draw attention to your Web site address. Order your next batch of giveaway pens printed with your URL as well as your company name, or send existing customers a small magnet or pad of stickies imprinted with it. One company, at *http://www.dotcomgear.com*, even specializes in labeling products like shirts and mouse pads with URLs.

Don't forget to update your packaging. Labels on everything from Quaker Oatmeal at *http://www.quakeroatmeal.com* and Michelob Beer at *http://www.hopnotes.com* now carry a URL along with a toll-free number for customer service.

Word-of-Mouth, Word-of-Net

Community efforts require more time than money, but the investment can pay off in goodwill and credibility. It doesn't have to be as expensive as a postseason college football game like the Insight.com Bowl sponsored by the discount computer software/hardware house or an extensive as the event program sponsored by Jelly Belly shown in Figure 6.57 (*http://www.jellybelly.com/events/html*). You could

Figure 6.55. eTown print ad. Courtesy etown.com: The Home Electronics Guide.

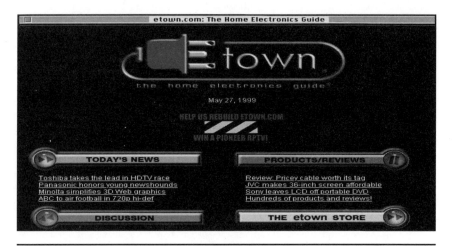

Figure 6.56. eTown Web site, *http://www,etown.com*. Courtesy eTown.com: The Home Electronics Guide.

Figure 6.57. Promoting special and community events, *http://www.jellybelly.com/events.html* ©1998 Herman Goelitz, Inc. All rights reserved.

sponsor several runners (or walkers) in a 10K race who agree to wear T-shirts with your company name and URL. The URL for your RV or powerboat Web site might work well on the back of shirts worn by a local bowling team.

If you deal in computer-related products, enlist in one of the many business-to-school partnerships. See if any of your employees, wearing that ubiquitous T-shirt with your URL, will volunteer for litter or graffiti cleanup campaigns. Doing good for others often does well for you.

We've now looked at all the major elements in creating, maintaining, and promoting a basic Web site. In the next chapter, we'll get fancy. We'll explore the trade-offs of incorporating multimedia—audio, video, animation, and 3D or virtual reality graphics—on your site.

7

Multimedia on Your Web Site

For many companies, a sign of successful marketing is return customer visits. On the Web, that translates to creating a site that attracts visitors—not just once, but repeatedly. This is often done by making the presentation exciting, attractive, and on the edge. To achieve these goals, more and more Web sites incorporate **multimedia,** the presentation of two- or three-dimensional graphics, animation, video, sound, real-time information feeds, and/or virtual reality simulations. This chapter will help you better understand

- The possibilities and limitations of multimedia technology on the Internet, so you can decide whether it is appropriate for your business

- Details about animation, audio, video, and virtual reality on the Web

- How to select a multimedia vendor

- What to expect from the multimedia design process

- How viewing sites rich in multimedia can stimulate your imagination

The Technology: Promise and Peril

A few multimedia options—simple animations and short audio files—now run automatically on browser software. More elaborate multimedia files can always be downloaded to a user's machine to be played back at any time. Assuming users have one of the newer computers that come with the built-in capability to play back certain types of stored video and audio, downloading for delayed playback is more straightforward than viewing multimedia as it is transmitted online.

Remember, though, that it can take a long time to download anything more than a short file. People may be reluctant to spend time downloading a long video clip they watch once and discard. Worse yet, they could end up resenting a business that requires this method to obtain information.

To view multimedia online, users must usually reconfigure their machines and install **plug-ins,** special pieces of playback software, into their browser. Most player plug-ins are compatible with the major browsers and can be downloaded free from the developer's site. (Plug-in developers make their money by selling or licensing the software designers use to create the media and/or the software that must be installed on host servers.)

Usually, it is straightforward to download and install plug-ins, but the process can be time-consuming and may deter a harried, casual, or inexperienced user. As new versions of browser and plug-in software are released, users may have to repeat this process. You must continually monitor multimedia on your site for compatibility with various combinations of new software versions. The most recent browsers for the newest machines already contain many of these plug-ins.

Streaming media, whether video or audio, play out as they are transmitted over the Internet to the user's computer. This is particularly valuable when files would be too big to fit into memory, when they would take an unacceptably long time to download, or when you want interactivity. By definition, you can't interact in real time with a downloaded file except to start, stop, fast-forward, or reverse it.

Streaming media may be played from files stored on a server, such as those at *http://www.virginrecords.com/index4.html,* or they may be real-time transmissions, such as a video teleconference or concert occurring at that very instant at *http://www.pluggedin.com.* In this case, multimedia is used not just as a teaser for another product, but to create a unique Internet-based form of entertainment.

The instant gratification of streaming media comes at a price. Most streaming media require fairly fast machines and modems to play well. Some sites combine the two forms of multimedia, using streaming media for instant previews of short file clips, so that viewers can decide whether they want to invest their time in a download.

Limitations

Several things contribute to the agonizingly slow delivery of full multimedia online: low-speed modems, the number of people online at any one time, and the limitations of telephone **bandwidth** (how much information can be transmitted). If you think of optical fiber or television cable as a water main, the bandwidth of a telephone line is that of a garden hose. As discussed in Chapter 1, means of Internet access remain in flux, varying by geographic region and demographics. No one knows what the configuration will be three months from now, let alone three years. For now, bandwidth constraints limit the size and scope of multimedia on the Internet.

Hardware Requirements for Client and Server

Compared to static sites, multimedia sites require that your users have more memory, faster processors, more recent browsers and system software, and better skills. To play multimedia, your customers should have at a minimum a 28.8 modem and a PC that runs at least Windows 95 with a Pentium- or Celeron-equivalent processor (e.g., the Advanced Micro Devices K6-2). PC servers require a minimum of Windows NT on a high-end Pentium. Macintosh users should have a minimum of System 7.1 on a Quadra or Performa; a Macintosh server must be at least a PowerMac running System 8.

Users' online speeds may range from minimal to state-of-the-art. Some users will be on T1 lines; others may access a commercial service such as AOL with a 14.4 Kbps modem. These users will have a variety of browsers in a variety of versions with who knows what plug-ins. As you design your Web site, you must consider the importance of providing an alternative for users who lack adequate hardware and software for multimedia displays.

Staying Up-to-Date

Print magazines such as *Internet World, Small Business Computing & Communications, Hyperstand: New Media Magazine, Red Herring*, and *Wired* will keep you informed of changes in Internet and multimedia technologies. Check also the Multimedia listings found in Appendix A.

Making the Multimedia Decision

Multimedia technology beckons, dangling juicy grapes of streaming audio, real-time video, and three-dimensional animation on the Internet vine. One of the hardest lessons to learn in any design project, however, is that just because it can be done, doesn't mean it should be done.

Ask yourself always whether multimedia will enhance the communication goals for your site. Some companies add multimedia to their site simply because everyone else is doing it, because it's "in," or because their competitors have it. They haven't got a clue whether it makes sense for them.

Will it be easy for your target audience to download and/or play back? Think realistically about your target audience. Are they experienced Web surfers, or are they consumers at home with less than ideal equipment? Aim to provide the best quality for your average user at the time you post your site. As the installed base of higher-end machines, modems, and transmission lines increases, you will be able to increase the length and density of multimedia information on your site.

Can you assemble the technical and financial resources to produce multimedia? You've already seen that developing a good site, beyond a simple home page, can be a complex and expensive process. Multimedia only compounds the complexity and expense. You can spend tens of thousands of dollars developing an extravagant multimedia site that the majority of users either can't see or will view at a much lower quality than you intend. Unless you sell to very high-end customers, don't get too fancy.

Plans to incorporate multimedia may also affect your selection of a Web hosting service, Web designer, and network administrator. You should modify the checklists in Chapter 4 to include questions about their experience, services, and skills in all these areas. Later in this chapter we'll discuss how to select appropriate multimedia subcontractors.

Know Your Business

Given the current limitations and problems, are there any reasons to use multimedia? To find the answer, look to your business. Go back to the business and site plans in Chapters 2 and 4. What are you trying to do? Are you creating a new site or adding multimedia capabilities, such as streaming video or audio, to an existing one? Are you updating a current media module, perhaps adding downloadable video of a newly scheduled bicycle tour through southern France to clips of other packaged tours on your Wheels Away travel site?

Sound, video, and animation appeal to users' different learning styles. Their novelty makes them marvelous attention-getters. For some applications, they bring immediacy and importance. For others, such as an Internet broadcast from shuttle astronauts to junior high school students, a multimedia teleconference may be not only a good technical solution, but also a cost-effective one. It all goes back to what you are trying to accomplish.

Does your Web site inform? Are you trying to pointcast (send requested information to specific users), to deliver rapidly changing material, such as commodity prices for cattle or copper, or to access a virtual reality tour of a wildlife reserve?

Does your site sell? Do you want users to buy a book or bouquet, a music video, a carton of ladybugs, a loaf of bread, a jug of wine, or thou? Do you want real-life adventurers to model your Indiana Jones hats on an Egyptian archeology site? Or to have a virtual community of inline skaters tout the virtues of active brake technology on the roller blades you sell?

If you're running a stock footage or sound effects library online, then, of course, having streaming clips for preview makes sense (as does downloading purchased ones). If you are building an audience for a new jazz artist, then a real-time, streaming Web broadcast can be an excellent element in a larger media campaign. Multimedia makes sense if your site is designed to promote your corporate identity as an innovative Web designer or to entertain.

Before you decide to implement any multimedia elements, go through the installation process for plug-ins yourself and test the multimedia experience on some of the sites in this chapter or on others. Play with these technologies to enhance your personal home page. Amuse your spouse or friends; astound your employees; impress the opposite or same sex; but think carefully about what multimedia will add to your business site that a simpler representation cannot.

Would downloaded audio be more appropriate than streaming audio for President Nixon's infamous tape recordings when they are released for broadcast after the year 2000? (Now you can listen to them only on audiocassette at the National Archives.) Would a series of photographs suffice instead of video for a travelogue? Would videotape be as useful as one-way video over the Internet? If the information is not time-critical, tape is easier, and when something is easier, it will be cheaper.

As with your overall plan for going on the Web, you should be able to state your multimedia goal succinctly, preferably in one sentence. If you can't, perhaps there isn't a good reason for using multimedia.

Know Your Objectives

Just as you did with your overall site, decide what specific objectives should be measured to show the effectiveness of the multimedia component. Try to quantify objectives within a set time so you can see if an objective is approaching the desired range, or if success wanes after a while. Remember to measure visits to your multimedia pages, or sales initiated from them, independent of total hits or sales on the site. Here's an example of goals and objectives for the multimedia component of a Web site.

> *The goal for the multimedia pages of the fictional Wild Geesers' Web site is to increase support for an endowment fund that will protect wetlands for the annual migration of Canadian geese and sandhill cranes. Specific objectives for the multimedia component of the site are to:*
>
> * *Obtain memberships from 10% of those who access the video of this year's migration, every month after the first.*

- *Double the percentage of multimedia page visitors who register at the site compared to those who enroll from non-multimedia pages in a similar period. (Registrants will receive future direct mail and e-mail fundraising campaigns.)*

- *Within the first six months obtain donations of over $100 from at least 5% of those who sign up for basic membership after visiting the site.*

- *By the fourth month after launch, reach a target of $8,000/month in sales of sound and video merchandise demonstrated on the multimedia site. Demo items include bird whistles, cassettes and CDs of birdcalls, the Audubon Society bird clock, and videotapes of wild geese, national wildlife refuges, and the whooping cranes who migrated after imprinting on an ultra-light aircraft.*

Know Your Audience

To ensure the success of your multimedia design, compare the profile of expected users with that of your target audience. Will multimedia draw new customers or merely window-shoppers? Will their profile differ from that of your current viewers?

Consider the differences between the media-savvy, Internet-experienced readers of Wired magazine and the older, more conservative readers of *Reader's Digest.* You would write in two different styles for the two audiences, you might include quite different content, and your audience would attract very different advertisers. The same is true for the multimedia component of your Web site.

Casual surfers using the Internet for recreation often cruise for entertainment sites. If they have a passion for reggae music, for instance, they will seek multiple sites with audio clips, musician interviews, music videos, and live events. They forgive content duplication as long as the experience is enjoyable. Such visitors will compare and contrast their site experiences, with high expectations for new content, glorious graphics, and quality multimedia. If a site doesn't satisfy them or is difficult to manage, they will quickly click to another.

Be sure to offer instruction on the plug-ins users will need and incorporate hyperlinks to their source. If possible, mirror the plug-ins so that users can download them without leaving your site.

Before we consider how to produce multimedia, let's look at a site that belies the idea that moving images attract more interest than static ones. Commercial photographer Michel Tcherevkoff presents extraordinary images in Figure 7.1 (*http://www.pdn-ix.com/MasterMichel/08barfish.html*). The asymmetrical layout and custom typography give this page a sense of motion and energy. Notice the heightened contrast obtained by using saturated color (it's

Figure 7.1. Design without multimedia, *http://www.pdn-pix.com/Master Michel/08barfish.html*. Photo © Michel Tcherevkoff.

mustard yellow on the sides and white in the middle). Consider the function of the empty space (designers call this negative space) on the right of the glass; it frames the image just as much as the colored border does. This page would be much less powerful if it had any clutter. Check out this site for other, equally powerful images.

Multimedia Development Tools and Techniques

A wide array of multimedia options are available. The following sections describe a few of the more popular selections.

Real-Time Animation: GIF, Shockwave, and Java Applets

Most browsers now run simple two-dimensional GIF animations, without any special plug-ins, as soon as they appear on-screen. GIFs download quickly, although they are limited in size and scope. **Sprites**, static GIF images that can be juxtaposed to provide the illusion of animation, can be created by your Web designer or found for free at

http://www.beseen.com/beseen/free/

http://users.atnet.net/~mlosborn/

http://www.top100.net/Animations.htm

Shockwave, a free plug-in for Macs and PCs from Macromedia at *http://www.macromedia.com/shockwave* (see Figure 7.2) is included in recent versions of popular browsers. Shockwave, which claims over 30 million users, plays animation created with Macromedia's popular program, Director. A developer creates an animation file with graphics and sound files in Director, converts it to a Web-compatible format with Afterburner, and installs it in an HTML document. You can view a number of "shocked" sites or submit your own by pointing your browser to *http://www.macromedia.com/shockzone/ssod*, *http://www.macromedia.com/softwareflashguide* or *http://realguide. real.com*.

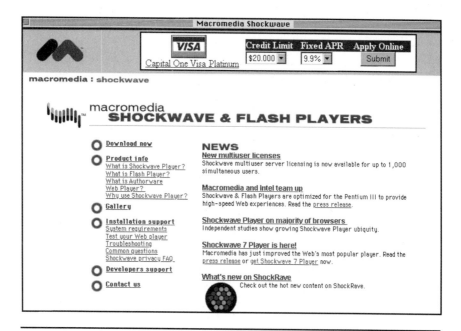

Figure 7.2.   Macromedia homepage for Shockwave, *http:www. macromedia.com/ shockwave* © 1999 Macromedia, Inc. All rights reserved. Used with permission.

Shockwave requires no expensive server software, just a few configuration changes that can be made by a network administrator. It is particularly useful for animating banners, logos, and simple objects. From the users' perspective, shocked files play automatically once the plug-in is installed. The only concern is that the version of the player usually must be at least as recent as the version used to create the animation. Users may have to wait for the animation to play while the site downloads to the user's system.

Java is a platform-independent programming language developed by Sun Microsystems (*http://java.sun.com*). Your Web programmer can create small application programs called applets to play animations, animate graphics, or generate interactive sequences. If the user's browser accepts Java, the applet is downloaded to the user's machine to perform its task. It's fairly safe to use Java on your site; some 76 percent of users had Java-enabled browsers by the end of 1998, compared to only 49% in 1997.

Downloaded Audio

Sound can add texture, depth, and personality to your site, as well as distracting users while images are downloading. MIDI, WAV, and Java applet files are downloadable audio file formats. Best used for short audio clips, simple tunes, and sound effects, these files may trade a fair amount of distortion, clipping, and dropouts in exchange for fast downloading. They can download automatically or on request, often appearing in a small window with a scroll bar. Sometimes the files play automatically (the sound can always be stopped); sometimes it is up to the user to decide whether to play them. Although bypassing the need for additional plug-ins, the need to request "play" makes the Web experience less immediate and interactive.

To hear an example of downloaded sound, try the moving audio narrative at *http://www.startribune.com/aids* or select a musical accompaniment to a greeting card at *http://www.marlo.com/card/*. Free sound effects clips are available at Sound America at *http://soundamerica.com.*

A much higher caliber form of downloadable audio, called MP3, debuted in 1998. MP3 technology uses a new file compression technique that allows users to download CD-quality sound off the Internet, compress it for storage in a small file (1/10 the size of a comparable WAV file), and play it back afterward. The drawback is that users need special player software, such as Winamp, which is also available for free on the Web at sites like Atomic Pop (*http://www.atomicpop.com*) or *http://www.mp3.com/software*. Some MP3 players, like Liquid Audio's, are not free.

The site *http://www.mp3.co*m, which registers some 200,000 visitors a day, has 10,000 licensed music titles to download, along with instructions. GoodNoise at *http://www.goodnoise.com* offers a similar list, as well as tracks for sale from the RykodiscUS catalog.

Additional software called a ripper allows users to transfer audio files from CDs to a computer, while an encoder converts CD format to MP3 so that an MP3 player can read it. (Winamp players, rippers, and encoders are all available at the *mp3.com* site.) Together with a

CD-ROM burner, these technologies allow users to create their own compact disks, mixing music in MP3 format from both recorded and Web sources.

Portable MP3 devices, such as RioPort by Diamond Multimedia Systems (*http://www.rioport.co*m), are available for about $200 at major computer and electronics stores. These devices, which can both record and playback on rewritable 60-minute disks, allow users to enjoy their MP3 files untethered from a computer. In an attempt to reduce music piracy from "serial" copies, the Rio player allows only one recording of a digital audio file.

The combined suite of MP3 technologies has thrown the music industry into a panic over potential copyright and piracy issues. The industry launched the Secure Digital Music Initiative which announced standards for security features to prevent piracy in Spring 1999; equipment complying with these standards will be available by Fall 1999. Microsoft is also trying to push its way into the music arena with its own audio compression/security technology.

At the same time, MP3 technology promises to revolutionize the way music is sold, with some forecasters estimating that the Internet will account for more than half of all music sold within 5 years. If you plan to use any MP3 files commercially on your Web site or off it, be sure to use only music in the public domain or pay a fee for copyright permission.

Streaming Audio

Streaming audio lets users listen to sound files as they are transmitted over the Internet. It can be used for long-playing radio dramas, such as those on the Seeing Ear Theater of the SciFi Channel at *http://www.scifi.com/se*t (Figure 7.3), or for radio stations that offer over-the-Web, real-time broadcasting. For example, listen to KOB FM in New Mexico at *http://www.kobfm.nmsource.com* or to other stations listed at *http://www.broadcast.com* or *http://www.radio-directory.com*.

RealAudio from RealNetworks (*http://www.realaudio.com*), the first well-received streaming audio product, has registered some 50 million users since its release in 1995. Free plug-ins for both Mac and Windows are available, but the server software, which comes with

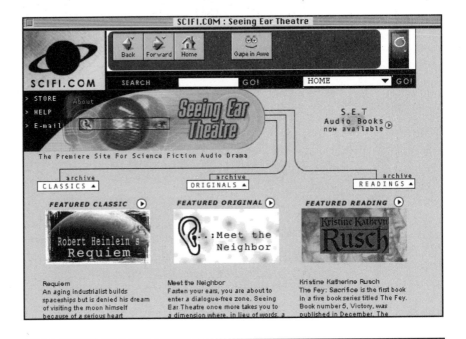

Figure 7.3. Streaming audio site, *http://www.scifi.com/set/*. Courtesy USA Networks.

audio development tools, is fairly expensive. Only some Web hosting services include support for RealAudio or RealVideo in their service packages. If you're planning to use streaming media, be sure to check.

As an alternative that requires no plug-ins, some producers use QuickTime audio files. Consider what kind of audio you will be transmitting and what equipment your desired users are likely to have. A 14.4 Kbps modem may suffice for listening to speech or sound effects, but 28.8 Kbps offers much better quality for music.

Downloaded Video

Apple's QuickTime for Macs and PCs and Microsoft's Video for Windows (AVI) allow you to create and play back multimedia, including audio, video, and animation. To develop a QuickTime or AVI file, you start with footage from a digital video camera and then add captions, banners, special effects, and sound. The latest developer's versions of QuickTime may be found at *http://quicktime.apple.com*. AVI is at *http://www.shareware.com*.

QT and AVI play after a download is completed. They look and sound as good once they are stored on a hard drive as they would if a user copied them from a CD-ROM. Most Macs come with QuickTime players installed, and most multimedia PCs include AVI. These movie players can also be downloaded at the sites mentioned earlier.

Streaming Video

One of several streaming video products is VDOLive from VDOnet Corporation (*http://www.vdo.net/default.asp*) as seen in Figure 7.4. Like RealAudio, plug-in players for VDOLive are available free for both Windows and Macs. VDOLive has an installed base of 15 million players and was integrated into Internet Explorer 4.0 in 1998.

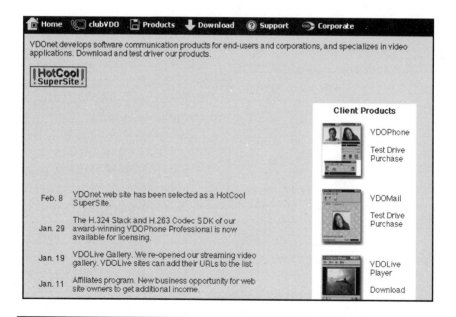

Figure 7.4. VDO homepage for streaming video, *http://www.vdo.net/ default.asp*. Courtesy VDOnet Corp.

You have two choices for implementation. One option, assuming you already have adequate hardware, is to license server software and development tools. The cost ranges from $1,500 plus $400 in annual support for 25 **streams** (simultaneous users) of 64 Kbps video to $10,000 plus $1,500 in annual support for 100 streams of higher-quality 512 Kbps video. The other option is to use VDOnet's new on-demand service, VideoDome Video NOW!, which allows you to submit VHS or Beta source footage. VideoDome will encode it and host the results on their server with a link from your site, starting at $30 per month for the first five minutes. Check their Web site for more details, including a VDOLive Gallery to which you can add your URL.

. VDOnet offers a free trial version to test streaming a maximum of 25 clips. If you are thinking about using streaming video, this is a good way to assess both the development process and viewer response. You will need to FTP the file from *ftp://ftp.videodome.com*. Enter the user name vdometrial (all lower case), and the password VDOLiveTrial or cdtrial (both are case-sensitive.) For download prices, contact VDO through *http://www.vdo.net/store/* or *http://www.videodome.com/*. Alternately, look at RealVideo (*http://www.real.com*).

Apple's QuickTimeTV is a potentially inexpensive alternative that combines downloading and streaming. Hoping for a compromise between download time and high-quality video, Apple plans a QuickTime plug-in that will start to play as soon as enough of a QuickTime movie is received. For more information on the status of this plug-in, go to *http://quicktime.apple.com*. For a peek at a QuickTime video, check out the Gallery section of *http://www. surfermag.com*.

Here are a couple of video hints, regardless of the format you use. Due to bandwidth restrictions, compression, and slow download time, video over the Internet displays in only a small portion of the screen and can appear jerky and disjointed. With clever design, you can integrate the screen width into the overall look of your Web page, perhaps even camouflaging the rectangular image and orientation.

Keep your video segments as short as possible. Treat them as live action video, cutting between several camera angles or images if appropriate. If you use on-screen talent, look for an actor with theatrical training and shoot for intimacy, as if he or she is speaking to the user one-on-one.

3D/Virtual Reality

Virtual reality (VR) refers to technology that simulates the experience of moving in space, adding drama and immediacy to an interactive experience. VR has proved particularly useful for showing models on sites for realtors, architects, and general contractors. (See the Bamboo.com site in Figure 7.5 at *http://www.jutvision. com/take_a_tour*). Realty sites typically offer three-dimensional rep-

Figure 7.5. QTVR house tour, *http://www.jutvision.com/take_a_tour/.*
© bamboo.com, Inc. All rights reserved. "bamboo.com logo are trademarks and service marks of bamboo.com, Inc."

resentations of rooms, houses, industrial buildings, or even castles. The many other applications are limited only by your imagination. If you sell games, entertainment products, travel, or unique objects enhanced by a tactile experience, VR may substantially enhance your marketing efforts.

Several different technologies are available. They use different techniques, produce a different experience for the user, and differ in costs. Whichever technology you select, producing virtual reality sites is best left to experienced engineers.

3D/VRML (Virtual Reality Markup Language). VRML offers an unusually compact form of data that can be transmitted more quickly than most video and animation. In this method images, usually of an abstract environment, are **rendered on the fly,** as the user points a cursor at different places. As you can see from the virtual reality mall in Figure 7.6 (*http://www.vr-mall.com/index3.html*), the images aren't very detailed. However, VRML offers more freedom, more flexibility, and faster playback times than QuickTime VR. Viewers need to download a plug-in to view VRML scenes.

General Motors uses VRML for a virtual tour of the model for its new corporate headquarters at *http://www.gm.com/about/info/overview/vrml.html*. Or check out the Cool Worlds page at Live3D

Figure 7.6. VRML house, *http://www.vr-mall.com/index3.html*. Courtesy Virtual Reality Mall.

(*http://www.home.se.netscape.com/su/eng/liv3d/index_v.html*) for some VRML fun.

QuickTime Virtual Reality (QTVR). QTVR provides a panoramic 180 or 360 degree view of anything from chairs to rooms, from parks to cities. San Diego Gas & Electric (*http://www.sdge.com/*) uses QTVR to take students on a tour of a power plant generator.

In QTVR a series of 12 static photos are patched together to create a 360 degree cylinder. Each 12-shot view is called a **node.** As users "turn" in a circle, they "see" the views around them. Alternately, QTVR can provide the sensation of the viewer standing still and the object rotating, as if the viewer were turning it over to see it from different angles. Simpler to create and more detailed than VRML, QTVR is also less expensive, averaging from $300 to $500 per node, depending on the number of nodes, although some vendors run as low as $150 or as high as $1000.

Prices for QTVR created with video are all over the block, depending on the particular technology involved. For instance, a higher-quality image created with Surround Video, which loads faster than regular QTVR and can be sized for larger viewing, costs $1,000 to $1,500 per page. Some companies enhance the images with PhotoShop postproduction.

At the other end of the scale, Bamboo.com *(http://www.jut vision.com)* offers quick-shots for realtors and construction companies. They use a nationwide network of video stringers who upload digital video to the Bamboo.com server. Within three days of receiving an order, Bamboo.com creates a set of four QTVR scenes for $99 and posts the results to one Web site. They offer the option of hosting the VR on their server, opening it with a link from your site. (For an example, go to *http://www.realty.com* or *http://www.royallepage.ca* and click on Virtual Reality.) Rimini Virtual Tours offers the opportunity to contrast VRML and QTVR at *http://www.iper.net/rimini-vrml* in Figure 7.7.

Remember that these VR technologies are not compatible with each other. A plug-in can play only files created with its corresponding development and/or server software. For more information and to obtain multimedia plug-ins, visit Netscape Software Depot at *http://www.software-depot.netscape.com/plugins/index.htmlcp+hom 03wplg*, or CNet at *http://www.cnet.com/Content/Reviews/Compare*/Plugin. You can also go to *http://www.plugins.com* or search Yahoo! for plug-ins.

Figure 7.7.   Virtual reality alternatives, *http://www.iper.net/rimini-vrml.* Courtesy IPER-NET.

Multimedia: Not a Do-It-Yourself Project

Professionals are best to handle all but the simplest multimedia. The dividing line is the sophistication of what you are trying to do; your budget, time, talent, and equipment; and the knowledge base of your staff. Before you begin, make a standard business decision: Is the money you would save worth the effort of doing it yourself?

Depending on your location and what you need, expect to spend $75 to $150 an hour for various multimedia services. As an alternate rule of thumb, budget $1,000 per minute of multimedia run time. Compare this to the $100 to $300 per page you would expect to pay for static pages on a Web site.

Establish a development team that includes both employees and the outside contractors, agency, Web designer, and multimedia developers you hire. You and/or your staff will need to participate in design, approval, monitoring, and maintenance of the multimedia pages, just as you do with the rest of your site. Be sure to include your director of Management Information Systems and your Webmaster, system administrator, or whoever will be responsible for installing multimedia elements on your server. This person will assess how much storage space will be needed, and whether increased traffic will affect communications requirements. He or she will also need to license and install the server side of plug-ins, if they are not already present.

Selecting a Contractor

Depending on your multimedia design, you may need a producer, content expert, HTML and/or Java programmer, graphic artist, photographer, audio engineer, videographer, or animator. Never hire any contractor until and unless you have seen some of their prior work. Check out the style of their work online as well as their references! This is just common sense. Certain production houses develop particular styles and specialties. You need to find a company that can do the job within your budget.

Multimedia professionals know the reputations of other specialists to hire, if necessary, saving you the hassle of locating everyone from a sound engineer to an illustrator. As a business owner, you might have a hard time knowing which of several competing plug-ins to implement, but professionals keep abreast of this rapidly changing world. They should select plug-ins and development software only from major companies, avoiding any beta software or "buggy" 1.0 releases. It's too expensive in time and money to redo your site if a product goes off the market, or to reach only a few insiders—unless, of course, that's your business base.

Evaluating a Contractor's Work

Multimedia designers have far more familiarity than nonexperts do with various creative formats, but you know your business better than anyone else. Here are some hints for evaluating the work you're shown in a contractor's portfolio or as part of the approval cycle for your own project. Just as you might rotate a lovely jewel to look at it from all angles, consider the results from four different perspectives.

1. *A design in two-dimensional space.* This is the familiar design problem of a static Web site, dealing with icons, typography, layout, and graphics.

2. *A design in time.* Users experience your site as a random sequence of pages and multimedia experiences. The concept of time applies not only to how your events flow through time, but also to how the user experiences elapsed time with downloaded or streaming media.

3. *A user-centric design.* Consider the point of view of a user coming to the multimedia elements for the first time. Try to erase your own knowledge. Imagine instead how users might cope with everything from installing plug-ins to an interrupted download.

4. *An element-centric design.* Each multimedia event is based on its own esthetics. Audio, video, and animation have distinct design vocabularies, criteria, and internal values. Try to look at each element independently, as well as how it works with all the other elements. Consistent? Repetitious? Complicated? Entertaining? Informative? Fun?

As you evaluate the design from each perspective, hold it up to the light of your goal and audience profile. Make sure your multimedia elements will serve your business purpose and meet your audience's needs. A word of warning, nothing in multimedia is ever simple. Creative projects generally cost twice as much and take twice as long as expected.

Multimedia Development Process

The pre-production steps described next are particularly critical in large projects, with multiple people on the development team. The larger the team, the more frequently you must ensure that they share your vision of what the multimedia elements will accomplish and how they will appear.

Don't be surprised to find that preproduction takes half the time allotted for your multimedia development. The better planned the project is, the more likely it is that it will be carried out within the time frame and budget allowed. A reasonable preproduction period provides time to watch for red flags (you can never find them all!) and allows for several cycles of review, changes, and approval.

The Treatment

Like an executive summary, a multimedia treatment provides a brief, high-level overview of the project. It should enumerate the goal and objectives, briefly describe each element, and specify how the project will be accomplished, in what time frame, and at what cost.

The Flowchart

The multimedia producer or Web site designer should create an abstract flowchart that shows how multimedia will be integrated with the rest of your site. The flowchart displays how viewers will enter and leave multimedia elements, as well as how they will move among them.

This exercise forces you to consider navigational issues. Do you want viewers to go first to a splash page that specifies site requirements? Can they link directly to your multimedia page from another site? How and when are viewers made aware of non-multimedia options or of downloaded versus streaming alternatives? Will there be an on-screen distracter while the media is loading? Who will create the alternative "lite" site, and how will it be reached? Are you providing links or mirrors for plug-ins?

The flowchart also helps your Webmaster design appropriate page layouts for downloaded and streaming media. It is important that visitors understand what they are doing, the size of the files they will download, and how long that process will take.

The Storyboard

Storyboards are a handy way to visualize the look and feel of multimedia for a Web site page by page or image by image. A storyboard shows images in the sequence they will appear after editing or assembly, not in the sequence they are produced. Visual thinkers often use a storyboard as part of the brainstorming process, producing the equivalent of a word outline in pictures.

Some Web producers prefer to storyboard early; others do them after a script is developed. Sometimes they do both: quick sketches of the overall site and detailed storyboards for animation or video. In the latter case, storyboards may indicate accompanying audio or text, if any, below the sketch.

In an agency or contractor relationship, the client usually receives several preliminary storyboards to chose from. These may show different layout styles, typography, colors, icon details, or navigational structures.

The Script

Your multimedia producer will ask you to approve the final script before she or he starts production. A script provides essential cohesion for multimedia elements, especially when the project calls for a variety of subcontractors, one doing animation, another doing video, and another doing audio. A script ensures that everyone literally sings from the same songbook. A script

- Provides precise audio narration or dialog, on-screen text, music, and special effects

- Anchors audio and text to a specific visual

- Indicates runtime

Estimates for costs and production time frames will be based on how many minutes or seconds an element is expected to run in real time. The timeline column also provides the relative time taken for each scene within the element.

Figure 7.8 shows a partial script for a downloadable video clip to be shot for a multimedia Web site. Note the Time column on the left. Location and talent are marked at the beginning of each scene, and the speaker is identified within the narrative column. This particular script includes an optional separate column for on-screen text.

Some producers use storyboard-like sketches instead of text within the Visual column of a script. They can then resequence the Visual column by similar scenes instead of time in order to create a shot list.

The Production and Testing Process

All the steps that went into the development and testing of static Web pages in Chapter 4 must be duplicated for multimedia elements. In particular, your producer should ensure that multimedia files will run on a variety of browsers and on a variety of machines. The network administrator or Webmaster will also want to test server software and plug-in installation. Test your site on a local area network, on an intranet, or in a secure portion of your Web site with limited access before posting it for all to see.

Once you have technical tests worked out, test the multimedia elements with real users. This allows you to discover whether directions are clear and navigation is easy. You can see whether users are frustrated or attempt to do things you didn't anticipate. Only when this process is complete are you truly ready to launch.

Surfing for Ideas

Check out the sites that follow for both appearance and operation from the user's point of view. Analyze them from your business's perspective as well. How can you adapt these ideas to suit your needs? Can you work your way backward to a statement of goals, audience definition, and objectives for each of these sites? Many of these multimedia-intensive sites are run by large companies with big budgets—

SCRIPT FOR: <u>Eating Well Website (diabetes education)</u>   Date: <u>8/2/96</u>
PAGE: <u>Chicken Mole Novela (streaming video) and interactive game</u>
TALENT: <u>Tia Tina and Maria; Narrator (audio only)</u>
LOCATION: <u>Dining Room</u>

Time	Visual	Audio	On-screen Text
0 00	Dining table set for big meal. Med. wide shot Tina serving large portion of food to Maria, sitting down	T: What's the matter? Don't you like my chicken mole any more? I made it special for you.	Banner 1: You can do it. Banner 2: Eating well makes you feel well. User frame below images: Click on the pictures to see some choices.
0 10	T sits and slow zoom to med. 2-shot; freeze image	N: How would you handle this situation? Click on the pictures to see some choices.	
0 14	Option 1: Hold med. 2-shot. throughout (no camera motion for QuickTime window. Minimal action within screen.) M holds up hand to stop serving. T nods with understanding. Freeze	M: I love it, but my blood sugar's been a problem.	
0 20	Option 2: Same med. 2-shot. M holds up hand to stop serving, but looks disgusted. T gapes and shrinks back. Freeze	M: I never liked chicken mole the way you make it.	
0 26	Option 3: Same med. 2-shot. M holds two open palms. T smiles; lifts dish for more. Freeze	M: Your chicken mole is too good to pass up.	
0 32	Option 4: Same med. 2-shot. M tilts head and holds up hand. T purses lips and shrugs. Freeze	M: Not now, Tia. Can you pack two servings for me to eat later?	
0 38	4 static poses remain on screen	N: Which is the best way to handle this situation? Click on your choice.	User frame: Click on your choice.

Figure 7.8. Sample script, courtesy Sandia Consulting Group.

multimedia can be an expensive proposition. Can you borrow their marketing know-how at a lower cost?

The children's site MaMa media is a good example of how to integrate several multimedia elements. This Web site (*http:// www.mamamedia.com/home/superdoorway/home.html*), shown in Figure 7.9, uses audio, animation, cartoons, and an interactive format to attract children. The site comes up immediately with both GIF animations and audio, making it simple to access.

If you market audio products, you might want to check out *http://www.mjuice.com/*, shown in Figure 7.10, a site that combines streaming and downloadable audio. To obtain music from this site, users establish an account, purchase Mjuice dollars, and download the Mjuice player. Each song they purchase debits their account.

The Blue Note (*http://www.bluenote.net/*, shown in Figure 7.11), a famous jazz club in New York City, uses RealAudio technology to present live jazz concerts on a regular basis. Their site is divided into frames that make it easy to update individual sections without redo-

Figure 7.9. Integrating multimedia elements, *http://www.mamamedia.com/ home/superdoorway/home.html*. Courtesy MaMa Media.

Figure 7.10. Streaming and downloadable audio, *http://www.mjuice.com.* © 1999 Audio Explosion, Inc.

Figure 7.11. Live audio events, *http://bluenote.net.* Designed and hosted by InterJazz.

ing the layout. The Blue Note brings repeat viewers to its page by presenting a live performance series. Every time people tune in to a concert, they have an opportunity to visit the gift shop or make reservations for their next visit to New York. If they enjoy these concerts, they'll be tempted to go for the real thing.

Other businesses incorporate online multimedia games to encourage return visits. The infamous BubbleWrap game may be found at OpalCat (*http://www.fathom.org/opalcat/bubblewrap.html*, shown in Figure 7.12). OpalCat is a Web design company; they handle the BubbleWrap trademark by providing a link to the manufacturer's site, Sealed Air Corporation at *http://www.sealedaircorp.com*. You can use similar games on your site from the Freebies section below to draw repeat visitors. Companies like Wallopware at *http://www. wallopware.com/* sell customized games with your corporate logo or other relevant imagery.

Figure 7.12. Multimedia game to draw return visits, *http://www.fathom. org/opalcat/bubblewrap.html*. Courtesy OpalCat's World Domination Headquarters.

To make life easier for viewers with slow modems, the Australian Museum, in collaboration with the Australian Cultural Network, offers stories from Autralia's indigenous peoples in text, audio, or two types of video at *http://www.dreamtime.net.au/creation* in Figure 7.13.

Haring Kids in Figure 7.14 (*http://www.haringkids.com*) uses images from the late artist Keith Haring to entertain children, while inspiring a sense of play and creativity. Full of activities for kids, free lesson plans for teachers, and giveaways like a Haring morph screensaver, the site combines sophisticated design with charming Shockwave animation. Nothing here is marketed, except a love of art and the Keith Haring Foundation. Buried deep in the site, without a link, is the URL for another Haring site at which items are for sale, *http://www.haring.com/popshop*.

For a real multimedia treat that unfolds in time, check out Monster Interactive's presentation at *http://www.monsteri.com*, shown in Figure 7.15. Using both Flash 3 and Shockwave animation, this site

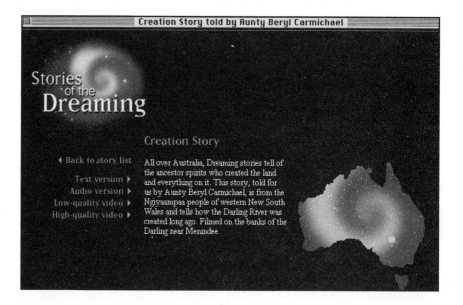

Figure 7.13. Allowing multimedia options, *http://www.dreamtime.net.au/ creation*. © 1999 Australian Museum.

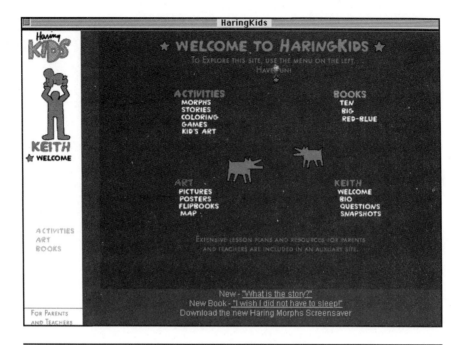

Figure 7.14.   Shockwave animation, *http://www.haringkids.com/master1. htm.* © Estate of Keith Haring. Web design by Riverbed Media.

is almost an animated short film, replete with excellent sound effects and high-resolution graphics. Monster Interactive, a multimedia and Web design company, uses this site as a portfolio and to demonstrate its capabilities. A static shot cannot do this site justice: Go see it.

Surfcheck (*http://www.surfcheck.com*), shown in Figure 7.16, demonstrates a very different use of multimedia. It incorporates an amazing number of live feeds for surfers: streaming video called the splash cam; daily video updates from over 100 live camera locations in California, Baja, Costa Rica, Hawaii, and South Africa; buoy data from the National Oceanic and Atmospheric Administration updated every half hour; and streamed tide information in graphical format.

Finally, there's a business site, shown in Figure 7.17, that makes ideal use of streaming RealVideo: The Web Traffic school displays videos for home study (*http://www.webtrafficschool.com/*

Figure 7.15. Loaded multimedia site, *http://www.monsteri.com*. Courtesy Monster Interactive, LLC.

default.htm). Users sign up for the class ($19.95) over the Web. This is an excellent example of using the Web as a cost-effective, interactive teaching tool. For ax video download site tied to a very different primary business, check out a stock footage distributor at *http://www.film.com*.

This review of sites that incorporate good multimedia may leave you panting to incorporate these features. Back down a minute, though, to reconsider the basic business issues that are the real key to deciding whether multimedia is appropriate for your Web site.

Regardless of what you decide about glamour and glitz, you must still deal with the nitty-gritty issues addressed in the next chapter: securing your site from hackers; processing transactions; accepting payment; and protecting the design and content of your site from ripoffs.

Figure 7.16. Live feeds, *http://www.surfcheck.com*. Courtesy Surfcheck. com. Designed by Tim Chandler (chandler @ netscape.net).

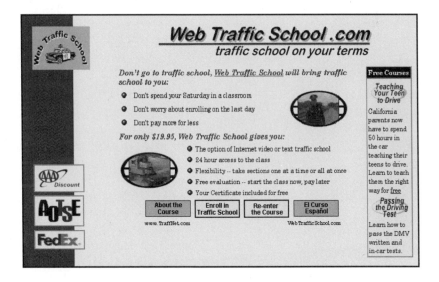

Figure 7.17. Streaming video for business reasons, *http://www.webtraffic school.com/default.htm*. Courtesy Web Traffic School.com.

8

Dollars and Legal Sense

It's time to move from the glittering aspects of Web sites to the nitty-gritty: privacy, security, transaction processing, payment, and legal issues. Data privacy and secure financial transactions are absolutely essential to maintaining customer confidence. Many consumers are reluctant to submit personal or credit card information over the Internet, especially after reading about the exploits of *hackers* (people with deep computer knowledge) who break into systems to steal data. By the end of this chapter, you'll know about

- The importance of a privacy policy

- Secure transmission of credit card, banking, and other private information

- Software for managing transaction activities, including catalog, auction, shopping cart, and checkstand programs

- Methods of accepting payment, from old-fashioned toll-free numbers to credit cards and **electronic data interchange (EDI)**

- Legal concerns, such as intellectual property, liability, and fraud

The Privacy Zone

Security concerns apply to the privacy and integrity of data as well as to financial transactions. Though the press has focused on issues related to payment, it behooves you to maintain security on any customer data that you obtain.

The basic step doesn't require technology: Develop and maintain a data privacy policy. Inform site visitors of your policy on any registration or order screen with a simple statement such as, "We do not sell or share our information under any circumstances. Your data will remain completely confidential." Your policy should apply not just to lists of e-mail and street addresses, but to demographic information such as the number of children in the household and to purchase records. Would you want someone to be able to obtain a list of all the books, CDs, or videos you buy?

Both the Federal Trade Commission *(http://www.ftc.gov/privacy/index.html)* and the U.S. Department of Commerce (*http://www.doc.gov*) acknowledge that if industry self-regulation doesn't work, federal legislation mandating online privacy rights is likely to result. A law passed in 1998 already prohibits Web sites from collecting personal information—including names, e-mail addresses, and zip codes—from children without parental permission. By mid-1999, legislators had introduced another 50 bills in Congress to protect Web users from such invasions of privacy as passing data from one company to another.

The FTC publishes a sample privacy policy, along with advice to consumers on its Web site. But perhaps greater incentives will come from companies like Microsoft, which announced it would buy ads only on Web Sites with adequate privacy policies. (The largest Internet advertiser, Microsoft, spent more than $34 million in online ads in 1998.)

Security: Raising the Barricades

Although the bigger risk with data may be misuse after transmission and collection, dishonest people do roam the Internet to obtain credit card information and make illegal charges. The files of one hacker arrested for breaking into a private computer system contained 20,000 stolen credit card numbers! How does someone intercept a card number sent over the Internet?

Messages are routed from one point to another, passing through many different servers on the Internet, potentially all around the world. Because you have no control over the security of these different systems, a message may be subject to snooping or modification. A variety of technologies have been developed to make it difficult for hackers to intercept or understand some messages, particularly financial ones. As a merchant, you face more risk than an individual does, since your files may contain the numbers of many cards.

Another risk arises because data over the Internet are transmitted without checking for accuracy. A 1 can change erroneously to a 0 during transmission, altering the amount charged or the number of the credit card! The design philosophy of the Internet is best effort, not no mistakes. This may be a good way to design a fast network, but it's not the best way to build a secure electronic system for financial transactions.

When it comes to transacting business, it's important that the person who receives the message be the person for whom it was intended. It's also essential that no one intercept it and that the message received be identical to the one that was sent. Unfortunately, Internet procedures don't keep transactions secure in any of these ways. Methods such as EDI, discussed later, offer a way to verify the accuracy and recipient of the transmitted message. Let's now look at ways that critical online data can be protected from interception.

Lines of Defense

The first line of defense is data **encryption** (putting a message into hidden code). The new standard for commercial encryption, called strong encryption, uses a 128-bit key, making it almost impossible to unscramble the message. Cracking the key would require the correct string of 128 ones and zeroes. Thus, even if an encrypted message is intercepted as it crosses the Internet, it cannot be read, as represented in Figure 8.1. The Digital Millennium Copyright Act of 1998 made it illegal to create or distribute devices that circumvent encryption codes or other means of security or copyright management for digital data.

A second defense is a **firewall,** a combination of hardware and software that separates a network into two or more parts to prevent

PRIME FACTORS
THE INFORMATION SECURITY COMPANY

Data Encryption:

Trouble with ~~~~~~ Trouble with
Far East Fund. ~~~~~~ Far East Fund.
Can't find a way ~~~~~~ Can't find a way
to withdraw bid. ~~~~~~ to withdraw bid.
Not sure what ~~~~~~ Not sure what
to do next. ~~~~~~ to do next.
Advise immediately. ~~~~~~ Advise immediately.

What you see is not what they get.

Figure 8.1. Encryption, *http://www.primefactors.com*. Courtesy Prime Factors, Inc.

unauthorized access. Your Web hosting service should have firewalls on its server. Your company may have firewalls on its internal computer network to make it difficult for people who access one part of shared information, such as a product database, to reach another, such as financial records.

Secure Socket Layers (SSLs)

Most browsers and computers can already exchange secure transmissions across the Internet, making it difficult for unauthorized people to view data sent between two points. Most browsers use a technology developed by Netscape called SSL (Secure Socket Layer) to enable authenticated, encrypted communications. Users can tell that SSL is in use by looking for an icon on the page: Netscape 4.0 and higher shows a locked padlock; earlier versions showed an unbroken key; Internet Explorer shows a lock on the status bar. In addition, the URL on the page requiring credit card information will generally change to one beginning with https://, with the s standing for secure.

One catch is that both the merchant's Web server and the customer's Web browser must use the same security system to exchange information. Because SSL can be used by all URLs that start with http, in most cases this is not a problem. SSL is included free on Netscape 2.0 or higher, Internet Explorer 3.0 or higher, and America Online 3.0 or higher. Users can set most browsers to provide notification when they connect to a nonsecure or suspect computer. If you intend to process transactions online, confirm that your Web hosting service offers a secure server with SSL and has firewall protections in place; some hosts charge an additional monthly fee of around $20 to use a secure server.

Digital Signatures

If you feel it's appropriate, you can authenticate (guarantee) orders with a digital certificate or signature. These forms of electronic identification can be used to verify personal identity and age, sign secure e-mail, confirm credit card charges, and offer other value-added services. They usually involve submitting proof of identity off-line to a digital ID company and receiving a coded ID number in return. Depending on the company, it costs $10 to $20 annually for an individual digital signature ID. It costs $250 to $1,000 for a company to obtain a license for its server, depending on the level of security identification desired. VeriSign (*http://www.verisign.com/client/index.html*, shown in Figure 8.2), is one vendor of digital ID products.

Managing Transactions

Transaction-based sites can be an order of magnitude more expensive than an ordinary Web site. A recent survey by NetMarketing (*http://www.net2b.com*) priced development of a 7,500-item catalog

Figure 8.2. Digital ID vendor, *http://www.verisign.com/client/index.html.* Courtesy VeriSign, Inc.

site at anywhere from $30,000 to $1.2 million, with a median price of $479,000! The adage that it pays to shop around holds as much for building Web sites as for buying on them.

In addition to secure server hardware, several pieces of turnkey software are required to construct a transaction-intensive site

- Catalog or auction display

- Shopping cart

- Checkstand or register

Optional software includes

- Automated payment processing

- Automated e-mail for order verification and tracking

- A means of feeding transaction data to your inventory and accounting software

Catalog or auction software, sometimes called store-building programs, allow you to display your products. **Shopping carts** let customers click on products they like as they review a catalog. They can view or change the contents of their cart at any time. To pay, a customer goes to a virtual **checkstand,** where the order is totaled and taxes and shipping charges are added, and enters shipping and billing information.

Depending on the software and your needs, automated payment processing may follow. The resulting order may then be stored in a database and e-mailed to both the merchant and the customer through a secure system. In the most sophisticated implementation, online catalog and transaction data tie directly into other management information systems. We'll take a look at all these types of software in the sections that follow.

The larger your catalog and the more sophisticated your financial processing, the greater the cost will be. Web hosts that specialize in handling transaction-heavy accounts are critical for medium-to-large sites. If you have a modest-sized site (10 to 1,000 items), you can usually find a Web host that includes necessary software as part of its hosting package for $25 to $50 a month. While pre-existing software from a host reduces design flexibility, it dramatically simplifies and speeds the development process.

On the other hand, if you plan to host your own site, you'll need to buy and install the software, which can be quite expensive. Hosting your own site on an internal server is usually viable only for large companies. Your decisions, as always, should be driven by your business needs and budget.

Just how sophisticated should you get? WebCom (*http://www.webcom.com*), a Web hosting service, recommends assessing your needs as shown in Figure 8.3. Keep this model in mind as you read through the software options that follow.

For the smallest businesses in the first column, hand-processing transactions is a cost-effective option. **Electronic funds transfer** (**EFT**), shown as a payment method, is the preauthorized transfer of funds from one bank account to another. It will be discussed in detail later.

Almost any Web software package can create an **electronic order form,** seen in the second column for order and payment information; just be sure your Web host can handle CGI scripts. If you accept purchase orders or maintain open charge accounts for your customers, such a form is an excellent, low-cost alternative to credit cards.

	1- 2 Products < 50 transactions per week	2-10 Products < 50 transactions per week	> 10 Products < 50 transactions per week	> 10 Products > 50 transactions per week
Order Method	Phone, fax, e-mail	Electronic order form	Shopping cart with checkstand	Shopping cart with checkstand
Payment Method	EFT or credit card by phone, fax, e-mail, check Money order	EFT or credit card by phone, fax, e-mail, check, Money order	EFT or credit card by phone, fax e-mail, check, Money order	CyberCash (real-time credit card processing)

Figure 8.3. Transaction needs by volume, *http://www.webcom.com.* Courtesy WebCom, worldwide host to small business. A member of the Verio Group.

The completed form can be e-mailed back through a secure server, set up for automatic fax-back, or returned by mail with a check or money order.

Real-time credit card processing follows the checkstand process with credit card authorization, the equivalent of running a card through an electronic swiper at a storefront. The customer is not charged until the product is shipped, while the merchant is assured that the card number is valid and the account holder has credit available to cover the transaction.

Catalog Software

You must set up your products to be viewed in an organized fashion, stocking your virtual shelves, so to speak. Many Web hosting services now offer store-building packages to create an online catalog. You enter the specifications and price of each product on a form and add thumbnail digital art if appropriate. Then you organize your store into departments, select shipping and tax options, and let the software do the rest. The more expensive packages are database driven, with sophisticated search features on multiple fields. Some have the capability to import existing product databases. Depending on the software, you may be able to

- Choose one of several prepackaged styles

- Modify colors, fonts, background, and layout

- Have your Web designer completely customize your catalog

- Search the database of products by name, type, or other variables

- Import product data from a pre-existing print catalog or inventory in electronic form.

Catalog software ranges in price from free to inclusion with certain Web hosting deals, to several hundred or several thousand dollars. The variables are catalog size, capabilities, searchability, flexibility, and operating system. Figure 8.4 shows the catalog software from Custom Catalog OnLine, Inc., (*http://www.customcatalogs.com*) in use by Boxer-Northwest, a wholesale restaurant supply company, for over 56,000 items at *http://boxernw.com*.

As an alternative to importing a database or entering individual items, Infosis Corporation (*http://www.infosiscorp.co*m) allows you to import your print catalog in Quark or PDF (Adobe Acrobat) format directly onto your Web site. Their software preserves existing layout, photos, and graphics, while adding a zoom-in capability, thus speeding the development of large or frequently changing online catalogs.

Sources for traditional catalog software include WebCom at *http://www.webcom.com* and Catalog.com (*http://www.catalog.com*), both of which include catalog and cart software as part of their Web hosting service. Catalogs and shopping carts can also be purchased from these sources as an add-on product for a free-standing site, with the price depending on the number of items. For other vendors, check *http://www.icat.com*.

Auction Software

The increasing popularity of auction sites has led, not surprisingly, to the development of prepackaged auction software. Vendors include OpenSite's Auction 4.0 (*http://www.opensite.com*) and Microsoft (*http://www.microsoft.com*), which has an auction extension to Site

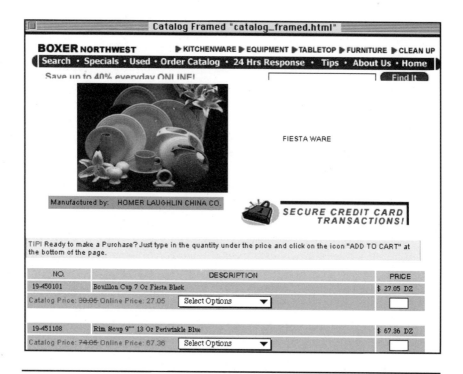

Figure 8.4. Catalog software from Custom Catalogs On-line, Inc. See at *http://boxernw.com/boxernw/images-f/b19-450.jpg.* Courtesy Boxer-Northwest Co.

Server 3.0. OpenSite has three levels of auction software beginning at $5,000, as well as a hosted auction "Coucierge Service" starting at $3,00 per month. More sophisticated—and more expensive—solutions are available for larger auction sites. Opensite handles the server installation and will help you configure the software to meet your needs.

Shopping Carts and Checkstands

Shopping cart programs generally incorporate checkstands. Like catalog software, cart programs have a tremendous range in price and capability, and are often incorporated with a Web hosting package. Elaborate shopping cart software may allow you to create a registration database of shipping and billing information so that repeat customers need not re-enter their data.

Depending on the nature of your product (fruit? flowers? medicine?), shipping volume, and customers' needs, you may want to automate shipping options from UPS Ground to Federal Express, and/or generate shipping labels as part of the process. Free shipping is becoming a competitive pricing feature on many merchandise sites. Since the costs are generally integrated into the overall price, you may want to adjust your own pricing and follow suit.

If you plan to sell internationally, you need software that supports international currency exchange and shipping requirements. If your Web host offers a shopping cart, check out the cart supplier's Web site to confirm that the product will meet your needs.

A sample shopping cart from Hassan Shopping Cart (*http://www. irata.com/products.html*) is shown in use at A. L. Van Houtte Fine Coffee (*http://www.finecoffee.com/cgi-local/shop.pl/*, shown in Figure 8.5). The Hassan Cart is a UNIX-based solution that supports both CyberCash and UPS shipping. Costs range from $200 for a single license to $1800 for a site license, plus per module charges of $200 to $300 for CyberCash or other secure transactions. For comparison with other cart programs, take a look at

- Precision Web (*http://precisionweb.net/shop.html*). This hosting service offers its free Ultrashop shopping cart software, otherwise priced at $100, with every site. Their shopping cart software is database driven, secure-server enabled, and customizable.

- Hamilton Associates (*http://www.hamassoc.com/*). Their basic cart product is EZshopper, which runs $500 for the server software, plus $75 per 10-item page. It has optional modules for UPS shipping at $125 and database administration/statistics for $200. Their Minicart option for $200 is useful for companies with only a few items. After calculating the sales total, shipping costs, and tax, their products send both company and customer a sales confirmation receipt with the individual order number.

- GTA NetOrderForm (*http://www.gta-tech.com/*). This free, simple-to-use, turnkey shopping cart system comes complete with online administration features, online credit card verification, customer feedback forms, and secure server capability.

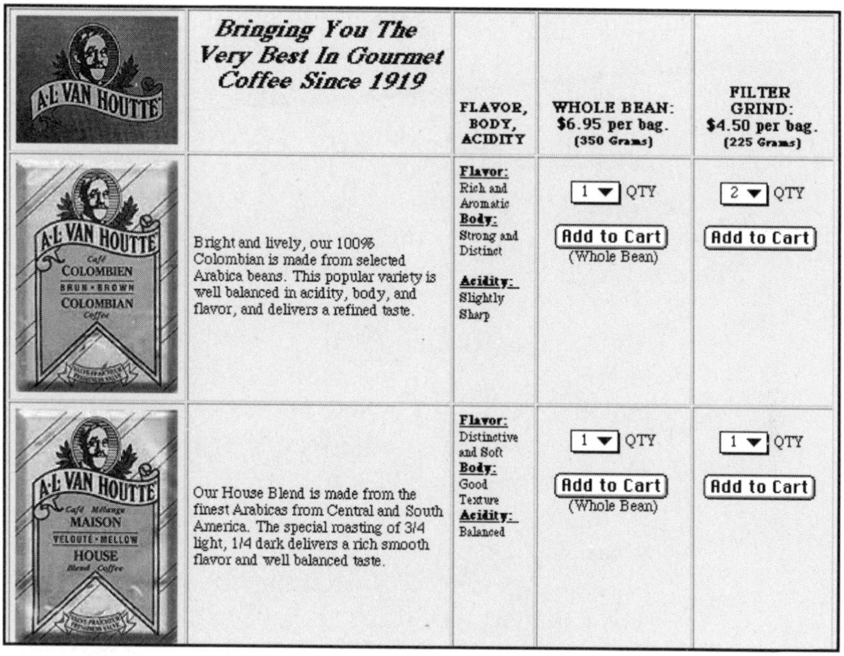

Figure 8.5. Shopping cart from Hassan seen at *http://www.finecoffee.com/cgi-local/shop.pl.* Courtesy Fruba, Inc. dba College Hill Coffee Shop.

You might also check out *http://www.pdgsoft.com* or *http://www.macrotec.com*, which "rents" cart software.

If one store is not enough, perhaps you would like to build your own shopping mall! The Mallsurfer turnkey solution (*http://www.mallsurfer.com/*) includes shopping cart, checkout stand, and store departments. It runs from Windows 95/98 or NT and can be uploaded to any Web site. The shopping cart and checkstand software are available as freeware or shareware, while the mall software itself starts at $199.95 for a single user, and $99.95 for five additional shops. Mallsurfer also offers a mall hosting service.

Integrated E-Commerce Solutions

Integrated e-commerce solutions are usually purchased by Web hosting services or by companies that host their own site. Integrated packages include standard modules for catalogs, shopping carts, and checkstands, as well as expanded administrative and statistical options. Most important, they provide linkage or export options to inventory, accounting, mailing list, and/or EDI (electronic data interchange) systems.

Web hosts may offer the complete package in one of their monthly pricing options. The first three sources listed are all vendor hosted. You don't need to buy software to create or maintain your site.

- iCat Commerce Online *http://www.icat.com/services*, shown in Figure 8.6), is an e-commerce service that includes store-building, order-processing, and promotional services to help you build, manage and drive traffic to your online business. Prices range from $10 a month for online stores containing up to 10 items to $350 a month for stores with up to 3,000 items. icat's e-commerce service will walk you through the process of setting up your online business and provide merchant support services. You can either build a new storefront from scratch with iCat Web Store, or you can enable an exist-

Figure 8.6. Web commerce solution, *http://www.icat.com/services*. Courtesy iCat, "a division of Intel Corporation".

ing site with iCat Commerce Cart. iCat hosts all Web stores and supplies you with your own URL, while only the commerce portions of the Commerce Cart are hosted by iCat. Owned by Intel, iCat has entered into a joint venture with Excite! to create a new e-commerce service designed to help consumers locate desired products and help online merchants reach a larger audience.

- webhosting.com in Figure 8.7 (http://www.webhosting.com/ pages/) offers a fairly typical e-commerce turnkey selection

Figure 8.7. Sample, *http://www.webhosting.com*. Courtesy Webhosting.com.

starting at $34.95 a month, with prices increasing by catalog size and features.

- The Yahoo Store (*http://www.viaweb.com*) offers electronic commerce Web hosting. Prices run $100 a month for up to 50 items, $300 a month for 1,000 items. This site offers point-and-click store building and lots of statistical and tracking tools. The downside is that you have to enter the individual items and process credit cards manually unless you have CyberCash. Users can post a storefront in a matter of hours.

- Advanced Internet Technologies, Inc. (*http://www.aitcom.net*) is another e-commerce Web hosting service. More sophisticated than Yahoo's Viaweb, it offers a card verification service, as well as store-building and statistical tools. Costs, in addition to a basic monthly fee of $70, depend on the options you select.

- INEX Corporation (*http://www.inex.com*) operates a little differently: You buy software to create your store and upload the finished store to one of the ISPs that supports the INEX package. Although you start development with canned templates, these options require technical know-how. Commerce Court Light ($595) handles up to 500 items, while Commerce Court Professional ($995) has no item limits and will interface with accounting and other systems. It offers reporting tools and customer-service features, such as recommending related products to customers. Such **intelligent agents** are available with other packages as well. These agents act like knowledgeable store clerks who **upsell,** encouraging additional purchases or suggesting upgrades to a more expensive model.

If you plan to host a huge site in-house, you'll want to look at an integrated hardware and software solution from one of the major companies. At this point you'll need not only dollars, but sufficient technical know-how to maintain the system. For instance, IBM (*http://www.ibmcom/ebusiness*) offers NetServer and Net.Commerce for $5,000 to $35,000 through value-added distributors. The ubiquitous Microsoft has an integrated electronic commerce solution called

BizTalk (*http://www.microsoft.com/WINME/030499com/clark28k/ html/BizTal_default.htm*). BizTalk not only sells products online, it tracks supply and demand and communicates with vendors. It has been tested by such huge sites as *1-800 Flowers*, *barnesandnoble.com*, *Best Buy*, *Dell Computer*, and *Eddie Bauer*.

Accepting Payment

Let's look at the options for accepting payment when you sell over the Internet. In most cases, payment is made by credit card, but taking that number and processing the payment may be handled several different ways. Credit card data may be delivered off-line, faxed or e-mailed after completing a form on the Web, or processed directly by a bank.

In spite of the perceived risk, credit cards are actually one of the best ways for individuals to make payment online. A cardholder's liability for unauthorized use is limited to $50, and most cards act as a guarantee of satisfaction. That is, a consumer can easily cancel a credit card purchase and return unacceptable goods. Your risk as a merchant is far greater than your customers' risk.

Phone, Fax, and Snail Mail

Old-fashioned ways are both safe and inexpensive, allowing customers to mail a check, call in, or fax a printed form with a credit card number. Preferably, you want to offer customers a toll-free number to place an order by phone or fax. The rates for setting up and running inbound toll-free numbers vary by vendor and location. As you can see in Figure 8.8, it's worth a few calls to get the best price.

For a monthly and/or per transaction fee, some Web hosts will establish an automated fax-back system. This allows consumers to fill out their form online (without bothering to print it out), but the information is faxed rather than sent over the Internet. This method also works for individual customers with established accounts who receive monthly bills.

You can accept an online purchase order from business customers without requesting sensitive credit card information. Remember,

Vendor	Set-Up	Monthly Service	Per Minute
AT&T	$35	$5	$0.113/min out-of-state .085/min in-state (CA)
MCI	free	$5, free if monthly charges are >$50	.09/min out-of-state, .06/local, .09 in-state
US West	$25	$3	$0.12/min (NM)

All prices vary by state

Figure 8.8. Sample rates for toll-free numbers.

75% of the commerce on the Internet is business-to-business, not retail. By 2003, online transactions are expected to represent 9% of all business-to-business sales.

Even if you accept credit card information online, always offer at least one alternative for customers who don't trust electronic methods. Given that 82% of small businesses themselves worry about security on the Internet, it's not a surprise that customers do. Resolve your concerns and theirs the way EyeWire does. This company, which sells images and tools to graphic designers, emphasizes its 800 number on its order information page at *http://www.eyewire.com/info /ordering.html* in Figure 8.9. The easier you make it for people to buy, the more sales you will make.

Credit Cards

In 1997, 10 million people charged an average of $100 in online credit card transactions; $1 billion out of $3 trillion worth of total credit card transactions. By 2002, an estimated 40 million people will be buying online and 80% of those purchases will be by credit card. After customers place an online order using their credit cards, their payments (minus a transaction fee) are transferred by the card issuer to your **merchant account.** Most card issuers provide free software to transfer information directly from your computer to theirs.

Although over a billion credit cards are in circulation, not all your potential customers have one, especially if your product sells internationally. In the case of unauthorized transactions, such as chil-

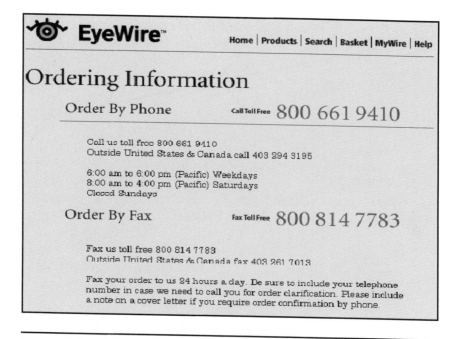

Figure 8.9. Offering the 800-number option, *http://www.eyewire.com/ info/ordering.html.* Courtesy *www.eyewire.com.*

dren using parents' cards without permission, the cardholder may refuse to pay and/or you may end up with the expense of processing returns.

In spite of these caveats, you could miss many sales if you don't take credit cards. Even the federal government now pays for most purchases under $2,500 (in some cases up to $25,000), using its own credit card equivalent, the IMPAC purchase card.

Setting Up a Merchant Account

Credit cards can be costly to you as a merchant. If you are not already set up to accept credit cards, research costs thoroughly. A card issuer may ask you to estimate the percentage of credit transactions to be handled electronically, by phone, or in person; your anticipated annual dollar volume on credit cards; and the average charge amount.

Most, but not all, commercial banks offer merchant card accounts. You will have to provide basic business financial data and possibly personal financial information, especially if you are a sole proprietor or have only recently established your business. You may also be required to create a second checking account into which all your revenues from credit card sales will be deposited and against which all charges will be debited. Some banks are reluctant to establish merchant accounts for new, mail-order, or Web-only companies. If your local banks don't come up with a reasonable rate, try one of the national commercial banks or a company like EMS Global that specializes in setting up merchant accounts (*http://www.eft.com*).

Most card issuers charge some combination of a one-time setup fee, a monthly fee for electronic swiping devices, a percentage of credit card sales, and/or a fee per transaction. All these fees vary, with the percentage of sales ranging from 1.2 to 6%. Generally speaking, the lower the value of receipts and the lower the volume of transactions, the higher the percentage rate you will be charged for each transaction. The table in Figure 8.10 shows some sample transaction rates for credit cards. Given highly variable fee combinations and percentage rates, it is definitely worth shopping around for the bank or service company that offers you the best rates for the type and amount of business you expect to do.

If these rates are too high or if your transaction volume is too low to qualify for a merchant account, consider using the services of

The amount from a sale that goes to the card issuer (called the Monthly Discount Rate) depends on your transaction volume, average transaction amount, and means of reporting transactions. Merchant Accounts have additional fees for initial application, monthly statement, equipment rental or purchase, and supplies. There are also differences in minimum monthly charges and how quickly payments post to your account. Shop around! For additional information, try these sites: *http://merchantcreditcard.com/rates.html http://www.wilsonweb.com/articles/merch-cc.htm*

Card Issuer	Monthly Discount Rate (% to Issuer)
MasterCard/VISA	1.30%-5.00%
Discover	2.25%-5.25%
American Express	2.95%-3.75%

Figure 8.10. Sample merchant account fees.

CCnow (*http://www.ccnow.com*), shown in Figure 8.11. For a 9.5% transaction fee, CCnow acts as a reseller to process credit charges for you. When they reach the checkstand, customers transfer invisibly to the CCNow secure site.

SET: Secure Electronic Transactions

To resolve conflicts among different types of encryption and improve security beyond SSL, the major credit card companies (VISA, MasterCard, and American Express) worked with a number of technology partners (including GTE, IBM, Microsoft, Netscape, RSA, SAIC, Terisa Systems, and VeriSign) to establish a single standard for secure credit card transactions on the Internet.

Combining encryption, digital certificates, specific content parameters, and secure transmission technology, the **SET** (**Secure Electronic**

Figure 8.11.   An alternative to your own merchant account, *http://www. ccnow.com.* Courtesy CCNow.

Transactions) protocol protects consumers' bank card information worldwide when they shop on the Web. The protocol not only increases transaction security, it authenticates the identity of the card user. This is particularly valuable if your products might tempt children to use a parent's card without permission.

Many software developers and electronic security providers are now implementing the SET 2.0 release. Products that conform to this protocol will display a SET-compliant icon. If you're curious, check out the SET specification at

http://www.setco.org/faq_usr.html

http://www.visa.com/

http://www.mastercard.com/shoponline/set/

Customers need two things to use SET: First, a digital ID or certificate, described earlier, as identification on electronic payment slips. Customers may request a digital ID from a card-issuing bank, or from a digital ID company, by filling out a form on a Web site. Rates range from $10 to $20 per year depending on the level of security desired. Second, customers need a digital wallet, a secure, encrypted envelope that seals personal information, including bank accounts, credit card numbers and expiration dates, shipping and billing addresses, and digital IDs. Shown in Figure 8.12, a wallet itself is a free plug-in that can be downloaded from the Web at *http://www.microsoft.com/wallet/default.asp* or from *http://www.cybercash.com/instabuy.how.html*. The Microsoft wallet also comes bundled with newer versions of browsers.

By invoking the wallet plug-in whenever they want to make an electronic purchase, consumers avoid the hassle of retyping their credit card information. Because multiple card numbers and addresses can be stored in a wallet, consumers can select both their payment method (confirmed by a password) and the shipping address with a simple click.

The MasterCard site (*http://www.mastercard.com/set/demo.html*) shown in Figure 8.13 illustrates the process of making a purchase under SET. First, consumers put items in their electronic shopping cart. At the virtual checkstand, they pull out their digital wallet (click on the Pay using SET icon). They are asked for confirmation on their

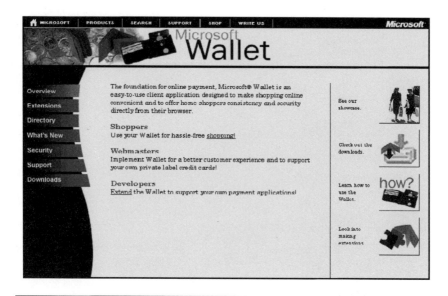

Figure 8.12. Digital wallet, *http://www.microsoft.com/wallet/default.asp*. Screenshot reprinted by permission from Microsoft Corporation.

digital payment slip. As in the tangible world, copies of the transaction are sent to the consumer, to the merchant, and to the bank card issuer.

CyberCash (see Figure 8.14) at *http://www.cybercash.com /cybercash/merchants* is one of many providers of server software designed to manage electronic transactions of all types (including returns, voids, etc.) in real time under the SET protocol. Their add-on module, which is available from many Web hosting services (sometimes for a monthly fee), automates all credit card processing and provides immediate confirmation that the cardholder has an adequate limit to make the charge.

The CyberCash site lays out a typical six-step process to become a CyberCash merchant. The process is simpler if your Web hosting service already offers the module. In any case, note that you must already have a merchant card account.

1. Notify your bank that you want to accept credit cards via CyberCash.

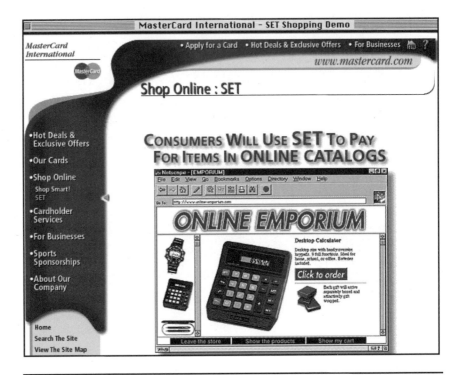

Figure 8.13.   SET Demo, *http://www.mastercard.com/shoponline/set/demo.html*. Reprinted with permission of MasterCard International.

2. Execute a service agreement and complete the online registration form.

3. Download Cash Register software from the CyberCash Web site and execute the Software License agreement.

4. Generate a public/private encryption key using the utility provided, and e-mail the public key and your merchant name to CyberCash.

5. Install and integrate the Cash Register software into the Web store on your server.

6. When you are ready, e-mail CyberCash that you are ready to go live with online transactions.

Figure 8.14. Provider of transaction software and services, *http://www.cybercash.com/merchants* © 1999 Cybercash, Inc.

Payment Alternatives

Another approach operates like a debit card, taking advantage of the wallet described earlier to create digital cash or e-money. Customers, who must purchase digital cash before they can spend it, tuck the "cash" into their wallet as an encrypted data file. For instance, Cybercash's InstaBuy service (*http://www.cybercash.com/instabuy.how.html*) in Figure 8.15 utilizes its own wallet technology for this service, which is particularly handy for small purchases, such as game playing time, database searches, and downloads.

Depending on your product, you could consider following the example of NewsLibrary (*http://www.newslibrary.com*, shown in Figure 8.16). Customers first set up a "library card" account guaranteed by credit card. NewsLibrary bills the account monthly for any articles downloaded from its worldwide newspaper archives at prices ranging from $1 to $2.95 per article.

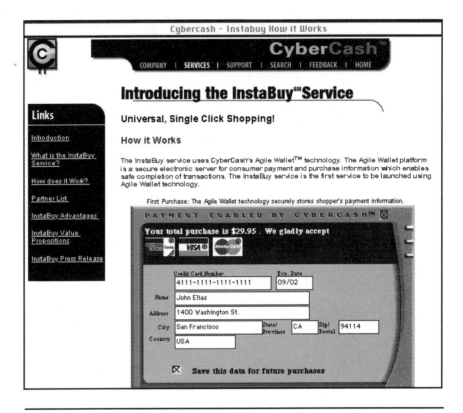

Figure 8.15. CyberCash's alternative to credit cards, *http://www.cybercash .com/instabuy/how.html.* © 1999 Cybercash, Inc.

EFT on the Internet

Electronic Funds Transfer (EFT) refers to electronic payments transferred between two checking accounts. It covers both an automated deposit to and a withdrawal from an account. EFT can be accomplished as part of Electronic Data Interchange (described later), or independently.

Many people are familiar with EFT without knowing the term. Applications include the automated deposit of Social Security or payroll checks and automated withdrawals for such payments as dental insurance, gasoline credit cards, utility bills, or donations to a local public broadcasting station. Perhaps you have received a letter ask-

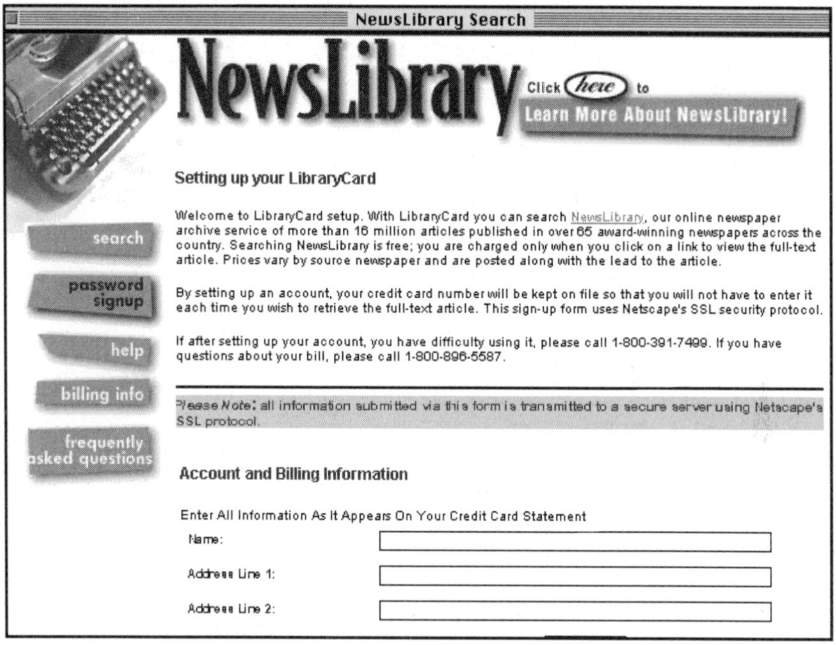

Figure 8.16. Guaranteed accounts for small purchases, *http://www.news library.com.* © 1998 Mediastream, Inc.

ing whether you want such a service instead of paying by check. By the year 2002 almost all businesses and over 15 million households are expected to do some form of EFT. The Federal government plans to make all its benefits payments via EFT starting in 1999.

EFT is extremely effective for the billing company because it guarantees payment (as long as there is money in the account!). It saves the individual customer the time and effort of writing and mailing a check while saving the merchant the cost of bill processing, mail and deposit delays, and bad checks.

This works particularly well with customers who buy from your Web site on a regular basis, and it is also cost-effective for one-time purchases over several hundred dollars from a number of different customers. With cost and labor for processing a standard check now running up to $4, it's worth seeing if you can save several dollars (or more) per transaction. If your company receives hundreds of checks on a regular basis, as do fitness centers, Internet service providers, online newsletters, or cable companies, this may be an excellent option on or off the Web.

To explore this alternative, first survey your primary customers to see if they would be interested. Then talk to your bank. Most commercial banks are capable of handling EFT through the Automated Clearing House (ACH), which facilitates the transfer of funds between member banks. In addition to a bank setup cost of $100 to $200, expect per transaction costs from 5 to 50 cents. Some banks charge a monthly fee and/or a per file transfer fee instead of, or in addition to, setup and transaction fees. Besides the bank's fees, there will be a charge for the software for your Website, generally starting around $900. You'll find general information about EFT at *http://www.prodigybusiness.com* or *http://www.pulse-efit.com*

Often called interactive online billing and payment software, some EFT products can be integrated into shopping cart/checkstand software. This option is available as a turnkey solution for your Web site and/or as a service from

http://www.cybercash.com/cybercash/services/paynow.html

http://www.electronicfunds.com/index.html

http://www.checkfree.com/index-ecommerch.html

http://www.electronicfundtransfer.com

It is possible to handle EFT without the automated software. If your transaction volume is low, consider an online form that users either fax or mail back. Since customers must provide a bank account number, a voided check or deposit slip, and a signature, they will need to print out the initial agreement form.

EDI on the Internet

Businesses that consistently trade with each other have one more option for secure financial transmission. **Electronic Data Interchange (EDI)** is the computer-to-computer exchange of structured business data, including invoices and payments, between two trading partners. EDI is also used for such purposes as shipping notices, responding to a request for quotation, and filing certain tax payments. Because it affects so many aspects of order taking, fulfillment, production, inventory, and bookkeeping, EDI has a major impact on business structure and processes.

Traditional EDI can be costly, running seven to ten times more than Internet-based forms of electronic commerce. Consequently, EDI fits the needs of only a minority of businesses. However, if most of your sales come from high-volume business-to-business customers, it may make sense. Recent advances in EDI over the Internet have begun to make EDI more available to small businesses.

With EDI, companies send each other business messages in a fixed format that moves information from one application to another without ever being rekeyed. This format is quite different from the unstructured nature of an e-mail message, as shown in Figure 8.17. Hundreds of different standardized business transactions, from waybills and EFT to customs reports and insurance claims, are available under EDI. The ANSI 3070 Committee of the American National Standards Institute develops the structured formats for these messages.

EDI is particularly valuable in industries in which inventory is kept at a minimum based on Just-In-Time (JIT) business practices.

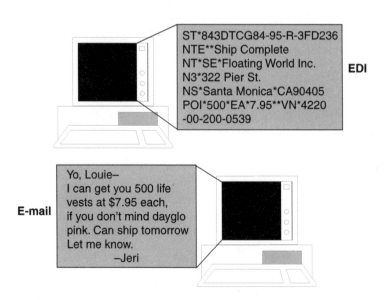

Figure 8.17. EDI versus e-mail information format.

With fully integrated EDI, a purchase order is received, a shipping notice and invoice are sent by the seller's system, the buyer makes an EFT payment, and new stock is ordered based on the usage or sale of items (tracked by bar code)—all without additional human intervention. For some sellers, EDI speeds payment and thus improves cash flow. You can expect EDI costs per transaction to range from 1 to 2 cents per data line plus startup costs.

Previously, EDI required a **VAN (Value Added Network)**, a private electronic network independent of the Internet, to act as the switchboard for transmitting messages between trading partners. As part of their services, VANs utilize very sophisticated encryption technology and guarantee the accuracy of electronic messages. In the past, both the buyer and seller, called **trading partners** in EDI lingo, had to subscribe to a VAN. In addition, both parties had to have special software to translate between EDI format and one that is humanly understandable on a computer screen. Dozens of vendors offer software for different platforms, but software from one company is not always compatible with software from another.

Within the past several years, VANs have developed Internet-compatible means of secure transmission. Many EDI software vendors now offer products that integrate a Web site with EDI applications. For instance, an auto parts manufacturer could accept orders from its electronic catalog on the Web, create an invoice, and receive payment from the buyer's bank without any additional human processing.

The latest advance in making EDI available over the Web is the creation of **XML (eXtensible Markup Language)**. XML packages data in a Web document in a way that can be understood by EDI software already installed in a business. In other words, business documents can move across the Web from the operations end of one trading partner to the back office of the other, thus eliminating a VAN.

Although sales of EDI-related products were $1.5 billion in 1997, only $50 million of this went to Internet-based EDI applications. Although Web-only EDI products represented only $10 million of this, the research firm Dataquest expects this segment to expand to $60–$70 million by the end of 1999. Since the next version of Microsoft Office is expected to be XML enabled, EDI on the Internet is likely to receive a significant boost.

Some large companies, particularly discount retailers and manufacturing firms, now require their suppliers to use EDI. For small businesses who want to sell to the WalMarts and General Motors of the world, an alternative solution may be a Web-based EDI service offered by some of the main EDI vendors, such as Sterling Commerce, Harbinger, and GEIS. These services allow small businesses to enter required information at the vendor's Web site. The vendor translates the information into EDI format and then transmits it to larger trading partners. Although small businesses must rekey the data into their internal systems, this approach makes EDI accessible to companies that cannot afford other EDI models. Figure 8.18 shows the site of Harbinger (*http://www.harbinger.com/products/edi/express*), which sells software for EDI on the Internet, as well as other EDI software.

For more information on EDI, see these Web sites:

http://www.geocities.com/wallstreet/floor/

http://www.edi-info-center.com

http://www.commercenet.com

Figure 8.18. Vendor of EDI on the Internet, *http://www.harbinger.com/ products/edi/express/*. Courtesy Harbinger.

http://www.saecrc.org

For selling to the government with EDI, try

http://www.acq.osd.mil/ec/

http://www.sbaonline.sba.gov

Selecting a Payment Option

In the unpredictable world of the Internet, one trend is predictable: More and more business transactions will be handled with some combination of electronic technologies, whether it be the Web, EFT, or EDI. In 1998 only 6% of sales transactions by volume came through electronic means, but projections are that this will increase to 24% by 2003.

As part of your online business plan, you need to weigh payment methods and their associated costs to decide which are best for you. If need be, make up sample spreadsheets estimating costs for transactions at various volume levels and average amounts. If it doesn't complicate your bookkeeping too much, you may want to hedge your bets by offering several payment options.

Make it clear on your site that you use SSL or other secure transaction methods. Advertise on your Web page which payment methods you accept, just as merchants on Main Street place Visa, MasterCard, American Express, and Discover logos in their windows. Offer links to vendors of payment methods you've selected, such as VeriSign for digital signatures, so customers can sign up quickly.

Make it as easy as possible for consumers to buy on your site with confidence. Try to allow customers to select secure transactions, digital signatures, or unsecured transactions based on their level of comfort and what their browser will accept.

Legalese

In its early days the Internet was an electronic Wild West. People grew fairly cavalier about intellectual property and linking to other sites. However, now that the Web has become such a popular commercial trading route, the chances of intellectual property infringement and incidences of fraud have skyrocketed. Everyone, from Web designers to merchants to ordinary users must be far more cautious.

You need to protect your own online material as well as ensure that you do not misuse the property of others. Legal issues are still murky, given the ease of moving information on the Internet from one place to another and of downloading it to an individual's computer. In most—but not all—cases, downloading by an individual is considered fair use. But republishing copyrighted material on another site without permission is a giant no-no. So is using someone else's high-design buttons for navigation or incorporating another company's trademark in a domain name or in keyword META tags.

Trademarks

A trademark or service mark confers the exclusive right of use of a particular name or logotype within one or more specific classes of commercial activity. Recent court decisions have held that trademark rights apply to domain names and legislation intoduced in 1999 would make it illegal to register someone else's trademark as a domain name.

A name may be available at the InterNIC database but still be trademarked and therefore not available for use in a particular category of goods or services. To determine trademark status and ownership, go to the free online search engine for the U.S. Office of Patents and Trademarks (PTO) (*http://www.uspto.gov/tmdb/index.html*), shown in Figure 8.19.

To trademark your own company or product name, you must file with the PTO at a cost of $245 per name per class of use. More information on what qualifies as a trademark and how to file is available from the PTO home page. Some states also maintain a trademark database for registration only within that state.

Many companies refer to their own trademarked names or the trademarks of other companies within their pages. Put the ™ symbol after a registered trademark the first time it appears, and provide a notice of trademark ownership somewhere on your site. (The symbol 0 is used when a trademark application is pending.) Use a statement such as "Quaker is a registered trademark of the Quaker Oats Company." For multiple trademarks, use a blanket statement such as "All trademarks…are the property of their registered owners" as ThirdAge does (see Figure 8.20). Or have fun with the legalisms as Ragu does does at *http://www.eat.com/site-credits.htm* (see Figure 8.21).

Copyright

Copyright is a form of intellectual property protection that applies to the design (look and feel) and content of audiovisual and print media. Copyright covers text, data, icons, graphics, audio, video, music and software programs. It ensures that you own your particular expression of an idea. A simple notice consisting of the symbol 8 or the word Copyright or Copr., followed by the year of first publication and the name of the copyright owner (usually your company name), confers common law copyright protection. At a minimum, this notice should appear on your site; you can supplement it with a statement of rights

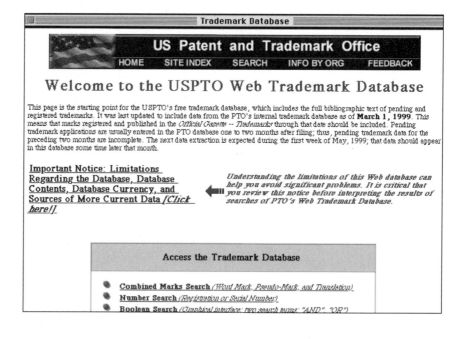

Figure 8.19. Patent and trademark search, *http://www.uspto.gov/tmdb/index.html.*

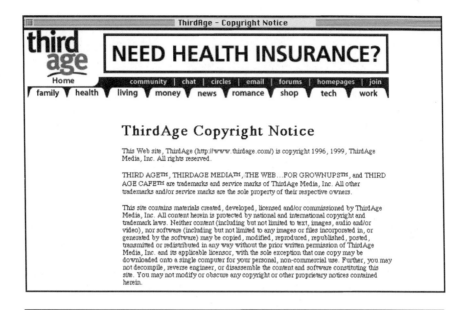

Figure 8.20. Sample trademark and copyright notice, *http://www. thirdage.com/copyright.html.* © 1997, 1999 Third Age Media, Inc. All rights reserved.

and permissable uses as ThirdAge (*http://www.thirdage.com/ copyright.htm*) does in Figure 8.20.

For a nominal fee of $30, you can obtain more complete copyright protection by registering your copyright with the Library of Congress (*http://lcweb.loc.gov/copyright/*) shown in Figure 8.22). Registration gives you greater rights in court and allows you to collect additional damages and legal expenses if you prove that someone else has infringed your copyright.

To file for protection on the design of your site, print out Form VA (Visual Arts) from the Library of Congress Web site. As directed, attach printouts of relevant pages of your Web site to the application. If you offer original information or an original compilation of information on your Web site, you can file Form TX (nondramatic literary works) as well. Read the information on the LoC Web site carefully to determine whether other forms of copyright, such as for sound or audiovisual works, would be appropriate. Mail the completed forms and your check to the Library of Congress at the address shown.

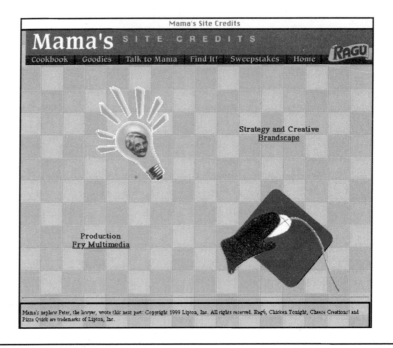

Figure 8.21. Fun copyright notice, *http://www.eat.com/site-credits.htm.* Courtesy Lipton Investments, Inc. and Unilever USA, Inc.

Figure 8.22. Library of Congress copyright page, *http://www.lcweb.loc. gov/copyright.*

Within several months, you will receive official notice that your copyright has been registered. Place copyright notices with other important legal documents in your safe deposit box or vault.

Whether or not a copyright notice appears on others' material, you cannot use it on your Web site without permission. (Government material is not copyrighted.) If you wish to republish or mirror the contents of a site, obtain permission in writing first. Start by sending a letter requesting permission, such as the one in Figure 8.23. It is very possible that the owner will give you permission for free or that you can negotiate a reasonable fee. If you are unable to negotiate permission, consider linking to the owner's site, allowing your Web viewers to jump to related information.

If you hire an outside Web designer or any other Web subcontractors, be sure that their contracts indicate that your organization has the right to use any material they incorporate on your Web site, making the contractors responsible for clearing ownership of whatever elements come from another source.

The contracts should also give your company all intellectual property rights to the contractors' work, which should be designated as "work for hire." If your page is designed in-house, your employment

---

The undersigned authorizes Maximum Press, 605 Silverthorn Road, Gulf Breeze, FL 32561 to print electronically, publish on its Web site at *http://www.maxpress.com*, and otherwise distribute throughout the world in all languages and versions, the following (information) (article) (screenshot) (art).

Material covered by this permission: (attached)

Please specify the credit line you would like to have appear:

Please sign this permission and enter your desired credit line. You may return it in the enclosed SASE or fax it back to:
Thank you.

Signature: Date:
Printed Name: Title:
Company
Address:
City: State: Zip:
T: F: E:

Figure 8.23.   Copyright permission letter.

contracts should include a notice that your company owns the intellectual property of all work performed by employees.

Hyperlinks

Although it is not required, notifying another site when you are planning to include it as a hyperlink is a good business practice. Because
you offer visibility, you may be able to obtain an agreement for that
site to link to you in exchange. Generally, linking is a legitimate activity. Be careful, however, that you don't eliminate someone's identifying information, implying that you have created their work. Also,
avoid manipulating a link to make it seem that others have endorsed
your site or company, unless, of course, they have.

Nasty Beasties: Liability, Disclaimers, Fraud, and Other No-No's

The Internet is still so new that no one is quite sure what liability
vendors will face. You should simply assume that any liability you
have off the Web, you also have on it. You can be just as liable for
unsafe products, false advertising, or financial fraud as you are off-
line. Many Web sites post an online disclaimer and/or consumer license, similar to the one that appears on their packaging. ThirdAge
uses a standard disclaimer, as shown in Figure 8.24.

Activities that are illegal off the Internet are illegal on it. For instance, you can't operate a pyramid scheme or other scams. The Federal Trade Commission (*http://www.ftc.gov*) has already warned more
than 500 Web sites and filed lawsuits against 33 companies alleging
online scams, such as illegal multilevel marketing schemes that focus
on recruiting members, not selling products.

Complaints of online fraud have escalated with the increase in
online sales. According to the Internet Fraud Watch, a system maintained by the National Consumer's League (*http://www.fraud.org*,
shown in Figure 8.25), complaints rose from 1,280 in 1997 to 7,752
in 1998. The biggest source of complaints was online auctions, as
seen in Figure 8.26. If you decide to run an auction on your site,
watch for the results of investigations undertaken in 1999 by the
FTC and state consumer affairs departments. The issue is whether an

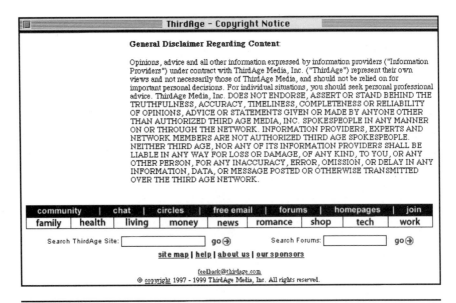

Figure 8.24. Disclaimer notice, *http://www.thirdage.com/copyright.html.*
© 1997-1999 Third Age Media, Inc. All rights reserved.

auction site can be held accountable for sellers on the site who falsely represent the sellers' goods.

If your Internet business falls into one of the categories in Figure 8.26, you might consider boosting consumer confidence by joining the Better Business Bureau (*http://www.bbb.org*). The Bureau allows members, who agree to certain methods of resolving customer disputes, to display the BBB logo on their sites. Customers can then check out your business history for customer complaints and see how they were resolved. Or offer to use a third party online escrow service, such as *http://www.safebuyer.com* or *http://www.iescrow.com.*

On the Internet, of course, dissatisfied customers can fight back with bad publicity. Prior to the Internet, a happy customer was likely to tell 3 other people; an unhappy customer would tell 20. Now, an unhappy customer can tell millions by posting an anti-company Web site or starting a negative discussion group. One company, Third Voice in Redwood City, California, claims to have created a way for surfers—including disgruntled customers—to paste a public comment on any Web page. The notes, which can't be removed by the site owner,

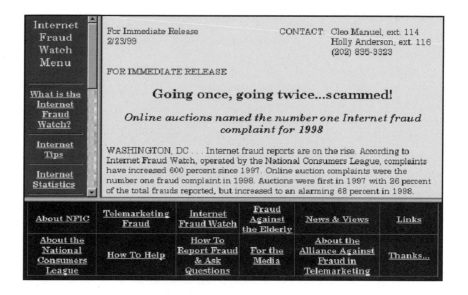

Figure 8.25. Internet Fraud Watch, *http://www.fraud.org.* Courtesy the Internet Fraud Watch, a program of the nonprofit National Consumers League.

could easily become a point of embarrassment at the point of sale. While the technology has other applications, such as group document review online, it may well prove to be a double-edged sword.

Content and the First Amendment

The content of the Internet is covered by the First Amendment. However, in some recent cases, courts have considered online and Web hosting companies to assume the responsibility of publishers for what appears on pages they host. You can't sell alcohol, gambling chances, or pornographic material to minors online, but so far these laws have proved difficult to enforce. Pornography, in fact, is one of the most lucrative businesses on the Web, with online earnings for the adult entertainment industry topping $1 billion in 1998.

The Supreme Court has upheld a federal law aimed at limiting obscene material in e-mail as well as Web sites. Many interest groups

---

Top 10 Sources of Online Fraud

1. Auctions
2. General merchandise sales
3. Computer equipment & software
4. Internet services
5. Work-at-home offers

6. Business opportunities
7. Marketing schemes
8. Credit card offers
9. Advance fee loans
10. Employment offers

Figure 8.26. Top 10 sources of online fraud, *http://www.nclnet.org/*. Courtesy the Internet Fraud Watch, a program of the nonprofit National Consumers League.

now demand that Web sites carry warnings if they contain material that might be objectionable, even if not legally obscene, if seen by children. Some organizations provide their own lists of "indecent," violent, or hate-filled sites; others recommend the use of blocking and filtering software. In the wake of episodes of school violence in 1999, ISPs will provide a link to a new site that offers technology for restricting children's access to sites, monitoring sites visited and limiting the time children are able to spend online.

There is bound to be a great deal of continuing litigation about these issues. If you're not sure whether what you want to do is legal, consult an attorney. Background information on computer law and current cases is available at such sites as The Computer Law Association (*http://www.cla.org*) or the American Bar Association Committee on the Law of Cyberspace at *http://www.abanet.org/buslaw/cyber/home.html*. Or contact the Electronic Freedom Foundation at *http://www.eff.org*, which seeks to protect the open exchange of ideas and expression on the Internet.

We have now covered both the glamorous and the gritty parts of creating, maintaining, promoting, and protecting your Web site. Let's have some fun in the next chapter looking at successful sites you might want to emulate.

9

Model Web Sites for Internet Marketing

Repeat this mantra: "Before adding a new feature or page to my site, I will check out the Web." Bring examples of sites you like and dislike when you meet with your designer. The more information you provide, the more likely it is that you will be satisfied with the results and the less expensive the process. Make sure that every feature adds benefits for both your customers and your business.

The model Web sites in this chapter might be among the ones you bring with you. Each of these successful business sites illustrates a different aspect of marketing on the Internet. We've already looked at multimedia sites, so the ones in this chapter focus on presentation style, content, and marketing techniques appropriate for the goals and target audiences of each business.

View these sites online to see how well their design matches their overall business concept. Flow through their Web pages as if you were a customer. Then look at each site from the standpoint of your own product or service. How could you adapt their ideas? Can you borrow their marketing wisdom? When you check these sites, the pages may well have changed from the ones presented here. Study the changes to see if you can determine the reason they were made.

Most business people are generous with advice and experience. If you find a noncompeting site that uses a marketing technique, such as a registry, that interests you, e-mail the owner and ask how well it works. You'll be surprised at the useful information a noncompeting owner will provide and the mistakes you can avoid as a result.

Almost all the sites in this chapter have something to sell, but only three quarters of them sell online. We'll follow the sequence of the business process as we look at sites that

- Draw customers to a cyber-storefront on the basis of location, activities, or original artistry

- Hold people on the site through content, links, real-time information, or humor

- Exemplify good marketing by demonstrating products, making purchasing simple with clear navigation, offering giveaways, or building a companion site for a product

- Maintain a strong customer focus that adds value through easy location of products, tailored support, customer contact opportunities, or input surveys

- Create an innovative marriage of a traditional service business with cyberspace.

Getting Customers in the Door

This is basic. Even in cyberspace you can't sell something to a customer who doesn't know your business exists. As you've learned, you need to make it easy for viewers to find (or want to find) your site by creating a desired destination, an extension of your corporate identity, or a smashing splash page.

Location, Location, Location: Mall of New Mexico at *http://www.mallofnewmexico.com*

As in real estate, location is one of the keys to Internet marketing success. It's hard for viewers to remember which generic "cyber–strip mall" they're in. Not so with Mall of New Mexico, shown in Figure 9.1, which draws viewers who have already self-qualified just by looking for this site.

The site is a helpful place for both tourists and New Mexico residents. The businesses linked here represent both classic tourist purchases, such as arts and crafts or Southwestern jewelry, and sites that a "local" might want to find, such as health clubs or financial services. Entertainment schedules, sports venues, and outdoor fun appeal to both audiences. Links bring visitors to each site's home page.

The Mall of New Mexico includes strong resource sections on New Mexico life and history, community groups, and healthcare facilities, as well as a large "Tourism" section that covers historical sites, museums, and lodging.

It offers New Mexico small businesses an excellent advertising value, ranging from a free link in small type to fancier links starting at $30 for 6 months or $50 for a year. Display ads start at $15 CPM for a banner ad and $10 CPM for a button (small box) ad. Changes are in progress to make the site "database-powered," allowing viewers to search by multiple parameters.

Similar malls have been organized in other states by governments or chambers of commerce, who often put local businesses on the state or regional tourism Web sites. You will also find malls specialized by category, such as music, food, sports, travel, or crafts. Or try a coupon mall tied to off-line direct mail coupons, like *http://www.nmcoupons.com*. At these sites, viewers print out coupons to use at local stores. If you want to be in a mall, look for one like the Mall of New Mexico to bring you the benefit of name, place, or category recognition.

Online Activities: Where's Waldo at http://www.findwaldo.com/city/city.asp

Figure 9.2 is a destination site for Where's Waldo Inc. The site trades on its name recognition with children who know Where's Waldo worldwide for its books, comic strips, and animated cartoons. Where's Waldo doesn't sell directly on this site (other than a buried note about licensing opportunities), which avoids problems with children misus-

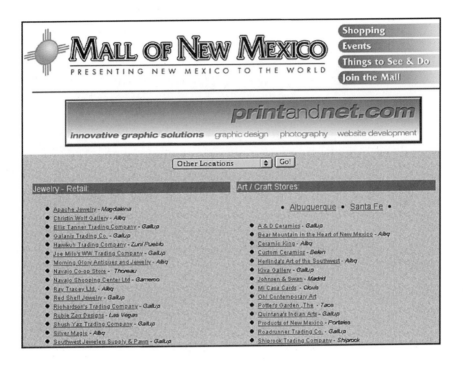

Company: Mall of New Mexico

Year Founded: 1998

Web Site First Established: 1998

Gross Annual Revenues: < $1M

Annual Revenues from Web Site: NA

% of Revenues from Sales on Web: NA

Site Start-up Cost: NA

Site Maintenance Cost (monthly): NA

Most Successful Feature of Site: The comprehensive information available about New Mexico.

Lesson Learned: We should have built the site based on a database platform. There was a lot of redundant data entry.

Advice about Marketing on the Web: "Never stay in one place." John Harris, President

Figure 9.1. Location, location, location, *http://www.mallofnewmexico. com/sales.html*. Courtesy Innovative Graphic Solutions, Inc. Webmaster, Joseph Talley; Graphic Designer, Russel Garcia.

Company: Where's Waldo? Inc.

Year Founded: Not Available

Web Site First Established: 1995

Gross Annual Revenues: Not Available

Annual Revenues from Web Site: Not Applicable

% of Revenues from Sales on Web: Not Applicable

Site Start-up Cost: $150,000

Site Maintenance Cost (monthly): $5,000

Most Successful Feature of Site: Interactivity of contests and games built an on-line community.

Lesson Learned: High level of sponsor commitment needed for e-commerce or revenue production.

Advice about Marketing on the Web: "Look to the Web as a vehicle for reaching audiences you are not currently hitting; use the interactive elements of the Web to drive value to a new audience."
Gail Smith, Principal, Sales & Marketing, at developer, inmedia, inc.:

Figure 9.2. Online activities, *http://www.findwaldo.com/city/city.asp.* Courtesy Inmedia, Inc.

ing parents' credit cards. Rather, it uses the site to build brand memory and consumer relationships.

The Where's Waldo site is stuffed with dozens of interactive opportunities to keep children busy: three shocked games and a zoom-in maze to find Waldo; giveaways to download, such as games, icons, color pages, and postcards; and a chat room. Hotspots over the buildings on the home page serve as navigation devices. The site does promote its off-line products, with descriptions of current books, cartoons, and artwork, and builds future demand by providing notice of soon-to-be-released books.

When the site first went up over four years ago, the use of Web sites for electronic commerce or generating advertising revenue was just beginning. With pre-packaged software replacing the need for custom programming, it is now much easier and less expensive to add these features to a site.

Too Cool: New York Cabbie at
http://www.nycabbie.com/

This site is a keeper! Trip once over New York Cabbie in Figure 9.3 and you'll bookmark forever this marriage of art and technology. The eye-catching, cab yellow background with checkerboard trim is hypnotic. More than 70 photographs of New York streets by artist (and taxi driver) Michael L. Krygier are viewable in glorious intensity. Each photo is well worth the 40 to 90 second download time (with a 28.8 modem) for a 90K JPEG file. To keep downloading to a minimum, the site wisely offers three pages of thumbnails that blow up to full screen art, with new photos added constantly.

NY Cabbie contains several other features that keep people returning to the site: a Dear Cabby advice column, a series of true taxi stories from around the world, and a set of Taxi Tips for both battle-scarred New Yorkers and harried tourists. Some photographic prints are sold online in three sizes at prices ranging from $60 to $160. To complete an online purchase by credit card, the order page links to *http://www.CCnow.com*.

Apart from the pleasure it provides viewers, the site provides recognition for Krygier as an artist. In essence, Krygier's site has become

Company: NYCabbie

Year Founded: 1998

Web Site First Established: 1998

Gross Annual Revenues: <$1M

Annual Revenues from Web Site: Not Yet Available

% of Revenues from Sales on Web: Not Yet Available

Site Start-up Cost: $25,000

Site Maintenance Cost (monthly): $900

Most Successful Feature of Site: Its all-around visual impact.

Lesson Learned: Information is worth dollars. Don't give ideas away for free.

Advice about Marketing on the Web: "Be creative, simple, and focused with a strong visual appeal; always strive to improve your Web site."
Michael Krygier, Artist and President

Figure 9.3. Too cool, *http://www.nycabbie.com*. © 1999 MLK (tps); Webmaster, Paul Wallace.

a multimedia performance piece. As he describes it, "I was thinking of making a coffee table book when I woke up one night thinking 'Internet.' I had never even seen the Internet, just heard about it....The whole site [was] intuition. It [came] very fast."

It had to be intuition: Before the site went up, Krygier didn't own a computer. He now uses WebTV to answer e-mail, which has become so voluminous he plans to create a book. His friend and Webmaster, Paul Wallace, handles layout and programming, while Krygier provides the images and content. To establish the site, Krygier obtained financial backing from a patron, Thomas Savitsky.

New York Cabbie is a premier example of the power of off-line promotion. Following the site's announcement on Yahoo! and other search engines, the BBC in Scotland called for an interview. This recognition was quickly succeeded by other awards, capped with a feature story in the Sunday City section of the *New York Times* on February 14, 1999. As the story cascaded through the media, Hot Link lists, and word-of-mouth, traffic to the site zoomed from a few hundred to over 61,000 hits.

Krygier's only paid advertising consisted of several hundred 5½" × 8½" reproductions of the Broadway photograph (#8) on the site that he occasionally mails out. He also printed 300 wallet-sized, laminated versions of the photo with the NY Cabbie logo to hand out to his passengers. This site, which has no links, is proof positive that you don't have to spend a fortune on advertising as long as you offer something unique that people want to see.

Hold Onto Them Once You Have Them

Okay, you've caught your customers' attention. Now you want to reinforce their interest. Providing useful information is one of the best ways, especially when it's in a medium, such as audio or real-time feeds, that can't be transmitted easily any other way. Don't forget humor, which gets people talking about your site.

The Medium Is the Message: Rachel Barton at http://www.rachelbarton.com

A violinist with a mission, Rachel Barton plays heavy metal, rock, hard rock, and grunge to show young people the classical roots of contemporary music. She is also an acclaimed classical violinist, recognized for her extensive repertoire and dazzling technique. Barton, who has appeared with symphonies in Chicago, St. Louis, Montreal, Vienna, and Budapest among others, also recorded a album of concertos by Black European composers from the 18th and 19th centuries.

Her site, shown in Figure 9.4, is aimed at two audiences. First, it provides information to a professional audience—orchestras and music directors that need her schedule, repertoire, history of appearances, published reviews, training, and resume. Second, the site serves the members of the public who want to buy her music. Although her music is carried by Borders and Tower Records, some of her albums, particularly the rock-based *Stringendo*, are difficult to find outside the Web site.

In addition to liner notes and reviews on each album, the site offers multiple WAV files from three of her most popular recordings. CDs are sold online through a simple electronic order form. Payment can be made by check or mail order, or online by credit card on a secure link.

For another music site filled with WAV files, try *http://www.seline. com/korb2.html.*

Creative Linkages: Thingamabobs at http://www.thingamabobs.com

Thingamabobs (Figure 9.5) turns the concept of links from a means to an end. Offering a little bit of everything to everyone, it uses a department store elevator as an organizing concept. However, it is more reminiscent of a flea market with a traveling carnival, linking to an ad hoc conglomeration of "stalls" to explore for bargains and freebies, such as an extensive collection of screen savers. The carnival part comes in the games-laden Arcade Area.

The site, which sells computer and office accessories on the "bargain floor," draws repeat visitors by allowing people to add free links to their own sites. Owner Lance Nakamura acknowledges that at first he tried to do too much. He couldn't keep up with the volume of responses, maintain the site, and fill orders. Now he's focusing on a product niche with less competition and better margins. For a nominal startup cost (and a significant investment of sweat equity), this site turns over a tidy supplemental income.

Company: Rachel Barton, Concert Violinist Cacophony Records

Year Founded: 1998

Web Site First Established: March 1998

Gross Annual Revenues: $5M-$20M

Annual Revenues from Web Site: Not Available

% of Revenues from Sales on Web: 33%

Site Start-up Cost: $500

Site Maintenance Cost (monthly): $50

Most Successful Feature of Site: Wide variety of information presented in easily accessible format.

Lesson Learned: Wish we had invested more money and time into higher quality graphics. It would have been very beneficial to approach other sites for links.

Advice about Marketing on the Web: "Keep your site and product information straightforward and do not over-stimulate your audience with extensive visuals and layers of information." Gregory Pine, Manager

---

Figure 9.4.   The medium is the message, *http://www.RachelBarton.com/*. Courtesy Cacophony Records.

THINGAMABOBS

Screen Savers

We carry one of the largest screen saver archives on the Internet. Our archive comprises of over 800 linked and direct downloads!

Jokes and Fun Stuff

Our Joke Section comprises of over 1000 jokes! One of our features is our Arcade Area that will amuse you for hours! Don't for get to grab our Fun Downloads too!

Bargain Floor

A great place to find useful and unique items! From CD Holders / Cases to Funky Computer Mice, you'll never know what you will find! A fantastic Secure Server site that will allow you to shop till you

Please press the above elevator

Recipes and Stuff

The Recipe Section holds some of our award winning recipes that will tantilize your taste buds! The Recipe Board is a great collection to post your favorite recipe or to add to one that's already there!

Site of the Moment

Do you think your site deserves a Thingamabobs Award or know of one that does? Enter your favorite URL for site recognition!

Contact Us

E-Mail Addresses:
-webmaster
-administration

Company: Thingamabobs Enterprises

Year Founded: 1997

Web Site First Established: Late 1997

Gross Annual Revenues: <$1M

Annual Revenues from Web Site: $70,000

% of Revenues from Sales on Web: 30%

Site Start-up Cost: $600

Site Maintenance Cost (monthly): None

Most Successful Feature of Site: Not a dry download; attracts people of all kinds and ages.

Lesson Learned: Should have had more realistic initial goals. The KISS (Keep It Simple, Stupid!) principle really applies!

Advice about Marketing on the Web: "Design a site that will entice people to visit; offer something free, fun, useful. [Need more than] shopping because the majority of sales on the Web are made impulsively!" Lance Nakamura, Partner

Figure 9.5. Creative linkages, *http://www.thingamabobs.com.* Courtesy Thingamabobs Enterprises.

Information Is Value: GoFish at http://www.gofish.com/login.asp?page=default.asp

"Cockles and mussels and shells! Cockles and mussels and shells!" GoFish, a buyer-driven seafood exchange (Figure 9.6), is proof positive that the Web is tailor-made for business-to-business commerce. It provides a wholesale fish market—not an auction site—for a product that cries for real-time transactions in a $46 billion industry.

The site pairs member buyers, who have a proven record of timely payment, with member sellers, who have a proven record of delivering high-quality product in a timely manner. In this industry, like most, there are good guys and duds. GoFish reduces the risk for both sides by checking references (sort of a Better Business Bureau for fish) while enabling parties to search for a match and make a trade in a way that would otherwise be impossible.

Buyers can submit the items they are looking for; sellers submit what they have in inventory and their offering price. Either side can conduct a database search, receiving a list of matches whose ratings they can then review. Actual sales are negotiated by e-mail between the trading partners, who pay for access to the database and marketing software.

GoFish offers links to home pages on the match reports, as well as advertising in its Go Fish Supplier Showcase, sorted by—what else?—type of fish. A very complex site, GoFish uses a real-time database and extensive forms to make this process work. Check out the steps on its very well-executed demo pages. Another section of the site, Channel SeaFax, provides seafood industry news, updated every 15 minutes.

The owner of the GoFish site, Neal Workman, started out working offline for the seafood industry and invested his savings to make this site successful. His risk has paid off beyond his wildest dreams. The site has now been featured as a premier example of e-commerce in *Fortune, Business Week*, the *Boston Globe* and *Computer World*.

Tickle the Funny Bone: Joe Boxer at http://www.joeboxer.com/joeboxer2/index.html

The off-the-wall humor on the Web site (Figure 9.7) of underwear manufacturer Joe Boxer positions the brand as "creative, enterpris-

Company: SeaFax, Inc.

Year Founded: 1984

Web Site First Established: January 1997

Gross Annual Revenues: $5M-$20M

Annual Revenues from Web Site: Not Available

% of Revenues from Sales on Web: 50%

Site Start-up Cost: $70,000

Site Maintenance Cost (monthly): $1,200

Most Successful Feature of Site: Facilitate purchase and sale of seafood over the Internet.

Lesson Learned: Make the functionality of the site more practical. Wish site were compatible with more browsers and AOL.

Advice about Marketing on the Web: "Don't offer fluff, only facts and pertinent information." Eric Reynolds, Webmaster

Figure 9.6. Information is value, *http://www.gofish/login.asp? page=default.asp*. Courtesy SeaFax, Inc.

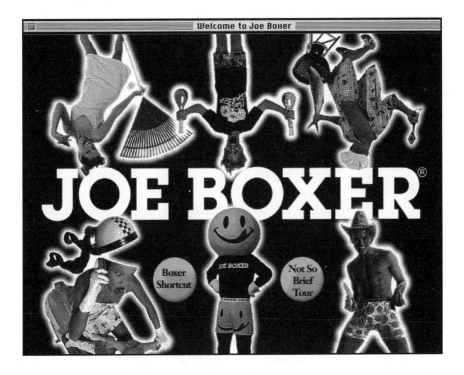

Company: Joe Boxer Corp.

Year Founded: 1985

Web Site First Established: 1994

Gross Annual Revenues: >$50M

Annual Revenues from Web Site: Not Applicable

% of Revenues from Sales on Web: Not Applicable

Site Start-up Cost: Not Available

Site Maintenance Cost (monthly): Not Available

Most Successful Feature of Site: Timessquare@JoeBoxer.com.
Allows people to e-mail to New York City billboard.

Lesson Learned: Wish we could update it more often.

Advice about Marketing on the Web: "The key to being on-line is getting off-line. Make sure your on-line presence is well marketed off the Web!"
Tessa Graham, VP Brand Development

Figure 9.7. Tickle the funny bone, *http://www.joeboxer.com/joeboxer2/ index.htm.* Courtesy Joe Boxer Corporation.

ing and unique. According to vice president of Marketing Denise Slattery, the company's motto is "a brand is an amusement park and the product is a souvenir." The underlying concept is that people recall best what they laugh about.

Joe Boxer doesn't sell underwear on this site, they sell an entertainment experience, with the intent of having users remember the brand when they shop in department stores. The site isn't loaded with multimedia files that take forever to download, relying instead on simple GIF animations. Joe Boxer uses great graphics with clever, but deliberately unclear, navigation to deliver its punch (see Figure 4.6).

Assorted games are buried among random smiley faces on a secondary screen, along with product descriptions and stores carrying Joe Boxer products. Check out the well-integrated catalog display under the tag "What We Make. Each screen includes stylized product shots and a pop-up menu for every category. Make no mistake, Joe Boxer is a marketing site: lists of stores are provided through another clever graphic display under Where to Buy.

Intentionally weird, loaded with verbal and visual jokes, the Joe Boxer site gets this review from users, "That was fun!" One of the most unusual features of the site is the offline presentation of e-mail. Mail addressed to *Timessquare@joeboxer.com* is displayed on the "World's Largest E-mail," attached to the Joe Boxer billboard at 42nd and Broadway in New York City. According to Vice President of Brand Development, Tessa Graham, "People have proposed marriage, said hello to visiting relatives...they love it!"

Here's proof, if you need it, that technology can bring creativity to the most unexpected places. Don't rush through this site; it's worth the exploration time—which is exactly what Joe Boxer intended.

Marketing Magic

We saw in Chapter 6 that the advertising industry has quickly adapted its techniques to the Web, finding ways to carve up space, time, and audience for dollars. Advertisers have created the equivalent of classifieds, display ads, event sponsorships, product placement in movies, and logos, logos everywhere.

If your business carries a variety of products, it's worth contacting manufacturers to see if they will let you use co-op advertising dollars for Web promotion as long as their logo appears on the page. Check out manufacturers' home pages, too. You might get them to link to your site, or pay you to place a link from your site to theirs. (Careful, though, that they don't pull a sale from you.)

Marketing specialists have created Web equivalents for forms of promotion and customer interaction besides advertising. These range from product demos to catalog displays, from giveaways to product tie-ins. Let's take a look at some companies that have applied these marketing techniques to increase their cybersales.

A Product Demo is Worth a Thousand Words: My Two Homes at http://www.mytwohomes.com/cal4page.htm

My Two Homes is a one-person business with an unusual set of products: items that help children ages 6 to 12 and their parents cope with the stress of divorce. My Two Homes' flagship product is a write-on calendar with colorful stickers for kids to track custody arrangements, as seen in Figure 9.8. My Two Homes also sells a Magic Words Handbook, My Two Homes Photo Album, and The Mom & Dad Pad, a duplicate message pad for parents who can't speak civilly to one another and who shouldn't use their children as intermediaries.

The calendar, which has sold over 3,000 copies since its introduction on the Web three years ago, is demonstrated on the site. Users can see how to apply some of the 444 activity and Mom, Dad, or Mom/Dad stickers to track their rather complicated lives. The site takes credit cards for purchases, either online or by mail, and also offers toll-free phone and fax numbers.

For marketing, My Two Homes uses Link Exchange, Banner Exchange, and a guestbook, serves as an Amazon.com associate, and makes reciprocal, strategic links with other sites dealing with divorce and custody issues. For an example of a good strategic link from this site, check out *http://www.makinglemonade.com*. In turn, Making Lemonade directs its viewers to My Two Homes and receives a small commission on referred sales. In spite of her success, owner Roberta Beyer wishes she "had paid more attention to the marketing aspects of her page."

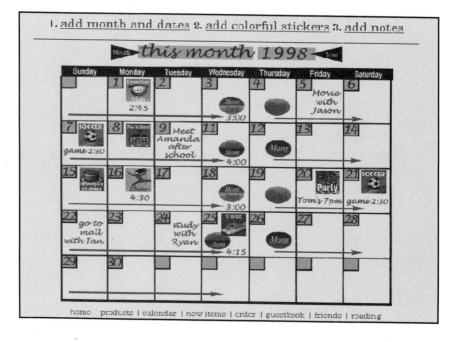

Company: My Two Homes from Ladybug Press

Year Founded: 1996

Web Site First Established: 1996

Gross Annual Revenues: <$1M

Annual Revenues from Web Site: Not Available

% of Revenues from Sales on Web: Not Available

Site Start-up Cost: $0 (Bartered!)

Site Maintenance Cost (monthly): $30

Most Successful Feature of Site: Very visual, not a lot of text.

Lesson Learned: Should have paid more attention to the marketing aspects of site.

Advice about Marketing on the Web: "Make the investment of hiring a marketing person in addition to a Web designer." Roberta Beyer, Owner

Figure 9.8. A product demo is worth 1,000 words, *http://www.mytwo homes.com/cal4page.htm*. Courtesy LadyBug Press.

Easy Does It: The Bead Gallery at http://www.beadgallery.com

Along with this Web site, the Bead Gallery operates two retail stores in suburban Buffalo, New York. The site and shops sell beads, bead kits, and other materials needed for jewelry, beaded lampshades, and zipper pulls. According to the owner, Bonnie Smith, average sales on the Web are about $40, more than triple an in-store sale. She finds that Web customers are used to making larger purchases from catalogs or can't find what they want from a local supplier.

Another explanation for her success is that she's made it so easy for Web shoppers to buy from her site, shown in Figure 9.9. The site is attractive—it helps to have a photogenic product—with strands of beads used to divide the screen into grids and to frame important information. The navigation is transparent, the catalog well laid out. Customers can easily order a print catalog, purchase a gift certificate, or opt to send beads as gifts.

Thank goodness someone uses large, easy-to-read type—what a relief for any viewer over 25! A site that looks this good and is this easy to use means someone has spent a lot of time planning it. It wasn't all easy, Smith recalls, especially when her first Web hosting service went bankrupt!

One thing would make shopping easier: shopping cart/checkstand software, and a full catalog with thumbnail photos (big enough for beads!) for each item. Now, customers must make notes as they review the separate bead and bead kit catalogs. They then transfer their requests to separate electronic order forms that total their purchases and add shipping and sales tax if appropriate. It is not clear whether the three different order forms (bead kits, beads, and certificates) total on one bill as they would with checkstand software.

The Bead Gallery is a member of two electronic malls, ShopNetMall *(http://www.shopnetmall.com/retail.html)*, which hosts the secure server for its tenants, and a regional informational mall, the Western New York Mall.

Free Is a Four-Letter Word: Jelly Belly (Herman Goelitz Candy) at http://www.jellybelly.com

Many four-letter words are used in marketing, but by far, the most common one is "Free." A giveaway is an excellent incentive to provide marketing information, since viewers receive something of value in exchange for their time. Companies like Jelly Belly (seen in Figure 9.10) have long known the value of giveaways, acknowledging that the free samples of jelly beans are the primary vehicle for driving

Home Page

The Bead Gallery

About Bead Gallery
Books
Charms
Czech Glass Beads
**Findings & Bead
Supplies**
Fly Fishing
Gift Certificates
Japanese Delica Beads
Gifts & Kits
Knitting & Crocheting
Mixed Bead Bags
Seed Beads
Semi-Precious Stones
Swarovski Crystals
Online Ordering
Ask Us
Get the Bead List

Czech Glass Beads

Order Online Now! With Our Secure Online Order

Company: The Bead Gallery

Year Founded: 1994

Web Site First Established: December 1995

Gross Annual Revenues: <$1M

Annual Revenues from Web Site: Not Available

% of Revenues from Sales on Web: 15%

Site Start-up Cost: $1,500

Site Maintenance Cost (monthly): $30

Most Successful Feature of Site: Pictures of product,
pictures of store, and ease of navigation.

Lesson Learned: Starting with a Web host who went bankrupt created many problems.

Advice about Marketing on the Web: "Offer a toll-free phone number for questions.
We are real people." Bonnie Smith, Owner

Figure 9.9.   Easy does it, *http://www.beadgallery.com*. Courtesy The Bead
Gallery. Web Designer, TacWeb (*www.tacweb.com*).

traffic to their site. The samples have not only been a way to get
people to try Jelly Bellies, but have also generated a significant number of links and word-of-mouth referrals.

Company: Jelly Belly from Herman Goelitz Candy Company

Year Founded: 1898

Web Site First Established: April 1996

Gross Annual Revenues: Not Available

Annual Revenues from Web Site: Not Available

% of Revenues from Sales on Web: Not Available

Site Start-up Cost: in lowest 25% of average start-up costs for comparable commercial sites.

Site Maintenance Cost (monthly): Not Available

Most Successful Feature of Site: Free samples of Jelly Bellies jelly beans. The accompanying survey, which includes questions about flavors, has helped introduce more successful new products.

Lesson Learned: E-commerce was more difficult than the promotional aspects. Some products didn't work well online. Focusing on gift-oriented items actually improved sales.

Advice about Marketing on the Web: "Manage the technology to focus on the single most compelling way to engage your target market (in our case, it's free samples) and avoid doing things just because they are technically 'cool' to do." Rob Muller, Marketing Manager & Webmaster for Jelly Belly Online

Figure 9.10. Free is a 4-letter word, *http://www.jellybelly.com/sample_summary_frame.html.* © Herman Goelitz, Inc. All rights reserved.

Jelly Belly offers 500 free samples a day to United States residents, and 100 samples a day to Canadians. Since starting the Web site, they've given out over half a million free samples. To get a sample, visitors complete a brief survey about Jelly Belly products and programs, and offer their opinions on new flavor ideas. According to Marketing Manager Rob Muller, "Consumers like being part of the new product process."

The original focus on promotional programs exceeded expectations since the site launch, says Muller. However, getting the e-commerce program rolling was more difficult. The initial product line in the Jelly Belly Candy Shop was extensive. It included products that sold well in factory stores, but that didn't translate successfully to the online business environment.

Muller explains that they streamlined the Candy Shop, dropping about two-thirds of the items to focus on gift-oriented products. As a result, sales actually improved. Muller believes this was because "it was easier for visitors to find something they liked." The shorter product list presented compelling information to viewers with limited time "quickly and in an engaging way."

In addition to the free samples and Candy Shop, this well-designed site is loaded with other features, from Jelly Belly recipes in 14 languages to a Jelly Belly art gallery. (You have to see it to believe it.)

A Companion Site: ¡Burritos! at http://www.littleburro.com

The site shown in Figure 9.11 is a companion Web site dedicated solely to a book, *¡Burritos! Hot on the Trail of the Little Burro*, published by Gibbs-Smith. The site is a kick, inviting burrito aficionados to submit their recipes, write burrito haikus (really!), nominate their favorite taquerias, and play a silly burrito game with winners registering to win a T-shirt or copy of the book. Mariachi music (streaming audio) keeps viewers in the mood for an online adventure. In other words, it features anything crazy and entertaining you could ever think to do with burritos, besides eating them. Salsa anyone?

Fun aside, this site is a good example of complementary marketing. The book is sold online at a 30% discount or can be purchased

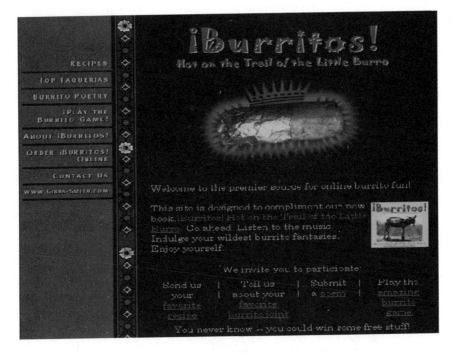

Company: ¡Burritos! from Minty Quinty Productions

Year Founded: 1998

Web Site First Established: November 1998

Gross Annual Revenues: <$1M

Annual Revenues from Web Site: <$5,000

% of Revenues from Sales on Web: Not Available

Site Start-up Cost: $700

Site Maintenance Cost (monthly): $0

Most Successful Feature of Site: Many areas that allow users to contribute; interactive game is very popular.

Lesson Learned: Costs limited what could be accomplished.

Advice about Marketing on the Web: "If you want to be successful, get exposure on something other than a computer screen." Quintan Park, His Royal Mintyness

Figure 9.11. A companion site, *http://www.littleburro.com.* © 1999 Minty Quinty Productions.

from *Amazon.com*, from *barnesandnoble.com*, or from the publisher's site. The site has been marketed as an independent product, drawing praise from reviewers. At once an advertisement for the book and a distribution channel, *littleburro.com* indicates that a creative marketer won't get caught with his burrito unwrapped.

Putting Customers First

Many Web sites demonstrate their commitment to customer service by making the ordering process easy, convenient, and secure. They may add online value through features such as retaining shipping information for future orders, keeping calendar reminders for gift purchases, and establishing gift registries, which are no longer restricted to brides. Most of all, they make product information easy to find. Let's look at some sites that focus on their customers through good indexing, tailored support, customer contact opportunities, and input surveys.

Find Once, Order Twice: Toys 'R' Us at http://wwwtoysrus.com/default.htm

Looking at one of the "big guys" is a great way to glean ideas. Although not the largest online toy store (eToys claimed that honor in Spring 1999) Toys 'R' Us is still a major seller on the Web. By turning its Web operation into a separate subsidiary called toysrus.com, the company hopes to leapfrog its way to dominance by Fall 1999, according to CEO Robert Nakasone. Toy retailing is one of the smaller sales segments on the Web, but it is the fastest growing. (Check *http://cyberatlas.internet.com/big_picture/toolbox_ecomm.html* for current shopping statistics.)

Recognizing that customers come to its site either to research purchases or to buy, Toys 'R' Us makes it exceptionally easy for customers to find what they're looking for. The home page allows customers to search by keyword, brand (such as Lego) and category (such as baseball or skates). A scrollable menu is available for theme or featured (branded) name such as Winnie the Pooh.

Company: TOYS'R'US

Year Founded: Toys'R' Us, Inc. 1949

Toys'R'Us.com 1999

Web Site First Established: 1998

Gross Annual Revenues: Not Available

Annual Revenues from Web Site: Not Available

% of Revenues from Sales on Web: Not Available

Site Start-up Cost: Not Available

Site Maintenance Cost (monthly): Not Available

Most Successful Feature of Site : The Toy Finder

Lesson Learned: Make sure of all the back end functionality (to the site and the fulfillment center if you are doing e-commerce) to be prepared to handle the load of successful marketing efforts.

Advice about Marketing on the Web: "Be sure to take advantage of the tracking capabilities of any online marketing effort, leverage e-mail marketing efforts, and don't ignore the power of offline marketing." Coleen Corbett, Marketing Manager, toysrus.com

Figure 9.12. Find once, order twice, *http://wwwtoysrus.com/default.htm.*
© 1999 Geoffrey, Inc. All rights reserved.

The Toyfinder pager seen in Figue 9.12 offers a customized search by multiple parameters: manufacturer, keyword, age, and price range. Thumbnails of each toy appear in a scrollable column as a result of any search.

In addition to a standard search of the toy database by product name or manufacturer, Gift Ideas offers a customized search by three parameters: type of toy, age and price range. Thumbnails of each toy appear in a double-column, scrollable list as a result of any search. *Zoom In* and *Buy It* buttons on each toy make the viewer's options obvious.

The left index of the home page offers other important shopping features: customer service, a baby gift registry, a store locator, and notice of in-store promotions. Since shipping information and a privacy policy may be critical to Toys 'R' Us customers, these options, too, appear in the index instead of being buried in the site.

Toys 'R' Us account options include registering billing and shipping information to make check-out faster in the future, an address book for gift recipients, a reminder service for birthdays and other events, and special online offers.

The site is easily understood in spite of its complexity and the extensive inventory carried by Toys 'R' Us. This isn't an exotic site that relies on expensive multimedia, gimmicks, or high-flying design. But it is a well-organized, well-programmed site that makes it easy for customers to locate toys, compare selections, and buy.

A Helping Hand For Customers: Mind Your Own Business at http://www.myob.com/us/home1.htm

Mind Your Own Business (MYOB) makes integrated accounting software for small to medium-sized businesses and competes with products like QuickBooks and Peachtree. MYOB uses its site to answer questions from prospective buyers, consultants, potential employees, and the press, as well as from current owners of the product.

Very few sites are smart enough to do what MYOB does on its splash page, shown in Figure 9.13: It asks viewers to categorize themselves in a pop-up menu so that the following screen can be tailored to the viewer's needs. Each option in the menu leads to a different secondary screen with its own pull-down menu of appropriate choices. This requires some sophisticated planning.

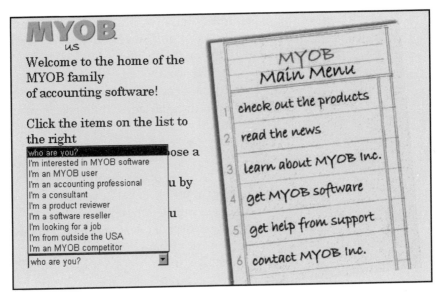

Company:	MYOB US, Inc. (Mind Your Own Business)	
Year Founded:	1982	
Web Site First Established:	1995	
Gross Annual Revenues:	Not Available	
Annual Revenues from Web Site:	Not Available	
% of Revenues from Sales on Web:	Not Available	
Site Start-up Cost:	Not Available	
Site Maintenance Cost (monthly):	Not Available	
Most Successful Feature of Site:	Interactive contact with our customers	
Lesson Learned:	Not Available	
Advice about Marketing on the Web:	Not Available	

Figure 9.13. A helping hand for customers, *http://www.myob.com/ us/home1.htm* © MYOB US, Inc. 1999, used with permission.

The MYOB site cleverly carries the graphic metaphor of office documents throughout the site, with navigational choices variously appearing on a note pinned to a bulletin board, a torn sheet of ledger paper, a To Do memo list, and an intra-office envelope. Although the site is actually quite deep, it never seems complex to the user, with margin notes or a rotating list of explanations for each menu option appearing on the page. Pull-down menus are used frequently to expand choices. Subsequent pages duplicate the carefully organized layout of the one shown.

Many businesses, from Adobe to Federal Express, have found that the Internet is a cost-effective way to offer customer support. Like MYOB, they have found that the immediate gratification of answers on the Web reduces the need for costly, labor-intensive telephone support while building loyalty and increasing customer satisfaction.

In addition to support, MYOB offers an opportunity to download a free trial version, buy online, or locate certified consultants or local resellers. The underlying message from MYOB is, "We're here to help." This site is a great example of delivering customer service through a menu.

Fly the Friendly Web: Trimline Medical Products at http://www.trimlinemed.com

No matter how much information and support your Web site provides, it makes customers feel more secure to know that they can always reach a real, live human being. Trimline Medical Products does that and more on its Web site, shown in Figure 9.14. Trimline, which manufactures blood pressure devices and accessories, started out seeking to provide just basic information about its products and the names of its distributors. It ended up selling online with a graphic catalog, reaching markets far beyond what it anticipated.

Besides its initial target of hard-to-reach small clinics and doctors' offices, Trimline now reaches the consumer market. Selling to that market would not have been cost-effective except online. In addition, the Web has brought Trimline customers from South America, Africa, and the Far East. Rich Jacobson, Trimeline's president, says, "The Web has really spurred us on to pursue international opportunities."

At least part of their success is attributable to how well they've handled their Web site. From the animated blood pressure cuff on the home page to product descriptions that specify detailed differences between products, this site is customer friendly. The friendliest feature of all is the promise of an instant phone call to a customer who has a question or wants to place an order. The animated ringing phone

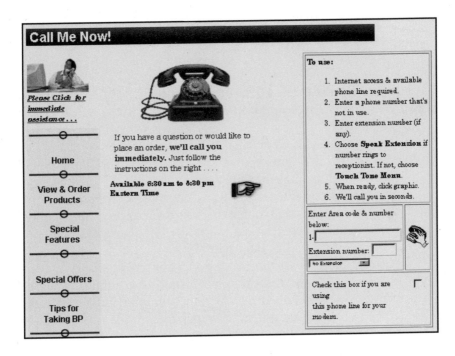

Company: Trimline Medical Corporation

Year Founded: 1996

Web Site First Established: February 1998

Gross Annual Revenues: $1M-$5M

Annual Revenues from Web Site: Not Available

% of Revenues from Sales on Web: Not Available

Site Start-up Cost: Not Available

Site Maintenance Cost (monthly): Not Available

Most Successful Feature of Site: Complete display of product line, easy navigation, information on how to take blood pressure correctly.

Lesson Learned: Try to understand customers' buying patterns before designing the site; use an experienced design firm that understands selling on the Net.

Advice about Marketing on the Web: "Think strategically—have very clear objectives, understand your customer, and get professional help before you proceed."
Charles Levin, Webmaster

Figure 9.14. Fly the friendly Web, *http://www.trimlinemed.com*. Courtesy Trimline Medical Products. Web Design, Pathfinder Consulting Group LLC at www.outofchaos.com. Courtesy Trimline Medical Products. (Web design Pathfinder Consulting Group LLD at *www.outofchaos.com*).

(a sprite) on the Call Me Now page allows users to type in their phone number and receive an immediate call back without leaving their computer screen. Talk about service!

Consumers Know Best: Forever Cigars at http://www.forevercigars.com/surveycigar_intro.html

Forever Cigars is an unusual, so far non-commercial resource. The purpose of the Web site, shown in Figure 9.15, is to "help both new and seasoned cigar smokers share their purchasing and smoking experiences." A consumer-oriented site, Forever Cigars recognizes that its users know cigars better than anyone else. Built for friendship and comraderie, its success "has been priceless," says site originator, Alan Discount.

Specifically, the goal of the site is to create two databases that can be searched for recommendations, one rating cigars that match the user's preference and the other rating tobacconists. The on-site surveys are a model of data collection, obtaining information that would take many weeks and much more money to collect any other way. The cigar and store surveys focus not on user demographics, but on product quality and buying experience.

Details about price, shape, draw, and burn characteristics the brand names of recommended beverages, and personal comments turn cigar amateurs into experts while educating them about the terminology used to judge cigars. Simultaneously, the cigar database provides marketing intelligence to tobacconists and smoking lounges about products to stock, and to cigar makers about features to emphasize in their marketing. According to Discount, the site has already gathered data that will be quite valuable; he's already declined offers to write a book about their findings.

The names of those who submit a survey entry (and other members who e-mail a request) are entered in a weekly drawing for cigar-related products from the site's sponsors. Other features on the site include a cigar discussion forum (users must register, but membership is free) and a scrapbook of photos from various cigar-related events.

At the moment, nothing except advertising is sold online, and the creators maintain the site as a labor of love. Site development and maintenance is donated by Vallon, Inc., a large-volume producer of full-service Web sites. Alan Discount, its CEO and a long-time cigar

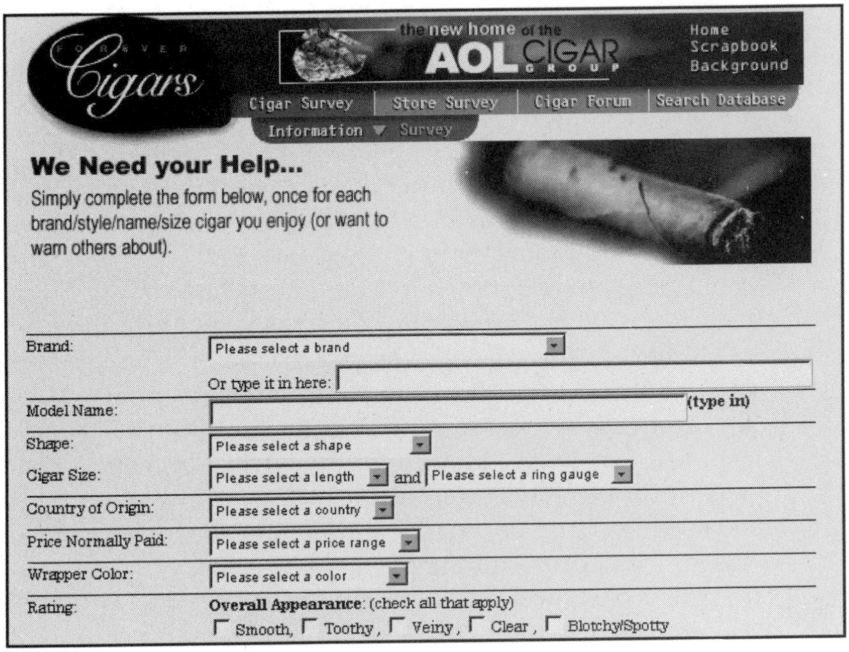

Company: Forever Cigars sponsored by Vallon, Inc.

Year Founded: 1996

Web Site First Established: August 1997

Gross Annual Revenues: Not Applicable

Annual Revenues from Web Site: Not Applicable

% of Revenues from Sales on Web: Not Applicable

Site Start-up Cost: Not Applicable (donated by Vallon, est. retail cost over $25,000)

Site Maintenance Cost (monthly): Not Applicable (server and site administration donated by Vallon)

Most Successful Feature of Site: Interest and support from other cigar lovers/hobbyists

Lesson Learned: Originally, didn't intend to keep site active, but had to respond to volume of user and sponsor demand.

Advice about Marketing on the Web: "Having a Web site for your business can be powerful, but most people don't realize that it is as much an exercise in marketing and promotion as it is about technology. Make sure you put your best foot forward in both areas to set yourself up for success." Alan Discount, CEO, Vallon, Inc.

Figure 9.15. Consumers know best, *http://www.forevercigars. com/surveycigar_intro.html*. Courtesy Alan Discount; Vallon Inc. Web Developers.

buff, explains that the site fuels his hobby, enabling him to "share [his] love of fine cigars, learn more about them and meet people who share the same passion." Indeed, hundreds of active users, many of whom visit daily, have created an online community (and apparently from the photos also an off-line one).

The Forever Cigars site acts as a testbed for some of Vallon's new products, such as online survey forms and message boards. After AOL decided to drop their cigar message boards, Forever Cigars donated its message board area to the AOL Cigar Group, which moved to its new home in February 1999.

Originally intended as a temporary tool, the initial development cost, underwritten as R&D, was high due to the complex underlying database and administrative features. According to Discount, Vallon expected to convert the site to demo purposes, rather than keeping it active. But users and interested sponsors, who donate prizes for the advertising exposure, provided an outpouring of support each time Vallon considered shutting down the site.

The company is now committed to keeping the site active as long as the AOL group calls it home, while continuing to use it to introduce new features of the Vallon product line. (There's a lesson here for non-profit organizations seeking a sponsor for their Web sites.) It will be interesting to see if this high-quality site can survive pressure for commercialization.

Service in Cyberspace

Some businesses take your breath away with the originality of their vision and the risks they take. Any small business that re-engineers its entire concept of service delivery to adapt to the electronic world deserves tremendous credit. Such is the case with our last model site.

Merging the Real and Virtual Worlds: The Shoe Guy at http://www.shoeguy.com

With imagination, personal services can indeed adapt to the Internet. Witness the Shoe Guy, a small business that transforms the face-to-face transaction between customer and cobbler into a hassle-free, convenient online service for busy professionals. By combining the Internet with modern shipping technology, the Shoe Guy intends "to be the best shoe repair and shoe care product business in the universe." They've made a great start with their Web site, shown in Figure 9.16.

As the animated home page shows, The Shoe Guy offers one-of-a-kind express shoe repair service directly from home or office. Fill out the online form to order service; receive a UPS box to ship your shabby shoes to The Shoe Guy; and welcome them back, repaired and polished, within a week.

The icons borrowed from the 1920s and 1930s are a thematic element of the site, which includes "shoe news," a catalog of shoe care products and accessories, and a shoe photo/story contest. The shopping cart and checkstand software by ActivCart, which keeps a virtual order form on-screen, is one of the friendliest cart interfaces available.

This was an expensive site. "It [took] longer to get things going and it [took] more capital resources than I originally thought," explains Shoe Guy President Jim Rice. The investment of working with an experienced Web design firm like Netopolis paid off, though, in the elegant details of the art deco design and the transparency of navigation.

The Shoe Guy achieves its claim to have "successfully merged old world craft with modern hi-tech abilities and management." Jim Rice has only one regret, "I wish I had put the site up sooner."

Moving On

We've now looked at a variety of sites that have utilized Web marketing techniques to achieve their business objectives. Although the larger companies spent a small fortune researching their customers' needs and developing their pages for maximum impact, some of the small businesses achieved their Web goals with relatively tiny budgets. If they can do it, why can't you? Regardless of cost, these successful sites have several things in common: They make the Web experience a pleasant one for their customers, follow through with support, offer quality products, and provide good service.

In the concluding chapter, we'll look at the impact of long-term business trends and a global economy on Internet marketing, as well as review the importance of integrating Web activities with the rest of your business.

Company: ShoeGuy.com

Year Founded: 1985

Web Site First Established: November 1997

Gross Annual Revenues: <$1M

Annual Revenues from Web Site: $100,000

% of Revenues from Sales on Web: 30%

Site Start-up Cost: $50,000

Site Maintenance Cost (monthly): $500

Most Successful Feature of Site: The new quick shoe service section.

Lesson Learned: It takes longer to get things going and more capital resources than originally thought. Wish I had put up the site sooner.

Advice about Marketing on the Web: "Work with a company...that has been successful marketing on the Web and has been in business for a long time and is forward thinking.
They must understand the ins and out of Web business and how it works. Take everything you know about traditional marketing and advertising and throw it out the window."
Jim Rice, President

Figure 9.16. Merging the real and virtual worlds, *http://www.shoeguy.com.*
© 1999 Netopolis at www.netopolis.net.

10

Conclusion

If you've learned one lesson by now, it's that online marketing is a technological variant of off-line marketing. If you forget the basics of business, all the fancy Web sites in the world won't make you rich. At the core of your business, you must have a solid product or service and the commitment to put your customers first. If your online activities reflect a desire to build a long-term relationship with customers—the most basic of business rules—the rest will be window dressing. This concept applies whether you're creating a signature file for a product news group, adding streaming video to your Web site, or running a print ad to draw attention to your new URL.

In this chapter, we will

- Look at long-term trends in corporate structure, legislation, and taxation that may affect Internet marketing in the future

- Consider the expansion of global markets and discuss how to implement international online marketing

- Summarize business basics and what we've covered in the prior chapters, including the importance of planning and of integrating online marketing with other business activities.

Trends to Watch

You might be able to ignore a ferret in your living room, but you can't ignore a gazelle. When the Internet was primarily an academic research tool, when only ten thousand Web sites had established residence in cyberspace, not many people in Congress, state legislatures, or single-interest groups paid attention. No one can ignore the Internet now.

The fastest growing communications technology in history, the Internet has drawn vastly different groups into action. Now state governments worry about losing sales tax revenue; not-for-profit organizations battle over censorship (pro and con), citizens complain to Congress about junk e-mail, and investors sue over profits lost when online stock brokerages shut down from overload.

If you market your business online, you need to keep your antenna up for trends that will affect your ability to survive and thrive on the Internet. Here are a few things to watch for in the next several years.

Legislation and Regulation

When it comes to the Internet, many people are saying, "there oughta' be a law." Pretty soon there will be—probably many of them! Legislation has been proposed at the federal and state levels to deal with such issues as data privacy, encryption, online fraud, spamming, access by minors to salacious information, and the prohibition of online gambling.

Spamming. In 1998 the state of Washington became the first in the nation to pass an antispamming law, requiring e-mailers to use real addresses and making it a crime to put false or misleading information in e-mail solicitations. A dozen more states and the U.S. Congress have considered similar laws.

The price you pay for spamming, even if it is not illegal in your state, may be high. ISPs have found that it's effective to sue spammers. For example, in 1998 Cyber Promotions had to pay a $2 million settlement to Earthlink Network and agree to stop sending unsolicited e-mail to Earthlink users. *You* don't spam, of course. *You* always obtain approval to send out newsletters and e-mail updates, don't you? *You* always make it easy for recipients to remove their names from your e-mail lists, right?

Encryption. Even the dry topic of encryption, which many consider key to electronic commerce, is a matter of hot debate, positioning U.S. competitiveness versus national security concerns. Current federal regulations prohibit exporting the strong encryption technologies described in Chapter 8. The CIA, FBI, and Department of Defense argue that this technology could make the U.S. vulnerable to terrorists and criminals, and want access to the key to monitor encrypted transmissions.

On the other side, businesses argue that the United States will lose its competitive edge and that encryption technology is needed to ensure the growth of global online trade. Recent Commerce Department regulations define Internet postings as exports, so even publishing encryption algorithms on private Web sites makes them subject to regulation.

A law proposed in 1998 to permit the export of encryption technology, incorporating concessions to law enforcement and security concerns, did not clear Congress. However, in September 1998 the Clinton administration relaxed export controls on strong encryption technology to 45 countries by industry sector, starting with banking, insurance, and health care. Some online merchants in these countries now have access to the same technology used in the United States to protect electronic transactions, an important step if you wish to sell internationally. For more information on encryption, try the Center for Democracy and Technology at *http://www.cdt.org/crypto/admin.*

Privacy. We spoke in the last chapter about the possibility of federal privacy legislation if self-regulation doesn't work. One proposed 1998 Senate bill would have empowered the FTC to regulate privacy protection during online commercial transactions.

A free-for-all policy on personal data ownership is unique to the United States. In Europe, individuals own their data by default, and must agree to its release; in the United States data defaults to the collector, with individuals needing to request that their names be removed from mailing lists or that demographic and purchasing data not be sold. As of October 1998, all firms conducting business within the European Union must certify that their data practices meet EU standards. This requirement, too, may affect your international online marketing.

As described in Chapter 8, your best defense is to establish and maintain a policy that honors the privacy of your customers. For an overview and updates on the privacy issue, see *http://www.cdt.org/* to learn about the efforts of the Internet Privacy Working Group.

Access.   So far, the U.S. Supreme Court has found that attempts to restrict access to the Internet in public settings run afoul of the First Amendment. Various courts have ruled against federal legislation requiring Web hosts and online services to restrict access to certain sites for those under 17, against mandating the use of software filters, and against attempts by libraries to install such software on publicly accessed computers.

Software filters are often used by parents at home and are offered as an option on online services. Filtering software may deny access to information on topics such as breast cancer or AIDS in an attempt to limit access to sexually explicit sites. Other filters prohibit access to information on subjects like homosexuality or Wiccan religions. If your Web site contains such content, monitor commercial filtering software; object to the manufacturer if its search algorithms block your legitimate site.

Regulation.   Some issues are more likely to be addressed through regulation than legislation. For instance, the Federal Trade Commission is attacking online fraud, while the Securities and Exchange Commission is strengthening oversight of day trading on online brokerages. Consumer affairs departments in several states are actively pursuing complaints about online auction houses.

To monitor the status of federal legislation on these and other Internet-related topics, go to one of the sites that tracks the progress of bills through Congress, such as *http://thomas.loc.gov/*. Similar efforts on state levels can be monitored state by state at such sites as *http://www.gse.ucla.edu/iclp/gen.resources.html*.

Taxation

You have to believe that $100 billion in e-tail commerce in 1998, with projections of hundreds of billions more within a few years, will get the attention of federal and state governments wondering how to tax these sales. State governments worry about the eventual loss of sales tax revenue, although state coffers are full at the moment as well as the loss of Main Street business. Most governors are searching for ways to tax Internet commerce, citing recent studies that estimated $170 million in lost sales taxes in 1998. (Compare that to $4 billion lost to mail order).

The U.S. Department of Commerce just began monitoring Internet sales independent of catalog sales to get a handle on the amounts involved. In 1998, Congress, heeding cries that taxation would impede the growth of online commerce and stifle small businesses, passed the Internet Tax Freedom Act. The Act initiated a three-year moratorium, which will expire October 21, 2001, on state and local Internet taxes, and established an advisory commission to study the whole issue. The consensus following the commission's initial meeting seems to be that Internet taxation is inevitable.

Keeping track of Internet transactions and deciding which sales would be subject to which taxes in which state would be a nightmare for both government and business. To some, the Internet should always remain a tax-free zone. But businesses that don't sell online argue that not taxing the Internet gives their competitors a cost advantage. For others, the impossibility of figuring multiple state and local taxes provides even greater impetus for a national sales or value-added tax. This will be a national issue; the Supreme Court previously ruled that Congress must authorize the imposition of state taxes on interstate mail order sales.

Opposition to Internet taxation could make the Boston Tea Party, the tax revolt that marked the original colonies' drive for independence, look like just that—a tea party. Stay tuned to events in the tax arena. They could affect your bottom line. You might want to check current information at *http://www.vertexinc.com/taxcybrary20/ CyberTax_Channel/taxchannel_70.html.*

The Corporate Carousel

It makes you dizzy just to read the headlines in the business press. AOL buys browser pioneer Netscape in a $9.6 billion deal. CBS announces $4 million in direct Internet investments and trades $200 million worth of in-kind advertising and promotion for a stake in Hollywood.com and storeRunner.com. Disney parts with $70 million to purchase 43% of Infoseek and launches its own *Go Network* portal, while General Electric, parent of NBC, antes up $26 million for a mere 5% of CNet and $38 million for 60% of the Snap.com portal. Verio buys Hiway Technologies to become the largest Web hosting service in the world. ·

On the retail side, Amazon.com diversifies, purchasing of *drugstore.com, pets.com*, and *accept.com* (an e-commerce company). Brick-and-mortar stores, like the pharmacy chain CVS Corporation, buy a cyber-equivalent (*Soma.com*), while eBay does the reverse, buying the long-established real-world auction firm, Butterfield & Butterfield. The conglomerates of Internet content companies mirror the conglomerates of distribution technology companies discussed in Chapter 1. Now that AT&T is the largest cable operator in the country, Microsoft invests in AT&T in exchange for AT&T's agreement to use Microsoft technology in cable set-top boxes! A lot of money is changing hands.

Yahoo! buys the online audio and video giant Broadcast.com for $5.6 billion, enabling Yahoo! to deliver broadband multimedia to more than 30 million monthly viewers. Yahoo! buys rival portal GeoCities for $5 billion. Yahoo!, which has several hundred acquisition deals underway at any one time, buys everybody.

iVillage goes public. Autobytel and AutoWeb go public. PC Flowers & Gifts.com goes public. Priceline.com goes public. Over one-third of **Initial Public Offerings (IPOs)** are now for Internet-related companies, drawing a flood of dollars into the stock market and unprecedented attention in the press. These darlings of the investor community drive the bull market with stock prices that rocket to the sky, even though *only* eBay and Yahoo! make a profit. According to one IPO firm, Renaissance Capital Corp., Internet stock has gained more than 200% over initial asking price, while non-Internet IPOs have gained only 2%.

What does all this hype and hyperactivity mean to small businesses seeking a mere hyperlink in cyberspace to call their own?

The concentration of corporate interests on the Internet is not without precedent in the history of communications, only the speed at which it has occurred. Watch for non-Internet companies, such as CBS, Disney, AT&T, and Hearst to acquire more and more Internet companies as adjuncts to their computer, cable, phone, news, and entertainment empires. Of the 15 most popular Web sites, only *one*—the e-card site Blue Mountain Arts, remained independent of large corporate ownership by February 1999. As compiled by MediaMetrix (*http://www. mediametrix.com/TopRankings/TopRankings.html*) these sites, arranged by millions of unique visitors per month in February 1999 are shown in Figure 10.1.

Watch for the increased importance of portals, those gateway screens people use as their entree to a multitude of Web services, from stock quotes to news and mail. Portals are seen as adding not only advertising value, but informational worth: they are expected to make the Web a more organized place to exchange both data and dollars. In theory, less confusion and greater ease of use will draw even more consumers into the Web.

Thus, when AOL bought Netscape not only for its browser software, but also for NetCenter, whose over 18 million vistors per month makes it one of the largest portals on the Web. The NetCenter site at *http://home.netscape.com* (seen in Figure 10.2) is an excellent complement to AOL's own portal and gives AOL ownership of two of the popular Internet destinations. (AOL itself receives over 38 million visitors monthly.)

Need more evidence? For $6.7 million, At Home, which provides Internet access over cable TV lines, will add Excite, a highly-popular portal, to its list of acquisitions. And in an unusually overt marriage of commerce and information, search engine portal Lycos is merging with USA Networks, a consumer goods company that already owns

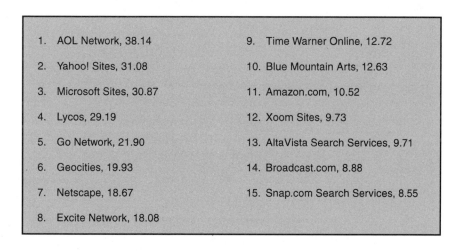

1. AOL Network, 38.14

2. Yahoo! Sites, 31.08

3. Microsoft Sites, 30.87

4. Lycos, 29.19

5. Go Network, 21.90

6. Geocities, 19.93

7. Netscape, 18.67

8. Excite Network, 18.08

9. Time Warner Online, 12.72

10. Blue Mountain Arts, 12.63

11. Amazon.com, 10.52

12. Xoom Sites, 9.73

13. AltaVista Search Services, 9.71

14. Broadcast.com, 8.88

15. Snap.com Search Services, 8.55

Figure 10.1. Most popular sites on the Web, *http://www.mediametrix. com/TopRanking/Top Rankings.html.* Courtesy MediaMetrix, Inc.

Ticketmaster, CitySearch, and the Home Shopping Network. Together, USA/Lycos Interactive Networks will be a $20 billion Internet/television conglomerate.

Portals are the mass marketing sites of the Web, like first-tier broadcast networks. To make the numbers work for their investors, these sites have to deliver one thing: eyeballs. They sell an audience to advertisers, particularly to huge corporations concerned with brand name imaging. Who else could afford their rates!

While portal advertising may be priced well beyond your means, do not despair. As you saw in Chapter 6, the best guerrilla marketing techniques for online success lie in niche markets. The rates for banner ads on most sites are dropping, making them more affordable. That's not bad, as long as the visitors to those niche sites are the very visitors you're trying to reach.

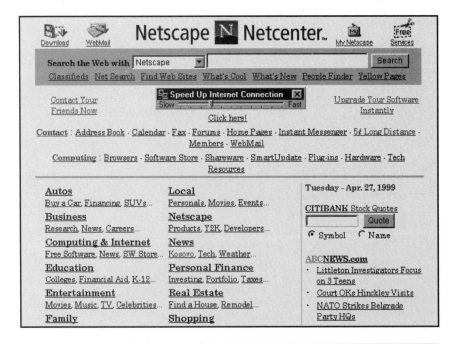

Figure 10.2. Portal site, *http://home.netscape.com.* The Netscape Communicator interface is © 1999 Netscape Communications Corporation. All rights reserved. Netscape, Netscape Navigator and the Netscape N logo are registered trademarks and Netscape Communicator is a trademark of Netscape in the United States and other countries.

To continue to draw audiences, portal sites may become increasingly a medium for multimedia entertainment rather than information. (Does this sound like the history of broadcasting yet?) Should you care? Yes, because the cost of creating those sites is part of the upward pressure on Web site creation prices overall, as you learned in Chapter 4. Yes, because entertainment on those sites crowds out the very thing you may be using to draw people to your site: information. This may bounce either way: forcing people to look at smaller sites to find what they are looking for, or forcing them off the Web altogether in frustration.

It also means that the Web will segment into monster sites, increasingly, albeit invisibly, linked to one another to reinforce marketing messages and to keep buyers within a cyber-conglomerate for purchasing. Several strategies exist if you are trying to reach the consuming public: You can affiliate with one of the mega-monsters, participate in a segment at a lower tier (equivalent to cable television), or stick it out as an independent. The answer, as always, depends on your business goals.

Remember that even a retail business involves a lot more than the Internet. Major retailers, while proceeding cautiously onto the Web, do not seem concerned that they will lose customers who prefer to touch goods and interact with knowledgeable sales staff. Only 18% of the top 182 general and specialty retailers were online by 1998, according to a Chicago research firm, the E-tailing Group. This compares with 50% of the top 100 catalog companies. Some are adamant about their storefronts. Jerry Storch, president of Dayton-Hudson Corp. (owner of Federated, Marshall Fields, and Target Stores), believes that the myth of lower overhead for online sales is just that: "Moving small quantities of products all around the country is vastly more expensive than store-based retailing. When they invent the transporter on *Star Trek,* then the Internet will be a real threat," he says.

Even if you agree with Storch about retail selling online (obviously, many people dispute his assessment of relative costs), you can focus on the ability of the Internet to reduce your costs for communication and inventory. Think how the Internet can create cheaper channels to reach your distributors or suppliers. As for your eyeballs: Keep one eye on trends influencing activity on the Internet, but keep the other on your bottom line.

International Online

Online services and the Internet are not restricted to the United States and Canada; it is the World Wide Web, after all. Growth of online commerce is likely to be greatest in Europe, where Internet access is growing quickly, the new Euro currency simplifies electronic currency exchange, and the globalization of trade has lowered barriers to commerce. Asian countries continue to suffer from their economic downturn in the late 1990s, though they represent enormous potential markets. At the moment, the use of the Internet and electronic commerce in Latin America is negligible. Apart from the United States and Canada, Germany and Japan are the most active electronic traders.

Although many people in Europe and Asia do speak English, they prefer to access the Web first in their native language. Only 15% of Europe's 500 million inhabitants speak English as a first language, and only 28% speak English at all. According to the marketing company Global Reach, only 32% of European Web surfers consult the Web in English. How are you going to sell to them? As former German chancellor Willy Brandt, put it, "If I'm selling to you, I speak your language. If I'm buying, *dann müssen Sie Deutsch sprechen* [then you must speak German]."

If you intend to market or sell internationally, consider targeting specific countries, perhaps only a few at a time. Translate several key pages of your Web site into the target language(s), and promote language-specific gateways to your site in each country. Companies like Global Reach (*http://www.glreach.com*) insist that this way you can raise the number of non-native English speakers visiting your site from 15–20% to 50% or more. Let's now consider what the world market looks like in more detail.

The Global Marketplace

About 56% of all those accessing the Internet speak English, about 30% speak one of the European languages, and the remaining 14% speak an Asian language. The distribution of languages apart from English appears in Figure 10.3. (Divide the numbers on the chart roughly in half to estimate percentage of all people online.)

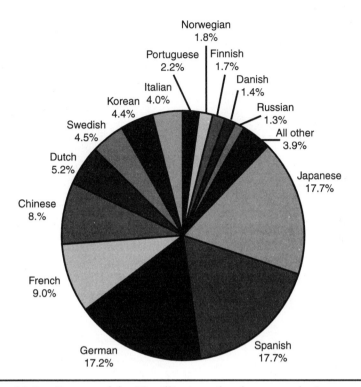

Figure 10.3. Percent of the 83 million people who access the Internet in languages other than English, *http://www.glreach.com/globstats/index.html.* Courtesy Global Reach.

Although 90% of direct online sales today are within North America, that, too, is changing. A French research company, Connectworld, anticipates the European market to double to 80–100 million users online by 2002, with e-commerce sites quintupling in that period. As shown in the table in Figure 10.4, significant growth in online activity is expected in France, Germany, and the UK. Note that the French have been purchasing goods online since 1981 through their own Minitel service, spending over $2 billion in 1997, triple what they spent on the Web.

In dollar terms, Visa International expects a broadly-defined European business-to-business e-commerce market to grow to more than $176 billion by 2004, with France, Germany, and the UK accounting

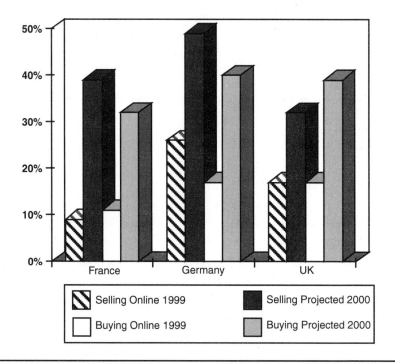

Figure 10.4. Percent of companies doing e-commerce in major European countires, *http://www.glreach.com.* Courtesy Global Reach.

for 80% of that volume. Revenues from European business-to-consumer online sales are expected to top $8 billion by that year.

Global How-To

If your product or service has international appeal, you will need to think about multilingual versions of your Web site and info-tools, as well as strategies for localizing your products. Localization addresses cultural issues, offers local contact points, and includes items of country-specific relevance, such as a local singing star on a site that sells CD-ROMs.

If you're not certain where to start, you might want to begin with Japanese and German (the languages after English with the greatest number of Internet users). Add Spanish and French when you can afford it. Major computer dealers, such as Apple, Dell, Cyberian Outpost, and Cisco have taken the lead in international marketing. Dell Computer, for instance, has unique Web sites for 44 countries in 21 different languages, and 34 of those sites conduct e-commerce. But major multinationals are not the only ones out there. Look at Spyzone (*http://www.spyzone.com/*) or Eagle Machinery Ltd. (*http://www.eaglemachinery.co.uk*).

Many European companies routinely use multilingual marketing on their Web sites to build sales, such as those for Swiss Army Knives (*http://www.victorinox.ch*), Floritel (*http://www.floripro.com*), Damart (*http://www.damart.com*), or Michelin *(http://www. michelin.com)*. The screen shots in Figures 10.5a-d and 10.6a-d show SpyZone's splash screens and Floritel's fully translated sites in four languages.

Figure 10.5.a. Spyzone English splash screen, *http://www.spyzone.com.* All four images courtesy C.C.S. International, Ltd. and the Counterspy Shops of Mayfair, London (continued on next page).

Figure 10.b-d. Spyzone splash screens in three other languages (Chinese, Arabic and Korean) *http://www.spyzone.com/foreign/index.html*. Courtesy C.C.S. International, Ltd. and the Counterspy Shops of Mayfair, London (continued from previous page).

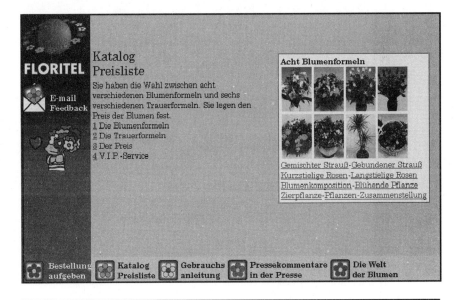

Figure 10.6.a-b. Floritel, English and German versions, *http://www. floritel.com/En/index.html?* Courtesy Floritel.com (continued on next page).

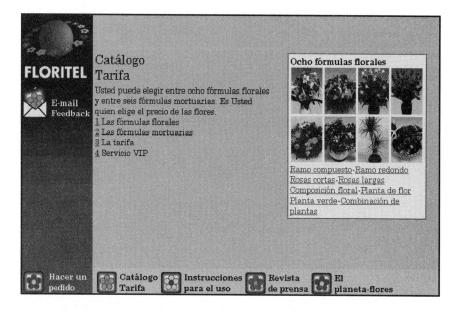

Figure 10.6.c-d. Floritel, Spanish and French versions, *http://www. floritel.com/En/index.html?* Courtesy Floritel.com (continued from previous page).

Site translation and localization services. A number of companies offer translation services. You can expect to pay about $50-$80 per Web page for translation, though many companies offer special packages for multiple languages or multiple pages. Take a look, for instance, at Global Reach: *http://www.glreach.com/GR/trans.html* or Intertrans *http://www.wetranslate.com.*

Localization might include anything from maintaining a virtual overseas office, with a local voicemail/fax contact point (an international version of MailBoxes Etc.) to advising on culturally relevant content.

Localization also addresses pragmatic issues. Should your product be marketed differently in different countries? Do you need to register your tradename? Is your product known by a different name in other places? Do you have different pricing structures in different countries? Can you consolidate pricing to a single price per item, and then add shipping, tariffs, and local taxes? That will make it easier to handle pricing through an electronic checkstand. Finally, given the issue of encryption discussed in the last chapter, you may have to accept a 56-bit key instead of 128-bit "strong encryption." Is this acceptable? Do you need to speak with a company like Baltimore Products (*http://www.zergo.com*) that specializes in global security?

From a practical point of view, you must also consider how you will handle payment and delivery. For amounts over $10, the simplest solution is to accept credit cards in any of the ways discussed in Chapter 8. You might want to explore other options in international currency exchange, such as the Virtual Trading Desk and other payment options offered by Thomas Cook (*http://www.fx4business.com*)

Delivering goods in a timely manner at a reasonable price is a difficult problem. You may find assistance from one of the resources described two sections below. Your options will vary by shipping location, size, weight, and type of product.

International promotion services. Many companies offer to promote your site in your target market using the same techniques in other languages and countries that you learned to use in Chapters 3 and 6. They will submit your site to international indexes and search engines in your target language. To be listed on those, you must translate, at a minimum, a localized page, a home page, or a one-page summary of your site, along with keywords, categories, and descriptive statements.

Like other firms, Global Reach (*http://www.glreach.com*) offers Web promotion services besides index listing: local domain name registration if desired; on-going monitoring for search engine placement; page optimization in the target language to improve placement; strategic linking; and banner advertising.

These services will handle a variety of Internet marketing tasks off the Web: posting to newsgroups and forums in the target language; preparing auto-responders, handling mailing list submissions, participating in chat rooms, and answering your e-mail. You can try using automatic translator software, but beware: Such solutions, while less expensive, can lead to some hilarious errors—and also to offensive ones. You would be better off with an e-mail translation service at $2 a pop. In addition to Global Reach above, try Blue Sky International Marketing at *http://www.blueskyinc.com*.

International search engines and indexes. Major search engines like Yahoo offer country-specific engines for Canada, Europe (Denmark, France, Germany, Italy, Norway, Spain, Sweden, UK & Ireland), the Pacific Rim: (Australia & New Zealand, Hong Kong, Japan, Korea, Singapore, Taiwan), Asia (in English and Chinese), and Latin America (in Spanish). Some of the many other international search engines are shown in Figure 10.7. More can be found at *http://www.glreach.com/eng/GR/regis.html*, along with other resources organized by country.

International Resources

You must be able to answer some essential questions before you can do business internationally. Are you set up for export? Do you know how to find distributors in other countries? Handle letters of credit? Process items for customs and international shipping? Take advantage of free or low-cost government programs to put your tax dollars to work. For information, check out the Office of International Trade at the Small Business Administration in Figure 10.8. Try a local international trade council, visit the International Trade Administration Web site in Figure 10.9, attend a Department of Commerce export training session, or check out some of the other sites listed in Figure 10.10. Most of these sites offer extensive information, including publications, links to export counseling services, trade statistics, financing options, and educational programs.

Name	Region/Language	URL
Alta Vista Canada	Canada/English	*http://ww.altavistacanada.com*
Alta Vista France	France/French	*http://www.i3d.qc.ca/*
Alta Vista Germany	Germany/German	*http://altavista.de/*
Ananzi	South Africa	*http://www.ananzi.co.za*
AusIndex	Australia	*http://www.ausindex.com*
El Faro (the lighthouse)	Spain/Spanish	*http://www.apali.com*
EuroFerret	Europe	*http://www.euroferret.com*
Euroseek	Europe	*http://www.euroseek.net*
Globe Page	Asia/Eng. Chinese	*http://www.globepage.com*
Heuréka	Hungary/ Hungarian	*http://heureka.hungary.com/*
In2 Ireland	Ireland	*http://www.iol.ie/~kasst/ in2ireland/*
India Search Engine	India	*http://www.indiaseek.com/*
Italian Spider	Italy	*http://rango.plugit.net*
Lokace	France/French	*http://195.242.78.15/* or *http://www.lokace.com*
Matilda	Australia	*http://www.aaa.com.au/*
MOSHIx2	Japan/ Japanese, English	*http://www.moshix2.net/*
Nordic Web Index	Scandinavia, Iceland	*http://nwi.dtv.dk/index_e.html*
Radar	International/ English, Spanish	*http://www.radar.com.mx/*
Search NZ	New Zealand	*http://www.searchnz.co.nz*
Search NL	The Netherlands	*http://www.Search.NL/*
Sesna	Ukraine	*http://www.uazone.net/sesna/*
Simmany	Korea/Korean	*http://simmany.chollian.net/*
Swiss Search	Switzerland/ English, German	*http://www.search.ch/*
TechnoFind	Singapore	*http://www.technofind.com.sg/ index.html*
Ugabula	Latin America, Spain/Spanish	*http://ugabula.com/*
UKMax	United Kingdom	*http://www.ukmax.com/*
WebIndex	Greece	*http://www.webindex.gr/*
Zebra	South Africa	*http://beta.zebra.co.za/zebra- cgi/webdriver*

Figure 10.7. Some International search engines, *http://www.glreach.com /eng /GR/regis.html.* Courtesy Global Reach.

Figure 10.8.   Resource site for international trade, *http://www.sba.gov/oit.*

Back to Basics

Let's come back from our globetrotting to consider the basic issues of doing business, wherever your location, wherever your customers are found.

The Customer Is the Measure of All Things

Regardless of the online task in front of you, put yourself in your customer's place. Is the message clear? Will the customer know how to take the next step toward a purchase? Does the message impart a sense of trust?

A site that indulges multimedia fantasies but frustrates users who lack the necessary software or hardware does not put its customers first. A site that takes hours to download sends a message that the user's time is not important. A site that forever hangs out a sign "Under Construction" loses viewers as fast as a retail store that never flips over its "Closed" sign.

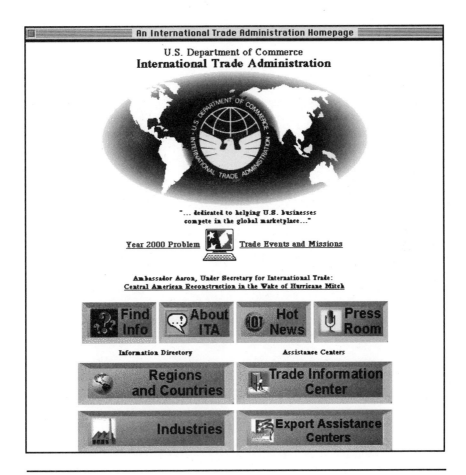

Figure 10.9. Resource site for international trade, *http://www.ita.doc.gov.*

Customers, clients, future employees, even suppliers like to be stroked and made to feel important. Successful online marketing makes it easy for customers to do business with you. They can find you easily; they can communicate with you easily; they can navigate through your Web site easily. When you offer useful information or entertainment, you offer value that tells customers they are worth the effort.

We have talked about tracking many forms of hits and winning awards for site design. In the end, the most meaningful measures of success are the return of existing customers and the arrival of new ones.

Name	URL
Small Business Administration, Office of International Trade	*http://www.sba.gov/oit*
Dept. of Commerce homepage	*http://www.doc.gov*
DOC, International Trade Administration	*http://www.ita.doc.gov/uscs*
DOC, Trade Information Center	*http://www.ita.doc.gov/tic*
DOC, Bureau of Export Administration	*http://www.bxz.doc.gov*
DOC, Trade Compliance Center	*http://www.mac.doc.gov*
Trade Fairs International	*http://www.tradefairs.com*
Export-Import Bank	*http://www.exim.gov/*
U.S. Export Directory	*http://maingate.net*
U.S. Customs Service, Automated Export System	*http://ww.customs.ustreas.gov*
U.S. Census Bureau, Foreign Trade Statistics	*http://www.census.gov/foreign-trade/www/*
National Trade Data Bank	*http://tradeport.org*
Global Marketing Discussion List	*email: globalmarketing-request@ListService.net* with word Subscribe in body and subject of message

Figure10.10. Government trade resources.

Sell More Than Air

A solid Internet marketing effort starts with something of value, whether that is a product, service, technical support, or additional information. A washing machine maker can offer a list of hints for removing stains. A car manufacturer can provide a maintenance checklist. The Federal Express site enables customers to track their package locations instantaneously. Not only does that feature meet its customers' needs, it reduces costs for Federal Express.

Customers who hear of others' bad experiences often shy away from purchasing online. They worry about guarantees, quality, service, and misuse of credit cards. Although you are not responsible for online problems created by others, you must overcome misgivings about using the Internet. Offering alternate ordering methods, warranties, solid return policies, and secure forms of electronic payment.

Plan Before You Program

Throughout this book, we've talked about the importance of planning your activities and following that plan during the implementation phase of Internet marketing. Figure 10.11 is a checklist of the various planning tools, surveys, questionnaires, and record logs you've learned about in previous chapters. By now you have created the Web notebook described in Chapter 2, so you have an organized place to store the results from all these tools and questionnaires.

Whew! So much for the paperless office! To be sure, you can keep many of these documents electronically as databases, spreadsheets, or word processing tables. However, you may as well set aside shelf space for your Internet marketing notebooks now. You will need some way to remember the hundreds of details required to implement your ideas successfully.

Apply Existing Marketing Know-How to Online Efforts

The more you know about the results of your marketing activities, the better off you will be. Closely monitor hits to your site and the rate of response to other forms of online marketing. Just as you monitor the results of any other promotional or sales activities, you should monitor your electronic results for individual Web pages, for visitors arriving from different links, for changed wording in ads, or for response to different giveaways.

Whenever possible, use source code numbers or modify entry pathways so that you know the effectiveness of each kind of advertising or promotion that you do. Don't be afraid to experiment with several approaches until you find the ones that work best. Then repeat the successful ideas and drop the losers. Online marketing takes work, but it is not rocket science.

If you have an online catalog, apply known techniques to make it alive with animation, photos, and careful use of color. Your Web site is like an ad that needs constant freshening. Update it frequently with new products, special offers, announcements, customer service tips, games, or new information.

Remember that an online site still needs off-line marketing. Every time you send a message, write a letter, put up a sign, print your business cards, go to a conference, join a news group, or create a

- Business plan: basic strategic guide showing where your business is going over the coming 1-5 years.
- Marketing plan: subset of business plan that lays out overall marketing goals and quantifiable objectives for all marketing activities combined.
- Internet marketing plan: subset of marketing plan that lays out the goals and objectives for all types of online marketing, including e-mail, mailbots, mailing lists, news group announcements, classified advertising, and Web site.
- Customer/user survey: if appropriate, a survey (online or off-line) of current and/or prospective members of target audience to understand their online activities, computer resources, and interest in electronic information, purchasing or service..
- Info-log: a schedule for regular maintenance, updating, and creation of non-Web electronic marketing tools, including news group postings, electronic press releases, and blurbs; log shows when activities were performed and by whom.
- Telecommunications survey: analysis of in-house computer and communications resources and needs.
- Web designer questionnaire: tool for selecting the best Web designer for you.
- WHISP questionaire: tool for selecting the best Web Hosting Service Provider for you.
- ISP questionnaire: tool for selecting the best Internet Service Provider for you.
- Team list: shows all participants in Internet marketing efforts, including Web creation, promotion, maintenance, and monitoring activities both in-house and outside.
- Budget: costs, cash flow, and/or revenue streams for Web and other Internet marketing activities.
- Schedule: timeline of activities for implementation and maintenance of Web site and other electronic marketing activities.
- Web site planning worksheet (treatment): goals, objectives, and outline of elements for a Web site.
- Scripts and storyboard for Web site (may be produced by contractor): depiction of narrative content, navigation pathways, links, and proposed design (look-and-feel) for Web site and/or its individual elements, especially multimedia.
- Web site maintenance plan: schedule of activities for repairing, updating, linking, and adding to your site.
- Web site monitoring schedule: list of which Web statistics will be collected and how often; results kept individually and with a historical log for comparison.
- Web promotion log: list of methods, cost, and frequency for promoting a Web site, with a record showing when activities were performed and by whom.
- Web site advertising plan: plan for paid advertising and sponsorships, including costs, CPM, frequency, and results.
- Copyright and trademark forms for filing if needed.
- Merchant card application if needed.
- Other electronic banking application forms if needed.

Figure 10.11. Checklist of Internet planning tools.

mailing list, you should funnel attention to your Web site, listserver, and e-mail address. As you already know, constant promotion is another key to business success.

Above all, don't be afraid to talk to your online customers to see what they like or don't like about your site, your service, or your products. Ask how they found you and what else you can do for them. Your customers know you better than anyone else.

Integrate Online Marketing with Other Business Activities

Even if you sell only in the virtual world, the rest of your business functions in the real world. From marketing to finance, order processing to supplier relations, banking to warehousing, a business deals with human beings in physical space and real time. Ignoring these elements of your business can lead to a downfall, no matter how brilliantly you execute your online marketing strategy. Think before you act electronically. Make sure you've estimated viewer response and have plans to handle it.

For most companies, online activities are only a portion of their overall marketing and promotion efforts, only one sector of their sales, and only one element in their customer service or employee recruitment tool kit. Staff buy-in and involvement will help you integrate online business techniques successfully.

Have Fun

Extrapolating from its growth, the Web—with its sizzle, graphics, entertainment, and information—will eventually draw almost everyone with serious intentions to market online.

Try to approach the Internet in a spirit of discovery and delight. You're going to spend a lot of time online researching, monitoring your site, and looking at what others are doing. If you experience sheer horror at dealing with computers, delegate Internet marketing tasks to someone who enjoys it.

Like anything else worthwhile in business, marketing online takes time. But you can make it fun for your employees, your customers, and yourself with realistic goals and the right attitude. Log on!

Appendix A

Resources

Category/ Company Name	URL	Descriptive Phrase
Advertising		
Ad Auction	*http://www.adauction.com*	Online ad auction
Ad Knowledge	*http://www.adknowledge.com*	Rates on major sites
Ad Resource	*http://www.adresource.com/*	Web advertising and promotion resources
Ad-Guide	*http://www.ad-guide.com/*	International guide to Internet advertising and marketing
Advertising Age	*http://www.adage.com*	Business marketing and analysis
Anancyweb	*http://www.anancyweb.com*	Advertising links
ClickZ	*http://www.clickz.com/index.shtml*	News about advertising trends
Congo's Money Maker	*http://www.globalserve.net/ ~bloemink/money/brokers.html*	Links to advertising information
CyberAtlas	*http://cyberatlas.internet.com /segments/advertising*	General advertising information
eMarketer	*http://www.estats.com/estats /net_ad_rev_exp.html*	Online advertising revenue
Media Awareness	*http://www.media-awareness.ca*	Canadian advertising statistics
Media Metrix	*http://www.mediametrix.com*	Advertising statistics
Nielsen	*http://www.nielsen-netratings .com/hot_off.htm*	Site ratings

Category/Company Name	URL	Descriptive Phrase
Computers		
Apple	*http://www.apple.com*	Macintosh computers
Dell Computers	*http://www.dell.com*	Computer manufacturer
IBM	*http://www.ibm.com*	The giant in PCs
PC World Communications	*http://www.pcworld.com*	Information about the Net and computers
General Business		
Better Business Bureau	*http://www.bbb.org*	Business information and links to local BBB
Business Marketing	http://www.netb2b.com	General ecommerce information
Business Week	*http://businessweek.com/ebiz*	General ecommerce news
CommerceNet	*http://www.commercenet.com*	Ecommerce resources
Economics & Statistics Admin., DoC	*http://www.ecommerce.gov*	Government report/projections on digital economy
Internet.com	*http://www.internet.com*	Ecommerce trends
Netscape	*http://home.netscape.com /netcenter/smallbusiness*	Ebiz basics
Real Estate Cyberspace Society	*http://www.recyber.com*	Online real estate information
Openmarket	*http://www.openmarket.com*	Internet commerce statistics
Time Warner	*http://www.pathfinder.com*	Business information from many sources
U.S. Department of Commerce	*http://www.doc.gov*	Export and statistical information
U.S. Small Business Administration	*http://www.sbaonline.sba.gov*	Multiple resources for small businesses
Internet Resources		
Bolt, Baranek & Newman	*http://www.bbn.com/support /resources/internetfaq.htm*	Internet history, use, FAQs
CyberAtlas	*http://cyberatlas.internet.com*	All-purpose information site
Discovery Channel	*http://www.discovery.com/DCO /doc/1012/world/technology /internetbest*	Internet history
Georgia Institute of Technology	*http://www.gvu.gatech.edu/gvu /user_surveys*	Web user surveys
HitBOX.com	*http://w21.hitbox.com/world/*	High traffic sites

Category/Company Name	URL	Descriptive Phrase
Iconocast	*http://www.iconocast.com/whatis /whatis.html*	Internet statistics
Internet Society	*http://info.isoc.org/internet/history*	History of the Internet
Internet Valley	*http://www.internetvalley.com /intvalstat.html*	Internet statistics
Internet.com	*http://www.internet.com /sections/news.html*	Internet news
Network Wizards	*http://www.nw.com*	Internet statistics
ngi.org (Next Generation)	*http://www.ngi.org/trends.htm*	Internet trends (downloadable slides)
PBS	*http://www.pbs.org/Internet*	Internet history
Web Com	*http://www.webcom.com/ walsh/stats.html/*	Tables of ecommerce growth
Wired	*http://www.wired.com*	Computer and Internet links

Legal

U.S. Federal Trade Commission	*http://www.ftc.gov*	Trade information
U.S. Library of Congress	*http://lcweb.loc.gov/copyright*	Copyright information
U.S. Library of Congress	*http://thomas.loc.gov/*	Legislative information about the Internet
U.S. Patent and Trademark Office	*http://www.uspto.gov*	Patent and trademark information

Marketing

Bannerworks	*http://www.bannerworks.com*	Sample banner exchange site
Hyperbanner	*http://www.hyperbanner.com*	International banner exchange
Interactive Traffic	*http://www.i-traffic.com*	Site traffic analysis
Links:2000	*http://www.2000.ogsm .vanderbilt.edu/links.cgi*	Marketing analysis
Linkexchange	*http://www.linkexchange.com*	Sample banner exchange site
New South Network Services	*http://www.nsns.com/Mouse Tracks/tloml.html*	Links to marketing resources
Online Advertising	*http://www.o-a.com*	Online marketing discussion list

Model Sites

eBay	*http://www.ebay.com*	Auction site
NYCabbie	*http://www.nycabbie.com*	Concept site with word-of-mouth promotion

Category/Company Name	URL	Descriptive Phrase
Ragu	*http://www.eat.com*	Creative site with excellent marketing
The Shoe Guy	*http://www.shoeguy.com*	Web selling for personal services
Virtual Vineyards	*http://www.virtualvin.com*	Well-structured, mature site

Multimedia

Broadcast.com	*http://www.broadcast.com*	Real time broadcasting
Listen to the News	*http://www.listentothenews.com*	Streaming audio site
Macromedia	*http://www.macromedia.com*	Shockwave and Flash plug-ins and more
Microsoft	*http://www.microsoft.com*	Downloads, products, support
MP3.com	*http://www.mp3.com*	Music player downloads
Netscape	*http://software-depot.netscape.com/plugins*	Plug-ins
Plug-ins.com	*http://www.plugins.com*	Multimedia plug-ins
Quicktime	*http://quicktime.apple.com*	Movie player
Radio on the Internet	*http://www.radio-on-the-internet.com/*	Radio links
RealAudio	*http://www.realaudio.com*	Streaming audio plug-in
Shareware	*http://www.shareware.com*	Quicktime applet
Sun Computer	*http://www.java.com*	Java applet
VDOnet Corp.	*http://www.vdolive.com*	Streaming video products
VR-Mall	*http://vr-mall.com/dabhome/vrst6-1.html*	Virtual reality mall

Site Monitoring & Tools

1-2-3 Webtools	*http://freeguestbooks.com*	free guestbooks and link pages
AccessWatch	*http://www.accesswatch.com/license*	Server statistics
HoTmetaL	*ftp://ftp.ncsa.uiuc.edu/Web/html/hotmetal/*	HTML editor
Htmlcheck	*http://www.uts.cc.utexas.edu/~churchh/htmlchek.html*	HTML syntax checker
Internet Profiles Corporation	*http://www.ipro.com*	Web and server statistical software
MOMSpider	*http://www.ics.uci.edu/pub/websoft/MOMspider*	Multi-Owner Maintenance Spider

Category/Company Name	URL	Descriptive Phrase
Netstore	http://www.netstore.de/Supply/index.html	Analysis software
RefStat	http://www.netimages.com~snowhare/utilities/refstats.html	RefStat freeware
The Counter	http://www.TheCounter.com	Hit counter
Toolzone	http://www.toolzone.com	Free guestbbook
University of California at Irvine	http://www.ics.uci.edu/WebSoft	Link checking software
VBStats 3.1	http://www.tech.west.ora.com/win_httpd/	VBStat software
Watson-Addy	http://watson.addy.com	Web page analyzer
Web Trends	http://www.webtrends.com	Statistical analysis software package
WWWstat	http://www.ics.uci.edu/pub/websoft/wwwstat	Basic log analysis
Yahoo!	http://www.yahoo.com/Computers_and_Internet/software/Internet/World_Wide_Web/Servers Log_Analysis_Tools	Log analysis tools
ZDNet	http://www.zdnet.com/yil/content/profit/soho/web1.html	Traffic tracking sites

Transaction & Financial Support

Catalog.com	http://www.catalog.com	Web transaction host
CheckFree	http://www.checkfree.com/products/cps/cf_web.html	Electronic bill paying
CyberCash	http://www.cybercash.com	Internet banking
E-commerce	http://www.electronicfunds.com/index.html	Electronic funds transfer and bill paying
EDI Information Center	http://www.edi-info-center.com	EDI links
GTA Net Order Form	http://www.gta-tech.com	Free shopping cart
Gomez Advisors	http://www.gomez.com	Ranks online banks
Mall Surfer	http://www.mallsurfer.com	Mall building software
MasterCard	http://www.mastercard.com/shoponline/set	SET demonstration
Merchant CC Services	http://merchantcreditcard.com rates.html	Card rates
Telebank	http://www.telebankonline.com	Sample online bank
Verisign	http://www.verisign.com	Digital IDs
Visa	http://www.visa.com	Merchant card information

Category/Company Name	URL	Descriptive Phrase
Wilson Internet Services	*http://www.wilsonweb.com/ articles/merch-cc.htm*	Card rates
WebCom	*http://www.webcom.com*	Web transaction host
Yahoo! Store	*http://www.viaweb.com*	Turnkey, online store

Web Site Creation

Brandy's Web Design Emporium	*http://www.geocities.com/ siliconvalley/heights/1288/ index.html*	Guide to Web publishing
CNet	*http://www.cnetbuilder.com*	Site building tips
InterNIC	*http://whois.internic.net/*	WhoIs domain name database
InterNIC	*http://www.networksolutions.com*	Domain name registration
NetCreations	*http://www.netcreations.com/ postmaster/index.html/*	Web registration site
Net Mind	*http://www.netmind.com*	E-mail notification service
PixelPen	*http://home.earthlink.net/~ thomasareed/pixelpen*	Guide to Web publishing
Submit It	*http://www.submit-it.com*	Web registration site
Totally Free Stuff	*http://www.totallyfreestuff.com*	Free stuff to put on a Web site

What's Cool/What's New Links

Cool Central	*http://www.coolcentral.com*	Cool Links
Mediacom	*http://www.mediacom.it/siti2 /hotsite.htm*	Cool Links
Netscape	*http://www.netscape.com/escapes /whats_cool.htm*	Cool Links
Netscape	*http://www.netscape.com/net center/cool.html?cp+hom07scul*	Announcement service
Newtoo	*http://www.newtoo.com /submit.html*	Announcement service
USA Today	*http://tech.usatoday.com/leadpage /usanew.htm1*	Cool Links
What's New	*http://www.whatsnew.com /whatsnew*	Announcement service
Yahoo!	*http://www.yahoo.com/new/ Computers/World_Wide_Web_ Announcement_Service*	Announcement service and more

Appendix B

Glossary

Above the fold   Ad placement on the top half of a page before a viewer would need to scroll down.

ADSL   Asymmetric Digital Subscriber Line   High-speed transmission method usable on standard phone lines to accommodate graphics, video and sound. Has a faster speed for downloading information than for uploading.

Agent log   A server record that shows which programs (e.g., spider, search engine, link verifier) have contacted a server.

Algorithm   A formula or model executed by a computer program.

Alias   An alternate e-mail address to which mail is forwarded from a Web site.

Applets   Small application programs that can be embedded within a Web page. Applets cannot be directly activated from the operating system.

AVI   Microsoft's format for packaging and playing video under the Windows operating system.

Backbone   Very-high-speed, wide-bandwidth transmission line forming a major pathway in a network.

Bandwidth   The information capacity, usually measured in megahertz or bits per second, that can be transmitted by a particular line or cable, or managed by a piece of hardware or software.

Banner ad   Standard, rectangular Web advertisement that links to another site.

Baud   Bits per second, also known as the baud rate. Measures the rate of data transfer within a specific time. (Also see bps.)

BBS   Bulletin Board System. Special-purpose electronic communications system in which messages can be entered or retrieved either privately or publicly.

Bit   Single item of information set to one or zero. It takes 8 bits to specify one byte, or one alphanumeric character.

Blurb   Short electronic message about a business, product, service or related topic.

Bookmark   On-line reminder that flags a desired Internet address for future reference.

Box ad   A square or almost square banner ad on a Web page.

BPS   Bits Per Second. Rate of information transfer. Modem speed is measured in K (kilo) bps. (See baud.)

Browser   Software that accesses the World Wide Web and other Internet resources.

Cable modem   Modem that uses coaxial cable to achieve greater bandwidth and thus faster information transfer.

Cache   Download information and store in memory for future use.

Call to action   A marketing and sales device that tells the customer how to take the next step towards a purchase or execute an activity; often uses an imperative verb.

CD-ROM   Compact Disk, Read Only Memory.

Centerless network   Network architecture that uses a redundant design so that multiple nodes remain running even if one becomes inoperative.

CGI   Common Gateway Interface. Web programming method that turns non-Web information into a Web document on the fly and vice versa. Used for interactive on-line elements such as registration forms.

Channel   One piece of information stored with an image.

Chat room   On-line communication in which typed messages can be exchanged in real time; some chat rooms on Webs run continuously; others are scheduled for a certain time for a certain topic. (See Conference)

Checkstand A Web software program that reviews and totals prices for items in a shopping cart, adds shipping and taxes, and arranges for customer payment. Also called a Register.

Classifieds Short text advertisements organized by category.

Computer network Two or more computers connected together to share resources.

Concatenate Chain together in a sequence.

Conference On the Web, a form of real-time chat, often moderated, with a guest speaker or speakers. Generally a specially-scheduled event; can also be convened for only invited participants.

Coop marketing Advertising subsidy in which a manufacturer underwrites some of the promotional costs incurred by its retailers or distributors.

Cookie Software implemented on client's machine that enables the server and client to "remember" previous transactions.

CPM Cost Per Thousand. Advertising rate to reach one thousand possible viewers or listeners (M is the Roman numeral for 1,000).

Cyberspace Term coined by William Gibson in his book Necromancer to describe an area that exists only online.

Data compression Method of reducing the amount of bandwidth required to transmit information, thus increasing the speed of transmission.

Digital cash Electronic money purchased in advance of expenditures, as with a debit card. Usually stored as encrypted data in a digital wallet.

Digital certificate Piece of identity in an on-line environment, often stored in a digital wallet.

Digital wallet Secure encrypted envelope that seals personal information including bank accounts, credit card numbers, expiration dates, shipping and billing addresses, and digital identification.

Directory Hierarchical database arranged by categories and subcategories. Used to locate sites on the Web.

Display Large Web advertisement, generally varying in size from quarter-, half- to full-screen, which links to another site.

Domain name Web site identification registered with InterNIC, usually ending in .com, .edu, .gov, .mil, .net, or .org. See URL.

Doorway page A page designated as an entry point for viewers arriving from another site or search engine. Can be an existing page on a site or a page independently created for that purpose. See splash page.

Download   Send a file or program from online storage to a personal computer for later use.

DSL   Digital Subscriber Line. High-speed transmission method usable on standard phone lines to accommodate graphics, video and sound. Speeds for uploading and downloading may be the same or different. See ADSL.

E-mail   Electronic mail. System that lets users exchange messages across a network.

Ear ad   A small banner ad usually found in the corner of a Web page.

EDI   Electronic Data Interchange. The structured exchange of standard business information.

EFT   Electronic Funds Transfer.

Electronic Order Form   An on-line document filled in by customers to indicate the items they want to purchase. Less sophisticated than shopping cart and checkstand software, it may or may not calculate totals.

Encoder   Software that converts "ripped" audio files into MP3 format.

Encryption   Coding of confidential, personal, or financial information for secure transmission.

Extranet   Wide area network with Web-like operations.

FAQ   Frequently Asked Questions. Appear often on news groups, mailing lists, forums, and technical support sites.

Firewall   Security procedure that sets up a barrier between an internal LAN (local area network) and the Internet.

Flame   Send on-line communication involving personal attacks and/or derogatory remarks.

Forum   Open, non-simultaneous discussion on an on-line service or Web site. Operates like news groups on the Net.

Forum message   Announcement in message section of a forum.

FTP   File Transfer Protocol. Method used to upload and download files between a computer and Internet servers.

GIF   Graphics Interchange Format. Compressed, bit-mapped graphics file.

Giga   Prefix for billion

Gigabyte   One billion bytes.

Hacker   Individual who forces unauthorized entry into a computer system. Also slang for computer enthusiast or amateur.

Hits   Number of times any file element of a Web site is downloaded.

Home page   Main page or welcome image for a Web site. Often shows a table of contents or refers to documents on other pages.

Host   Computer system (of any size) with a direct, high-speed transmission link to the Internet. Individual users connect to a host via LAN or dial-up modem.

HTML   Hypertext Markup Language. Used to author Web documents containing links, graphics, and multimedia.

HTTP   Hypertext Transport Protocol. Method used to transmit hypertext files.

Hyperlink   Same as link.

Hypertext   Any document with a link or links to other documents.

Icon   Graphical interface that, when clicked, accesses an object or program.

Inbound link   Viewed from the target business site, a one-way link coming from another site

Intelligent agent   A software program that performs a human-style processing task, e.g. upselling customers by suggesting additional products.

InterNIC   Internet Network Information Center. Maintains the master database for domain name registration.

Interstitial   An on-line display ad that appears between two destination pages.

Intranet   Internal network with Web-like operations.

ISDN   Integrated Services Digital Network. High-speed, wide-bandwidth, dial-up phone line for transmission of text, graphics and sound.

ISP   Internet Service Provider. Company that sells the use of its powerful servers and high speed transmission lines for access to the Internet.

Kbps   Kilo (thousand) bits per second.

Keyword   Important concept word in Web site text. Entered in search engines to locate information in a database.

LAN   Local Area Network. Links computers in the same building or area, generally less than one mile.

Leased line   Telephone line set up between any two sites for dedicated, continuously active transmission.

Link   A technique in HTML that allows a user to jump from one location on the Web to another. Can occur within a site or between sites.

Listbot Cross between list and robot. A type of mailbot that automatically processes requests, sending out information (e.g. a newsletter) or performing the specified task (e.g. entering a subscriber's name to a mailing list.) See Listserver.

Listserver Software that manages mailing lists on mailing list servers. Listserv and Majordomo are two of the primary mailing list-servers.

Live banners Ads that allow users to take an action without clicking through to another site.

Logo Name-only, paid advertisement on the Web, usually smaller and less expensive than a banner. May not link to named site.

Mail bomb Useless e-mail that clogs an electronic mailbox.

Mailbot Cross between mail and robot. A program that responds automatically to routine e-mail.

Mailing list List of participants who exchange electronic mail messages regularly, usually focused on a particular topic or concern.

Mall Virtual area on a server or on-line service where people can sell or advertise their good or services.

Media kit On-line or off-line package of information for potential advertisers, including ad sizes, rates, demographics, submission information, and contact names.

Merchant account An arrangement with a commercial bank or card issuer that permits a business to accept credit card payments and deposit those payments, less charges, to its bank account.

Message board Allows users to post messages on part of a Website for others to read. Like forums or electronic bulletin boards.

META tag In HTML code, a line that contains a list of keywords and the succinct description of a site that will appear when the site is listed as a search result.

Mirror Copy and display the material from one Web site on another.

Modem Modulator–demodulator. Converts computer data to a form that can be transmitted over phone lines and vice versa.

Moderated News group or forum checked by an individual with the authority to censor messages.

MP3 A file compression technique that permits rapid downloading of audio information from the Web with high quality replay.

Multimedia Combination of text, virtual reality, graphics, video, animation, and/or sound.

Netiquette   Guidelines for appropriate communication in news groups and mailing lists.

Network address   Electronic mail address.

News group   One of thousands of open discussion groups on USEnet. Requires a full-service Internet account and news group reader software provided by an ISP.

Node (1)   Any computer connected to a network.

Node (2)   In QTVR, one of 12 static images patched together to generate a panoramic view of a space.

Nonlink   Advertisement on the Web without a hypertext link. Usually less expensive than a linked ad.

Outbound link   Viewed from the target business site, a one-way link going to another site.

Packets   Means of dividing up and structuring information in a computer message for reliable Internet transmission to the correct address.

Plug-in   Applet integrated with a browser that enables users to view text, images, sound, and/or video in special formats.

Pointcast   A push technology that delivers requested information to a specific site. Also the name of a proprietary news/advertising product.

Portal   A large, multi-purpose Web site, often used as an entry point to the Web

POP   Post Office Protocol. Allows users to read e-mail from their operating system without logging onto a server.

Post   Enter a message on a news group or mailing list.

POTS   Plain Old Telephone Service.

PPP   Point-to Point Protocol. Type of Internet account needed to access FTP servers.

Protocol   Standard procedure for processing data.

Pull technology   Typical Internet interaction in which an individual must specifically request desired information. (Compare to push technology.)

Push technology   Internet interaction that enables data to be sent to an individual without a specific request. (Compare to pull technology.)

QTVR   QuickTime Virtual Reality. A method of virtual reality display that provides a 180 to 360-degree panoramic view from a fixed position, or alternately, of a rotating object. See VRML.

Quicktime Apple Computer's format for packaging and playing video and animation.

Raw hit Visit to a single file on a Web page.

Reciprocal link Two sites that have agreed to place links to the other on their own sites.

Referer log Server record of which sources or URL addresses have launched a link to a file on that server.

Register A Web software program that reviews and totals prices for items in a shopping cart, adds shipping and taxes, and arranges for customer payment. Also called a Checkstand.

Rendering-on-the-fly The method used by VRML to create images of a three-dimensional environment as the user points a cursor. See QTVR.

RFC Request For Comment. Method of open communication adopted in 1969 as part of the development of the Internet.

RFP Request for Proposal.

RFQ Request for Quote.

Rich media Ads that include animation, audio, or video.

Ringmaster Person who maintains the master database for a Webring.

Ripper Software that translates digital audio files from compact disk format to a computer.

ROS Run of site. When a banner ad is allowed to run anywhere on a site, not just at specific position or on a specific page; usually a less expensive rate.

Roulette Link on a page that sends visitors randomly to another page on the same site or to another site.

Search engine Software designed for the rapid location of information in one or more databases.

Server Computer used to control or manage a network.

Server report Operational information for host computer.

SET Secure Electronic Transactions. Standard for secure credit card transactions online that integrates SSL (Secure Socket Layer), digital signatures, digital wallets, and encryption technologies.

Shockwave Macromedia's format for incorporating multimedia objects on Web pages.

Shopping cart A Web software program that tracks items a customer selects from an on-line catalog.

Signature file Three- to six-line, text-only, electronic file used as an on-line identity. Like an on-line business card.

Sitecast   A Web-based, real-time event that incorporates streaming video, audio, graphics, and chat lines with pre-recorded information.

SLIP   Serial Line Internet Protocol. Type of Internet account needed to access Web servers.

Spam   Unwanted advertisements sent through e-mail or posted on inappropriate news groups.

Spider   Also known as a robot, crawler, or wanderer. A Web search program that automatically finds and stores pages and keyword information.

Splash screen   An introductory page or screen that users may see before they reach the home page for a Web site. Often created to allow software time to load, to identify a referring link, or to maximize a site for keywords.

Sponsor   Cost-effective type of advertising on the Web, usually featuring a small banner ad linked to another site.

Sprite   A small animated image in GIF format.

SSL   Secure Socket Layer. Netscape's protocol for sending confidential information, such as credit card numbers, over the Internet.

Stop words   Words ignored by search engines, generally articles, conjunctions, and prepositions.

Streaming audio   Sound files audible as they are transmitted over the Internet. (Compare to download.)

Streaming video   Video images that can be viewed as they are transmitted over the Internet.

Subscribe   Add one's e-mail address onto a mailing list or news group.

Syntax checker   Program that checks for "grammatical errors" in the structure of HTML code.

Sysop   Systems Operator. Manager of a bulletin board system, news group, on-line service, or special interest group site.

Thread   A topic of discussion in a news group or forum.

TITLE tag   In HTML code, the line that contains the words that appear in the title bar of a Web site.

Trading partner   A company that conducts business with another company using EDI.

TCP/IP   Transmission Control Protocol/Internet Protocol. The communications protocol for connecting hosts to the Internet.

Upload   Send a file or program from a personal computer to online storage.

Upsell To encourage a customer to purchase a more expensive item, an add-on, or a related product.

URL Uniform Resource Locator. Address designating the location of resources on the Web; it includes the user's registered domain name.

Vacation mailbot Mailbot notifying senders of e-mail that the recipient is away.

VAN Value Added Network. A subscription service that transfers secure EDI information between trading partners.

Virtual reality Computer-mediated method for interacting with a three-dimensional environment.

VRML Virtual Reality Modeling Language. Programming language for displaying three-dimensional space as if the viewer were moving through it in any direction.

WAN Wide Area Network. Links distant computer systems.

Web alliance A set of reciprocally-linked sites, usually joined by a common interest. Also called a Webring.

Webring A set of reciprocally-linked sites, usually joined by a common interest. Also called a Web alliance.

Whois Computer database of domain names.

WWW World Wide Web. Portion of the Internet that contains data, graphics, sound, and video, and is accessed through a graphical interface.

XML Extensible Markup Language. A method of packaging data in a Web document in a manner that can be understood by EDI software.

Y2K Year 2000. Refers to Year 2000 Bug, the problem older computers and software will have processing dates if the year is designated only by the two-digits 00.

Appendix C

URL Listings

The following is an index of the sites included in this book. For alphabetization purposes, the *http://* has been ommited, because most browsers add *http://* automatically if it is not typed in as part of the URL. Also, to avoid duplication, all listings include the home page URL, rather than the URL of specific pages.

Please remember that Web addresses change continually, therefore some sites listed may no longer exist by the time this book is printed.

Index

!Burritos!, 368–370
.com (commercial domain), 6, 149
.edu (educational institutions), 6
.net (network servers), 6
.org (not-for-profit organizations), 6
tags, 225, 227
3D/virtual reality (VR), 291–294

A

Abilene Project, 32–33
above the fold, space, 266–267
access and First Amendment, 346–347, 384
access to Internet, 7–8
AccessWatch, 193
Accrue Insight, 194
Accrue Software, 263
ACH (Automated Clearing House), 334
acq.osd.mil, 338
action (AIDA), 57–58
Adauction, 262
address information on Web sites, 169
Ad Resource, 258, 263
ADSL (Asymmetric/Digital Subscriber Line), 29–30
Advanced Internet Technologies, Inc., 322
Advanced Research Projects Agency (ARPAnet), 3, 4
advertisements, tracking, 195–196
advertising on the Web, 20–27. *See also* business on the Internet; dollar sense; Info-tools; Internet marketing; Internet marketing future; legal sense;

search engines and directories; Web site advertising on the Web; Web site advertising on Web sites; Web site creation; Web site marketing; Web site self-promotion
banner ads, 21–23, 24, 248–249, 263–266, 267
CPM (costs per thousand), 24, 258, 259, 267, 268
interstitials, 22
mass versus target marketing, 23–25
pull technologies, 25–27
push technologies, 25–27
sponsorships, 22, 252–253, 254
target versus mass marketing, 23–25
affiliate programs, 171, 174
African American Internetwork, 52
AfroNet, 52
agent logs, 188
AIDA (Attention, Interest, Desire, Action), 55–58
A.L. Houtte Fine Coffee, 318
algorithms (computer formulas) of search engines, 210
alliances (Web rings), 250–251
AltaVista, 151, 211, 214
ALT tags, 225
Amazon.com, 41, 47
American Bar Association Committee on Law of Cyberspace, 347
American Institute of Certified Public Accountants, 46
Another Company, 39
AOL (American Online), 30, 34, 52, 60, 83, 98, 99, 100, 102, 104, 105, 107, 232, 234
Apple's QuickTime, 288–289

Reader Feedback Sheet

Your comments and suggestions are very important in shaping future publications. Please email us at *moreinfo@maxpress.com* or photocopy this page, jot down your thoughts, and fax it to (850) 934-9981 or mail it to:

Maximum Press

Attn: Jim Hoskins

605 Silverthorn Road

Gulf Breeze, FL 32561

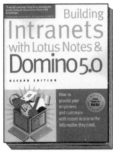